Nine Lives Are Not Enough

A Practical Guide to Caring for Your
GERIATRIC CAT

Dr. Mary Gardner

Copyright © 2022 by Mary A. Gardner, DVM

All rights reserved. You must get permission in writing from the publisher if you wish to reproduce any part of this book in any form.

This book may be purchased in bulk for educational, promotional or business use. Please contact the publisher for more details.

ISBN:
Hardcover - 978-1-956343-08-3/
Paperback: 978-1-956343-09-0 /
Ebook: 978-1-956343-11-3

Ed: 1

Library of Congress Cataloging-in-Publication Data

Includes bibliographical references and an index.

Researcher and editor: Dr. Theresa Entriken

Copy editor: Mindy Valcarcel

Doodles by: Portia Stewart and Moira Stewart

Illustrations by: Dusan Pavlic

Interior design by: Ljiljana Pavkov

Book cover design by: Victoria Black

Disclaimer

This book is not intended as a medical textbook or to replace the services of a veterinarian. Every pet should receive an examination by their veterinarian prior to starting any treatment. The author, editors, illustrators, and publisher disclaim any responsibility for and shall not be liable for any damages resulting directly or indirectly from information in this book.

I've shared my patients' stories in this book with their families' consent, and in a few instances where appropriate, I've changed their names and other identifying details.

I am not paid by any of the companies whose products I recommend. These are simply products that I have found useful for pets and their families. Except for Lap of Love Veterinary Hospice, of which I am co-founder and shareholder, and a company that I co-own with my brother called Monarch Pet Memorial Services, I have no other financial affiliations.

Publisher: Rolled Toe Publishing (iloveoldpets@gmail.com)

   /drmarygardner

This book is dedicated to all my cats who have taught me so much – Carcat, Princess, Herbie, Lilu, Bodhi, Goldie, and Mingo.

FOREWORD
Dr. Sheilah Robertson

> "The smallest feline is a masterpiece"
>
> —Leonardo da Vinci

If you live with an older cat, you know how unique they are and that taking care of them as they age can be challenging. As the title of this book infers, nine lives are not enough, but the information contained in it will help everyone who cares for cats make each of these lives, especially the latter ones the best they can be. It is an invaluable resource for cat parents but also for veterinarians and veterinary staff who are helping, advising and working as part of a cat's medical care team.

Dr Mary Gardner's professional and personal goal is to help older pets live well until the end; her book titled "it's never long enough" is full of practical tips and tricks to help care for geriatric dogs and was a unique addition to my library and this one is no different. She writes from personal experience having helped many of her own senior pets and uses this combined with her extensive veterinary medical knowledge to create an invaluable resource which has not existed before. She writes in a style that is easy for pet

 Drs Mary and Sheilah— good friends and fellow feline fanatics!

parents to understand and she writes from the heart, sharing the difficulties, the victories and the disappointments of geriatric care with compassion, leaving the reader feeling supported by someone who understands their struggles. Her commitment to senior cats and their families is unparalleled.

I first met Dr Mary when she sat down in my classroom at the University of Florida where she trained in veterinary medicine between 2004 and 2008. Her joy of being a veterinary student was as clear to me then as her joy of being a veterinarian is now. Her practical approach to veterinary medicine shone through when she started her clinical rotations – she was loved by the clients whose pets she was caring for and always went the extra step to make a patient feel comfortable and loved when they were away from their family. I interacted with her on many grueling rotations when her patients came to my service for anesthesia or pain management, and we worked side by side when she was learning anesthesia – she admitted it was a challenging task but as always tackled it head on and with energy, enthusiasm and an infectious positive energy to learn as much as she could. Fast forward to 2017 when I was lucky enough to be invited to join Lap of Love, the company she co-founded in 2010, as their senior medical director. I feel so lucky to be part of this amazing company where I call her "my boss" but also my colleague, fellow brain stormer and friend.

People and cats have been living alongside each other for at least 8,000 years, yet they are still mysterious creatures with secrets still to be discovered and myths unraveled. We may never know where the saying "cats have 9 lives" comes from – it could be a result of their survival instincts and ability to land on their feet when falling from a height or it could be based on nine being thought of as a magic or supernatural number. Regardless of where the saying originated, cats were worshiped in ancient Egypt – a fact they still know today! When you read this book, you will feel the love Dr Mary has for any older cat – the frail ones, the skinny fussy eaters and the ones who do not always cooperate with us. Her goal is to help you help them to live life to the fullest until it is time to say goodbye.

Dr Sheilah can almost always be found near a cat!

Table of Contents

Introduction: How my voyage began 15

PART ONE: GETTING TO THE GOLDEN YEARS LIFE STAGE 23

Chapter 1: A part of the family: A cat's place in the home sweet home 25
Chapter 2: Defining senior vs. geriatric: The fragility of life 29
Chapter 3: Aging in pets: Their clocks tick faster 37
Chapter 4: Dignity in aging: The mysteries of growing older 41

PART TWO: THE AGING BODY — COMMON AILMENTS THAT AFFECT GERIATRIC CATS 49

Chapter 5: Nose: The better to smell you with 51
Chapter 6: Eyes: "You looking at me?" Vision changes with age 61
Chapter 7: Hearing: "Say what?" Is it stubbornness, or hearing loss? 73
Chapter 8: Oral care: Keep them grinning 79
Chapter 9: Body condition and nutrition: Helping senior cats eat better and feel better 89
Chapter 10: Thermoregulation: Cool cats and feverish felines 119

Chapter 11: Skin: Scrappy cats—senior beauty is deeper ... 129

Chapter 12: Heart: Keeping the beat strong ... 137

Chapter 13: The kidneys: Little wonders ... 149

Chapter 14: Incontinence and other potty problems: Thinking outside the box ... 167

Chapter 15: The lungs: Keeping the wind in their sails ... 181

Chapter 16: Mobility: The creaky, shaky, and unsteady ... 193

Chapter 17: Cognition: Cross my mind... or not ... 219

Chapter 18: Endocrine disruption: Glands and hormones out of whack ... 243

Chapter 19: Cancer: Things that go bump in senior cats ... 257

Chapter 20: Pain: If only our cats could talk about discomfort, malaise, anxiety, and suffering ... 269

PART THREE: AGING WELL AND CARING FOR TIME-HONORED TABBIES ... 289

Chapter 21: Safety and environmental enrichment: Creating senior-cat-friendly homes ... 291

Chapter 22: Journaling: Tracking your cat's health ... 303

Chapter 23: Course of action: Therapeutic options and gaining acceptance from your senior cat ... 311

Chapter 24: Building your support team: Don't go it alone ... 335

Chapter 25: FAQs: Why not let your vet see your senior cat? ... 343

Chapter 26: Bucket lists: The joys of life ... 355

Chapter 27: Veterinary hospice: Living well until the end ... 363

Chapter 28: Goals of care: What matters most in the end ... 373

Chapter 29: Caregiver stress, burden, and burnout: When loving hurts ... 377

Chapter 30: Life quality: "Doc, when is it time?" ... 383

PART FOUR: ENDURING THE UNENDURABLE —PREPARING FOR AND SAYING GOODBYE ... 399

Chapter 31: A home divided: Conflicts between family members about end-of-life care ... 401

Chapter 32: Grief wellness: Anticipating and experiencing loss ... 405

Chapter 33: Young grief: When children bid farewell ... 413

Chapter 34: Housemates: Furry family members who lose their furry friends ... 421

Chapter 35: Natural passing: What to expect ... 427

Chapter 36: Euthanasia: The ending is what matters most ... 439

Chapter 37: Burial and cremation: A final place to rest and remember ... 455

Chapter 38: Keepsakes: Memorializing your cat to honor their life story ... 465

Chapter 39: After they are gone: The silence is deafening ... 475

Acknowledgments ... 479

References ... 481

ADDITIONAL

resources and supplements:

Designated website for this book that contains additional resources, tips, and product information organized by chapter.

Activity book to help children faced with the loss of their cat (**amzn.to/3dMZNQb**).

Workbook for journaling your cat's health status, care plan, and life quality, including organization (nutrition, symptoms, medications, test results) and assessment (cognition, cat and caregiver quality of life, goals of care, joys of living list) tools and more (**amzn.to/3dNvAkg**).

An Amazon shopping page for recommended products (**amazon.com/shop/drmarygardner**).

Dr. Mary Gardner's YouTube channel (**youtube.com/drmarygardner**).

Dr. Mary Gardner's website which has blogs, videos, and more (**drmarygardner.com**):

Nine Lives Are Not Enough

INTRODUCTION:

How my voyage began

> "The best way to approach happiness is expansion of yourself...
> with creation... with love... with sharing... with knowledge."
>
> — Jacques Cousteau

Of course I've always loved animals! But my childhood answers to the question, "What do you want to be when you grow up?" first revolved around the splashes Simone and Jacques Cousteau made in undersea exploration, rather than around veterinary surgeon James Herriot's storied experiences. My father owned a dive shop on North Caicos, a remote island within the Turks and Caicos. On summer breaks, I snorkeled and played tour guide from his dive boat as best as a kid could. I thought the ocean was my calling!

Besides those few summers on the island, I grew up in rural Orange County, New York. My brother, sister, and I dashed through cornfields, hid in an old barn, sledded down snowy hills, picked wildflowers, and chased wild critters. We also grew up with pet dogs—usually Great Pyrenees—and cats—usually strays who adopted us.

Me in North Caicos.
In hindsight, I should not
have done that to the fish!

 Me, our family dog Lump, a stray kitten, and my older sister, Sharon.

My parents divorced when I was 9. My brother and sister were older and lived with my father, but I lived with my mother most of the time. Finances were a struggle, so we lived in low-income housing. I desperately wanted my own pet, but we often rented rooms or had other temporary accommodations, which made it impossible. I was too embarrassed to have my friends visit, but a dog or cat wouldn't care about my humble dwelling!

When I was in high school, we moved into a 768-square-foot home that had a small backyard. I immediately went to the humane society to find a furry friend! I spotted a fuzzy, dirty beige, sweet-faced dog with dark eyes that melted my heart. Her name was Schmoo and the shelter identified her as a Samoyed mix. I had no idea what a Samoyed was, and I didn't care—I adopted her.

I took Schmoo home and immediately bathed her. To my horror, the dirt in her coat turned blood red when she got wet! I didn't understand why, but I quickly realized Schmoo had fleas. Later, I learned that most of that "dirt" was flea poop, which contained digested blood from the meals the fleas enjoyed at Schmoo's expense! I finished bathing Schmoo and toweled her off. Voilá! Her coat had turned pearly white as a Samoyed should be! We renamed her Snow White.

Snow White and I were instant buddies. She slept in my bed, helped me make new friends, and loved riding in the car. A few years later when I moved away for college, I had a rough time leaving Snow White behind. So while I studied marine affairs at the University of Miami, I got a job so I could pay for off-campus housing and bring Snow White to live with me. She remained my companion throughout college and my entry into the workforce as a college graduate.

Although I loved my boss, my first job working for a maritime lawyer was not what I envisioned for my future. So I moved on and became a trainer at my family's software company. Eventually I became a product manager who worked with the research and development team to design software, and I frequently had to travel.

During one of my work trips, my dog sitter reported that Snow White had gotten into a terrible dog fight and had been admitted to a veterinary hospital. I raced home the next day, and I vividly remember visiting her. Snow White's beautiful coat had been shaved so the veterinary team could find and clean all of her bite wounds. Tubes protruded from under her skin to help drain the fluid from her wounds, and her broken jaw was wired. Still, Snow White wagged her tail when she saw me.

After about a week, I got to take Snow White home. I tried to care for her for several days. But she wasn't eating well or taking all her pills, and I couldn't clean her extensive wounds sufficiently. I took her back to the veterinary hospital because I knew they would care for her better than I could.

After another week in the hospital, Snow White's condition worsened, and she had to have a blood transfusion. I left work immediately

Me and Snow White shortly before her accident.

to visit her. My beautiful Snow White was lying on a blanketed pad on the floor of the treatment room, being well cared for. But she looked yellow to me (I didn't know then that her abnormal color indicated liver failure). And again, she wagged her tail when she saw me! It seemed like Snow White could never have a bad day. A trait I wish I possessed.

I spent two hours sitting on the floor with Snow White, petting her head in my lap, and telling her about my day. She was now 12 years old. Besides this trauma, she had been healthy her entire life. What I didn't know then was that senior dogs have a harder time fighting infection and recovering from organ damage than young dogs do.

Then at 6:01 p.m., Snow White looked up at me. Her head suddenly arched back and her legs stretched out in front of her. I knew instantly that she was dying.

I screamed for the doctor, and the veterinary team ran in and lifted Snow White onto the exam table. The veterinarian started CPR. As hard as they tried, they could not bring Snow White back. I stood by, stunned. I had been certain Snow White would recover and return home with me one day soon.

Losing Snow White was horrible. And it hurt me when people would say, "Well, she was old," or "She was just a dog." I was so blessed to have had her in my life. Snow White will always be the first angel to watch over me.

Snow White's inspiration

Shortly after I lost Snow White, I realized I wanted to learn more about animal health and diseases and to start the journey to become a veterinarian! So at the age of 29, I began volunteering at the humane society. It was a mix of incredible fun—sharing my time caring for the animals and learning about anesthesia and surgery in the spay/neuter ward—and dreadful heartbreak—saying goodbye to animals who weren't adopted and had to be euthanized.

When I was 30, I quit my software job to work as a kennel assistant at a veterinary hospital. One week I was teaching CEOs of large corporations how to use their new software, and the next week I was cleaning kennels and picking up dog poop in the hospital lobby! I also enrolled in the undergraduate courses that were required before admission to veterinary school.

The moment I met those requirements, I applied only to the University of Florida College of Veterinary Medicine. The in-state tuition would allow me to graduate with less student loan debt. This was crucial, because the average annual starting salary for a veterinarian at that time was about $55,000. I was fortunate to be accepted after my first application, and in 2004 I started veterinary school at the age of 31.

My orange tabby, Herbie, grey kitty, Lilu, and calico cat, Princess, along with my two new family members, Serissa, a joyful Samoyed, and Neo, a handsome Doberman, helped me survive those fascinating, tough, tiring, fact-filled four years of veterinary school. I am proud to have graduated with the University of Florida College of Veterinary Medicine Class of 2008!

 I had the honor of delivering the student commencement address to my veterinary school class.

I've got the veterinary degree—now what?

I was lucky to be hired into a wonderful veterinary clinic in Deerfield Beach, Florida: Pet Vet Animal Hospital. I loved general practice! I loved the pets, I loved the clients, I loved the team I worked with, and I loved what I was learning. Yet

I began to feel the urge to make an even bigger impact with my degree and help more animals in a different way.

Right around that time, my friend and fellow University of Florida graduate Dr. Dani McVety called to catch up. She also asked whether I'd be interested in partnering with her in providing in-home veterinary hospice and euthanasia services. I knew of another veterinarian in Deerfield Beach who provided a similar service, and I thought that it must be depressing as a full-time job. But the way Dani explained her home visits—the comfort she saw in her patients, how the families reacted, and how much satisfaction and gratitude she received—I wanted to hear more about how I could help.

I visited Dani in Tampa and we brainstormed for two days straight. I fell in love with this idea, and something inside me lit up! The reason I had left my good software job, cleaned kennels, and went through veterinary school was because of the death of my dog Snow White. I realized I wanted to make an impact in my career by focusing on helping families who were losing their pets to advanced age or irreversible medical conditions. It was perfect for me!

Dani and I dreamt of ways we could grow and expand the business to help more families. We would also need a unique kind of veterinary practice software, and I started designing it in my head that night. I was so excited to start this new type of work in veterinary end-of-life care and grow the company to offer these services nationwide one day.

In the summer of 2010, our company, which is full-heartedly named Lap of Love, employed only Dani and me. We answered phones, scheduled appointments, and visited patients at home whenever and wherever families needed us. We were tired and nearly broke—but excited as the company started to grow.

Fast-forward 12 years, and in 2022 Lap of Love employs more than 300 full-time veterinarians who offer end-of-life care in over 115 locations across the country. We help over 120,000 families a year with end-of-life medical care for their pets who are terminally ill or have such advanced aging problems that their quality of life is poor. I have transitioned out of making in-home visits to full-time management of the company and helping our Lap of Love family.

Aren't I depressed?

One might imagine, as I once did when I first learned about veterinary end-of-life services, that hospice care and euthanizing animals as a full-time job is depressing. And, make no mistake, euthanasia can be heartbreaking, because I see the sorrow in the families' eyes. But it is rewarding to make a tremendously difficult experience a wee bit better for the pet and the family. The hugs I've gotten are fantastic! The thank-you messages I receive bring me tears of gratitude. For me, I cannot imagine a better niche of veterinary medicine than hospice and euthanasia. If I had a tail to wag or the ability to purr, I could better show how truly happy I am!

What has weighed heavily on me through the years were the visits I made to homes where the pet had not seen their veterinarian in a long time. I knew that veterinary care could have helped many of these pets sooner, such as with pain and anxiety relief as well as simple changes to manage the pet's ailments better. I knew that the pet and family could have had a longer, better quality of life.

I loved my hospice patients. I could do so much for them and their families before the end. But I wanted so many of them to see their veterinarian even sooner and more regularly because they could have received care for months to years to enhance and likely extend their pets' lives—long before my help was needed.

I realize that it may be difficult to get many older pets, especially cats, into the pet carrier for veterinary visits. I realize that some families may presume (or may even be told) that their pet is old and there is nothing they can do. But in so many cases, there is so much we can and should do!

Me and my cat Herbie (the love bug). I love getting love from old kitties!

Sailing on in my journey of sharing

I've spent years studying the ailments that plague our aging pets and the ways we can help manage and protect them in their homes. I travel the world teaching veterinarians at medical conferences and have written numerous articles in the veterinary literature and co-edited a veterinary textbook on these topics.

Because I also want to reach more pet parents directly, I was inspired to write this book and its canine counterpart, "It's Never Long Enough: A Practical Guide to Caring for Your Geriatric Dog." As companions to both books, I've created two toolkits specifically designed for caregivers of geriatric pets, "Geriatric Dog Health & Care Journal," and "Geriatric Cat Health & Care Journal." I've also coauthored a guide and activity books for children facing their final goodbye to a beloved dog and cat, "Forever Friend."

As you guide your cat's voyage through his or her* golden years, I hope this book gives you healthcare insights and guidance to spark new thoughts on how you can help your aging cat continue to live happily and comfortably. I also hope to spur smiles and maybe a few tears along the way. Throughout these chapters, I share lessons I've learned from my patients and their families' love and heartbreak,** and describe my experiences in caring for my own cats. You'll find the latest information on aging and common ailments of older cats, checklists to help you monitor your cat for aging changes and illnesses, questions to ask your veterinarian, tips to manage your cat at home, and product suggestions. I also cover the importance of checking in on yourself and other family members as you manage the challenges of caring for an ailing cat, how to assess your cat's quality of life, and what to consider before and after your cat earns their angel wings.

Where appropriate, and because the information may apply to pets and their families in general, some content in this book is the same or similar to that in "It's Never Long Enough: A Practical Guide to Caring for Your Geriatric Dog." Even then, I've updated the information where applicable based on research that's been published or new information that's come to my attention on those general topics in the short time since I completed the canine edition. We veterinarians know well and often say that "cats are not small dogs!" So rest assured that I wrote this book specifically for feline pet parents and the challenges you may face as your cat ages. Geriatric pets are my life's passion. I love the grey muzzle, golden-year pets—the wobbly dogs and the skinny, crusty cats. They are the best! And so are the families who love them.

---

* Instead of the impersonal pronoun "it" that you'll see in a lot of scientific literature when referring to a singular pet, throughout this book I wanted to be more personal and use "he" and "she" and related pronouns in the singular sense. All pets are loved, no matter their sex, so every "he" or "she" I refer to remains a cherished representation for your pet.

** It bears repeating that the content in this book is based on my professional and personal knowledge and experiences and is not intended as a substitute for a veterinarian-client-patient relationship. Always partner with, and consult your veterinarian about your pet's healthcare.

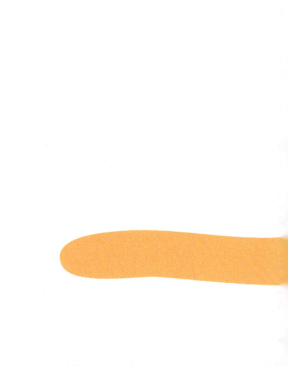

Part One:

GETTING TO THE GOLDEN YEARS LIFE STAGE

In every relationship there comes a time when many more days lie behind you than ahead. When we're granted the benefit of that keen awareness, our remaining days together become even more precious. You may have already begun to recognize the subtle changes that signal that shift in the sands of time as your cat ages… more struggles climbing to a top perch, diminished sparkle in his eyes, less body fat, and dwindling enthusiasm about exploring a new cardboard box or paper bag.

It may seem like only yesterday that you celebrated "Gotcha Day" (adoption day!) with your puffball kitten or mature feline family member. And our cats have indeed become family members, especially compared with many of their counterparts of years past. Although time typically marches on too quickly in many aspects of our lives, time seems to really sprint when it comes to our cat's lifetime. Why is that? Why can't they live as long as we do? Why do some cats age more successfully than others? What's the difference between a senior cat and a geriatric cat? Can cats become frail, like some elderly people do? Let's set off together in this chapter to explore these questions, and more, to help you ponder the mysteries and mechanisms of aging in cats.

CHAPTER 1:

A part of the family: A cat's place in the home sweet home

"I gave my cat a bath the other day. He sat there and enjoyed it. And it was fun for me. Oh, the fur would stick to my tongue a little bit ..."

—STEVE MARTIN

Dogs and cats have lived alongside humans for centuries. The human and non-human animals found mutual benefit in hanging out together. Classically, domesticated dogs were guardians, warning of threats or seeing off invaders. Cats were the rodent pest control patrol! Were friendships struck? Attachments made? Of course! But most pets were considered "just animals" and held a different place on a farm or in a household. Our relationships with pets have changed remarkably, and especially over the last few decades.

How times have changed ...

I remember as a child growing up with our family cats. They were typically strays who had found us, so we fed them and let them live in the barn. They were rarely allowed in our house, and never in our bedrooms! Contrast that with my household today. My cats now venture outside only with my supervision, climb *indoor* cat trees, and snooze wherever they please—my couch, bed, or dining room chairs! Pet hair everywhere is the decor of love.

According to a 2015 poll, more than 95% of pet owners consider their pets members of the family.[1] And we demonstrate this kinship love: 45% of owners bought birthday presents for their pets, and 81% of cat owners and 72% of dog owners let their pets sleep in their bed at night. The fact that you are reading this book shows that the four-footed critters who share their lives with you are cherished family members and will get attentive care as they age.

Where the pets are

So how many pets are out there in the U.S. today? How many families share their lives with pets?

Based on the 2021-2022 American Pet Products Association National Pet Owners Survey, 70% of U.S. households, or 90.1 million homes, have at least one type of pet.[2] The survey reveals that 69 million households have dogs, and 45.3 million households have cats and many times it is more than one cat. We're also pet parents to fish (14.7 million households), birds (9.9 million households), small animals (6.2 million households), reptiles (5.7 million households), and horses (3.5 million households).

FUN FACT:
BEST FRIENDS, BEST MEDICINE

Through the years, we've learned about the health benefits of sharing our homes with dogs, cats, and other pets. Most family physicians (97%) agree that pets provide health benefits for people. And 74% said that with medical evidence to support it, they would prescribe pets to improve their patients' overall health.[3] Studies show that pets help their owners be happier and more physically fit, with health benefits that include:

- More opportunities to socialize, exercise, and spend time outside
- Lower cholesterol and triglyceride levels and blood pressure
- Better cognitive function in older adults
- More companionship, less loneliness and depression, and decreased symptoms of post-traumatic stress disorder.[4]

Veterinary care for the ages

Veterinary education and the profession have shifted along with the changes in animals' roles in society and humans' overall relationship with pets. Most veterinarians today focus on dogs and cats. Some veterinarians even go on to become certified in feline medicine and see cat patients only. The American Veterinary Medical Association (AVMA) reports that more than 50,000 veterinarians (66.8% of private clinical practices) provide companion animal care (dogs, cats, pet birds, and exotics) exclusively. About 4,200 provide care for farm animals (e.g. cows, pigs, sheep), and 4,100 provide care for horses predominantly or exclusively.[5]

 Courtney is an amazing mom to her son Theo as well as her cat Cena!

Most veterinary students are still trained to care for many animal species. They complete medical and surgical rotations in equine and farm animal care, even if they plan to become dog and cat docs. And the education we receive in veterinary school continues to advance and expand. Of course we learn basic medical care, but we also learn about specialized orthopedic surgeries, heart surgeries, dialysis for kidney failure, chemotherapy for cancer, acupuncture, and so much more.

Pets' changing status in the family, along with advances in veterinary medicine that mirror those in human medicine, have increased pets' life expectancy. Just as healthcare is crucial to us, veterinary care for our pets is paramount. Routine care such as vaccinations and parasite preventives not only ward off disease in our pets, they help keep other pets and even people in the household healthy. Pets' veterinary care may range from a physical examination and quick nail trim to advanced joint surgery or radiation therapy.

Did you know that most any disease that can affect a human can affect a cat, too? Cats can have dental, kidney, gastrointestinal, and heart diseases. Arthritis, cancer, dementia, and diabetes are other familiar human ailments that cats may have as well. And similar to the opportunities available in human medicine, basic to advanced diagnostic tests along with simple to complex treatments are at the ready from your primary care veterinary team or veterinary specialists.

The great news is that basic, routine veterinary care goes a long way in keeping pet family members healthy during their lifetimes of happily shared adventures with you. Seeking veterinary advice and following veterinary recommendations can also help prevent some of the costly health problems that may otherwise emerge as a pet ages.

So how much do pet parents typically spend on pet care? The same 2015 poll that reported 95% of owners think of their pets as family members assessed how much the owners typically spend annually[1]:

- Food/treats—$476.60
- Medical costs (veterinary appointments, medications, procedures)—$425.70
- Pet sitting or boarding—$128.50
- Toys—$63.70
- Other (habitats, collars, litter)—$97.40
- Total—$1,191.90

Adjusted for inflation as of June 2022, that total equates to $1,511.18.[6]

We all vary in our abilities to care for our cats, especially when they are older. But we all care and don't want our cats to suffer. So this book focuses on the care we can provide, includes care options that you might not otherwise be aware of, helps you navigate what to expect as cats age, and suggests how senior and older cats with health problems can be managed in the home, including at the end of their lives.

The intent of this book is not to cover every disease a cat can get, but rather to focus on age-related changes. What causes them, and how can you care for a cat who may be plagued by them? The care suggestions in this book will range from those that are inexpensive and easy to implement to those that are elaborate and time-intensive.

Regardless, my intent with this book is to help you keep your beloved cat a healthy, active, engaged, and comfortable family member throughout her golden years—may they be many!

CHAPTER 2:

Defining senior vs. geriatric: The fragility of life

> "Choose to focus on what age gives you,
> not what it has taken away."
>
> —Arthur C. Brooks, American social scientist

When I was growing up, I vividly remember going to my Grandma Gardner's house in New Jersey every Thanksgiving and the phenomenal meal she prepared. After decades passed, our lovely tradition moved from the blustery Northeast to my father's house in South Florida, where Grandma had also bought a small condominium.

At the time of Grandma's move, my father and my grandmother were both senior citizens, but the years between them had highlighted many differences. My father was in his late 50s, yet his energy level and activities matched those of his 30s. He golfed three times a week, worked on his dive boat, treasure-hunted (my father is a real-life shipwreck diver!), and prepared a fantastic Thanksgiving feast (only a slightly less phenomenal one than my grandmother had cooked in years past!). My father was (and still is!) completely independent and mentally sound with no physical limitations or medical problems.

 One Thanksgiving holiday with my grandmother Margaret and my father, Allan.

FUN FACT:

Since 1943, when Jacques Cousteau and Émile Gagnan invented the Aqua-Lung, more than 28 million people have learned to use scuba (*self-contained underwater breathing apparatus*) gear and plunge into a fraction of the undersea world that covers 70% of our planet.[1]

My grandmother didn't have any known underlying medical problems either, and her mind was as sharp as a tack. She still baked her phenomenal apple pie to share with us at Thanksgiving! But she couldn't see or hear as well as she used to, and she had given up driving, so I would sometimes chauffeur her. She had little muscle strength and she held onto my arm and carefully shuffled her feet to maintain steady contact with the ground. Her hands were thin and her skin was dotted with wisdom spots. Her eyes had a grey haze (but they still sparkled!). She took her sweater along everywhere! The temperatures in Florida in November could still be 80 F, but Grandma got cold easily. She also tired quickly after an afternoon of socializing with family, so I'd drive her home before our Thanksgiving festivities ended. My grandmother needed help with various things, but not to the point of needing to move to a nursing facility. I realized that my grandmother was geriatric, but back then I didn't know the precise reasons why. She was fragile, while my father was not.

 My father, Allan, the treasure hunter near Jupiter, FL.

As I turned my career focus toward older pets, I went down a rabbit hole to learn about the differences between senior and geriatric. And I'm still learning! With all of the phenomenal achievements made in human and veterinary medicine over the last 100-plus years, people and pets are living longer than ever before. And with increased longevity comes a host of age-related ailments and diseases that researchers are studying so we can learn how to better prevent or manage them.

Senior or geriatric? An old cat by any other name would be as sweet

In pondering this question of senior vs. geriatric while co-writing the 2017 textbook *Treatment and Care of the Veterinary Geriatric Patient*, I turned to insight from the American Veterinary Medical Association (AVMA). I discovered there wasn't a strict definition for a "senior" or a "geriatric" pet then. They used the terms interchangeably and considered cats (and small dogs) as senior or geriatric at 7 years of age.[2,3]

In their 2009 Senior Care Guidelines, the American Association of Feline Practitioners (AAFP) stated that cats do not become senior at a specific age. They state that because individual animal and body systems age at different rates, cats can be classified as mature or middle-aged at 7 to 10 years, senior at 11 to 14 years, and geriatric at 15 years and older.[4]

More recently, the 2021 American Animal Hospital Association (AAHA) AAFP Feline Life Stage Guidelines define senior cats as older than 10 years, but they do not define geriatric cats.[5] International Cat Care, an animal welfare charity, goes a step further and calls cats "super senior" at age 15 years and older.[6] In a separate document, the 2021 AAFP Feline Senior Care Guidelines, the authors acknowledge cats as seniors at 11 to 14 years of age, but they go further and state that some cats are more appropriately considered senior at age 8 years — some cat breeds or cats with certain genetic predispositions may be considered senior at an even earlier age. The authors also recognized "the newer concept of 'frailty'" as it pertains to care for older people and the significance that frailty has in feline medicine.[7]

So in general, if the veterinary profession considers cats older than 10 years to be "senior," what about "geriatric"? People may be classified as "senior" beginning at some point between the ages of 50 and 70 years, depending on the organization or business that decides the age at which people are eligible to receive that organization's or business's benefits. In human medicine, people are considered to be "elderly" from age 65 years on, but the term "geriatric" doesn't apply to a specific age. For a person to be classified as geriatric, their age, health, mental status, and how well they can function in the world are all taken into account. The authors of the 2021 Feline Senior Care Guidelines indicate agreement on this point, linking the term "geriatric" to cats' health status, rather than to a specific age.[7]

The fragility factor: Handle with care

As our pets age, just like we two-footed folk, things get a little less automatic. For example, you may notice your cat is slower to pounce on toys and more reluctant to climb or jump than she used to be. Because many studies have been done to assess canine health, diseases, and aging, we know that aging is similar in people and dogs with respect to our nervous, immune, and muscle systems and gene alterations.[8] Dogs share our environments and develop many of the same age-related diseases that we do, such as cancer, heart and kidney disease, cognitive problems, and many others.[9] Of course cats share our environments and develop these diseases, too, but in general, cats and aging in cats haven't been studied with respect to their similarities in people as often as dogs have.

In people, the concept of the *Fragility Syndrome* (also known as *Frailty Syndrome*) is used in geriatric care, which stems from having diminished physical and cognitive physiological reserve. *Physiological reserve* is basically the body's ability to be resilient, and it helps organs function properly under stress. Physiological reserve decreases with age, but not equally in all people.[10]

Diminished physiological reserve makes elderly people more vulnerable to stressors—even seemingly mild stressors such as taking a new medicine, having a minor urinary tract infection, or undergoing a minor diagnostic or surgical procedure. With diminished physiological reserve, experiencing a stressor means a person has a higher likelihood of an adverse health outcome.[11] These stressors can cause a drastic change in a vulnerable person's health status. A seemingly healthy elderly person who has experienced a stressor but has diminished physiological reserve may go from having a stable posture and balance to being unsteady or experiencing falls, from being mobile to immobile, from being independent in daily activities to being dependent on others, or from being alert and aware to having severe confusion.[11] Thus, the person is considered to be fragile or frail.

People with fragility or frailty also have a greater risk of hospitalizations and death.[12] Keeping fragile people functioning well and safe becomes more and more of a concern. Nearly 10% of people 65 years of age or older are fragile, and fragility increases to 25% to 50% of people 85 years or older.[13]

The encouraging take from those statistics is that up to 75% of people over the age of 85 may *not* be fragile. So strategies to prevent fragility and tools to identify it in human medicine are crucial and have been studied.[11]

Signs of fragility or frailty in people

Physicians use various combinations of these indicators to classify fragility or frailty syndrome in people:

- unexplained or unintentional weight loss;
- weakness (including decreased grip strength);
- slowed motor performance (slow gait/walking speed);
- fatigue/exhaustion;
- impaired balance;

- decreased physical activity;
- social withdrawal;
- cognitive impairment (slow or muddled thought processes); or
- increased vulnerability to physiological stresses.

People are considered "geriatric" once they experience three of these signs of fragility or frailty:

- weakness (reduced grip strength);
- unexplained or unintentional weight loss (chronic [long-term] undernutrition);
- slowed mobility (slow gait speed);
- self-reported fatigue or exhaustion; or
- low physical activity level.

Now we know the same is true for older pets. They may be "old" in terms of age in years like my father (sorry, Dad!), but there may also come a point when they become fragile or frail, like my grandmother.

Signs of fragility or frailty in pets

In general, we can correlate these signs and classifications of frailty in people with similar signs in cats. Observations like:

- more difficulty with jumping or using stairs, slower to get up, more hesitant to use scratching posts or fully stretch out;
- less interest in food and unintentional weight loss;
- slower walking pace and reluctance to run;
- longer naps or restless nights; or
- less interest in play.

In fact, frailty assessments have begun to be studied in dogs, with veterinarians using the following categories and signs[9]:

- **Weakness**: Does the pet have normal muscle mass, moderate muscle wasting, or muscle atrophy (shrinking)? Muscle wasting and muscle atrophy can result from sarcopenia, which is skeletal muscle loss that occurs with aging, or cachexia, which is severe weight loss plus muscle wasting associated with disease.
- **Chronic undernutrition**: What is the pet's body condition (overweight or underweight based on assessment of body fat), level of appetite, and coat quality and density?

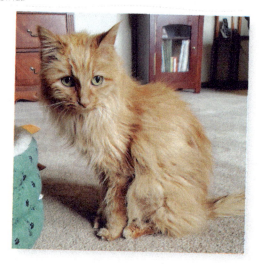

At 20 years old, Skittle still dishes out love full steam, even though he ticks a lot of the frailty boxes: muscle wasting, unintentional weight loss, reduced appetite, slowness (and stiffness), and low activity level (more sleeping, little self-grooming).

- **Poor mobility**: Is the pet's movement normal, or does the pet have stiffness, lameness, or incoordination? Does the pet have joint pain and, if so, is it moderate or marked?
- **Exhaustion**: Does the pet have normal exercise tolerance, or is exercise associated with tiredness or breathlessness?
- **Low physical activity**: Is the pet's activity level normal, moderately low, or low?

It doesn't seem unreasonable to expect that the categories and signs used to assess frailty in dogs could also be used to assess frailty in cats.

Frailty in cats appears to be even less studied than it is in dogs, but I'm confident we'll learn more as researchers continue to explore aging in people and other animals. The 2021 AAFP Feline Senior Care Guidelines suggest that veterinarians use two types of frailty scales adapted from use in human medicine to assess whether frailty factors are present in senior cats.[7] These scales indicate physical or cognitive (mental) states of decline in senior cats. The responses to each set of questions signify whether senior cats are *pre-frail* (answering 'yes' to two out of four questions) or *frail* (answering 'yes' to three or four out of four questions):

Phenotype (outward signs) frailty scale

- Has the cat lost weight unintentionally?
- Does the cat exhibit weakness?
- Does the cat tire easily or become exhausted earlier than would normally be expected?
- Does the cat exhibit slowness or have a low activity level?

Index frailty scale:

- Does the cat have deficits in normal function of any body system?
- Does the cat have psychological/emotional deficits?
- Does the cat exhibit cognitive, task-related deficits?
- Does the cat show reduced social capability?

All of these can be signs that the body is not quite working as it used to, and there can be many causes. But they do signify keeping a closer watch over our feline friends to ensure that they have all they need to continue to thrive and avoid stumbling blocks, to identify opportunities to investigate issues further and resolve some ailments or slow the progression of others, and to provide comforting care every day.

Keeping an eye out for changes

So how do we stay vigilant? In conjunction with your cat's physical examination findings, laboratory test results, and health history questions, the frailty scales for cats proposed in the 2021 AAFP Feline Senior Care Guidelines will help practicing veterinarians keep a closer watch on our elder feline friends and identify patients who are likely to need extra care and more follow-up veterinary visits than usual throughout their remaining years.

One of my dreams is for pet parents, together with their veterinarians, to better identify signs of advanced aging, vulnerability, and frailty in their cats. Developing, testing, and using standardized health and quality-of-life assessments of senior and geriatric cats should provide better evidence-based clinical tools. And in using better assessment tools, the care and treatment of geriatric cats can be more closely and individually optimized.

One easy way to monitor for changes in your cat's appearance and behavior is to take photos and videos of your cat every six months. (I'm betting you already do this more often than that!) Simply single out a couple photos or short videos at regular intervals, and keep them dated and organized for visual comparisons. Videos should show your cat walking, playing, using stairs, jumping onto and down from their favorite perch, and getting into the litter box. I've also created a journal as a handy companion to this book, called *Geriatric Cat Health & Care Journal: A Complete Toolkit for the Geriatric Cat Caregiver*. This journal can help you chart your pet's course during smooth sailing and squalls, and you can review it with your veterinarian during your cat's visits. In Chapter 22 of this book, I also guide you through tracking your cat's health.

What can be done for frail pets?

Research shows that frailty in people is preventable and its progression can be halted or even reversed–in essence, we can turn back time! By focusing on nutritional counseling and dietary support (ensuring the correct amount of protein intake and total calories), strength training to prevent muscle loss (individualized to the patient's abilities), mental stimulation, and health education, frailty can be prevented and corrected.[14-16] For people, physical activity has been proposed as an ideal way to prevent the abnormal processes that arise throughout the body and contribute to physical frailty.[17]

It isn't a stretch to think that frailty may also be preventable or reversible in cats. In this book, I highlight how you can help your cat best manage the aging process and the associated changes during his or her senior years, as well as the diseases that most commonly affect older cats.

CHAPTER 3:

Aging in pets: Their clocks tick faster

"How did it get so late so soon?"

— Source unverified
(the internet attributes this quote to Dr. Seuss)

Let's pounce on a popular topic of pet life—how old is your cat in people years? Turns out that simply multiplying cats' and dogs' ages by 7 to figure their age in human years is bad math. Instead, many charts and online calculators estimate relative ages of cats and dogs based on human years and they attempt to account for the age at which a pet reaches sexual maturity, as well as their breed and body size.

The 2021 American Animal Hospital Association (AAHA) AAFP Feline Life Stage Guidelines define four age-related life stages in cats similar to those that pet parents recognize: kitten (less than 1 year of age), young adult (1 to 6 years of age), mature adult (7 to 10 years of age), and senior (older than 10 years).[1] These age groups aren't absolute and can vary among individuals. So, for instance, a 12-year-old cat who is healthy and in excellent shape may be more similar to a mature adult cat than a senior cat (just as healthy, fit senior people may seem much younger than their age). The end-of-life stage is a fifth category, which can occur at any age.[1]

Biological clocks

Age in years reveals how long we've existed, and it's called *chronological age*. It differs from *biological age*, which accounts for factors that affect lifespan such as disease, environmental and lifestyle influences, and genetics.

Biological age can be estimated by assessing molecules called methyl groups that naturally circulate in the body and are added to specific parts of our DNA over the course of our lifetime. (A look back to biology class: DNA is *deoxyribonucleic acid*, a molecule that contains the genetic code in all known organisms and in many viruses. The genetic code essentially instructs an organism's development, life processes, and reproduction.) This addition of methyl groups to DNA (called *DNA methylation*) throughout life occurs in people, cats, dogs, and other species. DNA methylation gives researchers an accurate way to estimate biological age and it's known as an *epigenetic clock*.

Epigenetic clocks help us better understand many facets of the aging process. These clocks have been developed for people and mice, and recently they have

FUN FACT:

Genetic researchers have used an epigenetic clock for dogs to develop a new calculation that more accurately converts dog years to people years.[3] The new calculation was developed based on data from Labrador retrievers and shows that:

- an 8-week-old puppy is similar in age to a 9-month-old human baby;
- a 1-year-old dog is roughly 31 human years old (remember, most dogs can produce offspring by around 6 months of age);
- a 2-year-old dog is 42 in human years;
- a 4-year-old dog is about 53 in human years;
- a 7-year-old dog is around 62 human years old;
- a 12-year-old dog is about 70 in human years; and
- a 15-year-old dog is about 74 in human years.[3,4]

As you can see, the epigenetic clock "ticks" faster earlier in a dog's life than our human epigenetic clock does, then the canine clock slows later in life.

A similar calculation for cats hasn't been formulated yet. On average, cats live about 15 years and dogs live about 12 years,[5] so a cat-to-human-years calculation may differ from the dog-to-human years formula.

been developed for dogs and cats. Researchers expect that the feline epigenetic clock may be used in the future to monitor cats' health and allow additional studies in anti-aging interventions.[2]

Beyond the numbers: no matter our pets' ages in human years, most of us agree that they do not live long enough. But we can make the last life stage smoother—and potentially help them live a longer, better life.

FUN FACT:

Researchers have shown that animals can judge time. Time perception tests in mice and high-resolution images of a group of neurons in a part of the brain called the medial entorhinal cortex—a structure that helps with memory and navigation—revealed that these nerve cells switch on and count like a clock while an animal waits.[6,7]

If your cat sits on your pillow and paw-taps your nose five minutes before your alarm goes off, or sits next to her food bowl 20 minutes before dinnertime, it's probably no surprise to you that animals seem to know what time it is!

Is old age a disease?

A closing thought as we delve into more details about aging cats in the next chapters. A popular mantra among veterinarians (and most people) is that "old age isn't a disease." While that may be technically true, many health issues associated with aging exist and may develop more readily as fragility arises.

In human medicine, it has been suggested that aging *should* be classified as a disease, because such classification might promote more urgent aging research. Officially designating aging as a disease could enhance more development and rigorous

 Lou is well into his 20s–he's a bit dented (my affectionate term for overly skinny) and slow–but still living his best life!

study of therapies to address aging processes and age-related diseases. It could also increase funding for aging research and allow health insurance reimbursement for more treatments that have been proven to prevent, slow, or reverse aging processes.[8] Classifying age as a disease could affect pets as well, because developments in human medicine often influence diagnostic tests and treatments in veterinary medicine.

For now, age isn't classified as a disease in people or in cats, yet it's important to notice as changes occur in your cat and know the steps you can take to keep them comfortable and happy. I believe it's imperative that pet parents understand the aging process, how to recognize age-related conditions and what it means for their cat to have them, how to manage their cat's conditions, and where to find appropriate support to help them help their cat.

CHAPTER 4:

Dignity in aging: The mysteries of growing older

> "...it has been the providence of nature to give this creature [the cat] nine lives instead of one..."
>
> —Pilpay (also known as Bidpai), ancient Indian philosopher

As the years pass, like us, our cats nap even more (cats normally sleep or rest about 80% of the day as it is![1]), they lose muscle mass, and their get-up-and-jump attitude slumps. Most living creatures age (hydra–small, tubelike, freshwater organisms–and one type of jellyfish are exceptions and avoid aging!), and aging occurs at different rates across species.

How and why humans age has been debated for centuries! And in the last 100 years, oodles of studies have helped us better understand the aging process in people, along with age-associated diseases and other challenges.

FUN FACT:

Corals are the longest living animals on our planet—some can live for 5,000 years!

For people, it's generally accepted that living a long, healthy life is influenced by many factors, including genetics, relationships, environment, culture, education, occupation, income, and behavior. Behavior encompasses many other factors, such as the choices we make about diet, exercise, sleep, smoking, drinking alcohol, getting regular medical checkups, managing stress, engaging socially, and learning new things.

Many studies on aging focus on centenarians—people who live to be 100 and older. For example, large studies of centenarians in China revealed that mental resilience and optimism are keys to longevity,[2] along with following proven preventive healthcare strategies: eating a rich and varied diet full of grains and fruits, keeping up good dental health, not smoking, limiting alcohol intake, and sustaining a calm outlook.[3]

We can't study exactly the same health strategies in cats, but I do see many cats live good, long lives when they have environmental enrichment that supports emotional well-being and physical activity, healthy diets (and proper weights), routine veterinary medical and dental care, and positive bonds with their human and furry family members.

As biotechnology companies continue to attract billions of dollars from investors interested in investigating strategies to slow and even reverse the aging process in people,[4] the results of their research should benefit our pets as well. As our lifespans increase, we'll want our best furry friends' lifespans to keep pace!

Pets contribute to aging research in people

How and why cats age has been less studied than it has been in people and in dogs. Dogs are excellent models of aging in people.[5] Dogs receive similar healthcare and share our environment, yet they live shorter lives compared with people. So studies on the factors that influence dogs' longevity are relatable to people and can be completed much faster. Dogs, rather than mice, are now center stage for research in human aging, in part because dogs in North America, Australia, and Europe are living life most similar to humans.

How are we similar? Let us count the ways! Dogs have medical care similar to that of people: They are monitored and evaluated frequently, receive vaccinations, and get referred to medical specialists when needed. We share our homes, neighborhoods, exercise habits (walking, jogging, swimming, and even surfing!), and often our food with them. Dogs develop many of the same age-related diseases humans do, and they live with the same pollutants (e.g. secondhand smoke and other air

 Me and a yoga-loving goat friend.

contaminants, pesticides, herbicides) and disease-causing bugs that we do.

Sound familiar? Cats live close to the same lives as humans, too! Perhaps with the exception of exercise. (Even cat yoga is much more strenuous for humans, as is goat yoga!) Cats also tend to be pickier eaters than dogs when it comes to table foods. But, sadly, not a lot of research has been done yet on factors that relate to the aging process in cats. In fact, overall, dogs have been studied more often than cats, perhaps because dogs were domesticated thousands of years earlier than cats and comprise a vast range of breeds—400, compared with cat breeds, which number about 40.[6]

Two major lifespan studies in dogs are the Morris Animal Foundation's Golden Retriever Lifetime Study, which is monitoring more than 3,000 pet golden retrievers and celebrated its 10-year anniversary in 2022 (**morrisanimalfoundation.org/golden-retriever-lifetime-study**), and The Dog Aging Project, which involves more than 10,000 mixed-breed and purebred pet dogs. These studies hope to identify the factors that lead to better health and longer life in dogs, and they may shed light on improving lifespan in people. The good news for cats is that these dog lifespan studies will spark and likely have already encouraged researchers to design and implement similar studies in pet cats. For example, the University of Liverpool's Cat PAWS (Prospective Ageing and Welfare Study) research aims to evaluate the health and welfare of mature, senior, and geriatric pet cats (check out Feline Healthy Ageing Clinic on Facebook)[7]; and Basepaws, a pet genetics testing company has teamed up with a veterinarian-led research initiative called Project 25 to identify genetic markers linked to longer healthspans and lifespans in cats who are 17 years and older.[8]

A pill for the ages?

About 500 of the dogs who are enrolled in The Dog Aging Project will be chosen to also participate in a study that investigates whether rapamycin extends their healthspan, or disease-free period of life. Rapamycin is a drug approved for use in people who receive organ transplants, and it was originally discovered in soil bacteria on Easter Island. The drug has already been shown to boost longevity in mice, flies, and yeast—and much research into the potential anti-aging effects of rapamycin in humans is underway. Rapamycin is also being studied as a potential therapy for cats with a heart condition called hypertrophic cardiomyopathy,[9] and may hold promise in exploring treatments for cats with some types of cancer.[10,11] So I'm keeping my eye on further rapamycin developments!

Cats vs. little dogs vs. big dogs

In general, we know that larger animals live longer than smaller animals do, and one reason may be that larger animals encounter fewer threats than smaller animals do. For example, a rat lives about two years and a bowhead whale can live longer than 200 years. But the opposite is true for dogs, who have complex body characteristic differences and a wide lifespan range. This has always intrigued me. Why do small-breed dogs like Pomeranians live longer than large-breed dogs like Irish wolfhounds? While different dog breeds can look quite different from one another, and different cat breeds can also look quite dissimilar, the good news is that cats do not exhibit the extreme range of sizes that dogs do—most cat breeds are more or less the same size. So why do cats, in general, live longer than dogs?

One evolutionary theory for cats' longer lifespan relates to sociability and infectious diseases.[12] Cats tend to be solitary animals vs. pack animals like dogs, so cats have less risk of catching and spreading bacteria, viruses, and parasites. Cats also have better defenses against predators than dogs do: sharp claws and remarkable agility.

Why does aging occur?

Scientists are as yet unable to point to one simple explanation for all the differences between species' lifespans and the changes that occur as we grow older. A whopping nine major contributors to aging in mammals provide a few explanations![13] These and other aging mechanisms are hot areas of research that can help scientists identify treatments that directly target and prevent or reverse aging and age-related diseases:

1) GENOMIC INSTABILITY—occurs when DNA undergoes a range of irreversible and damaging informational changes. You'll recall that DNA is a molecule that contains our genetic code, and it's present in nearly every cell in the body—from fat cells to heart cells to brain cells. Most cells in the body are replenished throughout life because they can make copies of themselves, including their DNA. Cells can also repair altered DNA, but only up to a point.

2) TELOMERE ATTRITION—telomeres are repeating sections of DNA that protect the ends of chromosomes (chromosomes are "packages" of DNA inside cells). Telomeres get a wee bit shorter each time a cell divides to replenish itself. So telomere attrition is the gradual loss of these protective end caps (they're like the plastic tips on the ends of shoelaces that keep them from unraveling). Telomeres tend to break down faster in species that have short lifespans. When the telomeres get too short, the DNA gets damaged, and the cells stop dividing or die. (Quick dog fact: It turns out that large-breed dogs start life with shorter telomeres than small-breed dogs do, so this helps explain their shorter lifespans.)

3) **EPIGENETIC ALTERATIONS**—harmful but potentially reversible age-related changes in the ways genes are expressed.

4) **DISRUPTION OF PROTEOSTASIS**—age-related mishaps in cellular protein processes and production.

5) **DEREGULATION OF NUTRIENT SENSING**—the cell processes that ensure proper nutrition for optimal metabolism go awry.

6) **MITOCHONDRIAL DYSFUNCTION**—the energy-producing machinery of cells becomes defective.

7) **CELLULAR SENESCENCE**—cells no longer divide as they normally would. (Senescence can be a good thing when it happens to cancer cells because we want them to stop proliferating, but it's a bad thing when it happens to cells that should divide to replenish and replace themselves, such as with wound healing.)

8) **STEM CELL EXHAUSTION**—stem cells can develop into many different types of cells to replace those that are lost through normal wear and tear, disease, or injury, so when stem cell numbers or functions decline, this replacement stops.

9) **ALTERED INTERCELLULAR COMMUNICATION**—changes in the many ways that cells normally signal one another, such as through hormones and nerves. Hormones are the body's chemical messengers that tell many cells what to do. Hormones help regulate development and growth, appetite and thirst, digestion and metabolism, temperature, behavior, reproduction, and more! One big reason for disruptions in cell communication is called "*inflammaging*." This chronic (long-term), low-grade, age-related, stealthy stimulation of the immune system differs from the beneficial inflammation that routinely helps us fight infection and recover from injuries. Inflammaging also ties into other aging mechanisms such as cellular senescence and stem cell exhaustion.[13] Researchers are also examining whether inflammaging contributes to age-related frailty in people.[14,15]

Purebred cats vs. mixed-breed cats

What about purebred vs. mixed-breed cats—does one have a longevity advantage over the other? Selective breeding has given us our modern breeds, which are genetically isolated and, well, fairly inbred. Sadly, this practice can lead to breed-related genetic diseases and disease predispositions. And some diseases are more likely to occur in breeds with certain body shapes, sizes, or coats. Veterinarians can easily name common disorders in certain cat breeds. For example: Persian? Polycystic kidney disease and problems related to their flat faces. Tailless Manx cats? Incontinence and constipation related to their short spinal cord. Maine Coon? Heart disease. Cat breeds with white fur? Purebreds *or* mixed-breeds have a higher risk of skin cancer. Of course regardless of breed, any of these problems can reduce a pet's life expectancy.

Some lifespan variance exists between certain cat breeds, but on average, cats have a lifespan of about 12 to 15 years. A study of 4,009 cats in England revealed the lifespan range (of the middle 50% of the cats studied) was 9 to 17 years, with purebred cats living about 12.5 years and crossbred cats living a bit longer—about 14 years.[16]

FUN FACT:

According to Guinness World Records, the oldest cat ever was Creme Puff (1967–2005), who lived for an astounding 38 years and 3 days (more than double the average feline life expectancy)! The oldest dog ever was Bluey (1910–1939), an active Australian cattle dog who lived 29 years and 5 months.

The ultimate goal: Living longer together

We cat lovers can benefit in many ways from what researchers discover to help our furry family members. As scientists continue to look into why and how cats age, we will learn so much about how to prolong the lifespan and healthspan of our cats. One thing we know for certain… nine lives are not enough.

Dr. Mary's keys to slowing the sands of time for pets

We can help our cats live longer and happier by using these strategies throughout their lives:

- Feed a healthy, complete, and balanced diet appropriate for your cat's life stage or health issue.
- Exercise every day (play is a must!)—matched to your cat's abilities.
- Help your cat maintain a healthy weight and optimal body and muscle condition.
- Encourage play and provide mental stimulation (food puzzles!).
- Manage stress and anxiety.
- Provide regular veterinary medical and dental checkups and preventive healthcare.
- Be on alert to detect medical and behavioral issues earlier and seek veterinary treatment sooner. To help, keep a pet health journal with a photo diary.

- Consider spaying or neutering your pet (usually an early-life decision, but can be done later in life if indicated).
- Allow nature time—take your cat outdoors with supervision (walks using a harness and leash, catio, outdoor cat condo), but prohibit free roaming (to prevent car accidents, life-threatening wildlife encounters, neighborhood cat or dog fights, and exposure to infectious diseases from eating prey or fighting).
- Always give extra love!

Because these strategies can become more challenging to implement as cats age and after they have developed a medical condition or two (and unfortunately, geriatric cats often have multiple ailments), the chapters that follow provide more specific insight into how you can keep your senior and geriatric cats as happy, comfortable, and healthy as possible during their twilight years.

Part two:

THE AGING BODY — COMMON AILMENTS THAT AFFECT GERIATRIC CATS

From runny noses to blocked rear ends, in these chapters I focus on helping you manage the general ailments that most commonly plague senior or geriatric cats, and I highlight a few specific diseases that advanced age can bring. Whether your cat has achy joints (arthritis is quite common in older cats, and the signs aren't as obvious as you might think), overgrown claws, weak muscles, or is overweight, you'll want to manage his comfort and mobility. If your cat has pee and poop accidents outside the litter box because she has diabetes, urinary tract inflammation, cognitive dysfunction, or anal gland irritation, you'll still be dealing with stinky situations. In addition, sometimes what's ailing a cat isn't diagnosed—perhaps because ignorance can be bliss and you've been a bit tentative about visiting the vet, or because all those diagnostic tests and treatment options can be expensive, or because you did all the testing and still don't have a precise answer.

So even if you don't have a diagnosis to research online and are without a disease-specific support group to connect with on social media, you'll still want to focus on managing your cat's ailments. In this section you'll learn what ailments to watch for, what the signs look like, and what the signs may indicate. I provide caregiving tips specific to each ailment or disease, offer pointers based on home hacks that my patients' families and I have used, and suggest resources and products. I also list questions to ask your veterinarian that'll help spark discussion so you can take home more information from your visits.

CHAPTER 5:

Nose:
The better to smell you with

People often ask me about the correlation between the moistness or dryness of their cat's nose and whether it means he is "coming down with something." The quick answer is, no, probably not, unless of course he has a runny or crusty nose or is sneezing a lot. I'll delve into more details later, so let's first talk about the critical functions of that cute button beacon!

The nose's business

The sense of smell is a vital part of cats' lives and conveys critical information about their environments. Smell helps cats recognize their human family members and furry housemates and learn a little about where they've been. Cats also communicate by marking their territories and can detect the scents of other cats. It's been noted that cats can identify odors as well as dogs. But feline employment as medical detection or dangerous substance "sniffer cats" gets attention primarily as April Fools' Day internet pranks, possibly because cats are more challenging to train (at least in my house they are!).

Like people, cats breathe primarily through their noses. The nose warms and humidifies air and is a first line of defense against dirt, allergens, and pollution. It also helps the immune system recognize and protect against inhaled bacterial and viral invaders.

Noses trap air and scent molecules and shuttle them up the nasal passageways to specialized cells called *olfactory sensory neurons*. Each neuron has one odor receptor. Those scent molecules stimulate the odor receptors, which send signals to the *olfactory bulbs*—a collection of nerve cells involved in smell—in the brain and to the brain's frontal cortex to process and identify the smell.

The sense of smell and taste work together because food aroma travels to the same neurons. If the scent cannot reach the receptors, for example because of inflammation caused by a virus or a tumor, then the food's flavor isn't enjoyed as much.

FUN FACT:

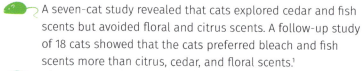

- A seven-cat study revealed that cats explored cedar and fish scents but avoided floral and citrus scents. A follow-up study of 18 cats showed that the cats preferred bleach and fish scents more than citrus, cedar, and floral scents.[1]
- Cats greet each other by touching each others' noses, and they may also sniff each others' sides and behinds.
- It's no longer considered conventional wisdom that humans' sense of smell is worse than that of other animals.[2] People can follow a scent trail and can improve with practice![3] And some evidence suggests people can tell when others are ill, emotionally stressed, or might make a good mate.[4,5]

So why are cats' noses often moist? Their moist noses help trap the scent particles that are passed to the neurons. A dry nose doesn't necessarily mean your cat is sick, but it can reduce their ability to trap odor (and therefore smell), so they may lick their noses often.

Who smells best?

Different species are more attuned to the scents that mean something to them in their environments, so it's difficult to compare the same scents across species to test which animal has the best sense of smell. The sizes of the olfactory bulbs and the number of olfactory neurons among different species also don't reliably predict smell abilities. For example, the proportion of a dog's brain devoted to interpreting smells (0.31%) is much greater than a human's brain (0.01%), but that doesn't mean humans can't detect certain smells as well as dogs can.[2]

For years it was thought that dogs have more smell receptors than cats do, but recent estimates suggest that cats have similar numbers of smell receptors. (Some dogs, such as bloodhounds, have more smell receptors than other dogs.)

Animal	Number of Olfactory Receptors
Human[6]	6 million
Cat[7,8]	200 million
Dog[6]	150 to 300 million

Along with the mammoth number of smell receptors, cats (and dogs, pigs, and horses) also possess a second olfactory organ called the vomeronasal organ.[9]

It's located at the bottom of the nasal passage and above the roof of the mouth. The vomeronasal organ is designed to pick up the scent of pheromones, which are chemicals unique to each animal (and some insect) species. Pheromones send messages that can alter a behavior or bodily function of the recipient. In fact, synthetic feline pheromones are available to use in a cat's environment to help comfort cats who have house-soiling, anxiety, or other behavior issues. Two examples are the Feliway (by Ceva) and Comfort Zone (by Central Garden & Pet) product lines.

To activate the vomeronasal organ and in response to certain odors, cats often exhibit a flehmen response or "gaping" (they curl their upper lip and open their mouth slightly—it's also sometimes called stinkface, peeface, funny face, and sneering) and dogs sometimes chatter their teeth. Humans also have this organ, but it is vestigial (still hanging around from a previous ancestor along the evolutionary journey but doesn't have its original function) and whether it works or not is still being debated![10,11]

Odoriferous influence

We know that smell evokes our memories, triggers our emotions, and sways our behavior. Does the scent of a fired-up charcoal grill transport you back to the first time you camped away from home as a kid? How about puppy breath—does it make you happy? Maybe a whiff of Midwestern air that somehow smells like a sea breeze prompts you to plan a beach vacation?

As for me, I'll follow the smell of warm chocolate chip cookies anywhere! And I'd love the chance to go back to my grandmother's living room and capture the

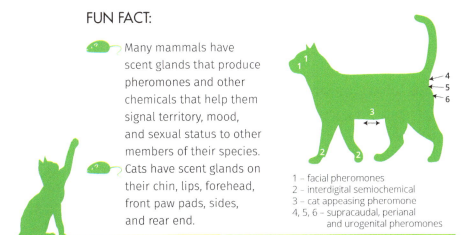

FUN FACT:

Many mammals have scent glands that produce pheromones and other chemicals that help them signal territory, mood, and sexual status to other members of their species. Cats have scent glands on their chin, lips, forehead, front paw pads, sides, and rear end.

1 – facial pheromones
2 – interdigital semiochemical
3 – cat appeasing pheromone
4, 5, 6 – supracaudal, perianal and urogenital pheromones

sweet smell of Grandma. I wish I could invent a way to forever hold onto her scent. Such special smells have the power to bring back vivid memories—ones that we might not otherwise readily recall. I often wonder whether our pets have similar responses to the smells they've learned.

What can go wrong with the nose?

Some of the common conditions associated with cats' noses as they age range from color change to cancer.

Color change

You may notice new dark freckles or "age spots" on your cat's pink nose, lip margins, gums, and eyelids. Some cells in these areas simply start to produce more pigment in senior cats, and it's known as *lentigo*. Such spots are harmless, but it's always a good idea to point them out to your veterinarian to assess because melanoma, a pigment-producing skin tumor in cats, can look similar. Melanoma is uncommon in cats, but it can be benign (harmless) or malignant (cancerous). Young kitties may have lentigo, too, especially orange, tortoiseshell, and calico cats.

Cancer

Nasal cancer in cats is uncommon, but the three most common types of feline nasal cancer are squamous cell carcinoma, lymphoma, and adenocarcinoma. The signs of nasal cancer? Cats may excessively rub their noses or sneeze and snort, or they may have nasal discharge, nose bleeds (also called *epistaxis*), snout swelling, or facial deformity. Some of these cancers grow quickly, and I encourage you to seek advice from your veterinarian as soon as possible if your senior cat has signs of nasal disease, because nasal cancer may be much easier to treat when the tumor is small.

Polyps, allergies, and infections

These problems can occur or be identified in cats of any age but tend to start in young cats. Cats may develop noncancerous growths in their nose and back of their throat called *nasopharyngeal polyps*, which can be surgically removed. Cats who have allergies may develop nasal cavity inflammation, so treatment focuses on managing the allergy and its irritating effects. Viral, bacterial, and fungal infections also cause inflammation of the nose (called *rhinitis*) and sinuses (called *sinusitis*), and they lead to a runny nose, watery eyes, and sneezing.

Foreign objects

Cats who spend a lot of time outdoors nosing around in the grass may inhale plant seeds that lodge in their nasal passages or pick up botfly larvae called *Cuterebra* (ick!) near rabbit or rodent burrows. Snorted materials and creepy-crawly invaders can cause sudden irritation, intense pawing at the nose, excessive sneezing, and long-term inflammation. If these signs are caught early, veterinarians, with careful examination, can sometimes find and remove the plant material or other unwelcome guest that doesn't belong.

FUN FACT:

Does someone in your life sneeze air-horn style, while you ahchoo as quietly as a kitten? Lung capacity along with nasal and sinus anatomy affect sneeze quantity and intensity, but our personality can affect the level of noise we make. A 2006 survey by the makers of Benadryl found that 45% of people sneeze differently in public than in private, and that people's personalities match their sneeze type 75% of the time.[9,10]

Autoimmune skin disease

Cats sometimes develop autoimmune skin problems (the body's immune cells malfunction and start attacking normal skin or mucous membrane cells) that affect the nose. It's always a good idea to have your cat checked out by a veterinarian if you notice oozing or bleeding erosions or other lesions that affect your cat's nostrils, lips, or gums.

Decreased ability to smell

We don't yet know precisely what happens with a cat's sense of smell as they age. But we know that our sense of smell declines as we age. People 65 to 80 years of age lose up to 50% of their sense of smell, and people over 80 years of age lose up to 80%.[11] As we age, oxidative stress (an imbalance between the harmful molecular reactions that can occur during normal cell processes and the mechanisms that prevent them) damages many of our cells, including our olfactory nerve and brain cells. A loss of nerve endings in a cat's nose can reduce the nose's ability to produce mucus, which decreases sense of smell.

In people, a diminished sense of smell is one of the earliest indicators of Alzheimer's disease.[15] In senior dogs, cognitive dysfunction has been likened to Alzheimer's disease. Smell disturbance is one of the physical signs of canine cognitive dysfunction syndrome, so a diminished sense of smell may be an early indicator of the disease in dogs, too.[16] We're not sure whether the same is true in cats, because it hasn't been studied yet.

Other factors that can diminish a cat's sense of smell include upper respiratory tract viral infections—such as feline calicivirus and rhinotracheitis (also known as feline herpesvirus, which is not contagious to people), severe dental disease, trauma, and cancer that affects the nasal cavity.

DOES COVID-19 AFFECT A CAT'S SENSE OF SMELL?

Many people who test positive for COVID-19 report a loss of their sense of smell and taste early in the infection, and sometimes this loss lasts for weeks or months and may be permanent. We also know that cats, dogs, ferrets, and other species are susceptible to illness from COVID-19. (People can transmit the virus to animals through close contact, but the risk of animals transmitting the virus to people is low.) As the virus does in people, it can cause problems in other animals that range from a mild upper respiratory tract infection to death.

We're not sure whether animals infected with COVID-19 have long-term loss of smell and taste. But because the virus leads to respiratory tract inflammation, it likely diminishes an infected animal's sense of smell at least temporarily. Long-term loss of smell is a serious issue because it affects our ability to taste, perceive threats, communicate, and recall memories, and it may affect some people's ability to work. Similarly, for working detector dogs recovering from COVID-19, a long-term loss of sense of smell could be career-ending and potentially disrupt national security.[17]

> **A nose for words**
>
> - Anosmia is the complete loss of sense of smell.
> - Hyposmia indicates partial loss of sense of smell.
> - Parosmia is a change in the normal perception of odors, such as when the smell of something familiar is distorted or when something that normally smells pleasant now smells foul.
> - Phantosmia is the sensation of an odor that isn't there.
> - Presbyosmia is the reduction in or loss of sense of smell that occurs with aging.

Dental disease

It may sound odd, but if a cat has nasal problems, I always look at their teeth! I have seen some nasty teeth in my years as a veterinarian. Unfortunately, dental disease can become unnecessarily severe in cats because many pet parents are nervous about the anesthesia required to have their cats' teeth cleaned. However, the risks of not treating dental disease may be far greater. Diseased gums and teeth can lead to pain, infection and even abscesses that disturb the scent pathway and cause many other problems throughout the body. So have your cat's teeth evaluated and cleaned regularly.

Sniffing out trouble: When to see your veterinarian

I can't stress enough how important it is to see your veterinarian if your cat repeatedly paws at her nose or face, snorts or snores excessively, or has nasal discharge, a bloody nose, or changes in her facial appearance.

To identify the cause of a nose issue, your veterinarian may recommend blood tests, clotting tests to check whether blood clots form normally, x-rays, a computed tomography (CT) scan, using a special scope to look up the nose, taking a biopsy, or referral to a veterinary dermatologist or other specialist.

It can be hard to tell whether your cat has an impaired sense of smell. Perhaps your cat may not be curious about sniffing a new piece of furniture or unfamiliar cardboard box anymore, nor your luggage when you get back from vacation. Cats with diminished smell often have a reduced appetite, or they may begin to show a preference for certain foods—presumably those with strong odors they can more readily detect.

A weak sense of smell can curtail a cat's appetite because smell and taste are linked. Taste buds play a big role, of course, but the molecules released from chewed food enter the nasal cavity and are processed by the olfactory cells to help detect complex flavors. (This is why pinching your nose can help you swallow bad-tasting medicine.) Scores of medical problems can cause a lack of appetite (called *inappetence*), so if your cat is otherwise in good health and has been checked for other possible reasons for losing interest in food, it may be related to a diminished ability to smell. A reduced appetite can, in and of itself, be of concern, so check out Chapter 9 "Body condition and nutrition: Helping senior cats eat better and feel better " for tips on appetite stimulation!

If it truly is simply an age-related loss of your cat's phenomenal ability to smell, there isn't much veterinarians can do to treat this just yet. Peg it up to one of the many joys of aging.

CAREGIVER TIPS AND HOME HACKS TO HELP YOUR CAT'S SENSE OF SMELL

- Humidify the air in your home to help keep nasal cells moisturized.
- Apply a balm made for pets (e.g. Nose Butter or Snout Soother) on the external portions of your cat's nose to help keep it moist.
- Warm foods to enhance their smell.
- Stay up-to-date on routine wellness veterinary visits and vaccinations to prevent upper respiratory infections.
- Give cats intriguing new things to smell to stimulate their noses and provide mental stimulation. Bring in leaves, pinecones, and logs from outdoors. Open different screened windows to let your cat enjoy the breeze. Offer catnip, silvervine, honeysuckle (wood and sawdust, not berries), valerian root,[18] and other herbs like rosemary, dill, and oregano. Avoid essential oils, as many are toxic to cats if they have skin contact or are ingested.
- Consider teaching your cat to use nontoxic scent markers, also known as *nosework*. These markers are typically used to help pets with vision impairment navigate their homes, but they can be used to teach cats to explore and find rewards. People who have lost their sense of smell—which has become a more common problem related to COVID-19 infections—may benefit from scent training, although it hasn't been widely studied. Scent training is likened to physical therapy for noses. (Human patients take a whiff of strong essential oils such as eucalyptus, clove, and lemon and attempt to identify the odors.[19]) This has not been studied in cats with impaired ability to smell, but teaching a cat to use pet-safe scent markers could help stimulate their olfactory abilities.

- If your cat is ill and must be hospitalized, send a favorite toy with him, or send a shirt that you've worn recently that you haven't laundered.
- When you pick up your cat from the hospital, put a towel or blanket from home inside the carrier.
- When your cat gets home from the hospital, rub her with a towel that you've first rubbed your other cat (or your dog) with. This transfers their familiar smells to your cat who smells like the veterinary clinic. Then consider rubbing the other cat (or dog) in the household again with the towel you've just rubbed on your homecoming cat (if your cat doesn't have an infectious condition). This way they'll all smell similarly strange and similarly recognizable to each other. Consider keeping housemate cats separate for the first day after one of them returns home, and supervise their reunion so they come back together peacefully.
- Check with your veterinarian for treatment updates. Ultra tiny molecules (called *nanoparticles*) of zinc delivered in a special spray have been shown to enhance odor detection abilities in dogs and in people,[20] so such therapy may someday be medically available for pets.

PRODUCT RECOMMENDATIONS

- Nose Butter (The Blissful Cat): **theblissfulcat.com/products/nose-butter**
- Snout Soother (Natural Dog Company): **naturaldogcompany.com**
- Snout Magic (The Happy Pet Company) **thehappypetcompany.myshopify.com/**
- SightScent™ Sight and Scent Mapping Program **sightscent.com/index.html**

CHAPTER 6:

Eyes: "You looking at me?" Vision changes with age

> "It is only with the heart that one can see rightly; what is essential is invisible to the eye."
>
> —A<small>NTOINE DE</small> S<small>AINT</small>-E<small>XUPÉRY</small>, <small>FROM</small> "T<small>HE</small> L<small>ITTLE</small> P<small>RINCE</small>"

Vision plays a fundamental, vital role in cats' lives—it helps them avoid hazards, find food, communicate, and play. Yet I have met many blind cats who live wonderful lives. As cats age, they become more susceptible to diseases such as kidney disease or hyperthyroidism that can cause high blood pressure and damage the eyes. Or cats may simply experience age-related changes such as lenticular sclerosis (hardening of the lens in the eye), which can lead to cataracts.

A glance at eye structure

Eyeballs are quite complex! It's helpful for pet parents to understand the basic structure of the eye to appreciate the things that can go awry.

The conjunctiva is a mucous membrane that covers the inside of the eyelids and front part of the eyeball. The eye consists of three chambers—the anterior (front), posterior (rear), and vitreous (gel-like goo that fills the eyeball and helps it keep its shape). Eyes also have three layers:

- The outer *fibrous tunic layer* consists of the cornea (clear portion of the front of the eye) and sclera (white portion of the eye that also contains tiny blood vessels). When you get an eyelash or dust in your eye, the conjunctiva, sclera, and cornea can become irritated and painful.
- The middle section is the *uveal layer*, which contains the iris (the colored ring that surrounds the pupil), ciliary body (sits behind the iris and supports the lens and produces the substances that fill the eye), and choroid

(blood vessels that supply the eye's inner layer). Many diseases can cause inflammation in this layer and lead to glaucoma, which is increased painful pressure in the eye from fluid buildup; excess fluid buildup can cause blindness.

- The inner *nervous layer* contains the retina (tissue that contains light receptors) and optic nerve, which carries the retina's signals to the brain for image processing. If the retina separates from the back of the eye (retinal detachment)—which can occur with some diseases (such as high blood pressure) or trauma—emergency treatment is required to reattach the retina to attempt to prevent permanent vision loss.

The lens is separate from these three layers. It sits behind the iris to help focus the light that streams through the pupil and onto the retina.

FUN FACT:

Did you know that cats "smile" at us by blinking slowly and closing their eyelids, then slowly opening their eyes to half open? And if we slow-blink at cats, they find us more approachable![1] A separate study found that cats living in shelters who respond to and exhibit a slow blink with people may be adopted faster than shelter cats who do not.[2] My cats Bodhi, a shelter kitty, and Goldie, a relinquished patient, must've charmed me with their seductive blinks!

Watch for age-related changes and signs of diminished eyesight

As cats age, different components of the eye can lose function. Luckily, age-related changes in the eye usually don't lead to total blindness, but they can hamper your cat's daily living activities and safety. If your cat shows signs of decreased vision, it's important for your veterinarian to examine your cat to determine the cause so that correct treatment and care can be provided.

When to see your veterinarian

The signs of eye disease and changes in vision range from subtle to obvious and include:

- excessive blinking or squinting;
- rubbing or pawing at the eyes;

- sensitivity to light;
- redness;
- watery eyes or gooey discharge;
- bulging eyes;
- cloudiness;
- persistently dilated pupils;
- one pupil that is larger than the other;
- bumping into furniture, doors, or walls;
- difficulty finding food or water bowls, toys, or treats;
- hesitancy to jump on or off furniture;
- reluctance to use stairs, explore new places, or navigate in dim light;
- new or increased anxiety or clingy behavior;
- increased vocalization;
- reduced eye contact;
- startling easily or exhibiting increased irritability;
- taking longer to recognize familiar people from a distance; and
- a persistently raised third eyelid.

FUN FACT:

In addition to their top and bottom eyelids, cats have an eyelid that moves diagonally from the bottom inner corner of each eye to further protect it. We call this the *third eyelid*, or *nictitating membrane*.

Eye conditions in older cats

Whether your cat has eye problems related to an underlying disease or exhibits common age-related changes, protecting your cat and alleviating discomfort is paramount. I'll cover ways to keep them safe and comfortable later, but first let's take a closer look at age-related changes and other conditions that may affect your cat's eyes.

Nuclear (lenticular) sclerosis

Made up of water and proteins, the lens is fairly elastic and can change shape to help focus light onto the retina. With age, the water and proteins decrease and the proteins become compacted in the lens center (nucleus), which reduces lens flexibility. (Reduced lens flexibility is the reason many older people need reading glasses.) As the proteins become more compacted, a white or blue-grey haziness appears in the center of the lens. This is called *nuclear* or *lenticular sclerosis*.

Pet parents often refer to this lens cloudiness as cataracts. But there is a big difference! Unlike cataracts, nuclear sclerosis doesn't usually affect vision. Nuclear sclerosis is usually seen in cats starting at around 6 or 7 years of age. It is not painful and no treatment is needed. However, your veterinarian should perform an evaluation to rule out other diseases that may look the same, and monitor your cat for cataracts during regularly scheduled examinations.

Senile cataracts

Age-related cataracts can develop in some cats who have nuclear sclerosis, so continue to monitor visual abilities in cats with nuclear sclerosis, in addition to taking them for their routine veterinary examinations. Senile cataracts can develop when the aging, compacted lens proteins start to degenerate, and it's important to catch this early, when surgery to remove cataracts is most successful.

Cataract surgery carries risks, post-operative complications can occur, and many eye and other medications are typically required afterward. Discuss your expectations and patient care capabilities with your veterinarian to determine whether cataract surgery is right for your cat. Your veterinarian must also determine whether your cat has senile cataracts or has cataracts caused by another underlying problem such as an infection or diabetes that also requires treatment.

Iris atrophy

The colored ring of tissue contains a sphincter muscle that alters pupil size in response to light, certain hormones, or drugs. In low light or scary

Charlie (meowing for attention in this photo) had lens dislocation (luxation) in his left eye. It's not necessarily a common condition in geriatric cats, but it is a painful, serious problem that requires immediate assessment and treatment, and it often results in blindness. It can happen because of glaucoma, cancer, an injury, or another eye disease, and surgery is usually needed to remove the lens.

situations, the pupils dilate to allow as much light in as possible. In bright light, pupils constrict to reduce the amount of light that reaches the retina.

Like many muscles in the body, the iris muscle shrinks with age, and this is called *iris atrophy*. This limits the pupil's ability to change size, so affected cats may not see as well at night or may squint more than usual in bright sunlight. With iris atrophy, the colored tissue may have a "moth-eaten" appearance or a wavy edge, or the pupils may appear to be misshapen or unequal sizes.

Iris atrophy is an aging change for which there is no treatment, but it shouldn't seriously affect your cat's vision or quality of life. However, it's important to have a veterinary exam to identify the cause of a cat's irregular pupil sizes because this can indicate other more serious problems.

Retinal detachment

High blood pressure, inflammation related to infections, trauma, and cancer can cause the retina to separate from its attachment inside the eye. Unless the retina can be successfully reattached surgically, the cat will be permanently blind in the affected eye.

Try not to look sideways at eyeball removal

Severe infection, a traumatic accident, glaucoma, or cancer may necessitate the removal of one or both of a cat's eyes—a surgical procedure called *enucleation*.

Minion lost his right eye but kept his handsome looks.

Simon not only masters steps just fine with one eye - but still achieves cuteness!

It's performed as a last resort because the eye is often painful and can't otherwise be repaired. After an eye is removed, the skin is permanently sutured (stitched) to close the gap. If a family requests it, a prosthetic globe can be placed for cosmetic reasons. Cats with one or both eyes removed can go on to live joyful, active lives with a little help from their loving families.

CAREGIVER TIPS AND HOME HACKS

If your cat has vision impairment, simple environmental adjustments can keep him happy and secure. Cats who are blind or have reduced eyesight miss visual cues from unfriendly cats and dogs as well as the danger signs of a swimming pool, stairs, an oncoming car, or an exuberant toddler who is waddling toward them. Keeping familiar routines, creating a safe zone, attaching bells to other pets' collars, using positive training techniques to teach new ways to navigate, finding different games to play, and providing opportunities for mental stimulation and physical activity allows cats with visual impairment to lead happy lives. They can still enjoy their favorite activities such as chasing toys that make noise, hanging out with the family, basking in sunlight, feeling gentle breezes, exploring outside while wearing a harness and leash, and dreaming of mice.

Preserve familiarity. To prevent your cat's injury or confusion, try not to move furniture or alter her routines.

Hinder hazards. Senior-pet-proof your home, similar to what you would do for a toddler. Ensure your cat is unable to wander into the street or off a balcony or deck. Place baby gates or "stack" tension rods (a lower cost option) to block off potential hazards. Attach soft pads to hard edges that your cat may bump into.

Heighten visibility. Many senior cats struggle to see in low light, so help them navigate hallways and stairwells with motion-sensor lights and night lights that turn on when it gets dark. Also place lights near food and water bowls and the litter box. Prevent run-ins with glass doors by adhering stickers to the glass at cat-eye level.

Be a lifeguard. Monitor your cat (visually impaired or not) at all times near a body of water! As a veterinarian in south Florida, I've encountered innumerable tragic accounts of cats who die from drowning in swimming pools, waterways, and even hot tubs and bath tubs. Pool

 Pause for paws! Stickers on a glass partition or patio door help cats avoid bumping into it.

alarms are also a helpful tool, and it's a good idea to keep the toilet lid closed, too. That closed toilet lid serves double duty for those dedicated toilet-water-drinking enthusiasts. Sorry, Charlie!

Provide nutritional support. Whether your senior cat has an eye disease or not, consider a supplement that supports eye health. I recommend Ocu-GLO (**ocuglo.com/**), which has been formulated by board-certified veterinary ophthalmologists.

Foster enrichment. Toys with sound and smell will thrill most cats—even older curmudgeons—and keep them engaged. Cats often enjoy catnip or honeysuckle-infused toys, as well as treat-dispensing puzzle toys and snuffle mats (small "carpets" that promote foraging for food or treats) or snuffle balls. Offer your cat's toys a few at a time on a rotating schedule to prevent boredom and keep toys feeling new rather than providing unlimited access to all their toys.

More tips for caregivers of cats who are blind

Most cats know their home well by memory and learn to rely more on hearing, smell, and touch as their eyesight diminishes. Sometimes they adapt so well that owners are surprised to learn their cat is blind. Understandably, cats who lose vision gradually or lose vision in one eye tend to adapt more easily than cats who suddenly become blind, which can be distressing, confusing, and sometimes depressing for them. With your patience, reassurance, support tools, and affection, cats can adjust to blindness and regain confidence in their environment and instincts remarkably well!

The comfort of a safe zone

Pick a room or specific location where all of your cat's basic necessities are readily accessible, such as his bed, food bowl, water, toys, and litter box. Geriatric cats who are blind are comforted by routine, such as being fed at the same time every day in the same spot. It helps when their necessities are in the same reliable places and that their established safe zone is always there for them, especially if they are distressed by visitors. Consider sprinkling the area with a special scent such as rosemary or dill as an added cue to help them easily locate their safe zone. Keep litter boxes in their normal locations (away from food and water bowls), and remember that it's best to have the same number of litter boxes as there are cats in the home, *plus* one litter box.

Some cats may need to relearn how to access their favorite perches or window sills. Create makeshift steps and use scent markers to help teach them how to climb.

Consider using a pet tracking device (e.g., Girafus Pet Tracker) to keep tabs on your cat. It's especially helpful if your cat often gets losts in your home, and can be a lifesaver if he accidentally wanders outdoors. And in case of inadvertent escape from your home or yard, also be sure your cat's microchip is registered (with your up-to-date contact information), and attach a medical alert tag to your cat's collar to indicate he is blind and include your contact information.

FUN FACT:

Cats do best if there is at least two feet between all of these things: their food/water bowls, their bed, and their litter box. So don't try to mush all of them into a small location.

A heaven-sent tool

If your cat isn't adapting as well to vision loss as you'd hoped, or if you have to move to a new home, you may want to consider trying a halo—a harness with a hard wire or plastic ring that serves as a bumper for blind pets. I've seen many canine pet parents successfully use halos, but I'm unsure how well cats adapt to wearing these. Cats rely on their whiskers to help them navigate. Several products are available and are designed primarily for dogs; families I know especially like Muffin's Halo for Blind Dogs, or the Walkin' Blind Dog Halo at **Handicappedpets.com**.

The nose knows

You can use your cat's good sense of smell to your advantage and develop a scent mapping system with special scent tabs. With repetition and positive reinforcement training techniques, you can teach your cat to associate specific scents with desirable objects such as bowls, beds, and crates, as well as locations such as specific rooms and hallways. You can also use this method to teach them about hazardous objects or places like the top of the stairs.

Auditory reassurance

Frequently talking to your cat brings much comfort, as it is helpful to be reminded of the family's presence. Using familiar short phrases are best, and use a calm, upbeat voice to convey happiness, comfort, and safety. Cultivating your own positive attitude and acting as a grounding anchor for cats is invaluable, especially for those adjusting to blindness.

Family members may consider wearing a bell or similar item that helps the cat easily identify the location of specific people. Teach visitors how to approach your cat without surprising her. Use a soft voice or other sounds to alert her to your presence and offer your hand near her nose to smell before touching her.

Cats who are blind will be unable to respond appropriately to the eye contact and body language cues that other cats use to communicate, so monitor their interactions. Attach bells to the collars of other cats (or dogs) in the home to alert vision-impaired cats to their whereabouts. Consider placing a bell on the cat who is blind, because it may allow you to more easily find him if he gets lost in the house!

And lap up this last quick tip: A drinking fountain placed in your cat's safe zone provides a continuous auditory cue and helps them locate their water.

Tactile reassurance

Maintain clear walking paths and consider placing carpet runners so your cat can feel where it's safe to walk.

Tips for administering eye medications

Ask your veterinarian to show you how to administer your cat's eye medications. Cats typically receive eye medications two or more times a day for several days or weeks, so to speed healing, make it a positive experience. Here are my tips:

- Give treatments somewhere in your home other than in your cat's safe place or favorite hangout or where their necessities are located, otherwise your cat may start avoiding those areas.
- Use a warm, damp washcloth to gently clean the area around your cat's eyes. Wash your hands and take extra care not to touch the tip of the medication container to your cat's eye or face, or to your hand. And don't apply the medication to your finger to rub in your cat's eye.

- You may want to wrap him gently in a towel with his head exposed and hold him in your lap or on a table. If your cat is especially wiggly or resistant, you may need a helper to hold him. Your cat's eyes may be sensitive and uncomfortable for the first few treatments until the medications start to work.
- Hold the medication container with your thumb and forefinger with the tip pointed down and gently steady your hand on top of your cat's head if needed. With your other hand, slightly tilt your cat's head up (use extra care in cats with neck pain) and use your thumb to pull the lower eyelid down to help catch the medication.
- Approach with the medication from the top or side of your cat's eye rather than straight on, and dispense the prescribed drug amount at the top outer corner or in the center of the eye. Don't allow the tip of the container to touch any part of the eye. The medication will feel odd or slightly cold, so your cat will blink and may jerk a bit and shake his head.
- Give your cat lots of praise and a favorite small snack after every treatment! And wash your hands again afterward.

Insightful help is out there

If your cat's vision declines or she becomes completely blind, remember that she can lead a wonderful, fulfilling life. I recommend that you meet with your primary care veterinarian to discuss causes, treatment, and environmental adjustments. You may also want to seek guidance from a veterinary ophthalmologist. To find one close to you, ask your primary care veterinarian, or visit the American College of Veterinary Ophthalmologists website at **acvo.org/**.

Questions to ask your veterinarian about your cat's eyesight

- What's the underlying cause of my cat's vision changes?
- Will additional tests be needed to confirm the cause?
- Should my cat be referred to a veterinary ophthalmologist?
- What is the expected progression of this condition?
- What treatment options are available, and what are the costs?
- What are the risks of treatment?
- What is the expected outcome of treatment?
- Will you show me how to give eye medications to my cat?
- What are my options if I'm unable to medicate my cat?
- Is my cat's condition painful, and, if so, how will pain be managed?

- What tests and how often will they be needed to monitor my cat's condition or response to treatment?
- What environmental changes can I make to enhance my cat's quality of life and ensure safety?
- What products can I use to make life easier for my cat?

READING RECOMMENDATION

- *Caring for a Blind Cat* by Sarah Caney (2008, Cat Professional Ltd.).

PRODUCT RECOMMENDATIONS

- Drinkwell Original Pet Fountain (PetSafe) **store.petsafe.net/drinkwell-original-fountain**
- SightScent Sight and Scent Mapping Program **sightscent.com/index.html**
- Babble Ball (Pet Qwerks) – found through many online retailers
- Snuffle Mat for cats: **catschool.co/products/snuffle-mat**
- Or make your own snuffle mat: **youtube.com/watch?v=nXzJsN6-Rzs youtube.com/watch?v=3s0cDtTlaxc**
- Ocu-Glo – **ocuglo.com/**
- Yeowww! Catnip Chi-CAT-A Banana Toy (DuckyWorld Products) **duckyworld.com/products/catnip-toys/yeowww-banana/**
- Chickadee Chirp Electronic Sound Cat Toy (SmartyKat)
- Cat Activity Fun Board Strategy Game (TRIXIE Pet Products) **trixie.de/heimtierbedarf/us/shop/Cat/ActivityGames/?card=62578**
- Girafus Pet Tracker **girafus.com/en/security-devices/girafus-pro-track-tor-pet-safety-tracker-rf-technology-dog-and-cat-tracker-finder-locator/**

SUPPORT RECOMMENDATIONS

- Blind Cats United Facebook group: **facebook.com/groups/1648311348814482/**

CHAPTER 7:

Hearing: "Say what?" Is it stubbornness, or hearing loss?

Your senior cat snoozes dreamily despite the buzz of your daily household activities, but as soon as you pop the top of a soup can, WHOOSH!—she instantly appears at your side! Yet, ten minutes before that, you'd tried calling her over to make a guest appearance on your video call, and she didn't even open one eye. To many cats, any sound associated with their food container is like saying "Hey Siri" to an iPhone! With that being said, some cats lose their hearing ability as they age, and the signs can be subtle.

Ear basics: Wired for sound and striking a balance

At the root of sound is vibration. Objects that vibrate create energy as sound waves that pass through air, water, or solids such as a wall. The eardrum (*tympanic membrane*) and three tiny bones (*ossicles*) in the middle portion of the ear catch and transmit sound wave vibrations, where they travel to a structure in the inner ear called the *cochlea*. The cochlea looks like a mini spiral seashell or snail shell. It contains teeny hair receptors that convert sound waves into electrical activity that the brain interprets.

You've no doubt noticed your cat perks up to seemingly imaginary sounds. Cats have better hearing than humans do for many reasons. Because cats' cochleas contain more spirals, they can hear a wider range of high-pitched and softer sounds than we can. Cats have the broadest hearing ranges of all mammals and detect much higher frequencies than people and dogs do, likely developed to give them stellar hunting abilities. Cats can hear sounds up to five times farther away than humans can![1] And their awesome outer ears use several muscles so they can swivel about 180 degrees, acting as funnels to capture sound waves. This helps them detect noises that are farther away, so they hear visitors pulling into the driveway— or an insect scurrying up the wall—much sooner than you do.

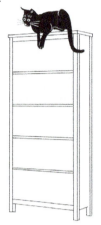

Another component of the inner ear is the *vestibular apparatus*—structures that help the body orient to stay balanced, maintain posture, and stabilize movements. Cats have an especially cool righting reflex that gives them amazing balancing abilities. Their vestibular system swiftly kicks in when they lose their balance or fall, plus they rotate their head, spine, and limbs with speedy acrobatic flair, which is why they usually land on their feet— ta-da!

Why hearing loss happens

Age-related hearing loss is called *presbycusis*. Deafness is classified in numerous ways, and presbycusis falls into the sensory classification, which means the cochlear structure is disrupted. With age, the teeny hair cells in the cochlea degenerate and lose the ability to transmit sound waves, or other ear structures may be affected. Presbycusis typically progresses gradually, and like people, pets may lose the ability to hear certain sounds before others. However, few studies have evaluated age-related hearing loss in pets, especially cats.

One study that tested hearing in 12 young cats (age range 3 to 5 years) and 15 older cats (age range 10 to 19 years) showed that the older cats did not have reduced responses to sound at any of the frequencies tested compared with the young cats. The results suggest that if age-related hearing loss does occur in cats, it occurs later in life than it does in dogs or people.[2]

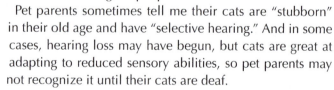

Pet parents sometimes tell me their cats are "stubborn" in their old age and have "selective hearing." And in some cases, hearing loss may have begun, but cats are great at adapting to reduced sensory abilities, so pet parents may not recognize it until their cats are deaf.

Other than presbycusis, deafness can result from many disorders. For example, some cats have inherited deafness–up to 85% of all-white cats with one or both blue eyes are born deaf, and some of these cats are deaf in only one ear; up to 22% of all-white cats with non-blue eyes are born deaf.[3] Total hearing loss can occur as a result of ear infections, which are also known as *otitis externa* (outer ear inflammation), *otitis media* (middle ear inflammation), and *otitis interna* (inner ear inflammation). Other causes of deafness include cancer, polyps (small growths), a foreign body (so *that's* where the tiny round Lego went!), a skull fracture, a ruptured eardrum, adverse reactions to drugs or inappropriate use of certain medications, birth defects, and exposure to extremely loud noises. (Flashback to my teenage heavy metal music phase in the 80s!)

Staying attuned to hearing changes: When to see your veterinarian

Because age-related hearing loss progresses slowly and can take years, you may first notice a subtle change in your cat's behavior—perhaps he sleeps more soundly or is less attuned to you shaking his treat container. Cats can rely more on their sight, sense of smell, established routines, and responses of other pets to household activities to navigate their world, so it's easy to miss signs of diminished hearing for quite some time.

You can screen your cat for hearing loss at home by making sounds with objects outside their line of vision—such as a crinkle ball, squeak toy, or bell—or by tearing paper or wadding up a plastic bag. A free online hearing test is also now available at **petacoustics.com/home-pet-hearing-test**.

Cats with hearing loss or other ear problems may:

- sleep more;
- not wake to sounds that would normally rouse them—like the garage door opening or a key or keypad unlocking a door;
- easily startle when touched;
- fail to respond to normal verbal cues;
- fail to respond appropriately to sound communication cues from other cats, resulting in aggression;
- fail to respond to sounds that normally elicit a tizzy (like their food bag or canned food being opened!);
- seem confused or disoriented;
- meow excessively or louder than normal;
- exhibit increased anxiety (which may be related to a fear of being startled by potential threats);
- shake their heads often, scratch or rub at their ears, or flinch or vocalize when; their ears are touched; and
- have unusually smelly, moist, dirty, swollen, or inflamed (reddened) ears.

If your cat's screening hearing test is abnormal or if you notice any of the above changes, visit your veterinarian to check your cat for causes of hearing loss that may be treatable, as well as for other conditions. Early assessment and treatment can help prevent permanent hearing loss in some cases. If you'd like a definitive answer about your cat's ability to hear, ask your veterinarian about a referral, because some specialty veterinary hospitals can evaluate pets' hearing with a nonpainful, noninvasive Brainstem Auditory Evoked Response (BAER) test that is relatively inexpensive. It involves delivering soft clicking sounds through foam earphones with electrodes placed on the pet's head that measure hearing pathway activity. The activity is recorded as waveforms on a graph by a special computer.

If you learn that your cat has age-related hearing loss, unfortunately there is no cure. Devices to improve hearing in people are technological wonders! But in cats, not so much. And no research has been done to evaluate the social or emotional effects of hearing loss in cats. However, cats are attuned to using other senses, so they can manage their environment well even when they are deaf.

 ## Questions to ask your veterinarian

- What is the underlying cause of my cat's hearing impairment?
- My cat won't let me touch his ears, so how can I best clean or medicate him when needed?
- What environmental changes can I make and what products are available to enhance my cat's quality of life and ensure safety?
- Will behavior modification techniques (such as counterconditioning—changing a cat's emotional response to a certain stimulus, and desensitization—safely and gradually exposing a cat to low levels of the stimulus before it provokes a response) help my cat respond more appropriately when she is anxious or afraid?[4]
- Will my cat benefit from anti-anxiety medications or supplements?

 ## CAREGIVER TIPS AND HOME HACKS FOR HEARING-IMPAIRED CATS

- My biggest concern when helping a family with a cat who is hearing impaired is that someone will startle the cat when he is resting, sleeping, or otherwise not expecting to be touched—and, in response, the cat scratches or bites them. Avoid startling your cat and teach others, especially children, how to approach him appropriately. Children may not understand that their geriatric cat is deaf and perhaps easily frightened, or may have painful joints that make quick retreats difficult. Teaching children the safe way to approach and "love on" their cat will mitigate many issues.

- If your cat is awake but turned away from you in a room, try flicking the room lights or pointing a laser toy on the floor to get her attention before approaching. If your cat is sleeping, make her aware of your presence by tapping firmly on the ground or pressing gently on the cushion she's sleeping on so that the vibrations or movements alert her. Then allow her to smell your hand or a familiar object. If she does not respond (let's face it, sometimes cats are simply in a deep sleep and dreaming about prowling!), rouse her another way. Gently fan air near her head. Avoid poking her face or touching her sharply and quickly. Many older cats have painful joints, so avoid their hips and limbs.
- Closely monitor your cat's interactions with visitors, and move him to a different location if needed.
- Use behavior modification techniques (as directed by your veterinarian) to help your cat manage fear- or anxiety-inducing situations safely.
- Always supervise your cat if she goes outdoors, and leash walk her or use a secure outdoor enclosure. Cats can easily wander off and may not notice oncoming cars, approaching dogs or cats, or other potential threats.
- Attach a bell and medical alert tag to your cat's harness in case she escapes from your sight.
- Learn and teach hand signals—a fun, additional way to communicate and keep that bond you have with your cat!
- Use different hand signals for different commands (e.g. come, get down, no) and situations (e.g. time to eat, I'm leaving, we have visitors). Give small treats or pet your cat as a reward, use lots of eye contact, and employ other communication cues (like a blinking penlight) as needed.
- If your cat seems to be more anxious, talk with your veterinarian about medications or supplements (also called *nutraceuticals*) that can help alleviate anxiety.
- Remember that your cat who is hearing impaired can enjoy a happy life—play, explore, cuddle, and do everything that a cat who has normal hearing can, except hear!

SUPPORT RECOMMENDATIONS

- Deaf Animals Facebook group:
  facebook.com/deafanimals/
- Deaf White Cats (DWC) Facebook group:
  facebook.com/groups/2358033161/about/

CHAPTER 8:

Oral care: Keep them grinning

> "...she noticed a curious appearance in the air; it puzzled her very much at first, but after watching it a minute or two, she made it out to be a grin, and she said to herself, "It's the Cheshire Cat; now I shall have somebody to talk to."
>
> —Lewis Carroll, from "Alice's Adventures in Wonderland"

In veterinary school I learned many things about many creatures. From infectious diseases and diabetes to skin problems and complex surgical procedures, I studied and helped treat dogs, cats, ferrets, rabbits, guinea pigs, hamsters, rats, mice, birds, chickens, cows, horses, llamas, Florida black bears, turtles (so many pet and wild turtles in Florida!), snakes, lizards, and even fish. One thing I wish I could've spent more time studying was the oral cavity. Yup—the mouth and teeth!

Nearly every cat and dog I see has some form of dental disease. And as pets age without proper dental care, their dental issues worsen. Senior pets *always* make me grin! But when I was in primary care practice and about to examine a senior cat's or dog's mouth, I braced myself for a hot mess that smelled like hot garbage!

A cat's first dental visit

Far too often, pet parents wait until their cats are middle-aged or older before scheduling their first veterinary dental visit and cleaning. But 50% to 90% of cats older than 4 years of age have some form of dental disease![1] And brachycephalic (short-headed)—also affectionately called "smoosh face"—breeds such as Persians are more prone to serious dental problems. They have a smaller bone-to-tooth-root ratio (less bone to support the tooth roots) and shorter skulls, so their teeth are crowded and sometimes rotated.[2] In these breeds, veterinarians may have to remove a tooth (that usually is not helping the cat chew anyway) simply to make room to treat the cat's other teeth or to provide overall better oral health.

The American Animal Hospital Association recommends that all pet cats have a professional veterinary dental cleaning starting at 1 year of age.[3] When I was a primary care practitioner, I typically didn't hear concerns from pet parents about their cat's teeth until their pet's breath smelled bad or they realized that their cat wasn't eating well. But by the time pet parents notice something amiss, the damaged oral tissues and infection have already wreaked havoc.

Many pet parents of older cats are shocked to learn from their veterinarians that not only is their cat long overdue for teeth cleaning, their cat's dental disease has progressed so far that the cat needs several tooth extractions! Many of my middle-aged cat patients had to have multiple teeth pulled during their first professional dental cleaning. And, sadly, many of their owners didn't bring them back for routine veterinary dental cleanings for the remainder of their cats' lives because their first experience turned out to be an extremely costly surgical procedure. Routine dental care and professional cleanings are important at all ages.

When dental care is irregular

Unlike people, cats rarely get cavities. But like people, they do get gum disease (also called *periodontal disease*), and it can begin when they're quite young. Periodontal disease is a common problem in the adult cat population because many cats do not receive consistent dental care. Cats can't brush and floss their teeth every day or schedule their own teeth cleanings, so accumulated food particles and saliva provide a great environment for their oral bacteria to multiply and leave deposits (*plaque*) on the teeth and below the gums. When plaque weasels its way beneath the gum line, the bacteria and their byproducts incite inflammation. Plaque that isn't removed by brushing continues to build up and hardens into dental tartar (also called *calculus*). Ultimately, tartar irritates the gums and other structures that support the teeth and causes infection.

Teeth, gums, and the bones that support the teeth are badly damaged after years of tartar buildup and infection, which leads to loose teeth and tooth fractures, necessitating tooth extractions. In one study, tooth fractures were found in one in four cats and dogs.[4] It breaks my heart to think how much pain so many pets have endured for so long because of a tooth fracture. At a veterinary conference, a veterinary dental specialist once shared something she learned from a dentist for people. Some patients who had been unable to seek immediate dental care described that eating with a fractured tooth is as painful as having to walk with a sprained ankle, or like chewing on broken glass!

Tooth resorption is another common, painful dental problem that affects 29% to 66% of cats.[5] The cells that normally help breakdown deciduous (baby teeth) roots to make way for permanent adult teeth inappropriately attack the adult teeth and lead to tooth erosions, progressive tooth destruction, and tooth fracture. Unfortunately the cause is unknown, and treatment requires tooth extraction or removal of the crown of each affected tooth.

In some cats, infection and inflammation from severe dental disease leads to bone loss around the teeth, which weakens the jaw bones. Weakened bones may allow small fractures to develop. So when diseased teeth are extracted during a dental procedure, the jaw may easily break, which requires a longer surgery to repair, as well as longer, more intense patient care afterward.

Untreated dental disease may also lead to trouble elsewhere besides the mouth. Bacteria from infected teeth and gums may travel through the bloodstream and cause abnormal microscopic changes in the heart, kidneys, and liver.[6,7] Pets with diabetes have a higher risk of gum disease, and, in turn, gum disease may hamper glucose metabolism, which can make diabetes worse.[8] In people, chronic inflammation associated with periodontal disease is recognized to adversely affect a person's overall general health.[9] Likewise, and especially in senior pets, if a pet's dental health can be improved, the pet's health overall will likely also improve.[10] I saw this with many patients. Not only do they show more zeal for life after professional dental cleaning (and tooth extractions if needed), but their blood test results return to normal.

It may be helpful to think of an infected, diseased mouth as a giant wound that's been left to fester. On top of that, if your cat has fractured teeth (keep in mind that broken teeth aren't always seen unless radiographs are taken), your cat likely endures tremendous pain every time she eats and drinks. You can easily imagine how much misery and poor health that causes.

FUN FACT:

Adult cats have 30 teeth and adult dogs have 42. Adult people have 32 teeth, unless their wisdom teeth have been removed!

Chewing on all the alarming details I've presented above, it's easy to see why regular veterinary dental examinations (at least once a year) and routine professional dental cleanings are necessary.

Is anesthesia really necessary to clean cats' teeth?

Wouldn't it be great if cats would cooperatively sit back once or twice a year, open wide, stay still, and let the veterinary technician examine, x-ray (bite down to hold the radiograph film, and hold still for the picture!), probe, scrape, rinse, suction, and polish their teeth for an hour?

Because—shockingly, I know!—pets won't allow this, they must be anesthetized for teeth cleaning. I know many pet parents are afraid to have their cat undergo anesthesia—particularly an older cat. This fear, along with the cost of veterinary dentistry (most pet insurance plans don't yet cover routine dental cleanings) and the well-meaning but mistaken pet parent belief that cats don't need regular dental healthcare like people do, all serve to justify some pet owners' decisions to forgo their cats' routine professional dental cleanings. That is, until a cat's oral disease has progressed so far that the problem can't be ignored. And at that point, a much longer time under anesthesia and a costlier procedure (typically with tooth extractions, as I mentioned earlier) are required.

This is why anesthesia-free dentistry, also called *nonanesthetic dentistry*, has gained popularity and appeals to many pet owners and to some veterinarians.[11] With this service, the cat is awake while the tartar—above the gumline only—is removed and the teeth are polished. While this makes the cat's teeth look shiny and white on the surface, tartar and other problems below the gums continue to lurk and can progress. This is especially concerning in areas like the tooth roots and jawbones that can only be properly evaluated with radiography (x-rays).

Anesthetizing cats for dentistry is needed to prevent patient pain or injury during a thorough examination and cleaning. It's also needed to prevent harm to the person cleaning the pet's teeth. Using a dental probe to measure tooth socket depths and a dental scaler to remove tartar under the gumline are often prickly and uncomfortable, plus these instruments are sharp and perilous to use in awake, wiggly cats who may also bite! In addition, cats who are not anesthetized can inhale the debris created by removing the tartar from, or scaling, the teeth, which can lead to a serious lung infection. (Cats who are anesthetized have a breathing tube in place that protects their airways from this debris.) The anesthesia also ensures cats stay still for correct x-ray positioning, and dental radiographs are a vital part of evaluating and maintaining oral health in every cat.

Some veterinarians and technicians believe nonanesthetic dentistry can be used successfully, when done under veterinary supervision and for those cats whose owners otherwise won't allow a full anesthetic procedure because of the cost or potential risks. But, of course, if a cat needs additional evaluation (which they do, because dental radiographs are considered the standard of care in veterinary practice) or treatment (e.g. tooth extraction), an anesthesia-free procedure is impossible.

The tradeoffs for cats who undergo nonanesthetic dentistry are that they may experience stress and pain during the service, and undetected or untreated dental disease may stay hidden longer, which leads to disease progression, further pain, and increased cost to treat later. For these reasons, I strongly discourage nonanesthetic dental procedures.

Keep in mind that the risks related to anesthesia can be greatly reduced with a proper preoperative patient history and examination, diagnostic tests (checking the blood and urine to assess a cat's health status, and performing other tests as needed), and high-quality anesthetic and supportive care techniques. If your cat has a medical condition that makes him a higher risk for anesthetic complications, such as diabetes, chronic kidney disease, or heart disease, your veterinarian may recommend referral to a veterinary dental specialist or that the procedure be done at a hospital with a veterinarian who specializes in anesthesia.

So don't be nervous if your veterinarian tells you your cat needs professional dental cleaning (all cats do!) and that he or she may (or does) need one tooth or several teeth pulled. It's crucial to remove the source of oral problems and pain and prevent future or more serious disease—both in the mouth and in other organs. Cats who have had some or even all of their teeth extracted can still eat well (and even better than with diseased teeth!). They'll also feel better and have a better quality of life, compared with living with rotten, painful, or fractured (like chewing broken glass!) teeth.

Other oral problems in seniors

Age-related muscle loss is called *sarcopenia* and it's common and expected in senior cats. This type of muscle atrophy is especially noticeable in the hindlimbs, and is also apparent in the muscles of the head. In people, sarcopenia can affect the jaw muscles and those involved in swallowing. It's possible that cats with sarcopenia may likewise have difficulty picking up, holding, chewing, and ingesting food.

Veterinary examinations that include a good look in your cat's mouth are important not only to assess the teeth and gums but also to look for swelling, wounds or sores called *ulcers*, masses, and abnormal color or changes in color. Oral ulcers can stem from irritation, infections, kidney disease, cancer, or even an autoimmune response to excessive plaque buildup. Senior and geriatric cats have a higher risk of cancer, and cancer can start in the mouth. Squamous cell carcinoma is the most common oral cancer in cats.

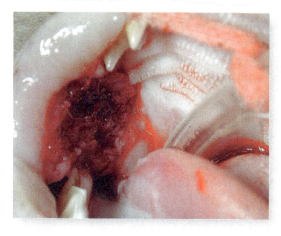

 Zaza (age 23 years) is anesthetized (a breathing tube is in place) in this photo. She had oral squamous cell carcinoma on the roof of her mouth. The first indication her family had that something was wrong was when she drooled blood-streaked saliva. Before she started drooling (which in addition to oral disease, may indicate nausea, pain, anxiety, high body temperature, or another problem), she had likely been swallowing her excess saliva for a while.

If detected early (which can be difficult without regular, careful veterinary exams), some oral cancers—especially those nearest the front of the mouth and whose tumor cells haven't spread to other parts of the body—can be treated to stop or delay progression. Surgery, chemotherapy, and radiation therapy may help.

News to savor

The good news is that the vast majority of periodontal disease in cats is preventable!

In addition to regular examinations and an annual professional dental cleaning, here are important ways to promote your cat's oral health at home:

- Brush your cat's teeth daily (use toothpaste formulated specifically for cats—do not use yours!). You can even teach many senior cats to accept this, with small steps and patience.
- Feed a therapeutic veterinary dental diet specifically designed to slow plaque buildup (discuss the options with your veterinarian).
- Provide safe, cat-specific chew toys. Some cats love to chew cardboard and tear up paper, which you can allow as long as they don't eat it. (Some cats like to chew on hair ties, rubber bands, ribbon, string, and tinsel, all of which are big no-nos because they're easy to swallow and can cause stomach irritation and intestinal blockages.)

- Offer treats formulated specifically for cats that help reduce plaque. Water additives and oral gels, sprays, wipes, and powders may also help slow plaque buildup. See the Veterinary Oral Health Council website at **vohc.org/** for a list of approved products for cats.

When to see your veterinarian

Keep in mind that signs of oral problems can be difficult to detect in cats. Your cat's broken tooth may not be obvious to you, but a tooth with even a minor fracture can be sharply or dully painful and ultimately lead to serious infection and an abscess. In addition to your cat's regular exams, schedule a veterinary visit if your cat:

- has foul-smelling breath;
- has yellow, brown, grey, or greenish discoloration or buildup on her teeth—this is tartar that needs to be removed from above and below the gum line;
- eats less—cats may seem hungry but eat very little or walk away from their food; because it's painful or difficult to chew
- drops food frequently, which may indicate that it's painful to hold onto or chew food;
- is reluctant or refuses to eat dry kibble, or swallows it without chewing;
- paws at his mouth or rubs his face or shakes his head often;
- drools;

Opal's mom called me after she noticed Opal pushing her food out of her bowl, not eating all her meals and not grooming herself anymore. Sadly, we found the culprit to be an oral tumor under her tongue. The signs can be mild so be on the lookout!

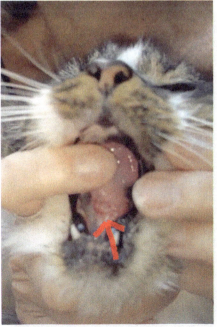

- has red or swollen gums, bleeding gums, or blood in her saliva;
- has oral ulcers;
- has swelling in or around his mouth, nose, eyes, or jaw;
- has nasal discharge;
- seems painful or gets defensive if you touch her mouth; or
- has obviously chipped or broken teeth, or loose or missing teeth;
- stopped grooming.

CAREGIVER TIPS AND HOME HACKS

Regardless of the cause of senior or geriatric cats' oral cavity problems, they should be able to consume enough calories to meet their nutritional needs and maintain basic daily activities, and they should be enthusiastic about eating and enjoy it. Embracing a love of eating factors into a cat's quality-of-life assessment.

- Feed moistened dry or canned food and soft treats to cats with muscle atrophy, those who have lost most or all of their teeth, or those who have had oral surgery to remove a tumor.
- Use low-sodium beef or chicken broth to soak kibble.
- Feed freshly made cat food (delivery options are available), such as Freshpet **freshpet.com**.
- Consider elevating food and water bowls, which may make swallowing easier and may also help cats with neck discomfort.
- Warm up room temperature or refrigerated canned/wet food to your body temperature before offering it. A study in cats older than 7 years showed that they preferred a chunks-in-gravy wet food that was warmed to 98.6 F (37 C) over the same wet food that was served at room temperature (69.8 F [21 C]) or just removed from the refrigerator (42.8 F [6 C]).[12]

- Teach your cat to accept having his mouth touched so you can look inside and eventually teach him to accept toothbrushing or dental wipes. Pair these lessons with a favorite treat or play activity afterward, so your cat starts to look forward to it!
- A soothing "cup of tea" may be helpful to a cat that has oral ulcers, swollen gums and/or bad breath. Mucositis is a common complication of cancer treatment and green tea has been shown to have beneficial effects in people and animals with this problem. Creating a green tea mouth rinse that you give 2-3 times a day could provide some comfort to your kitty. Click this QR code to learn more!

Questions to ask your veterinarian about your cat's professional dental cleaning

- If my cat's age or other medical condition increases the risk of complications from anesthesia, what measures are taken to help reduce this risk?
- Do you have a veterinary anesthesia-certified nurse available to assist?
- What is the cost of a professional dental cleaning?
- What is the cost if my cat needs tooth extraction?
- If my cat needs multiple extractions that exceed my budget, what will be the treatment plan?
- What pain management measures will you use before and after the procedure, especially if my cat needs tooth extraction? If my cat has serious oral disease and needs tooth extractions, will you prescribe medication to relieve pain for my cat to receive at home afterward?[13]
- Can my cat eat and drink normally in the evening after the dental procedure? Will my cat's food need to be softened for a few days? Will my cat need additional supportive feeding methods?
- What dental care can I do at home if I can't brush my cat's teeth?
- For diabetic cats: How should I fast my diabetic cat before a dental procedure? Should my cat's insulin dosage be adjusted? Will my cat need any diet alteration to ensure he'll eat on schedule afterward?

PRODUCT RECOMMENDATIONS

- Refrigerated, fresh pet foods: Freshpet **freshpet.com**

RESOURCES

- Animal Owner Resources. American Veterinary Dental College. **avdc.org/animal-owner-resources**
- Accepted Products. Veterinary Oral Health Council. **vohc.org/all_accepted_products.html**

CHAPTER 9:

Body condition and nutrition: Helping senior cats eat better and feel better

"Food is symbolic of love when words are inadequate."

— ALAN D. WOLFELT, AUTHOR, EDUCATOR, GRIEF COUNSELOR

Slowing the sands of time to help your cat through their ninth life as healthily and comfortably as possible is as easy as pie! If the pie consists of the perfect amount of a nutritious diet that suits your cat's life stage and health issue(s), and if you can entice your cat with engaging activities that burn calories and maintain strength. Sounds simple! But it's so hard to do!

Geriatric cats tend to be finicky princes and picky princesses when it comes to what goes into their tummy and what toys they'll bat at. Parents of husky senior and geriatric cats often tell me, "My cat doesn't overeat, he's just lazy!" Cat parents with skinny older kitties commonly ask questions like: "My cat eats a lot, why does he look so thin?" "Which food is best for my senior cat?" "How do veterinary diets differ from the cat food I buy?" "Why does my cat act hungry, then walk away from her food?" "How do I get my cat to eat when she doesn't feel well?"

I'll address these questions and more, and begin with why to keep an eye on your cat's physique. Unless we monitor our cats' weight and can tell whether they have a healthy mix of fat and muscle, gradual changes in their figures—whether they're packing on extra pounds or slimming excessively—can creep along and surprise us one day. Excess flab and measly muscles ramp up a cat's sands of time. Obesity and inactivity speed aging, while maintaining muscle strength and staying physically active slow aging.

Flabby felines and hefty humans

A few diseases cause weight gain in senior cats:

- Acromegaly—a tumor in the pituitary gland (in the brain) releases excess growth hormone.
- Hyperadrenocorticism—a pituitary gland tumor signals the adrenal glands (small glands in the abdomen that make many different hormones) to produce too much cortisol, a steroid hormone.
- Hypothyroidism—the thyroid gland underproduces thyroid hormone (an uncommon problem in cats.

I'll cover these conditions in more depth in Chapter 18 "Endocrine disruption: Glands and hormones out of whack." Treating this type of weight gain hinges on treating or managing the underlying disease and adjusting a cat's diet and activity as needed. Here, I'll focus on the biggest reasons cats become overweight or obese: overfeeding and inactivity.

Sadly, many adult cats of all ages in the U.S. are overweight. According to the Banfield Pet Hospital State of Pet Health report in 2017, 33% of pets in the U.S. are overweight.[1] In 2018, the Association for Pet Obesity Prevention estimated that 60% of cats (and 56% of dogs) were overweight or obese.[2] And in 2020, Banfield reported that veterinarians diagnose overweight or obesity in 38% of cats.[3] So although the precise percentages of overweight pets vary a bit, it's clear that excess weight continues to be a concern in a large number of pets.

Unfortunately, we've surpassed our pets in the realm of expanding waistlines. According to the Centers for Disease Control and Prevention, 73.6% of adult people in the U.S. are overweight or obese.[4] In people, obesity is considered

Andre (only 5 years old) was adopted as an overwhelmingly obese cat at 26 pounds! Fortunately, his new family is helping him slowly shed pounds, and his weight has dropped into the upper teens. He still has a ways to go, but if he were to remain obese, he'd be in store for a world of additional health troubles as he ages.

a disease and is a risk factor for developing diabetes, heart disease, osteoarthritis, cancer, frailty (which goes hand in hand with a poorer quality of life), and more. People with obesity also have a shorter lifespan and higher mortality risk. Likewise, our pets' health, quality of life, and lifespan can be negatively affected by obesity.[5]

> **NOT HAVING MUCH FUN FACT:**
>
> One 2017 study revealed that **adult people spend twice as much time on the toilet** (3 hours and 9 minutes) each week than they spend being moderately active (1 hour and 30 minutes), such as taking a bike ride or walking rapidly.[6]

A weighty topic

Many pet parents may not realize that their cat is overweight. A review of patient medical records at a university veterinary hospital in Sweden showed that 45% of cats were overweight or obese, but a separate survey showed that only 22% of cats were reported as overweight or obese by their owners.[7]

When I worked in general veterinary practice, weight loss in pets topped my discussion list with pet owners, with dental disease as a close second. (The irony, right? Pets with bad teeth can still overeat!) The veterinary technicians at our practice were always prepared for me to talk with clients about their chunky pets—typically a delicate topic.

Overfilling cats' bowls, giving table scraps, and offering treats are some of the ways that we show cats love every day. But if our cats have become rotund, we're also shortening their healthspan (the disease-free period of life) and diminishing their quality of life (which results in far fewer [and eventually none] of those joyous run-around-and-be-a-crazy-cat moments). And cats who are severely obese have shorter lifespans.[8]

I frequently talked with my clients about how much pet food, table food, and treats they could (and couldn't!) feed their portly pets. Plus, I helped them craft a pet workout plan (including food puzzle toys) and encouraged them to drop by the veterinary clinic for weekly weigh-ins to track their progress.

Metabolism slows in middle-age and older cats and they need less dietary energy—but only to a point. Unlike dogs, whose metabolism continues to slow as they grow older and they tend to gain fat, cats' metabolism shifts back into a higher gear at around age 11 years. So their energy requirements change and they need additional high-quality, highly digestible nutrients— especially protein.[9,10]

> ### Weighing food is the way
>
> Did you know that the only way to dish out the right amount of dry kibble or canned pet food is to weigh it, rather than use a measuring cup?[11,12] This goes for cats who need to lose weight, gain weight, or simply maintain their weight.
>
> First, you'll need to know how many calories your cat needs to eat each day. This depends on your cat's life stage, body condition, reproductive status, activity level, and health (or ailment) status. Your veterinarian will help you determine the correct number of calories for your cat.
>
> Second, you'll need to know how many calories are in the food(s) (and treats–which should be no more than 10% of the recommended daily calories) you feed. You may have to look online or call the manufacturer to get calorie information, because it isn't always on the pet food label.
>
> Third, you'll need to know how many calories the food contains per gram, then calculate the total number of grams to feed each day.
>
> Fourth, you'll need a kitchen scale that weighs in grams so you can weigh out the right amount of food at mealtimes.
>
> Finally, for cats, it's usually best to divide the total number of grams into two or more small meals each day, plus save some to feed in a food puzzle or Kong toy. This helps cats stay active and mimics their natural feeding pattern (to catch and eat several small meals throughout the day).
>
> Again, always consult with your veterinarian on what, how much, and how often to feed your cat, because these things depend on your cat's individual needs.

The cons (and one pro) of a glut of the gut

Overall, keeping fat at bay helps cats as they get older. Cats who have arthritis and carry excess weight into their senior years may end up with severe mobility issues (which limits activity and adds to weight gain). Arthritis in cats is strikingly common. In one study, x-rays showed that a whopping 90% of cats older than 12 years had degenerative changes in their joints.[13] In a separate study, x-rays showed that 92% of cats of all ages had signs of joint disease in their hips, knees, ankles, elbows, and backbone, and the signs were worse in older cats.[14] Also, cats with arthritis may have trouble grooming themselves, and obesity makes some spots harder to reach.

Other problems that cats may be able to avoid by trimming extra fat are a decreased lifespan, cancer, diabetes, and respiratory disease.[15] And because excess fat stimulates inflammation throughout the body, it puts cats at a higher risk of developing other conditions such as environmental allergies, asthma, high blood pressure, eye disease, and diarrhea.[16]

All of these conditions reduce cats' healthspans, so conventional wisdom suggests that cats with health problems have shorter lifespans. Yet surprisingly, one study of 2,609 pet cats revealed that mildly or moderately overweight cats live longer than underweight, just-right weight, or severely obese cats do.[8] So while mildly or moderately overweight cats are known to have more health problems, the study suggests that the extra weight doesn't shorten their lifespans (unless they become severely obese). The researchers concluded that overweight cats with longer lifespans don't necessarily have a better quality of life, because cats who live longer with chronic diseases likely have an unsatisfactory quality of life.[8]

How to assess fat mass

You can check whether your cat may be overweight or underweight by using a feline body condition scoring system, which is a tool veterinarians use. This assessment relies on feeling a pet's ribs, checking whether they have a "waist" as viewed from above, and evaluating whether their belly tucks up or hangs down as viewed from the side. To score your kitty, check out the World Small Animal Veterinary Association Body Condition Score scale for cats: **wsava.org/wp-content/uploads/2020/08/Body-Condition-Score-cat-updated-August-2020.pdf**

A handy way to check for scrawny or tubby kitties

Here's a less precise but quick way to assess your cat's fat cover.

Hold your hand out flat with your fingers extended, palm facing down. With your other hand, gently run your fingers over the knuckles on the back of your hand. This nears how your pet's ribs feel when their weight is ideal.

Then turn your hand over with your palm facing up and your fingers straight and feel your knuckles on the palm of your hand. If your pet's ribs feel like this or if you can't feel them at all, your cat may be too plump.

Turn your hand back over, palm down, and make a fist. Feel the knuckles on the back of your hand. If your cat's ribs feel this prominent, your pet is too thin.

FUN FACT:

As social media attests, some people positively adore fat cats and equate chubby with cute. What such posts don't show are the unattractive consequences of chronic health conditions.

A 2020 study from the Sydney School of Veterinary Science in Australia showed that cat owners who approve of portly pets are more likely to have overweight or obese cats than owners who frown on cat fatness. Perhaps not surprisingly, cat owners who believe that chubby or fat cats have a good quality of life are more likely to have overweight or obese cats.

The study also showed that cats who beg for food, are middle-aged, eat primarily dry food in unknown quantities, and spend a lot of time indoors are more at risk for being overweight or obese.[17]

Trimming the fat

Helping an overweight or obese cat lose weight can seem overwhelming, and cats must rely on their caretakers' willpower. Cats can't (usually!) help themselves to the food, so their route to a healthy weight starts with their pet parents simply dishing out less food and fewer treats. Overweight cats who are being fed free-choice need scheduled mealtimes (many small meals, preferably some that your cat has to seek out from food puzzles or kibble dispensers) on the menu instead. Talk with your veterinarian about a meal and weight loss program tailored to your cat's needs.

Keeping cats at an optimal weight while they're young, middle-aged, and senior—including while you're managing their conditions or illnesses throughout their lives—makes a world of difference in your cat's mobility, activity level, attitude, and ability to recover from sickness or injury. Feeding less of their regular food when appropriate or feeding a veterinary-recommended weight loss diet to help your cat stay trim also saves you money—both in food costs and potential future veterinary bills!

Getting your cat to move a bit more also supports weight loss and reduces boredom. And cats who are bored tend to eat more or beg for food to get attention. One study showed that lean cats are voluntarily more physically active and eager to socially interact with people than overweight cats are, so be patient and persistent![20]

FUN FACT:

One small study of 44 overweight cats who were participating in a weight loss plan unsurprisingly found that 32 cats exhibited annoying food-seeking behaviors such as meowing, opening cabinets to get food, and eating a housemate's food. But surprisingly, offering vegetables as a low-calorie treat to deter these behaviors helped the cats finish the plan!

Pet parents offered zucchini, broccoli, lettuce, green beans, cauliflower, and spinach. Four cats ate plain vegetables, and 28 cats ate vegetables sprinkled with FortiFlora (Purina Pro Plan Veterinary Diets), a probiotic supplement powder that was used as a low-calorie flavor enhancer.

On average, it took slightly less than 8 months for 29 of the cats to trim their body condition scores by two points or to reach an ideal body condition score.[18]

Bonus fun fact: Researchers have learned that obese cats have specific changes in their gut bacteria compared with normal-weight cats, so researchers think that in the future, diets, probiotics, and prebiotics can be formulated to normalize the gut bacteria and help treat obesity in cats.[19]

Caregiver tips for getting slack cats to act

- Short workouts hold a senior cat's attention. Even three to five minutes of activity a day that your cat wouldn't otherwise get counts. Gradually add time and increase the number of sessions a day if your cat is physically able, and as your cat sheds weight and starts feeling spunkier.
- Use an unswallowable-size magnet to stick an intriguing lightweight feather toy, crinkle ball, or crumpled piece of paper to your fridge just within your cat's reach, and allow him to stretch up to pull it down or knock it off.
- At mealtimes, place a third of your cat's meal in her bowl and wait for her to finish eating and walk away. Then put another one-third portion in the bowl so she has to walk back. Wait for her to finish and walk away. Then put the final third in the bowl. Extra steps add up!
- Try spurring your cat to chase a laser pointer toy–but don't run her to exhaustion and don't abruptly end the game. Allow your cat to slowly stalk and pounce near the dot as she would if she were attempting to capture prey, and always end the game with the dot landing on a toy or special treat. Your cat needs to "catch" the dot and win the game to avoid becoming frustrated, and to prevent possibly developing a compulsion

for chasing other reflected or flickering lights.[21] (And absolutely no pointing the laser in a cat's eyes!)
- With your cat watching, drop a crinkle ball, faux-fur mouse toy, or kibble into your old shoes or boots. Some cats like to stretch and fish around with their paws for items or stick their head in spaces they can't readily see into.

 Jack-Jack's workout program includes occasional deep-shoe fishing for toys.

- Encourage your cat to leap or stretch to pounce on a feather toy attached to a wand, including jumping into and out of a cardboard box or a laundry basket, if they're physically able.
- Entice your cat to climb a cat tree, jump onto the couch, or walk up and down a step stool by chasing a fabric ribbon wand toy or exploring intriguing items you've placed at different levels.
- Feed your cat on a different level of your house—upstairs or downstairs if applicable—to get her to use the stairs a few extra times every day.
- Provide vertical spaces for your cat to explore, and allow your cat to jump up to and down from heights that match his physical abilities.
- Use a slow feeder bowl, food puzzle, foraging mat, or food-dispensing toy

 Rita received her meals in a slow feeder bowl to prevent her from quickly wolfing down her kibble. It made mealtimes more interesting, gave her more time to feel full during meals, and helped her stay trim.

instead of a bowl to serve kibble meals. Or make a kibble dispenser by poking slightly larger-than-kibble-size holes in an empty cardboard paper towel roll, placing the kibble inside, and stapling the ends. Or punch holes in a clean plastic bottle or yogurt container that has a lid.

- Place kibble in various spots in your home so your cat hunts at mealtimes. For some cats, you may need to start by placing a few kibbles in their bowl and the rest in different spots near their bowl. Then gradually work outward and cover a larger area. Use more elaborate hiding spots as your cat catches on. Even if you use the same hiding spots and your cat quickly finds them, your cat will benefit from the additional exercise and mental stimulation at mealtimes.

- Toss your cat's serving of kibble around the room one piece at a time at mealtimes instead of placing all the food in a bowl. Wait for your cat to watch where you'll toss each piece so she'll walk or run to the right spot to catch and eat it. You can signal that mealtime is over by placing the last two or three pieces of kibble in her bowl.

- Depending on your cat's physical abilities and temperament, you may be able to teach your cat to wear a harness and walk on a leash outdoors, or to walk on a treadmill or use a cat exercise wheel. Such feline training tends to take more persistence and patience than teaching a dog does. Because overweight cats are likely already highly food-motivated, you can use tiny treats to encourage and reward their participation.

WallE and Eva get weekly weight check-ins!
Tip: Use a digital pet or pediatric scale, because if you weigh yourself with and without your cat, you'll miss small but meaningful weight differences.

Scrawny seniors

Each of my cats lost weight as they became geriatric. As they lost muscle and fat, their faces looked thinner, and their spines, hips, and shoulders became too easy to feel. They also each gradually showed less interest in their meals.

Unintended, unexplained weight loss always warrants a veterinary evaluation. If your cat has a condition that curbs his appetite or hampers nutrient absorption, he can lose weight because he doesn't eat enough calories or doesn't process nutrients effectively. Body condition changes in seniors can be dramatic and difficult to reverse. A geriatric cat health journal comes in handy for tracking your cat's zeal for food and treats, along with changes in his weight and appearance over time.

Cat Journal
(amzn.to/3dNvAkg)

Other than putting an overweight cat on a diet, many conditions in senior cats can cause weight loss. Dental problems can make eating too painful, and stressful changes in the home, refusal to eat a new diet, pain from any illness or injury, some medications, and a variety of illnesses can cause nausea, unwillingness to eat, and reduced nutrient absorption.

Kidney function declines over time in many cats, and it's a big reason senior and geriatric cats lose weight. Although I cover chronic kidney disease in more depth in Chapter 13, I include it here because gradual weight loss is one of the earliest signs. I also briefly discuss a few of the digestive system ailments that are likely to cause weight loss in senior cats—inflammatory bowel disease, pancreatitis, liver disease, triaditis, and constipation. And I address age-related and disease-related muscle loss and the consequences of each. Senior cats may also be scrawny because they have hyperthyroidism, diabetes, heart disease, or cancer, and I cover those topics in other chapters.

Kidney disease

Senior cats commonly develop chronic kidney disease (see Chapter 13 for more about this disease), and affected cats are usually thin and continue to lose weight. One study of more than 550 cats with kidney disease showed that they had lost about 9% of their body weight in the 12 months before their kidney disease was diagnosed.[22] And looking back further, it was clear that these cats had started losing weight three years before their kidney disease diagnosis.

The study also showed that cats continued to lose weight after their diagnosis, and that cats who weighed less than 9.3 lb (4.2 kg) at the time of their diagnosis did not live as long as cats who weighed 9.3 lb or more. The results indicate that tracking cats' body weights can help veterinarians identify kidney disease sooner. So cat owners can help by keeping a geriatric pet health journal and watching for weight loss trends.

Inflammatory bowel disease

With this condition, cells that normally help the body fight infections inappropriately invade and irritate the intestinal walls. Why these cells overreact isn't known, but affected cats have trouble digesting food and absorbing nutrients. They lose weight, vomit often, eat poorly, and have diarrhea.

To confirm a diagnosis, veterinarians use various blood tests, fecal tests, abdominal x-rays or ultrasound, intestinal biopsies (taking small samples of tissue to examine under a microscope), and diet trials (trying a different food to rule out a food allergy). Treatment can include dietary changes, probiotics, vitamins and other supplements, and medications that reduce inflammation and fight bacteria and parasites.

Pancreatitis

The pancreas is most famous for making insulin that controls blood glucose levels, but it also makes and releases enzymes into the intestine to help digest food. Pancreatitis means inflammation of the pancreas, and why it occurs in cats is unknown. But when the pancreas is inflamed, digestive enzymes leak inappropriately into the abdomen. This causes nausea, loss of appetite, vomiting, abdominal pain, diarrhea, and fever.

This digestive enzyme leak can turn serious quickly, and these cats need veterinary care quickly. Medical care such as medications that reduce pain and nausea and fluids given intravenously (into a vein) will be needed. Pancreatitis sometimes occurs with other conditions such as diabetes, inflammatory bowel disease, and liver disease.

Liver disease

The liver filters blood, helps with digestion, metabolizes drugs, removes harmful substances, stores vitamins and minerals, and produces proteins, fats and hormones. The liver also produces bile, a greenish-brown fluid that the gallbladder stores and releases into the intestine through the bile duct. Bile breaks down dietary fat for absorption in the intestine and processes harmful substances that shouldn't be absorbed. Liver disease in senior cats may stem from tumors, inflammation or infection, or fat infiltration.

Tumor cells that develop in the liver can be harmless (benign) or malignant (cancer). Tumor cells can also spread to the liver from cancer that started in other organs or tissues.

If the liver, gallbladder, and bile duct become inflamed or infected, this is called *cholangiohepatitis*.

When fat cells infiltrate the liver, it's called *hepatic lipidosis* or *fatty liver*. If cats—especially overweight cats or cats with another medical problem—stop eating for more than two days straight for any reason (illness or injury, moving, getting lost, refusing a new diet, boarding, losing or gaining a family member, houseguests), they are in danger of developing hepatic lipidosis, a life-threatening problem. So if your cat misses a few meals (aside from refusing to eat at the natural end of life, which is expected), veterinary evaluation is warranted.

Cats with liver disease typically refuse to eat, and they lose weight, vomit, have a fever, are weak or tired, become dehydrated, and develop jaundice—yellow discoloration of the skin, ears, gums, and white portion of the eyes because bile pigment builds up in their blood. Blood tests, ultrasound, and liver biopsies or abdominal surgery may be needed. Liver biopsies help sort out whether the disease is relatively harmless or seriously harmful.

Treatment for liver disease involves medications, supplements, supportive therapy, and careful attention to nutrition—ensuring that cats get back on the right track to eating well. This sometimes involves temporary placement of a feeding tube, which cats tolerate nicely and is very often life-saving. Surgery to remove a liver tumor can help some cats feel better and extend their lifespan.

Triaditis

When cats have inflammatory bowel disease, pancreatitis, and cholangiohepatitis at the same time, this is referred to as *triaditis* (which means three inflammatory problems at once), and veterinary medical care is needed, as mentioned above for these individual ailments.

Constipation

This uncomfortable condition occurs when too much poop builds up in the colon. Cats will strain to defecate in the litter box or may avoid the litter box. They may pass small, hard fecal balls, a tiny amount of diarrhea, or no poop at all. They tend to eat less, vomit, have a swollen tummy, hide, and walk stiffly.

Your veterinarian may give your cat fluid therapy, enemas, laxatives, and fiber supplements; suggest diet adjustments; and express (gently squeeze) your cat's anal sacs (glands located next to the anus that produce stinky secretions) if they're full.

Long-term or repeated bouts of constipation can limit the colon's ability to contract, leading to severe colon enlargement (called *megacolon*) and more constipation episodes. So it's important to relieve constipation as soon as possible and use preventive measures if repeat episodes occur. Cats who have megacolon may need surgery to remove the diseased part of the colon. Surgery may also be needed if constipation results from an abdominal tumor that presses on and narrows the colon.

Sarcopenia

As cats enter their senior years, they may also lose weight because of muscle loss, even without an underlying disease. This type of muscle loss is called *sarcopenia*, and it is a loss of muscle mass, strength, and function. Sarcopenia occurs as people age, too. I think of my Grandma Gardner, who was a fit woman her entire life. But as she aged, her hands looked bony, her face lost its fullness, and she was a twig. Most people lose muscle mass as they age, even if they are otherwise healthy. Sarcopenia starts at around 30 years of age, and, shockingly, we can lose 30% of our muscle mass by 80 years of age, as compared with the muscle mass we had at age 20.[23]

The danger of sarcopenia? In people, it reduces muscle strength and contributes to fragility, leading to falls and injuries as well as decreased immunity.[23] Sarcopenia is also linked to a risk of adverse outcomes such as physical disability, poor quality of life, and death.[24] Factors that likely contribute to sarcopenia in people as they age include being physically inactive, changes in muscle fibers, chronic inflammation, decreased protein production, insulin resistance, and decreased testosterone and growth hormone.[23]

Sarcopenia has been less studied in cats than in people, but evidence suggests that cats (and dogs) also lose muscle with aging.[23,25-29] Sarcopenia in cats probably results from similar mechanisms associated with aging in people and contributes to similar adverse outcomes.

Cats with sarcopenia often look thinner than normal. But fat can mask muscle loss, so in overweight cats, sarcopenia may not be as noticeable.

 Rumpleteazer had a good but robust body condition when he was 5 years old.

 At age 19 years, Rumpleteazer had sarcopenia and cachexia.

Cachexia

Another type of muscle loss in people, cats, and other species is associated with an underlying disease called *cachexia*. Cachexia is closely related to sarcopenia, but cachexia occurs when a disease leads to loss of muscle mass.[25] It most often happens in pets with chronic diseases, such as heart failure, cancer, or kidney disease. But cachexia can also occur in cats who have sudden severe illnesses and critical injuries.[25] Unfortunately, because senior cats often also have an underlying disease, they may have both sarcopenia and cachexia. Sarcopenia and cachexia also contribute to other health problems. Cachexia and frailty can also be considered as related components of malnutrition and aging.[30]

Animals with cachexia often have weight loss, which is sometimes extreme, especially as their disease progresses. But you may not notice weight loss in the early stages. The weight loss that occurs in pets with cachexia differs from weight loss that occurs in healthy pets. In healthy cats who lose weight because of reduced caloric intake, they lose fat first and preserve muscle. But in cats with chronic disease, muscle is catabolized (muscle protein is broken down to amino acids to use for energy) before fat stores are used.[25]

A distressing syndrome

In people, cachexia is also called wasting syndrome. As it is in pets, cachexia in people is a complex disorder that messes with the body's use of nutrients and is associated with long-term disease or sudden severe illness. People who have cachexia lose muscle with or without losing fat, have unintentionally lost 5% or more of their body weight in 12 months or less, and experience other problems such as less interest in food, being tired all the time, and muscle weakness.[31]

Cachexia can occur even in cats who are eating well. With cachexia, protein, carbohydrate, and fat metabolism go awry and the body doesn't properly process the energy it needs, even if the cat is eating normally. This faulty metabolism results in muscle breakdown and inhibits muscle growth, which contributes to weakness. Cachexia is also associated with triggering inflammation and immune system malfunction, which means the body has less ability to heal and is more susceptible to infections. And cats with cachexia often have a reduced appetite, which only makes the problem worse.

It's no surprise that cachexia diminishes quality of life in a number of ways. Affected cats become weaker (and wobbly), which can lead to accidents and injuries that require more caregiving. Cachexia can also hamper a cat's ability to respond to treatment, escalate symptoms of the underlying illness, and reduce life expectancy.

How to assess muscle mass

Your veterinarian should assess not only your cat's weight and body condition but also your cat's muscle condition to check for muscle loss associated with age or disease. The body condition score primarily assesses a cat's fat mass, so it can be misleading with respect to a cat's muscle mass. For example, despite being overweight or obese, cats may still have severe muscle loss, and this is called *sarcobesity*.[32] Thus, cats whose scale readout drops primarily because of muscle loss aren't necessarily making weight loss progress. Similarly, a cat who is underweight may have normal muscle mass but an insufficient amount of body fat.

Assessing a cat's muscle condition takes more practice than assessing a cat's body condition. It requires looking at and feeling the muscles next to the spine, on the head, and over the shoulders and hips. The score is graded as normal muscle mass or as mild, moderate, or severe muscle loss.

Duncan has arthritis and sarcopenia. From this angle, his muscle wasting is especially apparent over his lower back and hips, a result of him not wanting to use his back legs as much because of arthritis pain.

You can find information on how veterinarians assess muscle condition by reviewing the World Small Animal Veterinary Association Muscle Condition Score scale for cats: **wsava.org/wp-content/uploads/2020/01/Muscle-Condition-Score-Chart-for-Cats.pdf**

What can be done for cats with muscle loss?

The goals of therapy for sarcopenia or cachexia are to rebuild strength and reverse or slow the muscle loss associated with aging or disease. Unfortunately, cachexia can't be fully reversed, but it can be slowed. The most effective way to help cats with cachexia (or sarcopenia) is to treat their underlying chronic illness and provide supportive therapies. Supportive therapies that hold promise for helping cats with sarcopenia or cachexia include exercise, appetite stimulation, fish oil, and the proper diet in the right amounts.[25] Your veterinarian can help determine whether your cat may benefit from these or additional therapies.

EXERCISE. Increasing cats' activity through exercise that includes resistance training to slow or reverse muscle loss is key.[25] Endurance exercises build aerobic power generated by the heart and lungs, and resistance exercises maintain and build muscle. A three-day-a-week balanced resistance and endurance exercise program is physically and mentally beneficial for pets.[33] See the caregiver tips I listed earlier in this chapter, and talk with your veterinarian about a suitable activity plan for your cat. Also consider visiting with a veterinary rehabilitation therapy specialist to discuss an individualized exercise and strength-building program, especially if your cat has physical limitations or other medical conditions. Veterinary rehabilitation therapy is similar to physical therapy for people, and it's delivered only by healthcare professionals specifically trained in veterinary rehabilitation medicine.

FUN FACT:

A wee workout works! Scientists showed that in people, a mere *three seconds* of biceps weight training a day, five days a week, for one month increases arm strength.[35]

> "In my 30s I exercised to look good,
> In my 40s, I exercised to stay fit
> Then in my 70s, I exercised to stay ambulatory
> In my 80s, I exercised to stay out of assisted living
> In my 90s, I'm exercising out of pure defiance!"
>
> — Dick Van Dyke[34]

APPETITE STIMULANTS. Capromorelin (the brand name of this drug for cats is Elura, made by Elanco) is a liquid oral medication given once a day, so you don't have to get your cat to swallow a pill. It promotes appetite by stimulating receptors for a hunger hormone called *ghrelin*. Ghrelin also helps regulate other hormones that boost metabolism and affect muscle mass: growth hormone and insulin-like growth factor-1.[25] Cats usually show much more interest in food about an hour after receiving a dose of capromorelin.

Another great appetite stimulant option for cats that your veterinarian may prescribe is mirtazapine. The brand name is Mirataz (made by Dechra). It's available as a topical ointment that you rub on a cat's ear—at the top of the ear on the inside of their pinna (outer ear)—once a day. This allows the medication to be absorbed through the skin (wear a disposable glove to rub it onto the ear so you don't medicate yourself), and that's a huge benefit because getting cats to take oral medications can be a challenge.

FISH OIL. Omega-3 fatty acids (called eicosapentaenoic acid [EPA] and docosahexaenoic acid [DHA]) help reduce inflammation, decrease muscle loss, and improve appetite. Welactin (Nutramax Laboratories Veterinary Sciences) and Omega-3 Pet (Nordic Naturals) are omega-3 fatty acid supplements available in separate forms for cats and dogs. Some cat foods already contain omega-3 fatty acids, so talk with your veterinarian about whether your pet needs a supplement.

Avoid giving flaxseed oil (it contains an incorrect ratio of EPA and DHA) or cod liver oil (the amount of vitamin A and vitamin D are too high for the amount of this oil that would be needed to deliver the right dose of EPA and DHA) as fatty acid supplements.[36] Always ask your veterinarian whether fish oil or any other type of supplement is appropriate for your cat and, if so, what brands are best formulated for your cat's needs and what doses are safe.

DIET. Providing optimal nutrition formulated for your cat's life stage and, when indicated, feeding a therapeutic diet specifically designed to support pets with certain chronic diseases is crucial. Ensuring that cats with cachexia consume enough calories—especially protein and other nutrients—that also help manage their underlying disease is particularly critical. Pet foods labeled as senior diets won't necessarily provide optimal nutrients for seniors who have underlying diseases. For example, cats who have heart failure need a low-salt diet. Cats with kidney disease have special dietary protein and mineral needs. So, especially for cats with cachexia, consider asking a veterinary specialist in nutrition for help. A veterinarian who is board-certified in veterinary nutrition can tailor a pet's diet and feeding recommendations, and some provide remote consultation. Ask your veterinarian for help in connecting with one, or visit the American College of Veterinary Nutrition website **acvn.org/nutrition-consults/**.

Increasing food intake often involves making the food more

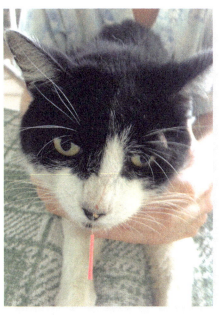

Acupuncture may help stimulate appetite in cats. Acupressure (without needles) may work to stimulate appetite, too, and this acupressure point is called "Shan Gen" or "Base of the Mountain." You can massage this area (between the haired and non-haired part of the nose) with your finger or a stylus pen 10 minutes before feeding.

palatable, which I discuss later in this chapter. Getting the most out of mealtimes may also mean you need to prevent competition for food from other cats and dogs in the household.

Which diet is best for senior cats?

Now that we've covered the pudgy and the scrawny issues that might pop up, let's look at nutrition in general and the topics pet parents often ask me about.

A plethora of diets have been formulated to support a variety of factors that make up the uniqueness that is your cat, including:

- life stage (e.g. pediatric or growth, adult, reproduction, mature, senior);
- breed (e.g. Persian, Maine Coon, Bengal);
- body system support (e.g. dental health, sensitive stomach, haircoat, weight management); and
- disease (e.g. diabetes, kidney disease, joint issues, heart disease, cognitive problems, intestinal disorders, seizures, allergies, urinary tract disease).

It can be overwhelming! Many diets are available over the counter (OTC) at grocery stores and pet stores, and others—veterinary therapeutic diets—are available only through veterinarians. You can face decision paralysis with all the options!

FUN FACT:

Cats are true carnivores, so vegetarian and vegan diets can't provide the protein and other nutrients from animal sources that cats need. An all-meat or almost-all-meat diet also harms cats—they need the right mix of animal and plant nutrients.[37]

What's the difference between veterinary therapeutic diets and OTC options?

Veterinary therapeutic diets must undergo extensive testing and research to show that they are precisely formulated to address the nutrient needs of pets who have a specific disease or condition. These diets often contain special high-quality ingredients or nutritional supplements that are not included in OTC pet foods. In addition, therapeutic diets have rigorous manufacturing controls, and the companies test every batch of food produced.[38]

Therapeutic diets typically cost more than OTC diets. The rigorous diet formulation, ingredient selection, and manufacturing technique all add up and make them seem expensive compared with OTC diets. This may be true if you compare them solely on a bowl-to-bowl basis. So if your veterinarian recommends a therapeutic diet for your cat, account for the amount you would spend on an OTC diet anyway, and then factor in the benefits of feeding a therapeutic diet as a component of your pet's overall medical treatment to prevent, slow, or reverse the ailment, thus potentially reducing future veterinary medical costs. You'll likely find that therapeutic diets provide invaluable support for your pet and you.

Why are therapeutic diets available only through veterinarians?

The FDA Center for Veterinary Medicine requires dog and cat foods that claim to treat or prevent disease be available to the public only through or under the direction of licensed veterinarians.[39] Pets with chronic diseases need veterinary evaluation and monitoring to help ensure that their therapeutic diet (which is often used along with medical treatment) is the right choice for that condition and continues to help the pet. Veterinary oversight is also needed to determine at what point it may be acceptable to discontinue the therapeutic diet and switch to a different therapeutic diet or back to an OTC diet.

It's vital to have a diagnosis before feeding your pet a therapeutic diet, especially if your pet has more than one health problem. You can inadvertently cause a nutrition-related medical problem if you feed a therapeutic diet that your pet doesn't need. The nutrients in therapeutic diets are specially formulated for pets with specific diseases, so the levels of these nutrients are not always suitable for long-term feeding in healthy pets, or the nutrients could be inappropriate for a pet who has multiple conditions. (Again, for pets with multiple conditions, consultation with a veterinary nutritionist about an optimal food is especially helpful!) The bottom line is that therapeutic diets are not available for sale at grocery and pet stores because veterinarians must approve of their use in each pet.[38] So along that line, don't presume that other pets in the household can eat the same therapeutic diet—ask your veterinarian.

On the other hand, OTC diets are most often based on a recipe that meets a healthy pet's nutritional needs and may have less rigorous manufacturing controls and product tests. Some OTC pet food labels suggest that the diet helps prevent specific health issues, but such diets may contain only one or two of the same supplemental ingredients that veterinary therapeutic diets contain and in amounts that may not be helpful in managing the pet's condition. This is why, for example, an OTC "stomach support" diet you find at a pet retail store probably costs less than the therapeutic diet that your veterinarian recommends for your cat's food allergies. And despite what a pet store employee may tell you, the OTC diet is not "the same thing" as the veterinary therapeutic diet.

Senior diets

Many diets marketed as senior pet diets contain fewer calories because as pets age they tend to have decreased energy requirements or may be overweight. Some senior diets contain additional fiber to support gastrointestinal health or to help with weight loss. Other senior diets may contain slightly higher potassium and lower sodium and protein to help support a pet's aging kidneys. But if your senior cat's kidneys function normally, she doesn't need these nutrient adjustments. Plus, protein restriction isn't needed in healthy senior pets, and, as we've learned, less dietary protein could make matters worse for pets who have sarcopenia or cachexia.

Diets marketed for senior pets must meet the same legal ground rules as diets marketed for younger adult pets. No best senior diet exists for all senior pets, and not all senior pets will benefit from a senior diet. Senior pets who are already receiving a good-quality commercial adult pet food may even be able to continue eating that diet.[40]

Precision home-cooked nutrition

Many pet owners consider venturing into preparing home-cooked diets for their dogs and cats. I tip my hat to those who do this well! I personally have a hard time feeding myself properly with home-cooked meals, let alone my pets! Shopping for all the ingredients and supplements needed, along with the preparation itself, can become time-consuming. But I know many pet parents who manage it and enjoy making meals for their furry kids.

FUN FACT:

Some cats may like to sneak a taste of your ice cream or lap up your leftover breakfast cereal milk, but did you know cats lack a sweet tooth? They can't taste sugary things. Cats *can* taste sour, bitter, salty, and meaty things.[41] They may like dairy products for their protein and fat content, but some cats may not tolerate lactose (milk sugar) either, leading to stomach upset.

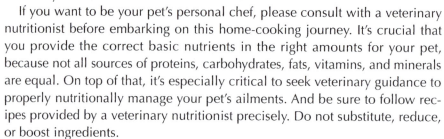

If you want to be your pet's personal chef, please consult with a veterinary nutritionist before embarking on this home-cooking journey. It's crucial that you provide the correct basic nutrients in the right amounts for your pet, because not all sources of proteins, carbohydrates, fats, vitamins, and minerals are equal. On top of that, it's especially critical to seek veterinary guidance to properly nutritionally manage your pet's ailments. And be sure to follow recipes provided by a veterinary nutritionist precisely. Do not substitute, reduce, or boost ingredients.

Quibbles about kibble

If you're looking for simple, healthy feeding alternatives or to add spice to your cat's weekly menu, alternatives to kibble or home-cooked diets include frozen, fresh, or freeze-dried options produced by companies whose pet foods are formulated by a veterinarian board-certified in nutrition or a PhD in animal nutrition. For fully prepared pet foods delivered to your door, I suggest Just Food For Cats.

Hitting a raw nerve

Raw meat diets for pets have sparked controversy. My recommendation—and that of veterinary nutritionists, most primary care veterinarians, and the FDA—is to avoid raw diets.[38,42] Raw meat diets are marketed to appeal to pet parents as being healthier for pets because they claim to be more natural and closer to what wild animals would eat. Yet studies have not been done to prove that raw meat diets are healthier for pets.

Pets aren't wild animals. Our domesticated furry family members don't have the same genetic makeup as their wild ancestors, and they have evolved alongside us (and as we humans evolved, we began to cook most of our food!). And, like us, our cats' nutrient needs have also likely evolved. Wild animals who live in their natural habitats suffer from more infectious diseases, parasites, and malnutrition than pets do. They also have a shorter life expectancy.[43]

The risks associated with feeding raw meat to cats aren't trivial. Compared with commercially available cooked pet foods, these diets are more likely to be imbalanced and not contain enough of certain nutrients or have excessive amounts of other nutrients—or both! Raw meat diets are also more likely to contain harmful bacteria. Infections with these bugs can make your cat (and you) sick and can sometimes be fatal. In addition, if the diet includes bones or bone shards, then mouth, esophagus, stomach, or intestinal injuries or blockages are also risks, as are broken teeth.[44] Without proven health benefits, and because of the potential for harm, raw meat diets are not recommended.

Heart problems in pets eating grain-free diets?

A concerning increase in reports of pets developing a specific type of heart disease called dilated cardiomyopathy (DCM) has occurred in recent years.[45] From January 2014 through July 2020 the FDA received reports of 1,100 dogs and 20 cats with DCM.[46] With DCM, the heart muscle stretches, thins, and weakens, which leads to enlarged heart chambers that pump blood less efficiently.

Specific diet ingredients that are missing or harmful haven't yet been identified as causing DCM. Early reports suggested that too little taurine (an amino acid important for heart function) played a role, but not all affected pets have low taurine levels.[47] More studies are needed to evaluate each potentially contributing factor.[48] In the meantime, veterinary cardiologists suggest that dogs with heart disease who are being fed a grain-free diet should be switched to a non-grain-free food that contains standard ingredients (beef, chicken, wheat, rice, corn) and is made by a well-established pet food company.

If your cat has DCM and is eating a nontraditional diet, veterinary nutritionists advise that you work with your veterinarian to follow the same recommendations as for dogs with this condition.[49]

Changing diets

If you need to switch your cat to a new diet for any reason, try to introduce it when he is feeling relatively normal. If he feels lousy when you try out a new food—such as a veterinary therapeutic diet—your cat may reject it and never take another nibble.

Veterinarians most often recommend that you switch to a new diet gradually. This gives your pet's gut microbiome time to adapt and helps prevent vomiting and diarrhea that sometimes occurs with sudden diet changes.

To begin, offer a small amount of the new diet in a dish separate from your cat's regular diet at mealtimes. When your cat eats the new food, pet and praise your kitty. You can then begin to switch gradually and reduce the total daily amount of your cat's regular diet and make up the difference with the new diet over a three-week period[50]:

- week 1, feed 75% of the regular diet mixed with 25% of the new diet;
- week 2, feed a 50:50 mix of each diet;
- week 3, feed 25% of the regular diet and 75% of the new diet; and
- week 4 and thereafter, feed 100% of the new diet.

Provide pets and praise at mealtimes to positively reinforce your cat's interest in eating.

If your cat shows signs of stomach upset at any time, decrease the proportion of new food and add back the regular food and lengthen the transition time. Also tell your veterinarian about the signs of your pet's upset stomach. And if your cat refuses to eat altogether, let your veterinarian know immediately. Cats who miss a few meals risk developing hepatic lipidosis.

One exception to a gradual diet transition is for cats who experience a sudden bout of vomiting or diarrhea, such as with pancreatitis or gastritis (inflammation of the stomach lining that can stem from ingestion of toxins or certain medications, or result from stress, hairballs, or a wide variety of other illnesses). In those cases, your veterinarian may recommend an abrupt, immediate switch to a specific type of bland diet for a few days, among other therapies if needed. But never fear, bland diets are intended to calm and help reset normal gastrointestinal function and gut microbiome balance.

> ### What's a gut microbiome? And did you say "poop transplant?"
>
> The gut microbiome consists of gazillions of tiny critters such as bacteria, protozoa, viruses, and fungi that live in our pets' (and our!) intestines. Some of these organisms are beneficial and others can be harmful, particularly when their balance is disrupted. The microbiome is crucial for proper digestion and helps produce vitamins and amino acids (the building blocks of protein). It also communicates with the brain through various complex mechanisms and influences metabolism, immune function, and mood.
>
> Every individual's gut microbiome is unique. It is delicate and can be disrupted by sudden diet changes (including overabundant treats or inappropriate snacks), various illnesses, stress, and some medications. Influencing or altering the microbiome has potential for treating or helping manage various diseases, and the gut microbiome is an intense area of new research in people, cats, and dogs.
>
> Therapy to modify the gut microbiome can include changing a pet's diet to better support an individual's microbiome needs, giving certain antibiotics to eliminate bad bacteria, adding good bacteria by feeding probiotics, and supplementing the diet with prebiotics—special plant fibers that supply nutrients that good bacteria like.
>
> In some cases, transferring organisms from a healthy gut microbiome to an unhealthy microbiome restores a healthy balance of good bacteria to keep the bad bacteria in check. This is called *fecal microbiota transplantation*, or poop transplant! It has been used successfully in people with overgrowth of bad gut bacteria and is gaining ground for use in veterinary patients.[51-54] Some researchers think a poop transplant may even help us better manage obesity in cats someday.[19]

Overabundant appetite

Flagging an overzealous appetite (also referred to as *hyperrexia*) as a problem can be tricky because many pet parents presume that cats who eat well must be healthy. It's true that sick or injured cats usually have a decreased appetite, but some behaviors, diseases, and medications produce an increased appetite.

For example, cats may learn that crying near the food bowl between mealtimes (or at your bedroom door at 3 a.m.) or begging for table food results in consistent food rewards, which can lead to obesity and an increased appetite.

Hyperthyroidism (overactive thyroid gland function) is a common disease-related reason that cats chow down excessively. These cats' hunger can seem almost insatiable! But ironically, cats with hyperthyroidism are skinny. And it's been said that *hyposmia* (partial loss of sense of smell) can lead to hyperrexia in cats,[55] although I'm unsure how commonly this is seen in veterinary practice.

Of course, obese or overweight cats who are on a weight loss diet often act ravenous, too. During these times, distract your cat with petting or brushing him, playing with toys, a walk, or offering a small amount of nutrient-enriched water such as Hydra Care (Purina Pro Plan Veterinary Diets) or low-sodium chicken or beef broth, or zucchini sprinkled with FortiFlora (Purina Pro Plan Veterinary Diets).

Diabetes, some gastrointestinal disorders, hyperadrenocorticism, or a diet with insufficient nutrients can also cause *polyphagia* (another word for abnormally increased appetite and eating). Medications such as corticosteroids and appetite stimulants make pets hungrier. So if your cat eats like a horse and isn't receiving a medication that's known to spark his appetite, a veterinary evaluation is warranted!

Apathetic appetites

Decreased interest in food caused by an underlying disease or other ailment is worrisome, and it is common in older cats. Lack of appetite (called *inappetence*) is one of the main reasons pet parents elect to euthanize their cat. Many diseases can cause a decreased appetite. Cancer; kidney or heart failure; pancreatitis (inflammation of the pancreas); stomach, intestinal, or liver diseases; upper respiratory infections or nasal problems that affect a cat's sense of smell; nerve disorders; osteoarthritis; and even cognitive decline can bring on:

- hyporexia (decreased appetite);
- dysrexia (altered appetite that manifests as a pet rejecting his or her typical balanced diet and accepting only certain other foods, such as extremely tasty treats; it may also manifest as disrupted patterns of eating); or
- anorexia (complete absence of appetite).

Many mechanisms are at work in causing disease-related decreases in appetite, and nausea and pain are two of those culprits. In addition, non-disease-related stress, such as stress from environmental changes (e.g. a new human or pet housemate, moving, being stalked or attacked by a housemate cat after returning from the veterinary clinic) can affect emotional well-being and cause inappetence.

It's also easy to confuse unwillingness to eat (I won't eat!) with inability to eat (I can't eat!). So cats who in fact have a normal appetite may eat less because they have an injury or disease that makes it painful for them to chew—such as teeth, gum, or jaw problems—or because they have an ailment that makes swallowing difficult (called *dysphagia*).

Talk with your veterinarian about your cat's waning appetite, without delay. Cats who stop eating or don't eat enough, even if only for two or three days, can make matters worse for themselves. Consider keeping a food diary—measure or weigh the food before you feed your cat and measure or weigh any leftovers your cat leaves. Your veterinarian can help reignite your cat's appetite by treating or adjusting treatments for underlying diseases, resolving injuries, recommending how you can reduce household stressors, and prescribing anti-nausea and appetite-stimulant medications, and can determine whether your cat will benefit from a feeding tube.

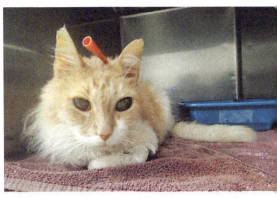

Charlie is patiently waiting to be discharged from the veterinary hospital after his esophageal feeding tube was placed.

Try not to pooh-pooh a feeding tube

If despite all efforts, your cat is still not consuming enough calories, consider a feeding tube. Cats tend to tolerate feeding tubes well, and feeding adequate calories keeps the gastrointestinal cells functioning and promotes overall strength, immune function, and comfort. A bonus: a feeding tube better ensures your cat gets the oral medications he needs.

Your veterinarian will evaluate which type of tube is best for your cat: a feeding tube inserted through the nose (nasogastric) or one surgically placed through the esophagus (which connects the mouth to the stomach) (esophagostomy) or stomach (gastrostomy). Your veterinarian will teach you how to use and clean the tube at home, and what, how much, and when to feed your cat. Cats with feeding tubes can still eat and drink on their own, and the amount they consume helps gauge when your veterinarian can remove the tube. Some critically ill patients may need a tube placed in the intestine (called *jejunostomy*), or they may need intravenous feeding (given into a vein, also called *parenteral nutrition*), and these patients stay in the hospital while the tube is in place.

> Pet parents sometimes draw the line on feeding tubes for their pets for many reasons. But feeding tubes can be incredibly beneficial to support cats through an illness that they might otherwise succumb to. Feeding tubes can also provide support near the end of life to give owners more time with their pets, yet still allow a good quality of life for the pet.

Veterinarians can also suggest other ways to nourish your cat's interest in food that are specific to your pet and his or her environment. I've garnered oodles of tips from my experiences with my patients, which I share here.

Encouraging cats to eat

For senior cats who aren't feeling well or who have a chronic condition that requires a special diet, we often need to change diets or add special goodies to their regime to encourage them to eat. And as the end of life draws ever closer, the nutritional goal focuses more on getting calories and protein into their bodies vs. worrying about maintaining a delicate balance of nutrients related to their specific disease. So if your cat is receiving a veterinary therapeutic diet that he refuses to eat despite your attempts to make it tastier or to address his reduced appetite with medications, then talk with your veterinarian about changing the diet to one he will accept.

A senior cat's finicky tendencies can really stress a caregiver. But likewise, avoid stressing your cat—keep mealtimes low-key and calm. Gently pet and sweet talk your cat while you're offering food to encourage them, but avoid hovering while they eat (unless they seem to like company during meals!), and never force feed them. Force feeding leads to caregiver aversion–your cat may run away from you when you approach, or find other ways to avoid you. Your creativity comes into play during these troubling times.

CAREGIVER TIPS FOR GETTING RELUCTANT CATS TO EAT

- Avoid putting medications directly into your cat's food because she may reject the food altogether. (For tips on giving medications, see Chapter 23 "Course of action: Therapeutic options and gaining acceptance from your senior cat")
- Feed fresh food in a clean bowl.

- Remember to refresh water frequently to keep it inviting. Cats with inappetence may not drink as much as they should, and dehydration makes inappetence worse and can contribute to constipation. Fill the bowl to the brim, and move the bowl away from the wall so your cat can choose which direction to face. If your cat's water bowl is next to their food bowl, offer at least one other bowl in a different location, because some cats prefer separate eating and drinking spots.
- Keep in mind that cats who refuse to eat their dry kibble may gobble up canned food, and vice versa.
- Keep in mind that cats who were not introduced to a wide variety of the different types of food early in life (kibble, different shapes of kibble, canned, pate, chunks, gravy) may not readily accept any unfamiliar new formulations, shapes, or textures.
- Offer a mix of a small amount of dry kibble and a small amount of canned food.
- Avoid competition for food from other pets in the household, and keep in mind that some cats prefer to eat alone.
- Try warmed (to body temperature) food.
- Try refrigerated food.
- Stick to your cat's usual mealtime routine. But if this isn't working, try changing it up: change your cat's mealtime or change the location in which you feed your cat, or change who feeds the cat. Every cat is different!
- Move the food bowl away from the wall so your cat can choose which direction to face, and avoid feeding near high-traffic areas in the home, noisy appliances, litter boxes, cat flaps, and full-length windows.
- Try feeding in a different bowl (ceramic, stainless steel, plastic or paper) or in a bigger bowl, or on a plate.
- Offer elevated food and water bowls (to ease discomfort in cats with arthritis).
- Keep small amounts of food available at all times so your cat can eat whenever he feels like it. Leaving large portions of food out isn't recommended and may be unappealing to cats with inappetence, because they tend to feel full after eating only a little. Or offer scheduled, smaller meals more often throughout the day and before bedtime.
- Add unsalted beef or chicken broth to your cat's food.
- Ask your veterinarian about adding an omega-3 fatty acid supplement made from fish oil to your cat's food. It may help stimulate appetite and has the added benefit of supporting muscle mass. If your cat refuses to eat their regular food with the added supplement, try it on a new food. If they refuse that also, don't force the fatty acid supplement, because you don't want your cat to develop an aversion to the food she enjoys.

- Add high-value treats such as small bits of cooked chicken or all-meat baby food to your cat's food (don't feed baby foods that have garlic or onion in them, which can be toxic to cats). FortiFlora (Purina Pro Plan Veterinary Diets) is a probiotic supplement powder that also enhances the flavor of food. Cats especially love an appetite motivator such as Churu by Inaba (**churuvet.com**) and Bonito Flakes by Cat-Man-Doo **catmandoo.biz/1oz-bonito-pouch**.
- Always provide clean, fresh water to help your cat stay hydrated and support nutrient absorption. Consider providing filtered water if your cat doesn't seem to like the taste of your tap water. Simply adding water to dry kibble or canned food, or making a dilute, flavored broth from gravy that remains in the can helps. Drinking fountains may entice some cats to drink. Juice from tuna packed in water can be especially appealing to cats, and you can make ice cubes with it to save for use throughout the week. Flavored broths for pets and nutrient-enriched water supplements such as Hydra Care (Purina Pro Plan Veterinary Supplements) are also available.

Then, once you think you have finally found the new food or the treat-enhanced diet that your cat will eat and you have their meal routine back under control, they decide to turn away from their food bowl again!

When you've reached that point, and perhaps before then, appetite stimulants prescribed by your veterinarian can be extremely helpful. I find appetite stimulants work great, especially for cats in the later stages of chronic kidney disease who tend to have spurts of inappetence—which usually indicates that they need a boost with subcutaneous (under the skin) or intravenous fluid support, which helps their appetites as well, so ask your veterinarian about that, too.

Research revelation: What's the fuss about whisker-friendly feeding?

Whiskers are delicate sensory tools that help cats understand and navigate their environments and communicate their moods. Although "whisker fatigue" and "whisker stress" haven't been scientifically validated, they're popular terms used to describe distress or discomfort that cats could potentially experience when their whiskers are overstimulated, for example, by constantly touching the sides of their food bowls during meals. The idea's origin isn't exactly known, but it's often used to market specially designed, "whisker-friendly" or "whisker relief" cat food and water bowls that have wide, shallow dimensions. Veterinary researchers got curious and wanted to test whether these bowls would affect cats' eating habits.

The results of their study showed that pet cats didn't eat more, drop less food, or spend more time at a "whisker-friendly" (wider, shallower ceramic or stainless steel) food dish compared with when the cats ate from their normal (narrower, deeper ceramic or stainless steel) food bowl.[56] But the study also showed that when pet parents offered the food in both bowls at the same time, 24 of the 38 cats (63%) chose the whisker-friendly bowl. Many of the cat parents decided to continue using the whisker-friendly bowl and even bought more for their other cats. The researchers cautioned that cats' preferences could have been related to cats choosing the bowl closest to them, or choosing the bowl that was different.

In short, the study's authors found that although whisker-friendly bowls didn't affect these cats' eating habits or support the whisker stress theory, more cats preferred the whisker-friendly bowls. The authors also suggest that further research will help evaluate whether whisker-friendly dishes are useful in cats.[56]

When there's no need to encourage or force cats to eat

Eventually cats will dramatically reduce their food intake at the end of their lives, and this is natural. There are few more emotionally loaded issues than the loss of appetite at the end of life. I have heard an insightful saying from human hospice caregivers that I share with all the families whose pets I help. "Food and water are for the living. A body won't eat or drink for a future it doesn't know." In the late stages of terminal illness, bodies will not desire and will even reject food and water. This is a symptom of death approaching, it is not the cause of death. Offering or forcing food during this time can make pets feel nauseated and distressed, and they will not appreciate your efforts.

 ## Questions to ask your veterinarian

- Has my cat's weight changed? Has my pet's weight shown an increasing or decreasing trend?
- What is my cat's body condition score? (Or, is my pet underweight, just right, overweight, or obese?)
- Will my cat benefit from a food puzzle toy or other type of food or treat dispenser?
- What is my cat's muscle condition score? (Or, is my pet's muscle mass normal, or does my pet have mild, moderate, or severe muscle loss?)
- How can I help prevent muscle loss in my cat?
- Does my cat need any dietary adjustments or nutritional supplements?
- Is a therapeutic diet available that is specifically designed to help manage my cat's illness or condition?

- Will my cat benefit from an appetite stimulant or anti-nausea medication?
- What other measures can I take to help my cat eat?
- Will a feeding tube help my cat?

 READING RECOMMENDATIONS

- Petfoodology. Articles/blogs on a variety of nutrition topics. Clinical Nutrition Service. Cummings School of Veterinary Medicine. Tufts University. **vetnutrition.tufts.edu/**
- How to Evaluate Food for Your Pet. NC State Veterinary Hospital. **cvm.ncsu.edu/wp-content/uploads/2019/01/Evaluating-Pet-Foods-v2-1.pdf**
- The Savvy Cat Owner's Guide: Nutrition on the Internet. World Small Animal Veterinary Association Global Nutrition Committee. **wsava.org/wp-content/uploads/2020/01/The-Savvy-Cat-Owner-s-Guide-to-Nutrition-on-the-Internet.pdf**
- Cat Carer Guides. International Cat Care. **icatcare.org/advice-cat-carer-guides/**
- Inappetence. Managing the cat that won't eat: information for owners/caregivers.
- Feeding tubes. Managing the cat with a feeding tube: information for owners/caregivers.
- *Geriatric Cat Health & Care Journal: A Complete Toolkit for the Geriatric Cat Caregiver.* By Dr. Mary Gardner (2022, Rolled Toe Publishing).

CHAPTER 10:

Thermoregulation: Cool cats and feverish felines

"No animal is a better judge of comfort than a cat."

— James Herriot, British veterinary surgeon and author

My cat Bodhi was the epitome of a lap cat. Wherever I sat, he would find a way to lie in my lap, which I welcomed most of the time! But his heat-seeking insistence also became uncomfortable or inconvenient at times. Even when I managed to sit alone for a few minutes, he had an uncanny sense of recognizing when I was on the verge of getting up again. He seemed to appear from nowhere and would leap onto my lap and settle in. (How do they *know*?!) So invariably I'd put off what I had planned to do for another 10 minutes. "I can't load the dishwasher right now, Bodhi is on my lap!"

The only place Bodhi liked better than my lap was... my laptop! Because he'd lost weight from his chronic kidney disease, Bodhi was a skeleton wrapped in fur with a few whiskers and a whole lot of love. He had barely any fat and not much muscle to keep him warm,

 My coworker Bodhi's first office chair.

and my computer laptop seemed like a perfect heating pad to him, especially if a sunbeam wasn't available. Luckily, I used an external keyboard and could turn off the laptop keyboard, which prevented him from accidentally sending emails or deleting my hard drive!

Regulating normal body temperature

In the exam room, pet parents often got wide-eyed during a routine wellness visit when the veterinary technician reported their cat's temperature: "It's 101.5, Dr. Mary." The cat's owner would immediately ask, "Why does he have a fever?"

Many pet parents don't realize that normal body temperature in a healthy cat ranges from 98.1 to 102.1 F (36.7 to 38.9 C).[1] This is slightly higher than humans' body temperature range, which is 97 to 99 F (36.1 to 37.2 C).

COOL FUN FACT:

Chickens' normal body temperature range is a whopping 105 to 107 F!

Typically we think of maintaining a comfy body temperature by adjusting the ambient temperature or altering our exposure to the environment. We change the room thermostat setting, cozy up near a fireplace or best furry friend, open a window to allow breezes to drift through, jump into a swimming pool, and dress appropriately—shorts in summer and sweaters in winter!

We and our cats also have an internal "thermostat." The anterior hypothalamus is the part of the brain that helps maintain core body temperature within a narrow range, called the *hypothalamic set point*. This narrow temperature

FUN FACTS:

The temperature range in which we and our feline friends don't have to burn extra calories to stay warm or cool off is called our *thermoneutral zone*. Cats' thermoneutral zone is 86 F to 100 F (30 C to 38 C).[2] As we know, cats seem to prefer a toasty ambient temperature, and their warm thermoneutral zone is one possible explanation for their love of sitting in boxes! (Other proposed reasons for cats' attraction to square spaces are that they feel secure in boxes, plus they like to hide and explore. One study showed cats will even sit in two-dimensional shapes on the floor that look like squares![3])

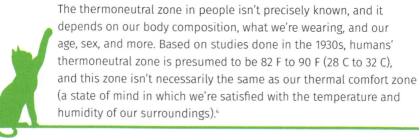

The thermoneutral zone in people isn't precisely known, and it depends on our body composition, what we're wearing, and our age, sex, and more. Based on studies done in the 1930s, humans' thermoneutral zone is presumed to be 82 F to 90 F (28 C to 32 C), and this zone isn't necessarily the same as our thermal comfort zone (a state of mind in which we're satisfied with the temperature and humidity of our surroundings).[4]

range is essential for cells to function normally and to prevent tissue damage and organ failure.

Temperature sensors (called *thermoreceptors*) throughout the body send messages to the hypothalamus about cold and hot within the body and in the environment. This helps the hypothalamus control the ways in which the body conserves or loses heat to maintain this set point temperature. This process is called *thermoregulation*. A healthy thermoregulation process maintains core body temperature despite big differences in ambient temperature.

Generating heat

Cats (and people) produce heat internally through metabolism, which involves all the chemical reactions in the body that keep cells functioning, including muscle activity, food digestion, and nutrient processing.[5] To retain body heat when the surrounding temperature is cold, blood vessels near the skin surface can narrow (called *vasoconstriction*) so that less heat is delivered to be transferred out through the skin. Fat cells under the skin also help hold heat in.

In addition, a pet's hair can stand up (called *piloerection*, also known as goosebumps in people) in response to cold. Raised hair traps air next to the skin, which insulates against heat loss. Piloerection also happens when pets are upset—like the raised hackles on those iconic black cats of Halloween! Many cat breeds also have undercoats to help them stay warm. Another way cats (and people!) conserve heat is by curling up, because exposing less body surface area to the environment retains heat.

Cooling off

Cats (and people) cool off by reducing activity to produce less heat, and by seeking shade when applicable. Like us, cats can reduce body heat by stretching out to expose more body surface to the environment and lose body heat through evaporation—cats can sweat a little through their paws, and they groom themselves to wet their fur (like us running through a sprinkler to cool off). Cats also pant when they're really hot—another evaporation technique. Like us, cats' blood vessels also widen (called *vasodilation*) to deliver more blood to the skin surface to release heat.

 LIFE-SAVING TIP: This heat-releasing vasodilation is why you never want to dip an overheated cat in cold or ice-cold water or pour it over them. Cold water contact with the skin makes those blood vessels constrict, which reduces blood flow to the skin and hampers a cat's ability to cool off. Instead, use cool water or fans, and never use isopropyl (rubbing) alcohol.

Staying hydrated

Proper hydration provides many health and well-being benefits, including body temperature regulation. People get to slurp slushies in the summer and savor hot chocolate in the winter. For cats, access to fresh water at all times—and especially on hot days or during exercise—is crucial to keep them comfortable.

Hydration is essential because it supports thermoregulation in other important ways. Staying hydrated replaces fluids lost during sweating and panting (which cats don't really do), eases the heart's workload, and boosts the blood flow needed to transport heat that's released through vasodilation.[6,7]

How aging and disease affects thermoregulation

Changes in body functions can throw a monkey wrench into regulating body temperature. As cats (and people) age, thermoreceptors and other thermoregulation mechanisms may change, which can lead to easily getting chilled or overheated.

For example, in people, age-related muscle loss (called *sarcopenia*) is one of the changes that may thwart thermoregulation and contribute to both heat and cold intolerance.[8] I remember how we always had to be sure my Grandma Gardner took her cardigan wherever we went—even during Florida's summer heat! With advanced age, her body had difficulty maintaining the hypothalamic set point. Geriatric cats also have sarcopenia, so it likely contributes to their cold and heat sensitivities. Older cats can't put on a sweater at will, so those who have a hard time conserving body heat seek a sunny spot or your lap! On the flip side, sarcopenia or other functional changes and diseases that affect older cats may predispose them to hyperthermia and even heat stroke.

Overall, with diminished ability to regulate body temperature, geriatric cats don't adapt as readily to ambient and internal temperature changes as younger cats do. This leaves geriatric cats more susceptible to their cells not functioning as they should, which can lead to illness and slower recovery from illness.

As I mentioned earlier, staying hydrated also helps with thermoregulation. But common conditions in older cats such as kidney disease and diabetes can cause dehydration and, therefore, also make it harder for them to maintain a normal body temperature. Medications that geriatric cats may be receiving such as diuretics (prescribed to help cats with heart disease retain less water), can cause extreme dehydration if the cat's water intake is insufficient. Prolonged or severe vomiting and diarrhea associated with a variety of illnesses can also quickly cause dehydration.

Why older cats feel colder

Muscles generate heat during physical activity and shivering, and geriatric cats have less muscle mass overall as a result of sarcopenia. On top of that, geriatric cats may have cachexia, which is severe muscle loss related to an underlying ailment such as cancer or heart disease. Just like us, cats shiver when their core body temperature drops, and the muscle activity from shivering helps restore normal body temperature. But shivering also takes lots of oxygen. This can lead to *oxygen debt*, a particularly dangerous situation in cats with conditions like heart or lung disease, because oxygen delivery to tissues is already stretched.

Geriatric cats also tend to lose some of the fat layer right under their skin, which allows heat to escape. In addition, blood vessels lose elasticity with age, so they don't constrict well in response to cold. And senior cats who have a reduced appetite and eat less have fewer nutrients available, which may slow their metabolism and reduce heat production.

You're as cold as ice! The chilling effects of hypothermia

Hypothermia occurs when body temperature drops below normal because cold input or heat loss surpasses body heat production. Being exposed to cold ambient temperatures for too long, or low blood pressure from profuse bleeding or from a sudden drop in blood flow, can cause hypothermia. Cats become hypothermic during anesthesia, too, so veterinarians use warm fluids and warming devices (pads, blankets, forced air) to support patients' body temperatures during dental and surgical procedures.

Signs of hypothermia in cats include intense shivering, tiredness, weakness, decreased awareness, and pale gums. If your cat has these signs or if your cat's temperature is below normal, wrap your cat in a blanket and seek veterinary care right away.

If you need to help your cat warm up at home, use blankets or towels warmed in the dryer or other types of heat sources (see "Tips for warming up" below). Check your cat's temperature every 10 minutes. You can remove the heat source (such as a towel-wrapped hot water bottle) once their temperature is above 100 F (37.8 C) and if they no longer seem chilled, but keep them cozy with a blanket in a warm room.

Take your cat's temp

Keep a separate pediatric rectal thermometer at home for your cat! Yup—the old-school method. Put a dab of petroleum jelly on the end and insert it just past the silver tip.

Remember, normal body temperature for healthy adult cats is 98.1 to 102.1 F (36.7 to 38.9 C). Call your veterinarian if your cat's temperature is outside this range or if your cat has signs of hypothermia or hyperthermia.

Why elder cats swelter

Sweating profusely is one way humans cool down, but cats only have small sweat glands in their paws, so they cool off in other ways. Cats seek shade, stretch out on a cool surface, lick their fur, and—when things get really heated—pant to promote evaporation from their mouth and upper breathing passages.

It's like a heat wave! The stifling effects of hyperthermia

Hyperthermia occurs when body heat production or heat input exceeds heat loss and causes an abnormally high body temperature.

Fever is a natural, *controlled* form of hyperthermia. Substances in the body called *pyrogens*, which are produced by activated immune cells (or by bacteria), turn up the body's thermostat to conserve more body heat to try to reach this new set point. Fever is the body's protective reaction to a disease or other insult because it activates immune cells, slows growth of bacteria and viruses, reduces appetite (which leaves more energy to fight infections), and promotes sleepiness.[9] Most cats who have a true fever have body temperatures in the range of 103 to 106 F (39.5 to 41.1C).[10]

Heat stroke is a form of *uncontrolled* hyperthermia where the body's thermoregulation system fails. Heat stroke can cause dangerous malfunctions in many organs and damage the brain. Heat stroke can result from external factors like a high ambient temperature and a lack of shade or water. Internal factors such as short upper airway passages in flat-faced breeds or obesity increase a cat's risk of heat stroke. When any of these external or internal factors affect an already fragile senior cat who has diminished thermoregulation ability, the cat could be primed for an emergency situation!

Signs of hyperthermia in cats include prolonged panting, drooling, dark reddish gums, confusion, weakness, labored breathing, vomiting, diarrhea, and collapse. With hyperthermia, the body can reach dangerously high body temperatures of 106 F (41.1 C) or higher. If your cat has any of these signs of if your cat's body temperature is above 104 F, seek immediate veterinary care.

Otherwise, you can cool your cat at home by spraying cool (not cold or ice-cold) water on them and directing a fan to blow air on them (see "Tips for staying cool" below), and placing cool, wet towels under them until their temperature is 103 F (39.4 C). Call your veterinarian, and continue to monitor your cat's temperature.

Mind trickery

In addition to its cooling effects, did you know a fan can "trick" the brain into thinking it has adequate oxygen?[11] Receptors in the nose sense rapidly flowing air, and they send signals via the trigeminal nerve to the hypothalamus. You can play this "mind game" by placing a fan in front of a cat who is panting or breathing heavily. It helps them calm down while you check with your veterinarian about what else needs to be done to assist them. I recommend this to help manage cats who have a chronic disease that impairs breathing, such as a cat who has asthma and is overexcited or anxious.

Which is better—a cold spot or a warm spot?

The simple answer is to let your cat decide! Providing a comfy environmental temperature with additional opportunities for your cat to warm up or cool down is important for all cats. Imagine what it would be like to live where you have no control over the temperature and to be perpetually uncomfortable.

Giving geriatric cats options that allow them more control over their comfort helps keep them healthy, reduces stress, and allows quicker recovery from illness or injury. Cats will pick warm or cool places depending on the ambient temperature and what feels best to help them relieve their pain or other discomfort. So offer a buffet of options. Each day they'll decide whether they want to feel as cool as a cucumber or hot as a potato.

Tips for warming up:

- Use your fireplace (if applicable), open curtains to allow sunbeams in, and keep areas near heating vents clutter-free.
- Create a cozy resting spot in a small draft-free room that has its own warming device, such as a space heater (with automatic shutoff for overheating or tipping over and a cool-enough-to-touch external surface) or a heated pet bed.
- Put an extra blanket or flannel pillowcase on your cat's bed and place blankets or towels in various spots around the house, including inside various sizes of cardboard boxes, and inside their carrier. Enclosed spaces

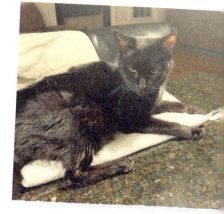

 Bruce has sarcopenia, so he especially enjoys his heating pad.

help create a microclimate, so you can avoid turning up the heat for the whole house.
- Dress them up if you have to go outdoors—hairless cats who live in particularly cold and windy climates benefit from wearing a jacket if they'll tolerate it and if you have to venture outside.
- Place a fresh-from the dryer towel or blanket in your cat's carrier and a blanket over the top if you're taking a car trip on a cold day.
- Brush your cat to remove dead hairs from his coat and undercoat, which helps prevent matting, permits hair to fluff up, and allows more air to act as an insulating layer near the skin.

 Spike had a variety of heating pads to choose from.

- Help your cat maintain an optimal body weight with good nutrition. Cats who are too thin have less fat and muscle to keep them warm.
- Provide a heated blanket under their favorite bedding, or provide a heated pet bed, radiant heat lamp, heated rice bags, or heated water containers in their resting spots. A great option is the Snugglesafe Microwave Heatpad (Lenric), which provides nonelectric, long-lasting warmth for pets: **snugglesafe.co.uk/**. Ensure your cat has no direct contact with a heat source because it can cause burns, and when using one:
    o At least 60% of the cat's body surface area must be close to the external heat source for warming to work.

 A Snugglesafe Microwave Heatpad for pets

 A Snugglesafe Microwave Heatpad with its own fleece cover.

- The cat must be able to move away from the heat source if she becomes too hot. I have seen many burns and overheating in cats from heat sources that are used inappropriately, such as in a kennel where the cat cannot move away or near or under a cat who cannot move without assistance.
- Place a barrier like a towel or blanket between the heat source and your cat.
- When using electric heating pads, keep liquids such as water bowls away from the area because of electrocution risk.

 Lance enjoys his warm Snugglesafe disc.

 Tips for staying cool

- Place a fan near your kitty.
- Keep the ambient temperature at a comfortable level. This is especially important for cats who are "at risk" of overheating such as brachycephalic (short head, "smoosh face") breeds, cats who have lung disease, or cats who are obese.
- And remember, if your cat loves car rides, being left in the car while you run errands can be dangerous for them. Cats may experience heat stress in less than 10 minutes (which can progress to heat stroke) inside a parked car, even when the windows are cracked and the temperature outside is a pleasant 70 F (21 C).

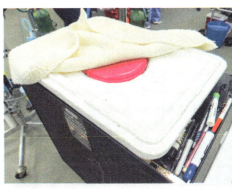

You can tuck a Snugglesafe Heatpad in a styrofoam lid or box to help retain the heat, and place a fleece blanket over it for your cat to rest on.

 LIFE-SAVING TIP: Leaving a cat unattended in the car is dangerous in any season—they may rapidly become too hot or too cold!

- Brush your cat to remove dead hairs from the coat and undercoat, which prevents matting and keeps air moving near the skin.
- Help your cat maintain an optimal body weight with good nutrition. Cats who are obese are more susceptible to heat exhaustion and heat stroke.
- Remember, do NOT cool an overheated cat by pouring ice water or cold water on them or placing them in it. Applying cold water causes the blood vessels under the skin to constrict and impairs heat loss from the body. You can use cool to lukewarm water and put cool wet towels under your cat.
- Help cats stay cool with special products:
    - Cooling mats and cooling cots or beds, which are available in many sizes at many retailers.
    - Cat beds that allow air flow.
- If you suspect overheating or heat stroke, call your veterinarian. Heat stroke can occur suddenly.

Comfy is key

Remember, be especially mindful about providing the appropriate temperature support for geriatric cats who have any chronic disease, whether it's kidney disease, respiratory system dysfunction, heart disease, arthritis, diabetes, cancer, or thyroid dysfunction. Help your cat warm up (and towel them off if they're rain-soaked or covered in snow) or cool down (perhaps with a fan) after outdoor excursions, and help them stay warm if you're giving your cat subcutaneous (under the skin) fluid therapy at home (like Bodhi!).

Bodhi's persistent laptop heat-seeking behavior continuously interrupted the work I needed to do. So I searched online for a heated cat bed and had it delivered the next day. I plugged it in near my desk (he loved hanging out with me) and voilà! Problem solved. Bodhi LOVED his heated bed and spent hours lounging there, always watching me!

My coworker Bodhi's new heated office chair!

CHAPTER 11:

Skin: Scrappy cats—senior beauty is deeper

> "Why are people afraid of getting older? You feel wiser. You feel more mature. You feel like you know yourself better. You would trade that for softer skin? Not me!"
>
> — ANNA KOURNIKOVA, PROFESSIONAL TENNIS PLAYER

Our cats don't share the vanity trait that many humans have, so does their senior appearance really matter? In my eyes, the sweetest, most beautiful furry faces belong to senior and geriatric pets. Their years of love and companionship—or for some, their years of endurance—are sculpted within their bony heads; reflected in their hazy, wise eyes; and sprinkled throughout their grey-speckled faces. I treasure every one of them!

I approach geriatric cats' skin issues from two perspectives: Does the crusty cat with dry, flaky skin and an untidy coat have any discomfort? Is the human-pet bond strained by the cat's condition or appearance? Helping ensure that ailing cats are comfortable and not smelly, scabby, greasy, bloody, goopy, excessively scratching, or otherwise repulsive in any way is an important part of my work as a veterinarian.

Age-related skin and fur changes

Hair, nails, and skin are made of a protein called *keratin*. The skin, along with its diverse population of bacteria, viruses, mites, and fungi—collectively called the *skin microbiome*—is the largest organ in the body. It protects us from infections,

FUN FACT:

Genes influence hair length and determine whether we and our cats and dogs will be long-haired or short-haired (or no-haired!). Humans' hair tends to grow long and bountiful on our head (and is genetically programmed to stop growing at a certain length, which differs among individuals), but it grows short and sparse on our arms and legs. Pets' fur tends to be short and cover most of their bodies.

regulates our body temperature, and gives us the sensation of touch. And like other organs, it can start to fail as the effects of age creep in. The barrier to the outside world that skin provides weakens and can lead to problems that are often overlooked under all that fur. (If you have a Sphynx or other hairless breed, problems are easier to spot—lucky you!)

With aging, senior cats' fur can go grey in spots, particularly around their chin and eyes, as the skin loses pigment-producing cells. Their coats may thin because old hair follicles are less active. Believe it or not, some senior cats also get harmless age spots (known as *lentigo*) on their nose, lip margins, gums, and eyelids because cells in those areas churn out *more* pigment.

Cats' claws may become thicker, drier, too long, misshapen, and more brittle. And like our skin, cats' skin thins and loses elasticity with age, so their skin becomes more prone to infection or injury. Skin wounds can take longer to heal.

Odd growths on skin, footpads, and noses

Senior cats may develop "senile warts" (*sebaceous adenomas*) and fatty tumors (*lipomas*) that are benign growths on or under the skin, but your veterinarian will need to check every one of them to determine whether they're cancerous.

Some geriatric cats have an overgrowth of keratin, called *idiopathic hyperkeratosis* (also known as *horned paws*), which isn't well understood. Or they may develop a callus on their footpads that is thought to be caused by long-term friction. These problems can be mild or can cause mobility problems.

Keratin overgrowth on the nose can cause discomfort and excessive nose-rubbing, or it can block cats' nostrils and make breathing difficult. A veterinarian may be able to use a surgical laser to remove the excess tissue in severe cases and provide some comfort for your cat.

Skin and fur flaws that reflect skin disease or an underlying disorder

Much research is done to investigate various diseases that affect people's skin, but it's also done in relation to the multi-billion-dollar (and growing) anti-aging skincare and cosmetics industry. For cats, it's not about keeping their youthful appearance. Skin research in cats focuses on combating disease—especially allergies, cancer, infections, and autoimmune disorders.

Skin problems that began during your cat's wonder years can carry on throughout their advanced years. So if your cat had itchy skin because of an environmental allergy (called *atopy*, or *atopic dermatitis*) or from a food allergy as a young cat, their allergies may continue to flare and need additional treatment as the years pass. Skin growths or masses that pop up at any age need to be checked out by a veterinarian to determine whether cancer is present. Keeping up with parasite prevention during the geriatric years is still essential, because fleas, ticks, mites, and mosquitos won't refuse the chance to latch on for a meal—no matter your cat's age.

Structural changes in the skin during the golden years can increase a cat's risk of skin infections or ear infections (also called *otitis externa*) and can hinder skin healing. Microscopic bugs can overgrow on the skin, so cats with allergies or parasites can more easily develop skin and ear infections caused by bacteria or yeast—another reason to stay on top of allergy management and keep up with parasite preventives. And if your senior cat undergoes surgery, the incision site may heal more slowly and have a higher risk of bacterial infection than it would have in her youthful days. Postoperative care for a senior cat is often more intensive than that for a young cat.

Arthritis or obesity curbs a cat's ability to self-groom, so elder cats' coats can become lusterless and matted. Inadequate nutrition—from a poor-quality diet or a chronic disease that hampers nutrient uptake or use—also contributes to a bedraggled look. Cats with gastrointestinal, kidney, or liver disease; diabetes; or thyroid hormone imbalances often have coat and skin abnormalities. An affected senior cat's coat may be thin, dull, and brittle and have patchy hair loss; the skin may also be either excessively dry or oily. Sebum, a natural, protective oil

 My cat Koala is showing off that she can still groom herself, but when her arthritis gets so bad that she can't, I'll need to help her (with pet wipes and a comb, of course!).

made by small sebaceous glands in the skin, keeps skin from drying out. Too much sebum can cause both flaky and oily skin, and it can stem from an infection, hormone imbalance, or other underlying condition. Skin problems also sometimes produce body odors in cats. Pet parents have asked me why their cats smell "musky" or "like a mildewed basement."

You can reduce or resolve many skin problems with a veterinarian's help to identify the cause and direct treatment appropriately—and to correct nutritional imbalances and supplement your cat's diet when needed. For puzzling or recurring skin, nail, coat, or ear problems, a visit to a veterinary dermatologist early in your cat's evaluation process is worthwhile, and it will likely save you time and money overall on diagnostic tests and treatments.

All the while, help your cuddly friend stay clean and combed—most cats savor this tender touch, attention, and assistance!

See your veterinarian if your cat has:

- itchy skin, which is characterized by your cat frequently licking, scratching, chewing, or rubbing her skin, fur, or ears; shaking her head often; or scooting on her bottom;
- red, swollen, scaly, flaky, crusty, greasy, or smelly skin;
- scabs, skin sores, or skin that is excessively moist or has draining pus or pimple-like bumps;
- matted fur that is difficult to groom;
- a thin coat or bald patches, or has been pulling out tufts of hair;
- skin lumps or bumps, especially any growth that is pea-sized or larger;
- overgrown claws; or
- nose or footpad lumps or bumps.

Tests your cat may need:

- blood and urine tests to check for underlying medical conditions;
- a fecal examination to look for intestinal parasites (fleas cause skin problems and carry their own parasites, known as *tapeworms*, that can inhabit your cat's intestines if your cat swallows fleas while grooming themselves);
- skin tests to obtain cells for examination (your veterinarian may use a cotton swab, Scotch tape, or a glass microscope slide pressed to the skin or use a surgical blade to scrape the skin surface);
- microscopic examination of lumps or bumps by drawing cells out with a needle;

- biopsies or surgical removal of lumps or bumps (these samples are sent to a diagnostic laboratory for evaluation); or
- a food trial (also called a *diet elimination trial*) to check for food allergies.

Questions to ask your veterinarian

- What is the underlying cause of my cat's skin condition?
- What tests will my cat need?
- What medications does my cat need?
- Should my cat be evaluated by a veterinary dermatologist?
- My cat excessively licks and chews his fur; does he need treatment for a behavior problem?
- Does my cat need a different diet or nutritional supplement?
- What shampoos or topical treatments are available for my cat's skin condition?
- How do the medications you prescribe work—will they cure my cat's allergies?
- Is this lump or bump on my cat something serious?

CAREGIVER TIPS AND HOME HACKS

- Regularly brush your cat to keep his fur mat-free and clean. When bathing is necessary, use a high-quality shampoo designed specifically for cats. The ZoomGroom (KONG) brush is fantastic.
- Cats with dry, flaky skin benefit from brushing because it stimulates their sebaceous glands, which produce sebum to lubricate the skin.
- Your veterinarian may prescribe a therapeutic shampoo specific for your cat's skin condition. Follow the instructions for how often you'll need to bathe your cat and the length of time the shampoo needs to remain on her coat.

Minion loved getting groomed with the KONG ZoomGroom.

 My dad loves to use a grooming glove to brush his cats. Here he is with Tabby, Whity and Fluffy – and they all want to get groomed/loved daily!

- Use dry shampoo made for cats to help them freshen up when needed.
- Keep your cats' nails trimmed. This helps them get around easier and reduces their risk of snagging and tearing a nail.
- Trim long hair between the toes if needed to keep the areas dry and clean and help prevent infection. Beard trimmers work wonders here.
- If your cat's fur becomes easily or frequently matted, have a professional groomer remove them. It's difficult for an unskilled person to remove these mats and it's painful for the cat.
- Apply cat nose balm to dry noses and cat paw balm to dry or callused paws.
- Prevent sores and infections from urine scalding by placing absorbent pads under your bedridden cat or use diapers if needed for incontinent cats, and change them right away when they become soiled. It's crucial to keep your cat's skin clean and dry to prevent serious skin issues.
- Provide comfy, clean, thick-padded bedding.

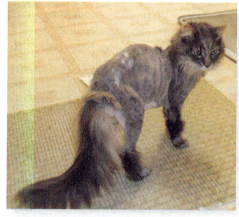

 Hobbes regularly had a close shave to keep his hair mats at bay.

- If your cat is recovering from surgery or is otherwise laid up, help your cat turn over so they can rest in a different position every two or three hours. Be vigilant about preventing pressure sores—these are painful and can quickly become infected.
- Helping your cat maintain his optimal weight helps prevent pressure sores.
- Use pet wipes or unscented, hypoallergenic baby wipes (and keep them in a wipe warmer) to help spot-clean areas when needed.
- Avoid "quarantining" your cat if possible—isolation leads to emotional stress for your cat and for you. Help your cat stay in the areas close to you and other members of your household.

 A baby wipe warmer comes in handy for messy pets, too.

Prevent decubitus ulcers (bedsores, pressure sores) in ailing pets

Pets need clean, soft, absorbent bedding to help keep their skin clean and dry. Prevent skin abrasions that can result from friction if a partially immobile pet drags himself from place to place: bring your pet's food and water to him, help him get where he wants to be, or consider using a drag bag (such as **barkertime.com/product-category/drag-bag/**) if appropriate.

Reposition immobile pets every two or three hours to relieve pressure on bony points—pressure sores can develop on your pet's elbows, shoulders, hocks, knees, and hips, and even on their head. Protect these points with orthopedic padding or memory foam. Reposition your pet by turning him from his right side to sternal (chest and abdomen facing the ground). Then in about two hours turn him from sternal to his left side. After another two hours, turn him from his left side to his right side. Repeat this pattern of repositioning throughout each day and night. Avoid friction from the pet's bedding or from your clothing while repositioning a bedridden pet.

Wash your hands and check your pet's skin for redness, heat, moisture, and abrasion. Carefully clip the fur over areas of concern so you can more easily monitor it, make cleanup easier, and allow air to reach the skin. Use hypoallergenic pet shampoo to spot-wash the fur and skin to remove food, urine, or feces. Always thoroughly dry the skin and fur. Avoid using rubs such as petroleum jelly that block airflow to the skin. Your veterinarian should advise you on whether your pet needs a specific skin ointment or other treatment for irritation or infection. If a skin sore develops, notify your veterinarian right away, because severe infections can develop quickly in immobile pets and be difficult to treat.

 PRODUCT RECOMMENDATIONS

- Nose Butter (The Blissful Cat)
  theblissfulcat.com/products/nose-butter
- Paw Butter (The Blissful Cat)
  theblissfulcat.com/products/paw-butter
- KONG ZoomGroom (available from many online retailers)

CHAPTER 12:

Heart: Keeping the beat strong

"The best and most beautiful things in the world cannot be seen nor even touched, but just felt in the heart."

— Helen Keller

Unlike people, cats rarely have heart attacks. The blood vessels within cats' heart muscles don't develop hardened cholesterol deposits like ours can as we age. These deposits can cut off the blood supply to portions of our heart muscle and cause a heart attack—also known as a *myocardial infarction*. Cats can have a heart attack in the rare event that a blood clot—a sticky mass of blood cells—blocks the blood supply to their heart muscle. But typically, cats who have heart trouble encounter disease of the heart muscle itself, known as *cardiomyopathy*, which makes their hearts work harder and grow weaker.

Some cat breeds, including Maine Coon, Ragdoll, Sphynx, Persian, Chartreux, and British Shorthair, are genetically prone to heart problems. But any cat is at risk of being born with a heart abnormality, or of developing a heart disorder later in life.

FUN FACT:

Cats help our heart health! Studies show that pet ownership may protect us against heart disease and help lower blood pressure and cholesterol.[1]

Near and dear to the heart

The heart is the engine that pumps blood to the lungs to pick up oxygen and travel around the body via blood vessels to deliver it. Blood then circles back to the heart to be pushed to the lungs for oxygen again. The heart sits in a delicate but tough sac called the *pericardium*. It contains a small amount of fluid and is like a pillowcase for the heart. It helps lubricate the heart and protects it from injury and infection.

The heart is basically one big muscle with four chambers: the right and left atrium sit above the larger right and left ventricles; the left ventricle is the strongest. Four valves within the heart act as doorways (like old-time saloon doors, but they normally swing only one way) to direct blood flow through the chambers and into two of the body's major blood vessels.

Breathing in (inhaling) brings oxygen into the lungs so it can be transferred to the blood. This oxygen-rich (oxygenated) blood from the lungs travels to the heart's left atrium, where it is pumped through the mitral valve into the left ventricle. The heart's left ventricle then pumps the oxygenated blood through the aortic valve and into the aorta (the body's largest blood vessel) where the blood travels far and wide by branching off into other blood vessels (called arteries) leading to the body's organs and tissues. Blood circulation is an amazing oxygen, nutrient, hormone, and immune cell delivery system! In addition, the blood circulation system allows byproducts from cell metabolism to be picked up in the blood and shuttled to organs such as the kidney and liver to process—and also back to the lungs to further clear up.

FUN FACT:

Blood vessels that carry blood *away from the heart* to the rest of the body are called arteries. And in most cases, that blood is oxygenated. Blood vessels that carry blood from the body back *to the heart* are called veins. And in most cases, that blood is deoxygenated. But when it comes to the vessels carrying blood between the heart and lungs, their roles are reversed!

The blood vessels that carry blood *away from the heart* to the lungs are appropriately called arteries. But these pulmonary arteries carry deoxygenated blood *away from the heart* to the lungs. The blood vessels that carry blood from the lungs back *to the heart* are appropriately called veins, but these pulmonary veins carry oxygenated blood from the lungs *to the heart*. Clear as mud?!

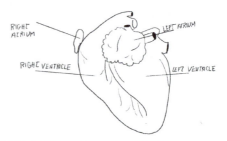

When blood delivers oxygen to the cells of tissues and organs, the cells use the oxygen and produce carbon dioxide. Carbon dioxide travels back with the blood through vessels (called veins) to the heart. This oxygen-poor (deoxygenated) blood in the veins ultimately travels to the heart's right atrium and is pumped through the tricuspid valve to the heart's right ventricle. The right ventricle pumps the blood through the pulmonary valve into the pulmonary artery, a major blood vessel that's like a one-way "highway" to the lungs. The carbon dioxide is then expelled by breathing out (exhaling), and oxygen is picked up again during the next breath in (inhalation).

The oxygenated blood in the lungs again travels to the left atrium and left ventricle and the process repeats—about 140 times a minute (more or less, depending on a cat's activity level and health status); in other words, at the speed of a cat's heartbeat, or heart rate. Many nerves and specialized heart muscle cells control this pace. They send electrical impulses that choreograph the rhythm and speed of the heart's pumping action.

FUN FACTS:

Normal heart rates at rest (beats per minute)[2]:

- Cat 120 to 140
- Dog 70 to 120
- Guinea pig 200 to 300
- Elephant 25 to 35
- Dairy cow 48 to 84
- Baby chick 350 to 450
- Goat 70 to 80
- Rabbit 180 to 350

Manatees' heart rates drop by half during long dives!

Octopuses have three hearts![3]

Some heartbreaks

The usual suspects that cause trouble elsewhere in the body—infections, inflammation, nutritional deficiencies, and tumors—can cause heart problems in cats. Heart tumors are fairly uncommon in cats, and, like other tumors, they can be benign (affecting only the surrounding area) or malignant (cancerous and spread to other parts of the body). Cats who have a heart tumor may need to be evaluated by three veterinary specialists—a cardiologist (heart specialist), an oncologist (cancer specialist), and a surgeon.

Heart trouble may stem from a problem with the heart's electrical system, which disturbs the nerves and signals that coordinate the heart's rhythm and rate. Structural problems that involve the heart chamber walls and muscle, the heart valves, or the pericardial sac also cause heart trouble. Structural issues can in turn lead to electrical issues, and electrical issues can lead to structural issues!

By far, most cats with heart disease tend to have a heart muscle disorder (called *cardiomyopathy*) that weakens the heart's ability to pump blood and can disrupt the heart's rhythm. In cats, three types of cardiomyopathy cause the most problems and they typically affect the left ventricle:

- *hypertrophic cardiomyopathy*—abnormally thick and stiff heart muscle (this is the most common type of heart disease in cats) that develops possibly because of gene mutations or occurs under the influence of an overactive thyroid gland (hyperthyroidism);
- *restrictive cardiomyopathy*—excessively stiff heart muscle from scar tissue buildup (called *fibrosis*) that may be associated with aging; and
- *dilated cardiomyopathy*—abnormally thin, stretched heart muscle that occurs when a cat's diet lacks taurine, an essential amino acid the body uses to make protein.

Research revelation: We *can* mend a broken heart

Veterinarians have identified a new type of heart muscle disease in cats, called *transient myocardial thickening (TMT)*.[4] It looks like hypertrophic cardiomyopathy and can result in serious symptoms, but it can resolve with treatment, whereas hypertrophic cardiomyopathy continues to get worse.

The cause isn't known, but TMT seems to affect cats who have recently experienced a stressful event and who tend to be younger than cats who have hypertrophic cardiomyopathy—about 2 years old vs. 8 years old. I point out TMT because some affected cats may be older (they were up to 11 years old in the study), and because this condition has a better long-term prognosis than hypertrophic cardiomyopathy.

So, for pet parents who might otherwise be discouraged about their cat's heart problem and the prospect of giving lifelong medication and who, therefore, might prematurely consider euthanasia, keep in mind that TMT is a possibility. Talk with your veterinarian or veterinary cardiologist and, if appropriate, consider trying treatment for a few months and monitoring for improvements in your cat's symptoms and heart muscle function. In the study, twenty of 21 cats with TMT were able to stop receiving heart medications within seven months, ultrasound showed that their heart muscle had gone back to its normal size and function, and the cats had no further symptoms.[4]

Heartworms

Heartworms are parasites that can infect cats of all ages. I mention them here because I often see cat parents who have stopped giving heartworm preventive medications to their senior cats because they think older cats no longer need them. But cats need heartworm (and flea, tick, and intestinal parasite) prevention throughout their entire lives. Parasite prevention protects not only the cat, it protects other pets in the household and neighborhood, and human family members, too.

Mosquitoes transmit heartworms to cats. Young heartworms (called *heartworm larvae*) develop in a cat's bloodstream, and the adult worms live in the heart, lungs, and large blood vessels associated with the heart. These parasites are super creepy and can cause serious lung and heart disease and death in cats. Signs of heartworm disease in cats may include vomiting, weight loss, decreased activity, labored breathing, and coughing. If an adult heartworm dies, it can release toxins into a cat's blood that cause sudden death.

Once cats are infected, there is no medical treatment available to eliminate the parasites, but medications can be given to manage a cat's signs of lung disease. In some cases, heartworms can be surgically removed, which is a risky and costly procedure. So please continue heartworm preventive medication regardless of your cat's age! And when you adopt a cat—no matter his age—talk with your veterinarian about heartworm testing and starting a preventive medication.

When the heart is not content

Heart disease differs from heart failure. Your cat could have heart disease and you might not know it. The heart itself and many other mechanisms in the body compensate for diminished heart function, so some cats with heart disease have no outward signs. And cats have skills in limiting their activity when they feel ill, so you may not notice subtle changes. Many cat parents are surprised to learn that their cat has a heart problem because veterinarians often discover heart issues brewing during a cat's yearly physical examination—or during the examination that is done before a cat's surgical procedure or professional dental cleaning.

As heart disease progresses, cats have signs that range from subtle to severe, and you'll know that your cat needs to be evaluated. Cats may lose their appetite and lose weight, be less active, and breathe faster and harder with exercise.

Cats who have heart disease (or heart failure) are prone to developing high blood pressure (hypertension) and blood clots (thromboembolism), so severe ailments can pop up, seemingly out of the blue. High blood pressure can make cats suddenly lose their eyesight. Blood clots can lodge in blood vessels and cut off blood flow to the legs (known as *aortic thromboembolism* or *saddle thrombus*), the lungs (called *pulmonary thromboembolism*), the heart itself, or other organs. Cats with blood clots may abruptly cry out in extreme pain and be unable to move one or both of their back legs, or they may suddenly have trouble breathing and collapse. Cats with sudden blindness, abrupt pain, or collapse require emergency veterinary assessment and treatment.

Counting beats and breaths

You can feel your cat's heartbeat on her left side, right behind her front leg. Tally how many beats you feel in 30 seconds (use the stopwatch on a smartphone, or a clock with a second hand), then multiply it by two to get the heart rate per minute.

To count your cat's respiratory rate, wait until your cat is quietly resting or sleeping. Count the number of breaths your cat takes in 30 seconds and multiply it by two. This equals your cat's respiratory rate per minute.

FUN FACT: COUNT ON AN APP

Did you know you can download a nifty free app—such as Medtimer—that calculates heart and breathing rates for you? Simply tap the number of seconds you'll count for (15, 20, 30, or 60 seconds), and when the timer starts, tap the screen each time you feel your cat's heartbeat, or each time you see a breath! Count the beats and breaths for separate periods of time—once for the heart rate and once for the breathing rate.

The app lists a range of normal heart and breathing rates for people at different ages, so remember to compare your cat's numbers with the normal cat resting heart rates range: 120 to 140 beats per minute, and the normal cat resting respiratory rates range: 15 to 30 breaths per minute.

When the heart fails

Heart failure occurs when the heart can no longer efficiently pump blood. As the heart's pumping ability continues to decline, blood flow through blood vessels throughout the body slows. This eventually leads to fluid buildup (congestion) in the lungs or in the abdomen and other parts of the body. This is called *congestive heart failure*.

Heart failure is classified based on whether the left or right side of the heart is affected. Left-sided congestive heart failure is the most common type of heart failure in cats. When oxygenated blood from the lungs is not properly pumped from the left ventricle (because of a structural or electrical heart problem), it eventually strains the left atrium. Then the left atrial blood pressure rises, which in turn leads to fluid buildup in the lungs (called *pulmonary edema*). The fluid sometimes triggers coughing in cats, but it primarily makes breathing a struggle. Long-term left-sided heart failure can lead to right-sided heart failure.

Right-sided heart failure means that the blood returning from the body to the heart does not adequately flow into the right side of the heart and on into the lungs. So fluid builds up in the veins, which then leaks out into the abdomen (called *ascites*) and causes a swollen belly, and also leaks into the limbs and causes swollen legs (called *peripheral edema*). Right heart failure is less common in cats than it is in dogs.

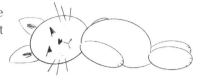

Heart failure sometimes leads to fluid buildup in the pericardium, the protective sac around the heart. The pressure from the fluid-filled pouch severely restricts the heart's ability to pump, and emergency treatment is needed to remove the fluid.

See your veterinarian if your cat:

- tires easily or sooner than she usually does with normal activity;
- breathes faster or harder than normal or pants with mild exercise or at rest;
- seems restless or has trouble getting comfortable;
- has a reduced appetite;
- has unintentional weight loss;
- vomits frequently or has diarrhea;
- has pale or bluish gums or a bluish tongue;
- has pale or bluish nail beds or footpads;
- has a nosebleed, blood in the eye, sudden blindness, or wide pupils that don't respond to light;
- cries in pain;
- seems weak;
- limps, has a cold and painful rear or front leg, can't walk, or can't move his legs;
- has a swollen belly or legs; or
- faints or collapses.

Looking into your cat's heart

Veterinarians listen with a stethoscope to assess a pet's heart's rate and rhythm, and to detect a heart murmur. Murmurs occur when blood flow through the heart is disturbed, such as when a heart valve doesn't close completely or when a pet has anemia (low red blood cell count). In a young cat, a murmur may occur because the cat is born with a small hole inside the heart chambers. Heart murmurs are graded on a sound scale of 1 to 6, with 6 being the loudest.

Depending on your cat's symptoms and complete physical examination findings, your veterinarian may want to do standard blood tests (complete blood count and serum chemistry profile) plus blood tests to look for specific markers of heart disease (called *nT-pro-BNP* and *cardiac troponin-1*). Chest and belly x-rays allow a closer look at a pet's heart size and whether fluid is present in the lungs and abdomen, an electrocardiogram (ECG) evaluates the electrical signals that spark the heart's rhythm and rate, and blood pressure measurement helps detect high blood pressure. An ultrasound of the heart (echocardiogram) is the most useful assessment, and cats often need a referral to a veterinary cardiologist for this test. Veterinary cardiologists also sometimes use a Holter monitor—a portable ECG that a cat wears as a vest for a prescribed amount of time to continuously record the heart's rhythm during routine daily activities and when they are resting or sleeping.

Doing your cat's heart good

Both heart disease and heart failure can be managed—to a point—with medications, diet changes, and activity adjustments. Medications help the heart muscle pump better, dilate blood vessels to reduce resistance so the heart can more easily push blood through the body, and reduce congestion in the lungs and other parts of the body. Cats with heart disease may also receive medication to prevent blood clots. And cats who have heart disease related to hyperthyroidism need treatment to lower their thyroid hormone levels.

A veterinary therapeutic diet formulated specifically for cats who have heart disease is also beneficial. These diets are low in salt and contain other nutrients at optimal levels for cats with heart disease. It's important to have a conversation about diet with your veterinarian or with a veterinary nutritionist, especially if your cat has another condition (e.g. kidney disease, obesity, thyroid disease) that also requires dietary adjustments.

Because dental disease may contribute to heart problems and heart disease progression, veterinarians may also recommend a professional dental cleaning and treatment of gum disease, or tooth extractions for cats who may not have received regular dental care.

Surgery may be an option to treat some types of heart disease. In rare cases, a pacemaker can be placed to regulate the heart rate and rhythm, just like in people with arrhythmias! Advanced treatments like these require referral to a veterinary cardiologist and may also require help from a board-certified veterinary surgeon.

Cats with heart disease can often maintain a great quality of life for several months or many years if we manage their signs, and they can continue to enjoy most activities and even undergo anesthesia when necessary. It's crucial to continue to give cats their heart medications as directed, even when they seem like they feel normal, because treatment is lifelong.

Watch out for cardiac cachexia

Cats who have congestive heart failure—that buildup of fluid in the lungs, abdomen, or elsewhere—often develop cardiac cachexia, a loss of lean muscle mass.[5] Cats who have chronic kidney disease or cancer also have increased risk for developing cachexia, and geriatric cats often have multiple ailments.

Cachexia can cause weakness, a decreased ability to fight infection, and a reduced survival time. It can occur even in overweight pets, and veterinarians need to help pet parents monitor cats who have heart disease for muscle loss and help prevent its progression. Monitoring a cat's body weight alone isn't sufficient, because muscle loss can occur before weight loss is noticed, especially in cats who retain fluid because of their heart disease.

Cats with cardiac cachexia may still have a good appetite, or cachexia may cause a reduced appetite. Changing your cat's diet to more palatable foods and making a few feeding schedule adjustments (smaller amounts more frequently) may be needed, and consultation with a veterinary nutritionist is especially helpful. Diet supplements such as fish oil (omega-3 fatty acids) or certain amino acids (taurine or L-carnitine, depending on the type of heart disease) may help. An appetite stimulant or anti-nausea medication may be needed at times. If dietary adjustments aren't successful, your veterinarian may suggest placing a feeding tube, which allows you to provide the calories your cat needs without worrying whether he'll eat enough. A feeding tube can also make medication administration easier. Cats tolerate feeding tubes well, and using a feeding tube can reduce your and your cat's stress associated with their care.

End stages of a failing heart

During the later stages of heart failure, veterinarians can use a special needle and catheter to remove the fluid buildup in a cat's chest (called *thoracocentesis*) or abdomen (called *abdominocentesis*) as needed—sometimes every two to four weeks—or by placing a tube to drain the fluid and help the cat stay comfortable. Fluid buildup in the pericardial sac is uncommon, but when it occurs it's an emergency situation, and the fluid can be removed with a needle and catheter (called *pericardiocentesis*) or with surgery (called *pericardiectomy*). But when the heart can no longer pump blood effectively even with our best efforts, the disease becomes life-threatening.

Congestion in the lungs from left-sided heart failure causes respiratory distress and, eventually, death. Congestion in other parts of the body from right-sided heart failure leads to uncomfortable pressure on the abdominal organs and the diaphragm—a muscle that helps with breathing.

Any disease that affects a pet's ability to breathe comfortably is a major cause of concern for me. I cannot imagine any worse form of suffering than the inability to breathe well and the intense anxiety and discomfort it causes.

Questions to ask your veterinarian

- What tests will my cat need to evaluate his heart?
- What caused my cat's heart disease?
- Does my cat need a referral to a veterinary cardiologist?
- What medications will help?
- What are the possible side effects of my cat's medications?
- Are the medications a lifelong treatment?
- What is my cat's prognosis?
- How often does my cat need rechecks?
- What will be done during the rechecks?
- Does my cat need a special diet?
- Will my cat benefit from specific dietary supplements?
- What kinds of treats can I give my cat?
- Will you monitor my cat's body condition and muscle condition for cardiac cachexia?
- Does my cat have exercise restrictions?
- What are the signs of distress I should look out for?
- What is the normal heart rate for my cat while resting? (Ask your veterinarian to show you how to check your cat's heart rate.)

CAREGIVER TIPS AND HOME HACKS

- Help your cat maintain a healthy weight and feed the appropriate diet for your cat's condition.
- Avoid high-salt treats and most of the foods that people eat, especially potato chips, pretzels, cheese, and processed meats. Low-sodium drinking water may be needed if your tap water contains lots of sodium.
- Continue providing parasite prevention, routine vaccinations, and dental care.

- Use a pill organizer to help keep track of your cat's daily medications. Giving heart medications at the correct dosages and on time each day is important. Be mindful of when medication refills will be needed. Plan to request and pick them up or have them delivered before the medication is gone.
- Keep a cat health journal to routinely note your cat's heart and respiratory rates, activity level, appetite, weight, and the timing of any medication dosage changes that your veterinarian prescribes. Your help in closely monitoring your cat's signs at home helps your veterinarian better determine whether medications need to be added or otherwise adjusted.
- If your cat's respiratory rate increases by 20% or more over two or three days (for example, from 25 breaths per minute to 30 breaths per minute or more) it may mean that fluid is accumulating in or around the lungs and a medication adjustment or other therapy is needed, so call your veterinarian.
- Schedule and keep all your cat's veterinary recheck appointments. Cats with heart disease need more frequent monitoring and checkups. Take your cat's health journal with you to each appointment.
- Keep cats calm and shield them from things that can get them worked up, like children chasing them or unfamiliar people visiting.
- Allow easy access to quiet places so your cat can "get away from it all" if needed.
- Cats who are well managed with medications and diet can still enjoy their regular mild to moderate levels of activity. Just avoid allowing them to overdo it and become short of breath or exhibit weakness.
- If your cat loves to go outdoors on leash walks with you, slow the pace or reduce the duration of the walk, or go every other day instead if needed.
- Engage cats in quiet, low-stress activities like food puzzles and other interactive, low-key toys. Use a variety of toys and rotate them to prevent boredom. Passive range-of-motion exercises or massage may help and they provide mental stimulation for your cat, too.
- Maintain the environmental temperature and humidity at comfortable levels and take care to avoid heat or cold stress when outdoors.
- Keep food and water bowls and litter boxes easily accessible.
- Place ramps or stairs where needed to make your cat's favorite perches easier to get to.
- Place nightlights where needed.
- Direct a tiny desktop fan toward your cat's bed if needed. The increased airflow on cats' faces and in their noses helps them breathe easier.
- Massage limbs gently–from the paws toward the body–to help alleviate pressure from fluid retention.

PRODUCT RECOMMENDATIONS

- Music:
  Feline Calm for Pet Tunes (Pet Acoustics)
  petacoustics.com/shop?category=Cat and
  iCalmPet (BioAcoustic Research)
  icalmpet.com/
- Calming pheromones: Feliway (Ceva)
  us.feliway.com/
- If home oxygen treatment is needed: Oxygen for pets (Pawprint)
  pawprintoxygen.com/
- Pillbox organizers (available at many pharmacies, online retailers, and pet retailers)
- Come With Me Kitty Cat Harness & Bungee Leash (Pet Safe)
  store.petsafe.net/come-with-me-kitty-harness-and-bungee-leash
- Cooling mats to prevent heat stress in hot climates:
  arfpets.com
- Do not ring or knock signs:
  amazon.com/dp/B01BL4MP3I/?ref=exp_drmarygardner_dp_vv_d

RESOURCES

- HeartSmart: Information on Pets with Heart Disease. Heart Diseases – Cats. Cummings School of Veterinary Medicine. Tufts University.
  heartsmart.vet.tufts.edu/heart-diseases-cats/
- Heartworm informational tools and resources for pet owners. American Heartworm Society.
  heartwormsociety.org/pet-owner-resources
- Parasite information for pet owners.
  petsandparasites.org/
- Information about veterinary specialists in cardiology, oncology, and surgery.
  - VetSpecialists.com.
    vetspecialists.com
  - American College of Veterinary Surgeons.
    acvs.org/

CHAPTER 13:

The kidneys: Little wonders

"It has long been an axiom of mine that the little things are infinitely the most important."

— SHERLOCK HOLMES
(FROM "A CASE OF IDENTITY" BY SIR ARTHUR CONAN DOYLE)

When I adopted my cat Bodhi, he was already a geriatric and was being treated for kidney disease. His disease was no surprise to me because I see so many older cats with this condition. Somewhere between 35% and 81% of geriatric cats (more than 12 years old) have kidney disease.[1] Many younger cats are affected too, and studies suggest cats of all ages should be screened for it.[2]

I was prepared to manage Bodhi's kidney disease, so this probably nudged me into adopting him right then and there. I knew Bodhi had a slim chance of finding a home otherwise, since few people are willing to take on this challenge with a newly adopted cat in the midst of his golden years. Plus, I'm a sucker for an old, skinny, grey-chinned, brown (or any color!) tabby cat! What a treasure he was to have found.

 Me with Bodhi on his adoption day (he looks thrilled!).

Kidney duties

Like our kidneys, cats' kidneys perform vital functions:

- They filter toxins from the blood and send water-soluble waste out of the body through the urine.

- They stabilize electrolytes and other bloodstream components.
- They help regulate blood pressure and blood pH (pH relates to acid-base balance, a chemical harmony in fluid that allows cells to function normally).
- They produce certain hormones, including one that helps make red blood cells.

> **SIDEBAR: Get to know your electrolytes!**
>
> Sodium, potassium, phosphorus, and calcium are a few of the electrically charged essential minerals present in blood, urine, tissues, and other liquids that the kidneys are hard at work stabilizing. These electrolytes maintain hydration and proper blood pH, and play important roles in nerve, muscle, bone, and heart function and much more. When electrolyte concentrations are imbalanced in the body, fatigue, vomiting, irregular heart rate, seizures, and many more symptoms occur.

Kidney design

Most mammals, including ourselves and our dear felines, have two kidneys that sit in the upper part of the abdomen—one on each side. The kidneys are part of the urinary system (also called the *renal system*). The urinary system also includes the ureters (tubes that carry urine from the kidneys to the bladder), bladder (the hollow organ that stores urine), and urethra (a tube that allows urine to pass from the bladder to outside the body).

FUN FOOD FACT:

Healthy, nutrient-packed kidney beans derive their name from the kidneys' shape and color.

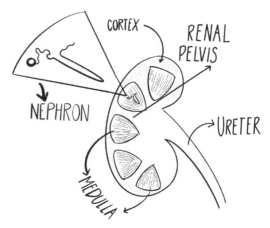

The kidney's structure is pretty cool. Its outer protective shell is a fibrous capsule embedded in fat. Inside are the renal cortex, medulla, and pelvis. Hundreds of thousands of nephrons run through the cortex and medulla.

The nephrons are amazing, teeny, blood-filtering systems that shuttle nutrients, sort electrolytes, and help pass waste products. These little powerhouses in the kidneys vary in numbers among species, with people estimated to have up to 2,000,000 nephrons! Beagles are estimated to have between 445,000 and 589,000 nephrons per kidney.[3] Cats are estimated to have about 190,000 nephrons per kidney.[4,5]

The renal pelvis is the funnel-shaped, innermost section of the kidney. It provides the pathway for urine to flow into the ureter—a muscular tube that runs from each kidney to carry urine to the bladder. The bladder stores urine until urination occurs, when the bladder releases urine to flow through the urethra to be eliminated from the body.

Chronic kidney disease: A common, complex condition

Urinary system troubles include acute (sudden) and chronic (long-term) kidney disease. I'll focus on chronic kidney disease (CKD) here because it's an all-too common urinary system problem in senior cats. Around 30% to 40% of cats older than 10 years have CKD,[6,7] and estimates show that up to 80% of geriatric cats have CKD.[2,8] Chronic kidney disease is also known as *chronic kidney failure* and *chronic renal failure*. (Renal is another term that refers to the kidneys.)

A single, precise cause of CKD in cats has not yet been found. Several factors probably play a role in sparking kidney disease and allowing it to progress: age-associated changes in kidney tissue structure and cell function, environmental influences such as stress and improper diet, and damage from intermittent injuries that reduce oxygen or induce inflammation in some parts of the kidneys.[1,3] Kidney damage may stem from:

- medical conditions such as diabetes,[7] high blood pressure, thyroid disease, heart disease, or immune system dysfunction;
- severe dehydration or blood loss;
- blockages or irritation anywhere in the urinary tract—such as urethra, bladder, ureter, or kidney stones (kidney stones are also called *nephroliths*), cysts, or strictures; or urine crystals;
- tumors;
- bacterial infections (these usually start as serious infections in the bladder [called *bacterial cystitis*] that move to the kidneys [called *pyelonephritis*]);
- chemicals, plant toxins, or medications that harm kidney function (never give aspirin, ibuprofen, or any of your own medications to your cat because they can be deadly)
- Genetics (some cat breeds are predisposed to kidney problems, e.g. polycystic kidney disease in Persians, amyloidosis in Abyssinians);

- viral infections such as feline leukemia virus; or
- parasites (uncommon unless cats eat earthworms or groom themselves after contact with urine eliminated by another parasite-infected animal).

Damaged kidneys allow waste products to build up in the blood and helpful nutrients to be lost in the urine. Less water is reabsorbed and electrolyte balance is disrupted, so dehydration and other abnormalities can occur. For example, when too much potassium is lost in the urine, muscle weakness or weight loss (from lack of appetite or nausea) and heart rhythm problems can occur. When too little potassium is passed in the urine, the extra potassium stays in the blood and can also disrupt the heart's rhythm. When too little phosphorus is eliminated, it builds up in the blood and leads to further kidney damage. Damaged kidneys also allow protein to leak into the urine (called *proteinuria*), and sometimes glucose inappropriately escapes (called *glucosuria*) as well, so these nutrients aren't reabsorbed properly for the body to use. In the late stages of kidney disease, waste product buildup in the blood can cause mouth ulcers, which make eating and drinking painful.

See your veterinarian if your cat:

- drinks more water;
- urinates more often or urinates more than normal (more or larger urine clumps in the litter box);
- urinates in odd locations;
- strains to urinate;
- has pinkish, reddish, or brownish urine (indicates blood in the urine);
- has unkempt fur;
- is weak;
- has unintended weight loss;
- has a loss of appetite;
- has nausea;
- salivates or drools excessively;
- has bad breath;
- has sores in her mouth;
- vomits;
- has diarrhea;
- is dehydrated (signs include decreased skin elasticity [to check this, gently pinch and lift a fold of your cat's skin between their shoulder blades, then release it; if it doesn't immediately fall back into place and stays "tented" for a second or longer, your cat may be dehydrated]; dry or sticky gums, weakness);

- is constipated;
- is lethargic;
- sleeps in odd locations or hides (cats tend to do this when they don't feel well for any reason);
- breathes rapidly; or
- has vision problems (can be a sign of high blood pressure).

Testing for kidney disorders

If your cat's symptoms point to the urinary tract, blood and urine tests, x-rays, or ultrasound will help identify the cause. But keep in mind that those handy blood and urine tests (along with weight checks and blood pressure measurement) done as part of your cat's routine yearly or twice yearly checkups allow your veterinarian to monitor for changes in kidney function as your cat ages, perhaps even before outward symptoms occur.

> ### A smart crystal ball for CKD
>
> A new test called RenalTech (Antech) uses machine learning—a branch of artificial intelligence that analyzes patterns in data—and allows veterinarians to predict whether a cat will develop CKD in the next two years, potentially long before a cat shows symptoms.
>
> The test is over 95% accurate and it evaluates six components of a cat's blood and urine test results. Two sets of test results are needed for comparison. The tests must have been completed within the past two years and at least three months apart. For more information, see **antechdiagnostics.com/renaltech/**.

Tracking a cat's body weight can also help veterinarians identify CKD sooner. Cats with kidney disease may begin losing weight up to three years before the problem is typically diagnosed, so identifying a trend of unintentional weight loss should prompt further tests to assess kidney function.[9] As kidney disease takes hold, cats start eating less because they don't feel well or they become picky and eat only highly tasty foods, so they consume fewer and fewer calories and ever so gradually lose fat and muscle mass.[10]

The body's normal metabolic processes produce two waste substances that can be measured with blood tests to check kidney function: blood urea nitrogen (also called BUN; medical savvy tip—say each letter separately [B-U-N]) and creatinine (pronounced kree-*at*-n-een). However, these waste products don't excessively build up in the blood until kidney function is seriously diminished, and they can also be elevated because of other problems.

Another substance that's measured in the blood that can detect kidney disease sooner than BUN and creatinine can is called symmetric dimethylarginine (pronounced si-*me*-trik dahy-*meth*-uhl-*ahr*-juh-neen), or SDMA. Blood concentrations of SDMA, BUN, and creatinine correlate with kidney damage and increase as kidney disease progresses.

When both BUN and creatinine levels are too high, it's called *azotemia* (pronounced ey-zuh-*tee*-mee-uh). Azotemia occurs when the kidneys have trouble filtering blood for one of three major reasons:

1. blood flow through the kidneys is reduced, possibly because of dehydration or blood loss;
2. kidney function itself is badly compromised; or
3. urine can't be expelled from the body (because of a blockage from a urinary stone, for example), so waste products in the urine are reabsorbed and they build up in the blood.

Urine tests give additional clues about kidney function. Veterinarians can check whether protein, glucose, ketones (chemicals the liver creates by using fat for energy when there is not enough insulin around to help cells use glucose for energy), or blood cells are improperly leaking into a cat's urine. And because the kidneys conserve water and concentrate urine, veterinarians also check urine concentration by measuring its specific gravity. This test compares urine density to the density of water. The lower the urine specific gravity, the less concentrated the urine is, which may indicate kidney damage or that your cat drinks a lot of water. Based on urine and blood test results, veterinarians can detect whether a cat has one of the three types of azotemia.

X-rays and ultrasound allow veterinarians to look at the size and shape of the kidneys and bladder and to check whether bladder stones, kidney stones, tumors, or other abnormalities are present.

> ### SIDEBAR: Stages of kidney disease in cats
>
> According to guidelines developed by the International Renal Interest Society (**iris-kidney.com/**), veterinarians can determine what stage of kidney disease a cat has, which allows us to recommend the best course of treatment for each stage.
>
> **Stage I** – Blood tests show no azotemia, but blood creatinine concentrations may reveal a gradual increase; urine tests may reveal protein in the urine and a low urine specific gravity; and the kidneys may be abnormal in size or shape; cats show no obvious outward signs.
>
> **Stage II** – Blood tests show mild azotemia; cats may have no signs or mild signs.

Stage III – Blood tests show moderate azotemia; cats may have no signs or mild or moderate signs.

Stage IV – Blood tests show severe azotemia and cats have a range of clinical signs.

Managing CKD—and your expectations

Pet parents have told me they think CKD is a death sentence. But it isn't, especially when it's caught early enough.

It's true that CKD is not easily reversible and rarely disappears.[1] In fact, a kidney transplant is the only potential cure for CKD. The procedure is typically done at veterinary teaching hospitals, and not all cats are eligible. Your veterinarian can tell you more about this surgery and help you find a referral center if appropriate. Pet parents who elect kidney transplantation for their feline friend get a bonus feline friend—they must adopt the donor kitty! There is an valid debate on the ethics of kidney transplants. The donating cat has no 'say' in the matter and statistically they will probably have kidney disease themselves when older and need all the nephrons they can get. Therefore, ethically, I am against kidney transplants.)"

Because of cost ($12,000 to $25,000)[11,12] and patient eligibility factors, a kidney transplant is not an option for most cats. But if your veterinarian expects or detects reduced kidney function in your cat, you can start supportive measures to slow the disease. The disease tends to progress slowly in most cats, but in many cats (47%) it progresses within one year.[13] The good news is that cats with CKD can remain stable for long periods with supportive treatment. A veterinary therapeutic diet, medications, and fluid therapy can curb the rate of kidney damage, and these therapies also help cats feel better. And because cats with gum disease have a higher risk of developing CKD,[14] keeping up with professional dental cleanings and treatments remains important for cats with CKD.

Therapies to manage CKD are intended to minimize the buildup of waste products in the blood, stabilize electrolyte and mineral concentrations, control protein metabolism, support a cat's appetite and nutritional intake, balance adequate hydration and blood pressure, and support red blood cell production.

Cats with CKD often have high blood pressure (hypertension), either because their kidneys aren't working right, or because they have another condition that causes high blood pressure such as high thyroid hormone levels (hyperthyroidism) or heart disease. Regardless of the cause, high blood pressure further damages the kidneys, so identifying high blood pressure and treating it—along with treating other underlying conditions when appropriate—is crucial.

Some cats with CKD develop a low red blood cell count (*anemia*) because the kidneys stop making enough of a hormone (called *erythropoietin*, pronounced ih-rith-roh-poi-*eet*-n) that stimulates red blood cell production. Anemia is managed with medication that replaces this hormone and with blood transfusion if needed.

Food as medicine

Managing CKD with a special diet is the backbone of treating affected cats. Feeding veterinary therapeutic diets designed for pets with kidney disease curtails kidney disease progression and increases survival time.[10]

Veterinary therapeutic diets for CKD are highly recommended because they serve to correct many of the detrimental mechanisms at work in pets with kidney disease. Therapeutic kidney diets typically have low phosphorus and sodium content, modified amounts of protein, and more omega-3 fatty acids compared with adult pet maintenance diets. Therapeutic kidney diets may also contain more fat (which makes the food taste better and increases calories), additional antioxidants such as vitamins C and E (to reduce oxidative stress in the kidney), more potassium, added B vitamins, and more fiber. Bacteria in the colon like fiber, so feeding specific types of dietary fiber helps the bacteria do their job to reduce wastes that might otherwise build up in the blood of pets who have kidney disease.[15,16] Fiber also helps prevent constipation, which can occur in cats with CKD.

Many therapeutic diets designed for cats with kidney disease are available, and your veterinarian will discuss these with you. Rechecking blood and urine tests at regular intervals and monitoring symptoms are key in assessing your cat's response to a therapeutic diet, and the results will signal whether nutrient adjustments are needed. As with medication and dose adjustments, diet adjustments must be customized for each cat.[10]

What's oxidative stress?

As cells generate energy, they produce oxygen-containing molecules that can either damage tissue (called *free radicals*) or can repair tissue (called *antioxidants*). Producing these molecules is normal and necessary. But when too many free radicals are running about, an imbalance between free radicals and antioxidants occurs, which is called *oxidative stress*. This stress damages cells, and cell damage leads to tissue and organ damage. Disease, a poor diet, and environmental pollution can also cause excess free radical production. Antioxidants can be supplied in the diet to help cells vanquish excess free radicals, which reduces oxidative stress and restores balance.

The dietary protein debate

One characteristic of veterinary therapeutic diets for pets with kidney disease is that they contain less protein than a maintenance diet for healthy adult pets. However, therapeutic kidney disease diets still meet, and typically exceed, the Association of American Feed Control Officials minimum crude protein content recommendation.[10] Yet veterinarians debate whether protein restriction is necessary for pets with kidney disease, or question which stage of kidney disease protein restriction should be started. The debate continues because the benefits of feeding therapeutic diets for kidney disease can only be attributed to the diets as a whole, and not to an individual component of the diets such as reduced protein. Evidence that dietary protein intake plays a role in kidney disease progression is lacking.[1] But never fear, researchers are continuing to explore the optimal balance of dietary protein and other nutrients in cats who have different stages of CKD.[17-19]

Restricting dietary protein in pets with kidney disease may be beneficial because it reduces buildup of nitrogen wastes in the blood, and these wastes cause many of the signs of illness. On the other hand, veterinarians worry that protein restriction leads to protein malnutrition and loss of lean muscle, especially in cats. Loss of lean body mass is common in pets with CKD, and it may contribute to weakness, hamper immune function, reduce wound healing, and decrease overall survival time.[20] But studies that evaluate feeding a higher protein diet (a diet that is not protein-restricted) to pets with CKD have not been done.[10]

The bottom line is that your veterinarian should assess your cat to determine what stage of CKD your cat has and whether dietary protein restriction would be beneficial or potentially harmful. Your veterinarian will consider your cat's protein intake in light of the amount of protein loss in your cat's urine, the degree of waste product buildup in your cat's blood along with your cat's symptoms, and whether your cat has muscle loss.[15]

How (and how not) to switch your cat to a therapeutic (or any new) diet

Introduce your cat to her new diet gradually, and avoid starting the switch while your cat feels unwell, because she may associate the new diet with feeling sick and never venture to try the new food again, even when she feels better. This is why veterinarians try to avoid introducing pets to therapeutic foods while they are hospitalized and will instead send samples with you to feed after your cat feels better at home. A cat should be reliably eating their regular diet before starting a switch, because if they're not, they're unlikely to accept a new food. It's important that your veterinarian look for and try to address as many causes of decreased appetite as possible—such as nausea, anemia, dehydration, and electrolyte imbalances—before switching to a new food.[10]

Bruce has chronic kidney disease and a sweet setup for his fluid therapy sessions. He lounges on a comfy cover placed over a heating pad, with easy access to his favorite drinking fountain and a litter box—and careful oversight from his dog sister Luna. He also receives nutritional support and medications through an esophageal feeding tube (under his neck bandage), which was placed because he wasn't eating enough on his own. After he feels better and his appetite returns to normal, the tube can be removed.

First offer a small amount of the new diet in a dish separate from your cat's regular diet at mealtimes. After your cat eats the new food, provide lots of praise and petting. You can then begin gradually reducing the total daily amount of your cat's regular diet and make up the difference with the new diet over a three-week period[10]:

- **week 1**, feed 75% of the regular diet mixed with 25% of the new diet;
- **week 2**, feed a 50:50 mix of each diet;
- **week 3**, feed 25% of the regular diet and 75% of the new diet; and
- **week 4** and thereafter feed 100% of the new diet.

Pet and praise your cat at mealtimes to make the experience more rewarding.

If your cat shows signs of stomach upset or refuses the new food, decrease the proportion of new food and add back the regular food and extend the transition period. Also tell your veterinarian about your pet's upset stomach or refusal of the new food. And if your cat refuses to eat altogether, don't wait, let your veterinarian know.

Most important in Bruce's care is the TLC his mom, Dana, doses him with generously many times a day (Dana also happens to be a vet)!

Quench your cat's thirst and make mealtimes inviting

Because cats with kidney disease are unable to drink enough water to keep up with the amount of fluid they lose through the urine, veterinarians often suggest giving affected cats subcutaneous (under the skin) fluids a few days a week and up to once a day. Fluid therapy helps keep your cat hydrated and feeling good when their kidneys lose their ability to conserve water.

Cats usually tolerate subcutaneous fluid therapy, and even if they're hesitant at first, they tend to grow accepting of it with time. And once pet parents get the hang of it, it can be done quickly. Your veterinarian will show you how to do this and tell you how much and what type of fluid to give your cat. Videos are also available on YouTube that demonstrate this technique, so ask your veterinarian to point out a few. Check out my favorite from International Cat Care at **icatcare.org/advice/how-to-give-subcutaneous-fluids-to-your-cat/**.

Once kidney disease reaches the late stage, your cat may need to be hospitalized from time to time for supportive treatments, including intravenous fluid therapy. Intravenous fluids (fluids administered into a vein) must be given much slower and over a longer period of time than fluids given under the skin, so a hospital stay is needed. Typically, cats return home feeling good again and do well with continued subcutaneous fluid treatments at home.

Bodhi's wonderful pet sitter, Jean Martin, giving Bodhi his fluid therapy.

Eventually some cats seem to tire of their therapeutic diets—usually when they have nausea associated with their disease and lose their appetite. So talk with your veterinarian about whether your cat needs additional fluid therapy, anti-nausea medication, food flavor enhancers, and an appetite stimulant. These treatments can make cats with kidney disease feel better and eat more.

If treatment adjustments still don't entice your cat to eat his therapeutic diet, you may need to try a different therapeutic diet, temporarily switch back to feeding your cat's previous maintenance diet, or mix his therapeutic diet with his maintenance diet to ensure he eats enough. Keep in mind that your cat's quantity and quality of life will be extended if your cat eats enough of a diet designed especially for cats with kidney disease, and that sometimes their reluctance

to eat is not related to the food but to how they feel overall.[10] Yet eating enough calories to preserve body functions and provide energy is important, too, so compromises may be needed along the way, rather than insisting that your cat continue to eat only the therapeutic diet.

Also talk with your veterinarian about whether placing a feeding tube may be needed. A feeding tube can support cats through an illness setback that they might otherwise succumb to. Feeding tubes can be used long-term, or veterinarians can remove them once cats eat enough on his own. Cats tend to tolerate feeding tubes well, and the tube makes it easier to give oral medications. A helpful resource to learn more about feeding tubes is available from International Cat Care at **icatcare.org/app/uploads/2022/05/Managing-the-cat-with-a-feeding-tube.pdf**.

 Jonesy didn't seem to mind his esophageal feeding tube at all!

Keep a positive perspective

Many cats who have well-managed kidney disease can live several more happy, active years. My cat Bodhi lived well for years with dietary, medical, and supportive care to manage his kidney failure. He ate a special veterinary therapeutic diet made for cats with kidney disease, and I always had five other canned cat food varieties on hand to coax him to eat on the days his appetite waned. He learned to sit patiently and receive his "camel hump"—the subcutaneous (under the skin) fluids he needed to help him stay hydrated—at first only once a week, then every other day, then every night. He sometimes needed a boost with anti-nausea medication and an appetite stimulant. And later in the disease he sometimes had to stay in the hospital for a few days so he could receive his fluids intravenously. He always came home perky and eager to get back to my lap!

In the early stages of kidney disease your cat may not experience discomfort. Cats whose kidney disease is being well-managed can be likened to being on a sailboat in calm seas for long periods. As the disease progresses, their sailboat may be intermittently caught in bad storms, so rechecking your cat's blood and urine test results and addressing your cat's symptoms is paramount. Cats can feel quite sick and develop oral ulcers (because of toxin buildup in the blood). They can become dehydrated and have mobility issues from weakness related to electrolyte imbalances. Frequent veterinary rechecks are also needed because many drugs are metabolized by the kidneys, so some drug doses may need to be decreased in cats with CKD to prevent side effects.[8] But with treatment tweaks and medication adjustments, the calm seas return.

Eventually, worse storms arrive that make you wonder whether the boat will sink and it's time to jump ship. But, with further treatment tweaks, calm weather arrives again! Recognizing when the storm will not abate while carefully evaluating your cat's quality of life are key.

FUN FACT:

In 1938, two giraffes aboard the cargo ship *S.S. Robin Goodfellow* survived a hurricane at sea as they were en route from British East Africa to the United States. They then made a cross-country road trip via a makeshift giraffe RV from New York to the San Diego Zoo. Patches and Lofty lived nearly 30 years at the zoo, and during their residence they had seven baby giraffes (calves).[21]

Questions to ask your veterinarian

- Has my cat lost weight despite not being on a diet? Is my cat losing muscle mass?
- What stage of kidney disease does my cat have?
- Does my cat have an underlying problem that may be causing or contributing to kidney disease that also needs to be treated (a kidney stone or other urinary tract blockage, hyperthyroidism, infection)?
- Is treatment needed if my cat does not have outward signs of kidney disease?
- What is my cat's prognosis with and without treatment?
- Is my cat eligible for a kidney transplant?
- What kidney disease treatments will be needed, how will they be given, how often, and for how long?
- Does my cat need a special diet, nutritional supplements, or an oral fluid supplement?
- How is my cat's dental health? Does my cat need a professional dental cleaning?
- Will my cat need fluid therapy under the skin at home? If so, how do I do that?
- Will my cat benefit from a feeding tube?

- Does my cat need to be treated for high blood pressure? Does my cat also have a thyroid or heart condition?
- What follow-up tests and exams will be needed to monitor my cat and how often? What are the costs?
- Are there side effects of treatment?
- What problems do I need to watch out for?
- What do I do if problems occur after regular business hours?

CAREGIVER TIPS AND HOME HACKS

- Provide clean, fresh water every day. Consider providing filtered or mineral water or clean rainwater. Cats with kidney disease tend to—and need to— drink more water, so you'll want to encourage this.
- Provide more than one water bowl in different locations, and try different containers (bowls, tumblers, pitchers) in small, medium, and large sizes and made of different materials (glass, ceramic, plastic, or metal) to see what type of container your cat prefers. Keep the water filled to the brim, because cats tend to prefer this.
- Give your cat access to a clean water source outdoors if you take your cat out for supervised exploration and sunbathing.
- Try adding a ping pong ball to a large, wide, shallow bowl of water. It may spur your cat to play and get the water moving a bit, which encourages some cats to drink.
- Consider providing a drinking fountain designed for cats to entice your cat to drink more than she would from her regular water bowl, especially if your cat enjoys drinking directly from the faucet.
- If your cat prefers to drink from the faucet, consider installing an automatic motion sensor, so your cat can drink when you're not available to turn on the faucet. Continue to provide a bowl of fresh water each day in case your cat can't access the faucet.
- Offer (unseasoned) water left after poaching fish or chicken. Or offer flavored broths and nutrient-enriched water supplements (oral hydration supplements) designed to help cats stay hydrated—ask your veterinarian.
- Feed a veterinary therapeutic diet formulated for cats with kidney disease.
- Feed primarily canned or moist foods, or add water to dry kibble.
- Warm your cat's refrigerated canned food to body temperature before feeding.
- Add juice from chicken or tuna packed in water to enhance palatability (the yum! factor). FortiFlora (Purina Pro Plan Veterinary Diets) is a probiotic supplement powder that also enhances the flavor of food.

- Keep several varieties of extra tasty, "special" canned cat food on hand for the days when your cat's appetite needs a boost. Your cat may get to a point where you need to rotate these and offer a different flavor or formulation (gravy, chunky, slices, pâté) every day, or even at each meal to keep your cat interested.

A kitty "buffet"– lots of menu options!

Important tip: Rotate through the options one at a time—daily or on a per-meal basis. Avoid plating several options at one meal, because cats who aren't feeling great may find this unappetizing. Also pick up and discard wet food that your cat leaves in her bowl within two hours. If she leaves dry food in her bowl for 24 hours, toss it out and feed fresh food. Always wash and dry the bowl so your cat has a fresh opportunity to clean her clean plate!

- See Chapter 9 "Body condition and nutrition: Helping senior cats eat better and feel better" and Chapter 23 "Course of action: Therapeutic options and gaining acceptance from your senior cat" for more tips on getting cats to eat and on giving your cat medications.

- Remember that cats with kidney disease tend to urinate more, so they will need easy access to clean litter boxes. And cats who are receiving subcutaneous fluid therapy urinate even more, so be prepared for more frequent litter box scooping and cleaning duties so your cat won't balk at using a soiled box. Consider adding an extra litter box as well.

- Stock up on high-quality, low-dust, eco-friendly, lightweight cat litter if your cat is receiving subcutaneous fluids. They'll go through a lot more cat

 These low-entry litter boxes are easy for cats to access, and the potty pads help catch over-the-side misses and reduce litter tracking in the room.

163

Bruce had all the creature comforts: a heating pad, a water fountain, mushy delectable foods, and lots of love!

litter, and although higher quality litter costs more, it's easier to scoop and keeps its fresh smell longer. (The lightweight type is easier to lug and pour, and this adds up and saves caregiver energy!)

- Purchase a rigid, sturdy metal cat litter scoop—this makes scooping the large clumps of wet litter from the bottom and sides of the pan so much easier, faster, and less tiring! Avoid plastic scoops or the flimsy metal types if you can.
- Use a stainless steel scrubber when you wash the litter box. This helps you more easily remove the litter that tends to stick even after you've scraped it out. Thoroughly dry the litter box before adding fresh litter.
- When giving subcutaneous fluids, warm the bag (but not the injection port or injection set) in hot water for 5 or 10 minutes. Before giving the fluids, test the temperature of the water by dripping a few drops on your

As a reminder, kidney disease is not a death sentence. Bodhi (the cover model) lived for years with his kidneys not functioning properly – but not only did he live .. he lived well!"

wrist, similar to testing the temperature of milk in a baby's bottle. After each treatment, give your cat a treat and lots of praise and more petting!
- Frequently launder your cat's bedding, and rotate different types of blankets to different spots to increase their comfort and keep them clean. Cats especially like freshly laundered items and may appreciate variety. Consider lightly spraying these with a synthetic feline pheromone to further comfort your cat. And keep in mind that cats tend to sleep in odd locations when they aren't feeling well, so that may be a signal that they need medication adjustments or a hospital visit for intravenous fluid therapy.
- Provide heated cat beds, especially for underweight cats and those with decreased muscle mass who have trouble regulating their body temperature and are susceptible to getting chilled.
- Provide a calm environment to reduce stress. For example, if your cat doesn't adapt well to boarding, have a family member or cat sitter care for your cat if you have to travel. Reduce contact with other visiting family members' cats if they tend to make your cat anxious.
- Watch for mobility difficulties and place rugs, small stairs, or ramps where needed; also provide nightlights near litter boxes.

PRODUCT RECOMMENDATIONS

- Water supplement for cats: Hydra Care (Purina Pro Plan Veterinary Supplements)
- Veterinarian-prescribed appetite stimulants: Elura (Elanco) or Mirataz (Dechra)
- A probiotic supplement powder that can be sprinkled on food as a flavor enhancer: FortiFlora (Purina Pro Plan Veterinary Diets)
- Highly tasty, food-topping appetite motivators:
  Churu by Inaba (**churuvet.com**)
  Bonito Flakes by Cat-Man-Doo
  catmandoo.biz/1oz-bonito-pouch
- Synthetic feline pheromones (e.g. Feliway by Ceva or Comfort Zone by Central Garden & Pet Care)

SUPPORT RECOMMENDATION

- Feline Chronic Kidney Disease Facebook group
  facebook.com/groups/felinecrf

CHAPTER 14:

Incontinence and other potty problems: Thinking outside the box

> "I don't need you to remind me of my age. I have a bladder to do that for me."
>
> —Stephen Fry, actor/comedian/writer

As I carefully waddled to the bathroom in near-total darkness at 4 a.m., I made sure not to step on squeaker toys, bump into a dog bed, kick my cats' jingle and crinkle balls, or trip over any one of my many snoozing critters. I navigated this obstacle course pretty precisely most nights! So I sighed with relief as I made it to my destination without any disturbances.

But then, I instantly felt it. The cold, sopping wet bath mat against my bare foot—squish! I knew immediately that one of my cats had peed there (because I'm also an expert in sock-foot cat hairball detection and barefoot dog doo-doo discovery). I suspected that my cat Bodhi was the culprit. His chronic kidney disease made him drink more and pee more, and he had arthritis, so he sometimes didn't make it to the litter box.

After I washed my foot in the bathtub, I tiptoed to the laundry room with the bathmat and dropped it in the washing machine. I didn't want to wait up in the wee hours for the washer and dryer cycles to finish, so I sadly realized this would be an impossible accident to hide. Someone else would notice the missing bath mat, and I knew I'd hear some form of complaint shortly after the alarm clock buzzed. The frustration from others in my household about Bodhi's ailments was wearing on me. Not that I didn't care about Bodhi peeing on the bath mat—I would rather he didn't! But I also understood his medical issues and knew I could easily clean up after him. But oh boy, did my senior pets' accidents cause so much more trouble than wet feet! (I was relieved to be the one who stepped in it!)

Oops, my cat did it again!

Young and old cats alike can lose urine or bowel control—and sometimes lose both. Several conditions, many of which are more likely to affect senior cats, can cause or contribute to these problems. Whether a cat is incontinent and can't control peeing or pooping or is having "accidents" for another reason must be sorted out. A veterinary visit to find the reason that a cat isn't using her litter box or to find out why she is visiting her litter box too much is always necessary so that her medical condition or behavior issue can be corrected or managed. Urination troubles caused by urinary tract blockages are immediately life-threatening and require emergency veterinary care.

Why "wee" hours add up

Urinary incontinence means that a pet unintentionally leaks urine while resting, sleeping, or walking. With incontinence, a weak or overwhelmed urinary sphincter—a muscle that controls urine flow from the bladder—lets urine seep out. Urinary incontinence is uncommon in cats, but it can be caused by a problem with the nerves that control the bladder or by a urinary tract blockage.[1,2] For example, spinal cord injury or cancer can damage the bladder nerves and allow urine to leak from the bladder. Urinary tract stones, mineral plugs, strictures, and tumors can block voluntary urine passage, yet the fluid pressure builds and urine begins to leak around the obstruction. And sometimes, cats with urinary tract infections also involuntarily leak urine.

If your cat intentionally squats to urinate somewhere in your home other than the litter box, your cat is having urine accidents, which differs from urinary incontinence. Veterinarians used to refer to these types of pee accidents as *inappropriate urination*, however, the now-favored term is *house-soiling*, because it implies no misconduct by the cat. How appropriate!

Cats who have arthritis, diabetes, cognitive dysfunction, kidney disease, hyperthyroidism, or cancer may urinate in places in the home other than the litter box. And cats who have any type of urinary tract inflammation, irritation, or blockage probably have an urgent, uncomfortable feeling that they need to urinate every few minutes. They make frequent trips to the litter box, and pet parents often think their cats are constipated. Or affected cats may not bother to make so many trips to the litter box and go wherever they are when they feel the urge. Cats may even purposefully avoid their litter box because urinating is painful and they think it is related to the litter box. Cats who have urinary tract inflammation from an unknown cause (called *feline idiopathic cystitis, feline lower urinary tract disease,* or *feline interstitial cystitis*) or from a bacterial urinary tract infection often urinate somewhere odd (such as a bathtub, sink, or closet) or right next to the litter box.

In addition, some senior cats develop behavior issues and pee outside the litter box, perhaps related to stressful household changes or in association with new habits they developed during their medical ailments. They may suddenly avoid certain types of litter; prefer a different surface to eliminate on; dislike the litter box size, structure, or location; mark territory (cats typically stand and spray urine on household objects or in the litter box); or develop separation anxiety.

> **SIDEBAR: Separation anxiety?**
>
> You might be thinking, well, of course my cat is anxious when I'm not with him! But separation anxiety is a behavioral condition diagnosed in cats who react to being left alone by meowing excessively, having urine or fecal accidents, destroying household items, or overgrooming. Cats with separation anxiety may also demand extra attention when their pet parent is home. In one study, 75% of the cats with separation anxiety who didn't use their litter boxes urinated only on their pet parents' beds.[3]

Is it urinary incontinence or urine house-soiling?

Veterinarians can start to sort out whether a cat has urinary incontinence or is having accidents for other reasons by asking pet parents several questions, such as:

Does your cat—

- visit the litter box excessively?
- cry out in the litter box?
- leak urine while resting, walking, or jumping?
- lick his urogenital area or stomach often?
- squat normally to urinate?
- squat normally to urinate initially, but then stand up during urination?
- pee small amounts in unusual locations around the home?
- leave one large puddle on the floor?
- stand with his tail up and shake his tail while spraying urine on household items or in the litter box?

- dribble urine immediately after urinating normally?
- drink more water than usual?
- urinate outside of the litter box right in front of you?
- urinate outside of the litter box only while you're out of the house?

Your veterinarian will also ask about your cat's litter boxes—how many you have, how big and how tall they are and whether they're covered, what kind of litter you use, where the boxes are located, how often you scoop them, and how often you completely empty and clean them. They will also ask about medications and supplements your cat is receiving and whether other pets live in the household.

If your cat urinates small amounts often—whether in the litter box or in weird locations— it may be a sign of urinary tract stones or crystals, idiopathic cystitis, a urinary tract infection, or bladder cancer. If your cat urinates on the floor and leaves one big puddle, then kidney disease, hyperthyroidism, arthritis, or cognitive dysfunction may be the cause. If your cat urinates in the litter box but over the side of it at times, they may be standing up during urination because arthritis makes squatting uncomfortable. Veterinarians further sort out these possible problems with blood tests, urine tests (including a culture to check for bacterial growth in the urine), x-rays or ultrasound, and cystoscopy (looking inside the urethra and bladder with a tiny camera in a flexible tube called a *cystoscope*).

Because nerve dysfunction from spinal or other problems can cause urinary incontinence, your veterinarian can check your cat's reflexes and sensation by doing a neurologic exam, and, if needed, x-rays, a computed tomography (CT) scan, or magnetic resonance imaging (MRI) to help pinpoint the problem.

If your cat's symptoms and your responses to your veterinarian's initial questions suggest that your cat has a behavior issue, and if your cat's diagnostic test results are normal, your veterinarian will ask additional questions related to your cat's behavior and home environment to try to pinpoint the issue.

Depending on the cause of a cat's urinary incontinence or urine house-soiling, veterinarians can address the underlying medical or behavioral condition by prescribing medications, supplements, special diets, other therapies (such as veterinary acupuncture, chiropractic care, or rehabilitation therapy), or environmental enrichment. Enriching a cat's environment entails giving a cat multiple rewarding opportunities for activity and positive mental stimulation and reducing stressful situations.

If your cat has a urinary tract blockage, emergency care is needed. Cats with blockages caused by strictures (scar tissue that builds up in the urethra) or tumors may need surgery. If a urinary stone is blocking urine flow, some cats can be treated with a veterinary therapeutic diet and medication to dissolve the stones, some can benefit from a nonsurgical technique called *voiding urohydropropulsion* to flush stones out, and some need surgery to remove the blockage. And in some cases, cats with urinary stones can undergo a procedure called *lithotripsy* at a veterinary specialty hospital. With lithotripsy, a laser is used to break stones into tiny pieces that can be passed through the urine or removed with an instrument guided by a cystoscope.

When cats leave poop where you don't scoop

Similar to cats with urinary incontinence, cats who have *fecal incontinence* can't properly control pooping (defecation). Spinal cord trauma or other injury to the nerves of the anal sphincter (the ring of muscle that opens and closes the anus) can allow poop (feces) to slip out. Cats with fecal incontinence may not posture to poop, may be unaware of having a bowel movement, and may have a droopy tail. Cats with nerve damage sometimes have fecal and urinary incontinence.

Similar to cats who exhibit urine house-soiling, cats who intentionally squat to poop somewhere in the home other than the litter box are exhibiting fecal house-soiling.

So if your cat randomly drops poop around the house, leaves a "nugget" where he's been resting, produces a pile in an odd spot, strains or cries in the litter box, has diarrhea, or has off-color poop or feces that contains blood or mucus, schedule a veterinary examination.

Veterinarians take a careful history to help identify the cause of the poo mishaps and ask questions such as:

- Do you find feces next to the litter box? In your cat's bed? In random spots around the house?
- What is the color and the consistency of your cat's feces? (It's helpful to bring your cat's fresh stool sample or at least a photo to the appointment.)
- Does your cat posture normally to defecate?
- Does your cat sometimes seem to be unaware when stool comes out?
- Does stool come out when your cat is excited or when she gets up?
- How often does your cat defecate?
- Does your cat make frequent trips to the litter box?
- Have you changed your cat's diet recently?
- Does your cat lick her hind end frequently or scoot on her rear?
- How often do you scoop the poop (and clumps)? (Answer honestly, and remember, no one likes a nasty porta-potty!)
- How often do you completely change the litter?
- How often do you wash and dry the litter box after completely changing the litter?

Your veterinarian will also ask about your cat's litter boxes, medications and supplements your cat is receiving, and whether other pets live in the household. Your veterinarian may also do fecal, rectal, and neurologic examinations, along with blood tests and x-rays. Your veterinarian will also check whether your cat's anal sacs (glands near the anus that produce stinky secretions) are full and need to be expressed.

A cat who has normal poop (dark brown, formed, and a bit moist) but has fecal incontinence may have a nerve-related disease that causes anal sphincter malfunction. In affected cats, poop is evacuated and the cat may not be aware of it. If these cats have mobility disorders and an overfull bowel and struggle to get up, fecal balls may fall out.

Cats with cognitive dysfunction may also poop outside the litter box or sometimes seem to be unaware of defecation. Cats with constipation sometimes randomly pass small fecal balls and may or may not seem to be aware of it.

Other reasons cats poop (or pee) outside the litter box may be related to arthritis or other mobility problems or painful conditions. This may include cats who stand in the box but their rear end hangs over the side. Mobility problems can make it difficult for cats to properly get into position to poop or to get where they need to be in time to eliminate. So don't assume your cat is being sassy or lazy; you cat likely has a medical issue that your veterinarian should look into!

Depending on the cause of a cat's fecal incontinence or fecal house-soiling, veterinarians may prescribe an analgesic (for cats with arthritis) or medication that slows movement of food through the digestive tract, and recommend a change in diet to a low-fiber, more highly digestible diet. In some cases, they may suggest adding a dietary supplement such as pumpkin to boost dietary fiber. Cats may need surgery if a tumor is affecting the colon or anal sphincter. And cats who have chronic, severe constipation (called *obstipation*) can develop an overstretched colon that no longer moves as it should to push poop out. This is called *megacolon*, and surgery can be done to remove the diseased bowel. Cats who poop outside of the litter box because of a behavior issue will need environmental adjustments specific to their household, along with encouragement and litter box retraining.

Cats who have fecal incontinence also have a higher risk of urinary tract infections, so help them keep their heinies clean and watch for additional signs of discomfort. As I mentioned above, cats with urinary tract infections may make numerous trips to their litter box, urinate small amounts frequently, or urinate in odd locations like a sink or bathtub.

Questions to ask your veterinarian

- What is the cause of my cat's urine or fecal elimination issue and what is the expected outcome with treatment?
- Should I consult with a veterinary internal medicine or surgery specialist about options to treat my cat's incontinence?
- Is pain from mobility problems or muscle weakness preventing my cat from eliminating appropriately? Can my cat receive medications for pain management? Will my cat benefit from therapies that support muscle strength or joint function?
- Will my cat with fecal incontinence benefit from a diet change to a more highly digestible food? Or to a food with higher fiber content?
- Will acupuncture, chiropractic care, or rehabilitation therapy help my cat's incontinence, constipation, or arthritis?
- Do you offer special grooming for "sanitary cuts" (shaving around the rear end and groin —like a bikini trim—to help keep those areas clean)?

Regaining cleanliness control

No matter the cause, ongoing urine or fecal incontinence or house-soiling is tough to manage, and I empathize with caregivers of affected cats. It can become overwhelming for caregivers and for family members who share the household. Managing a cat with incontinence or other elimination issues requires a considerable degree of steady, dedicated care. So again, it's important to seek veterinary evaluation to identify the reason for a cat's urine or fecal incontinence or accidents.

Many causes of incontinence or house-soiling respond to appropriate treatment or can be well managed. With medications, surgical treatment (if needed), changes to the cat's diet (if applicable), and environmental adjustments, pet parents and their incontinent or otherwise potty-unrestrained cats can live contentedly together. Next up are tips to help you keep the peace!

Mack's cat bed is a comfy waterproof baby changing pad that helps keep him clean!

CAREGIVER TIPS AND HOME HACKS

- Keep consistent feeding schedules and easy access to fresh water.
- Place night lights near litter boxes for cats who may have poor night vision.
- Add a litter box or two so your cat has more options to get to where they need to be to eliminate.
- Use boot trays or oil drip pans (to protect garage floors from car oil) under litter boxes to catch over-the-edge mishaps.
- Repurpose and modify a plastic storage bin to use as a litter box. You'll have oodles of styles and sizes to choose from.
- Consider decreasing litter depth to one or two inches. Some cats with severe mobility problems have trouble maneuvering in deep sand (a bit like some of us on the beach!).
- Your cat's litter preference may change over time. Cats may also reject their usual litter or avoid the litter box location if they experience pain or anxiety while using it. "Ask" your cat which litter he prefers by offering different litters in different sizes or types of boxes. An uncovered box that is 1.5 times the length of your cat that contains unscented, low-dust, clumping litter typically works well. Or try alternatives to clay litter—pine-based clumping litter, newspaper-based litter, corn or other plant-based litter, or even shredded paper.
- Senior cats who start peeing in potted plants may have

 Cut out an entry point in a large plastic storage bin and pad the edges with pool noodle material to use as a covered or uncovered litter box.

 This low-entry litter box has a potty pad inside (with cat litter sprinkled on top) and a potty pad on the outside to catch mishaps.

This plastic storage container was converted into a litter box. The cat preferred a see-through box with no lid. The firm pillow in front of the entry point makes it easier for the kitty to step in and out of the box. A slip-resistant bath step is an alternative option as a booster step for this box or a standard size litter box.

discovered they like potting soil, or they may have tried and liked it when they had a medical problem (that veterinary care has presumably since resolved). If needed, restrict cats' access to the plants (urine can burn plant roots and kill plants). Using potting soil in the litter box is messier than most other types of litter and probably costs more because it needs to be changed more often, so you may want to encourage and retrain your cat to accept another type of litter.

- If you need to switch litter, offer the new litter in a separate litter box, and gradually mix in small amounts of the new litter with the standard litter in the standard box. Work up to a complete swap over a few weeks, for example, replace 25% of the litter each week until the switch is complete and your cat reliably uses the new litter.
- Cats love clean litter boxes! Scoop each box at least once a day. Scoop twice a day for cats with excessive urination related to conditions such as kidney disease and fluid therapy. "Top off" the box with a bit of clean litter if needed. Once a week, dispose of all remaining litter and wash and dry each box and fill it with clean litter. (A well-washed and rinsed box shouldn't have residual urine, strong soap, or cleaning agent odors.)
- If frequent scooping isn't feasible and your cat doesn't have mobility problems, a self-cleaning litter box may be an option. These litter boxes are pricey, so research them to help you decide whether they'll work as you expect them to, and keep in mind that some cats are afraid of them.
- If cats need extra encouragement to use their litter box, try a litter additive made specifically to attract cats to their litter box.
- Consider using a color-changing litter designed to alert you to certain cat health issues that warrant a veterinary visit.
- To help relieve anxiety, use feline synthetic pheromones in diffuser, spray, or collar form.

- Never discipline or punish your cat for incontinence or accidents in the house.
- If necessary, reduce your cat's access to the house when you're away and confine her to a room with a litter box (preferably non-carpeted), as well as her food and water bowls (as far away from the litter box as feasible), with a comfy place to rest (also as far away from the litter box as possible).
- Invest in a carpet cleaner and keep the machine, rug cleaning solution, and pet stain and odor remover products in a readily accessible location. These ick-extractors are lifesavers for pet parents!
- Use an ultraviolet black-light flashlight in darkened rooms to help you find urine spots you missed.

Use a puppy training pad holder with a wee-wee pad for cats with arthritis or other mobility issues who need a low-entry litter box. This photo of my cat Goldie—who had partial hindlimb paralysis—using her low-step potty isn't great, but you get the idea!

Should my incontinent cat wear diapers?

Because diapers increase the chances of urinary tract infections, I usually reserve recommending diapers until we are at our wits' end or until it is absolutely necessary. So please use them carefully and under your veterinarian's guidance. For diaper-clad cats or those resting on potty pads, be on alert and prevent painful skin rashes and infections. They commonly develop and if they do, they require additional time, attention, treatment, and cost.

For medium- or long-haired cats, do a "sanitary trim." Beard trimmers work great for this. Carefully clip the fur (avoid clipper burn!) around the areas where urine or feces may cling and not be easy to clean, including the back of the hind legs. Check diapers and potty pads frequently and change them regularly to keep your cat's fur and skin clean and dry. If needed, use wipes made specifically for pets, or use unscented, hypoallergenic baby wipes.

Cats with urinary incontinence can suffer from urine scalding—inflammation caused by urine sitting on the skin. If your cat's skin is mildly irritated, this is a warning sign, so wash the area with a mild cat shampoo and thoroughly dry it. Your veterinarian can prescribe specific skin care products to support healing as needed. After the skin is completely dry, you may apply a thin layer of a pet-safe skin ointment or baby diaper rash ointment to relieve irritation and leave a moisture barrier. Some ointments contain zinc oxide, which can be toxic to cats, so avoid those.

Extra tips for caregivers of incontinent cats

- Use washable, reusable potty pads to protect furniture, cat beds, or carriers.
- Use disposable potty pads where needed.
- Cover duvets and couches with washable, waterproof covers.
- Use easy-to-clean cat beds.
- Cover cat beds with waterproof mattress covers (crib mattress covers are the best!). A shower curtain under a blanket also works and is less likely to tear or bunch up than a plastic bag will. In a pinch, cover cat beds with trash bags and place old blankets or towels on top.
- Prevent sores and infections from urine scalding by placing absorbent pads under your bedridden cat, or use diapers if needed for incontinent cats and change them right away when they become soiled.
- Use puppy pads along with baby changing pads to help keep incontinent cats clean and comfortable and their beds dry.
- Some pet beds are "water resistant" and not waterproof, so they may not stand up to leakage that isn't immediately cleaned up. Some are designed with waterproof liners that sit between the bed cover and the bedding material. So if your cat is consistently incontinent, consider adding an absorbent layer of protection on top that's disposable or easier to remove and launder than the pet bed cover or liner.
- Organize your cat's grooming supplies and skin care products in a tote kept in a handy spot for quick cleanups.
- Consider keeping pet wipes or baby wipes in a wipe warmer for your cat's added comfort. (Who wouldn't like a warm wipe?)
- On frequently wiped areas of skin, apply diaper rash ointment to prevent or relieve irritation (be sure your cat doesn't ingest the ointment).

The cotton swab secret for pets with fecal incontinence

I learned a trick from pet parents who show their dogs or travel a lot and need their dog to defecate before stepping into the ring or during rest stops on car trips, and it works for cats, too. Place the tip of a cotton swab just inside the pet's rectum—not too far beyond the anal sphincter—and gently move the swab in small circles. The pet poops right away!

You can try this trick to stimulate your cat with fecal incontinence to poop right before bedtime, or before you leave for a few hours. This trick has saved me from hours of carpet cleaning and days of arguing with family members, and it has given me more precious time with my pets (and less time with the rug shampooer!).

PRODUCT RECOMMENDATIONS

- Dr. Elsey's Ultra–The Litter Cats Love:
  drelseys.com/
- Pretty Litter color changing, health-monitoring cat litter:
  prettylitter.com/
- Self-cleaning litter boxes (research these before deciding whether they're right for your household):
  - Litter-Robot (Whisker):
    litter-robot.com/
  - PetSafe Simply Clean:
    store.petsafe.net/simply-clean-litter-box
  - Nature's Miracle Multi-Cat:
    naturesmiracle.com/products/cat/litter-boxes-and-accessories/multi-cat-self-cleaning-litter-box.aspx
  - CatGenie
    catgenie.com/
- Feline synthetic pheromones
  - Feliway (Ceva):
    ceva.com/en/Products/Companion-animals/Behaviour
  - Comfort Zone
    comfortzone.com/
- Dr. Elsey's Cat Attract Litter Additive:
  drelseys.com/products/cat-attract-litter-additive
- Ultraviolet black light flashlight

Especially for cats with mobility problems

- Replace standard litter boxes with those that are roomier and have a shorter side for easier entry. Here are a few ideas:
  - Senior cat litter box:
    amazon.com/dp/B07QG4M7TZ?ref=exp_drmarygardner_dp_vv_d

- Easy entry, high-sided litter box:
  naturesmiracle.com/products/cat/litter-boxes-and-accessories/high-sided-litter-box.aspx
- Underbed storage tubs are extra-long and have low sides: **amzn.to/36IjANi**
- Canine litter trays make excellent litter boxes for senior cats, too. For example: Puppy Go Here (Avidog Essentials) **shop.avidog.com/products/puppy-go-here.**
- Cats with advanced mobility problems may appreciate an ultra low-sided tray, such as a boot tray or a puppy training pad holder lined with only a puppy pad and a dusting of litter on top. Eventually they may use the tray with only the pad and not need the litter. For example:
  - IRIS Dog & Puppy Training Pad Holder: **chewy.com/iris-dog-puppy-training-pad-holder/dp/133348**
- For additional advice on litter box types and products: See "The Conscious Cat with Ingrid King" at: **consciouscat.net/2017/06/28/litter-box-solutions-senior-cats/** and **consciouscat.net/litter-boxes-litter-and-accessories/**.

Cat diapers, waterproof blankets, and related supplies

- PeeKeeper
  Peekeeper.com
- Barkertime
  barkertime.com/
- Pet Parents
  petparentsbrand.com/
  petparentsbrand.com/products/premium-pet-blanket
- Hartz Disposable Cat Diapers
  hartz.com/products/cats/diapers/
- Diaper rash cream: A+D Original Ointment (Bayer) (Don't let your cat ingest the ointment, and don't use the A+D [or any] product that contains zinc oxide.)
- Your veterinarian may recommend Vetericyn (Innovacyn) or other veterinary skin care products to soothe irritated skin.
  vetericyn.com/product/vetericyn-plus-feline-antimicrobial-hydrogel/

Beds for incontinent dogs may work for cats, too

- SleePee Time Bed (Handicapped Pets)
  handicappeddogs.com/sleepee-time-bed-for-incontinent-dogs/

Washable, reusable potty pads

- Trendy Den Pet Mat (Trendy Den Creations) **thetrendyden.com/product-1-trendy-pet-mat/**
- Pawtect Washable Pads (Pet Parents) **petparentsbrand.com/products/puppy-pads**

Washable duvet and couch covers

- Floppy Ears Design **floppyearsdesign.com/**

RESOURCES

- American Holistic Veterinary Medical Association **ahvma.org/find-a-holistic-veterinarian/**
- International Veterinary Acupuncture Society **ivas.org/**
- American Veterinary Chiropractic Association **animalchiropractic.org/**

CHAPTER 15:

The lungs: Keeping the wind in their sails

My handsome orange tabby, Herbie, started having dry coughing spells when he was 10 years old. He'd crouch, stretch his neck out, and make wheezy, hacking sounds—and he'd gulp and lick his lips between coughs. At first I thought he might throw up a hairball, but his movements and the sounds he made were different from his vomiting motions and noises, plus he didn't puke. Back then I was still in veterinary school, and I was participating in an externship at a primary care veterinary clinic. So I took Herbie to their clinic to have him checked out. I remember clearly when the veterinarian put Herbie's chest x-rays up on the viewing light box. He gazed at them for a couple minutes, then he switched off the light box and announced, "Nothing to worry about. Herbie just has old cat lungs." And off he went to his next appointment.

Herbie was a friend to many species!

"But wait," I thought to myself, "What? Did you just say Herbie is *old*? He doesn't look or act old at all! And what does 'old cat lungs' mean?" I was puzzled *and* worried. But the cat got my tongue, and as a student, I didn't challenge the veterinarian by asking what that meant for Herbie.

Thinking back to that visit, I know that the veterinarian meant only to say that it was good news that Herbie didn't have a serious condition like heart failure, fluid in his chest, pneumonia, or an obvious lung tumor. But experience taught me that although infrequent coughing spells and age-related changes in the lungs are not necessarily life-threatening, coughing is a symptom that should be further investigated, especially in senior cats whose aging changes in the lungs can make even mild respiratory ailments harder to recover from.

That veterinarian taught me a lesson I'll always remember. After I graduated from veterinary school and began practicing, I realized that age-related lung changes, or age-related *any* changes, shouldn't be flippantly disregarded. When veterinarians look "WHOLE-istically" at a pet, we cannot think, "No big deal. It's just old lungs, or just old teeth, or just old ears, or just old legs, or *just old*." All of these changes mean something for the pet's quality of life, and they mean something to the pet's family.

Breathing basics

Inhaled room air—made up of about 78% nitrogen, 21% oxygen, 0.04% carbon dioxide, and tiny fractions of other gases, plus water vapor—begins its journey through the breathing passageway in the upper respiratory tract: the nose, mouth, and *larynx* (voice box—part of the throat that connects to the windpipe). It then travels through the lower respiratory tract: down the windpipe (*trachea*) and into the lungs, which are made up of large and small airway tubes (called *bronchi* and *bronchioles*) and millions of air sacs (called *alveoli*). Each air sac is surrounded by tiny blood vessels (*capillaries*).

Oxygen crosses the air sac membranes into the capillaries, where red blood cells pick it up for delivery to all the body's tissues. After delivering the oxygen, the red blood cells return with the byproduct—carbon dioxide—which is transferred back through the air sacs and out of the respiratory tract. Exhaled air contains about 4% carbon dioxide, 16% oxygen, 78% nitrogen, and a small amount of moisture.

The flow of oxygen in and carbon dioxide out is choreographed by brain signals that produce a rhythmic dance of alternating contraction and relaxation of muscles that assist breathing, including the diaphragm (the large muscle that separates the chest from the abdomen), intercostal muscles (the muscles between the ribs), and a few accessory muscles. Air flows into the lungs when the diaphragm pushes backward, the intercostal muscles rotate or pull the chest wall outward, and pressure in the lungs decreases. During exhalation, these muscles return to their resting places.

Some cells that line the respiratory tract produce mucus, and other cells have tiny hair-like projections called *cilia*. The cilia move together in rhythm (called *beat frequency*) to transport mucus-trapped invaders such as bacteria, viruses, and pollen that have been inhaled back out of the respiratory tract, banishing as many as they can before they reach the delicate air sacs in the lungs.

FUN FACT:

Plants mix sunlight, water, and carbon dioxide from air and soil to make the energy they need—and the energy we get when we eat plants—through photosynthesis. Luckily for us and other animals, plants create a byproduct called oxygen during photosynthesis.

Trees produce about half of the oxygen we breathe, and phytoplankton—teeny plants that live on lake and ocean surfaces (thousands per drop of water!)—puff out the other half! Oceans and forests are often called the lungs of the Earth.

Age-related breathing challenges

When I take chest x-rays and see aging changes in a patient's lungs, I counsel the pet parents about these findings. In senior pets, buildup of fibrous tissue (called *fibrosis*) and calcium deposits (called *mineralization*) throughout the lungs may be considered part of the aging process. So with age, the lungs become stiffer and less elastic, and breathing efficiency drops. Fibrosis can also result from various airway diseases, or because of long-term exposure to airway irritants (like secondhand smoke—yes, cats are at risk, too!). Even the little cilia deep in the lungs can develop a diminished beat frequency rhythm with age, or they can be hampered by secondhand smoke exposure or other airway insults. During regular day-to-day activities, geriatric cats usually compensate for age-related lung changes. But when they are faced with other respiratory system stressors, it becomes more difficult for them to recover.

Age-related changes in a pet's spine (decreased space between the vertebrae can adversely affect the intercostal muscles), the ribs (hardening of rib cartilage decreases flexibility of the chest wall), and the breathing muscles (weakening) can also hamper breathing. Weak contraction or diminished strength of the breathing muscles—the diaphragm and intercostal and accessory muscles—makes them less efficient. So as cats age, they may cough less effectively.

Cough strength can be measured in people and it indicates whether we can properly clear secretions from our respiratory tract and whether we have a high risk of inadvertently inhaling (aspirating) food. We can't ask our cats to cough on demand to check their cough strength, but veterinarians presume that senior cats who do have weak cough strength can't easily clear mucus and other particles from their breathing passageways.

If a senior pet's chest x-rays show that he has "old lungs" and he isn't coughing or doesn't otherwise have signs of a breathing problem, I suggest that pet parents monitor and record his breathing rate at least once a month, both while he is resting and after a walk or other activity. Respiratory rate recordkeeping helps pet parents see a trend in increased breathing rates, and helps signal when lung disease has progressed or when a new problem has developed. Then additional diagnostic tests can be done, and therapy and comfort can be started sooner. If I see aging changes on a senior patient's lung x-rays and the pet is coughing or has other symptoms, we can do additional tests right away to try to pinpoint the problem and provide therapies to resolve or manage the condition.

Cat Respiratory Rate Tracker

Common respiratory problems in senior cats

Disturbances anywhere along the respiratory pathway can impair breathing. Such changes increase cats' risk of developing serious breathing issues. Cats can develop inflammation in the airways that leads to asthma or chronic bronchitis, and they can catch infectious causes of lung disease such as bacteria, viruses, fungi, and parasites—especially heartworms. Regular checkups, vaccinations,

FUN FACT: CATCHING THOSE BREATHS

To count your cat's respiratory rate, wait until your cat is quietly resting or sleeping. Count the number of breaths your cat takes in 30 seconds (use a phone stopwatch or a clock with a second hand) and multiply it by two. This equals your cat's respiratory rate per minute.

Or use a handy free app—such as Medtimer—to calculate your cat's breathing rate. It's easy to use–just tap the number of seconds you'll count for (15, 20, 30, or 60 seconds), and when the timer starts, tap the screen each time you see a breath! The app lists a range of normal breathing rates for people at different ages, so remember to compare your cat's number with the normal cat resting respiratory rates range: 15 to 30 breaths per minute. If it's faster than that, let your veterinarian know, fast.

and parasite preventives remain important protective measures throughout cats' lives. Senior cats who have recurring upper respiratory tract signs may be having flare-ups related to reactivation of a feline herpesvirus infection, which can occur with stress or another underlying illness, and supportive care is needed.

Heart disease can occur for various reasons at any point in a cat's life, but it is more common in older cats. It, too, can result in breathing problems and is managed with medications. (See Chapter 12 "Heart: Keeping the beat strong.")

I will mention cancer here as well because cancer is so common, especially in senior cats. Cancer can start in the mouth, nose, or lungs or it can spread to the lungs from a tumor that develops elsewhere in the body. (See Chapter 19 "Cancer: Things that go bump in senior cats.") According to the American College of Veterinary Surgeons, about one in four cats who have a lung tumor will not show any signs and, instead, veterinarians find the tumor when they take chest x-rays for other reasons.[2]

Can my cat catch COVID-19?

It isn't common, but it is a concerning topic. Cats can catch severe acute respiratory syndrome coronavirus-2 (SARS-CoV-2)—the virus that causes coronavirus disease 2019 (COVID-19) in people—from people. Cats can also pass the virus to other cats, but it appears that the risk of the virus spreading from cats to people is extremely low to non-existent.[3]

Only one instance of COVID-19 transmission from a cat to a person has been documented.[4,5] In that case, a father and son in Thailand both had symptoms of COVID-19 and tested positive, and one of them likely passed the virus to their cat. The cat, who appeared to be healthy, then sneezed in a veterinarian's face (she was wearing a mask and gloves but no face shield or eye protection) while she was swabbing the cat's nose for a COVID-19 test. The cat's test results were positive for COVID-19, and the veterinarian became symptomatic and tested positive for COVID-19 five days later. Advanced tests later confirmed that the veterinarian had contracted the same strain of the COVID-19 delta variant that the cat and the cat's owners had—a strain that was not common in that area. Experts say that people are much more likely to pass COVID-19 to their pets, and that infected people should avoid contact with their pets.[5]

Pet cats with COVID-19 typically show no signs or only mild symptoms and quickly recover with supportive care, but in big cats such as tigers, lions, and leopards, the respiratory disease can be severe and life-threatening. Signs of COVID-19 in cats include sneezing, runny nose, coughing, fever, eye discharge, vomiting, diarrhea, lethargy, and trouble breathing.[6]

People who test positive for COVID-19 or have symptoms should isolate themselves from other people and from their pets and follow the current Centers for Disease Control and Prevention quarantine and isolation recommendations. And until they recover, people with COVID-19 should have someone else care for their pets whenever possible, or they should limit contact with their pets and wear a mask and wash their hands before and after interacting with their pets.

Pets rarely undergo COVID-19 testing, and a special test done by a veterinarian is needed to confirm the diagnosis. Pets who have COVID-19 should be isolated from other pets and people in the home during their illness (but don't put a mask on the pet), with their caregiver limiting their contact with the pet (no snuggles, kisses, or sharing food) and protecting themselves (wearing a mask, washing hands frequently) until the pet has completely recovered. Concern about COVID-19 spreading from pets to people is not a reason to give away or euthanize pets.

Vaccines against COVID-19 are available for people. People who are vaccinated against COVID-19 not only protect themselves, they also protect their pets and other people from this illness. COVID-19 vaccines aren't available for cats yet, but researchers are working on them![7] The ability to vaccinate other species against COVID-19 will further combat virus spread and curb virus mutations that may otherwise develop in other animals and potentially spread to people.

Reasons to pant

Cats can't sweat like we do (though they do have a small number of sweat glands in their paw pads), so if they're overly warm, they may pant to help cool off. Panting allows quick exchange of hot air from the lungs with cooler external air, and that speeds water evaporation from a cat's mouth (especially from the tongue), nose, and upper respiratory tract. This process helps regulate body temperature. This rapid, shallow, relaxed, open-mouth breathing is generally nothing to worry about, as long as the cat can otherwise access a cooler location. Still, cats don't pant as often as dogs do, so panting can be a sign of overheating. Their panting should subside when they cool down.

Cats sometimes pant after strenuous bouts of activity (e.g. exuberantly climbing, jumping, and chasing a toy through the house; being chased by another pet) or when they're seriously stressed or anxious, such as during car rides or being near an animal they perceive as a threat. Panting for these reasons should stop once a cat rests and calms down.

Pain and illness are other factors in the panting equation. Cats don't always show signs of pain that are obvious to us, but panting can be a sign of severe pain, especially when they wouldn't normally pant—like when they're resting or cooled down. Panting can also be a sign of heart or lung disease.

When taking a breath isn't as easy as breathing

Dyspnea means labored or difficult breathing and it massively adversely impacts a cat's quality of life. Human hospice patients equate the suffering associated with being breathless to the suffering associated with uncontrolled pain. I have seen many cats with dyspnea, and although they can't tell me whether they are suffering, I believe that they are. It's important for pet parents to understand the causes of respiratory system changes and the ways to help alleviate any stress and discomfort associated with their cat's dyspnea.

Some cats have physical abnormalities that make breathing a challenge. Brachycephalic (meaning a broad, short head) or "smooshed-face" cats (such as Persians and Burmese) are born with airway disadvantages. They may have narrow nostrils, an overlong soft palate (the area just behind the roof of the mouth), tissue in the larynx (voice box) that blocks air flow, and an underdeveloped trachea. Some cats are severely affected and require surgery to correct these problems. Even brachycephalic cats with mild to moderate physical abnormalities and who may not have needed surgery earlier in life may still have more breathing problems as they age than other breeds do.

Help keep the wind in your cat's sails

- Keep your cat up to date on vaccinations and parasite preventives to reduce the risk or severity of infectious diseases that can affect the respiratory system. The vaccinations cats receive protect against common viruses and bacteria that cause many problems, including those that damage the respiratory tract. Also protect your cat against heartworms by giving a heartworm preventive, because these mosquito-borne parasites cause severe lung disease.
- Help your cat maintain a healthy weight and body condition by feeding the right amount of high-quality food and promoting physical activity. Obesity can exacerbate respiratory distress from any cause.

- Help your cat quit being a secondhand smoker. Now *that's* a good reason for people to stop an unhealthy habit if they need another convincing argument—their cat's health! Your cat wants you to be well as well. Secondhand smoke can cause chronic respiratory problems and cancer in cats.

See your veterinarian if your cat:

- tires easily or sooner than she usually does with normal activity;
- breathes faster or harder than normal or pants with mild exercise or at rest;
- has unexplained weight loss or lethargy, which can be signs of lung cancer, among many other conditions;
- has a breathing rate consistently over 30 breaths per minute while he is relaxed and resting or sleeping;
- coughs or gags frequently (pet parents may think their cat is trying to "cough up a hairball");
- pants (more than expected after strenuous activity or in warm weather);
- has noisy breathing;
- seems distressed or anxious, is restless, or can't rest comfortably;
- has flared nostrils during breathing;
- breathes with an open mouth;
- uses her belly muscles to help her breathe;
- needs to stay upright or extend his neck to breathe; or stands or crouches with his head down and elbows out;
- has pale, bluish, or gray gums; or
- faints or collapses.

Questions to ask your veterinarian

- Will my cat benefit from receiving a feline bordetella vaccination in addition to other routine vaccinations (feline calicivirus and rhinotracheitis [also known as feline herpesvirus]) against respiratory illnesses?
- What tests will my cat need to evaluate her breathing problem?
- What medications will help?
- How can I help my cat breathe easier at home? Will my cat benefit from steam-room therapy, medications delivered through an inhaler, nebulizer, or coupage?
- Does my cat need oxygen therapy?
- Will my cat's condition resolve with treatment?

CAREGIVER TIPS AND HOME HACKS

Managing a cat's respiratory issues can be distressing for the family. But a simple rule applies: do everything to keep the cat calm and comfortable. These suggestions have worked for my patients and my cats:

- Maintain the home environmental temperature and humidity at comfortable levels and take care to avoid heat or cold stress.
- Keep food and water bowls and litter boxes easily accessible.
- Place ramps or stairs where needed to make your cat's favorite perches easier to get to.
- Place nightlights where needed.
- Play relaxing music, place "do not disturb" signs on your front door, and use cat synthetic pheromone sprays.
- Keep a cat health journal to routinely note your cat's heart and respiratory rates, activity level, appetite, weight, and the timing of any medication dosage changes that your veterinarian prescribes. Your help in closely monitoring your cat's signs at home helps your veterinarian better determine whether medications need to be added or otherwise adjusted.
- Schedule and keep all your cat's veterinary recheck appointments. Senior cats and those with respiratory ailments need more frequent monitoring and checkups. Take your cat's health journal with you to each appointment.
- Administer medications as directed by your veterinarian. When needed, cats can even be trained to use a specially designed medication inhaler called the Aerokat Chamber (made by Trudell Animal Health). Check out the International Cat Care website for more information on this topic. **icatcare.org/inhaler-training/**
- Keep cats calm and shield them from things that can get them worked up, like children chasing them or unfamiliar people visiting.
- Allow easy access to quiet places so your cat can "get away from it all" if needed.
- If your cat loves to go outdoors on leash walks with you, reduce the pace and duration of the walk, or go every other day instead if needed. In general, avoid allowing your cat to overdo it and become short of breath or exhibit weakness. Go out only during cooler times of the day to help prevent heat exhaustion.
- Engage cats in quiet, low-stress activities like food puzzles and other interactive, low-key toys. Use a variety of toys and rotate them to prevent boredom. Simple brushing and petting also provides mental stimulation for your cat.

- Cats with upper airway or lung congestion may breathe easier with steam-room therapy. Take your cat into a steam-filled bathroom for 10 minutes a few times a day to help loosen airway secretions.
- Coupage (firmly but gently patting your cat's chest) may also help cats who have pneumonia or bronchitis, but ask your veterinarian whether your cat needs it. If your cat will benefit from coupage, your veterinarian will show you how to do it and tell you how often to do it.
- Run a tiny desktop fan next to your cat's bed to promote more air flow into his nose. This helps alleviate distress in people with dyspnea and works well in my pet hospice practice. The cool airflow may trigger nerve receptors in the nose to send signals that "trick" the brain into thinking enough airflow is present.[8] It may help calm a cat in respiratory distress. Also make sure your cat is otherwise comfortable with the fan and not cold—drape a lightweight towel or blanket up to his shoulders if needed, because a heavy blanket may be too restrictive.

PRODUCT RECOMMENDATIONS

- Come With Me Kitty Cat Harness & Bungee Leash (Pet Safe) **petsafe.net**
- Music for cats:
    - iCalmPet (BioAcoustic Research) **icalmpet.com/**
    - Pet Tunes Feline **petacoustics.com/**
- Feline synthetic pheromones
    - Feliway (Ceva): **ceva.com/en/Products/Companion-animals/Behaviour**
    - Comfort Zone **comfortzone.com/**
- "Do not ring or knock" signs (check Amazon)
- Oxygen for pets (Pawprint) **pawprintoxygen.com/**
- AeroKat Chamber (Trudell Animal Health) medication inhaler for cats **trudellanimalhealth.com/product/aerokat-chamber**

Herbie's final harbor

Herbie's health sailed on smoothly until he was 15 years old, when his appetite began to waver. I knew his breathing rate had been slightly and steadily increasing, but he had suddenly become less active. He was also coughing again, and he was no longer the charming love bug that I knew him to be. His blood and urine test results showed no concerning abnormalities, but his chest x-rays showed a mass that wasn't there the year before, and it was most likely a lung tumor.

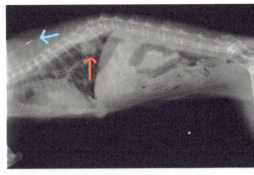

 On this x-ray you can see Herbie's tumor (red arrow) in the upper part of his lungs. You can also see his microchip (blue arrow) under his skin.

Herbie's quality of life declined rapidly after that. Within a month, he had seriously labored breathing. Difficulty breathing is one of the worst pains I think anyone can go through. I knew I had to give him his final sigh of relief, so Herbie could charm the angels.

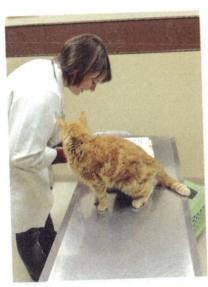

 Herbie, charming my veterinarian friend Dr. Elizabeth Hewit.

 Herbie soaking up the sunshine in his last week.

CHAPTER 16:

Mobility: The creaky, shaky, and unsteady

> "If a fish is the movement of water embodied, given shape, then [a] cat is a diagram and pattern of subtle air."
>
> — Doris Lessing, British novelist

When I started offering in-home end-of-life veterinary care, I thought I would be helping a lot of cats, because cats aren't brought to the veterinary clinic as often as dogs are. At that time, a typical veterinary practice saw about 70% dog patients and 30% cat patients, so my theory was that more cat owners would be interested in home veterinary services. But I quickly learned that the patients I saw most were large dogs with mobility issues. They simply couldn't get up and get around as well anymore, and their pet parents often couldn't manage getting them to the veterinary clinic, either.

Still, an alarming number of senior cats—nine out of 10 cats older than 12 years—have degenerative changes in their joints.[1,2] And even the most attentive pet parent may not think much of the subtle signs. Cats with arthritis may have trouble grooming themselves, be reluctant to jump up on or down from furniture, have trouble getting in and out of their litter box, experience discomfort when posturing to eliminate, and be less active overall. As a veterinarian, I have grown to more fully appreciate the impact that mobility problems have in my patients. And as a pet parent of three dogs and two cats with impaired mobility, I even more deeply understand these daily struggles. Each one of my patients and pets has taught me so much.

Goldie's broken back

When I was working in a primary care veterinary practice, I fell in love with and adopted Goldie, a gentle, sweet black cat with gold eyes. She had been

an outdoor cat, and a dog had attacked her and fractured her spine. Goldie had no feeling or function in her hind legs, but surgery to repair the fracture was not an option, and her pet parent could no longer care for her. Veterinarians are often faced with rescuing sick (and healthy) pets whose caretakers give them up for a variety of reasons. And we sometimes take home more pets than we should. But in Goldie's case, we had a connection that I could not deny!

 Me and Goldie on our first day together!

Goldie's treatment consisted of rest, supportive care to help her urinate and defecate, a high dose of corticosteroids to reduce swelling in her spine, and acupuncture, plus rehabilitation therapy (similar to physical therapy in people, but specific for pets) and a lot of prayers. About a month later, Goldie began moving her back legs herself—a massive improvement!

Within six months, Goldie regained about a third of her hindlimb mobility, but she would never walk normally. If she was on a rug or another surface with good traction, she could get her legs under her body and walk several wobbly steps. Then she would fall to one side and drag herself the rest of the way.

When most people heard about Goldie, they would tell me to euthanize her because that was "no way for a cat to live." But Goldie was extremely happy and well cared for. She was my "slider." She slid around the tiled parts of the house like a racecar, faster than my fully functional four-legged cats. She could climb up a cat tree and into my bed. She would even climb up my legs to my lap, which admittedly hurt like hell when her claws pierced my jeans. But she was happy!

Goldie loved to get out for supervised fresh air. (In addition to partial paralysis of her hind legs, she had a slightly wayward left eye related to a previous injury.)

One big problem: Goldie could not use a litter box. Squatting normally to urinate or defecate was impossible for her. So I set up wee-wee pads in the house that she learned to use, or I supervised so she could go outside. She would slide to the grass and tilt her hips to pee, and then slide back to the house. Goldie had the most serious mobility issue of any pet I had ever adopted, but she weighed only 10 pounds, so she was easy to manage and still got herself around fairly well.

Mobility issues in senior cats

Dozens of diseases or conditions can cause mobility trouble in cats. A broken leg or a sprained ligament not only causes short-term incapacity, it may lead to joint changes and lifetime lameness. A wound infection that spreads to a bone or joint can cause limping and other serious consequences. A blood clot (such as a saddle thrombus that blocks blood supply to the hindlimbs in some cats who have heart disease) or a fibrocartilaginous embolism (a clot that consists of soft spinal column material that breaks away and lodges in a spinal cord blood vessel) can cause inability to walk.

Diabetic cats who don't receive diabetes treatment or who don't respond well to treatment may end up with nerve damage and reduced sensation in their limbs, called *diabetic neuropathy*. These cats stand and walk flat-footed in their hindlimbs (called *plantigrade stance*)—their ankles are sunk close to or are touching the ground. The front legs are also sometimes affected (called *palmigrade stance*). This mobility issue can improve with treatment that controls the cat's blood sugar levels. About 30% of diabetic cats, especially those who don't respond to insulin treatment, also have a disorder called *acromegaly*, in which the body produces too much growth hormone. A double whammy: excess growth hormone can also harm a cat's bones, joints, and muscles.

With aging, the intervertebral disks that sit between the spinal bones (vertebrae) to provide cushioning and spinal flexibility can degenerate. These "shock absorbers" are made of fibrous cartilage that surrounds a soft gel-like material. If the disks stiffen with age, they can slip out of position (herniate) and put pressure on the spinal cord. This condition is called *intervertebral disk disease*. Depending on the amount or force of the pressure, a gradual or a sudden onset of back or neck pain, limb weakness, and paralysis occurs. Fortunately, cats infrequently experience intervertebral disk herniation (unlike dogs and people do).[3]

Instead, geriatric cats often have bone spurs along their vertebrae, called *spondylosis deformans*.[4] These bony growths develop with aging, perhaps to support the spine as the intervertebral disks stiffen and reduce spinal joint stability. Cats with spondylosis may show no signs of discomfort, and veterinarians identify it when they take x-rays for other reasons. But if the bony growths are large or press on a nerve, cats may have stiffness or show signs of pain (crying out when being petted or brushed, or limping). In one study, cats with spondylosis of the lower back showed less willingness to be petted and greet people, became more aggressive, and had a poor quality of life, according to their pet parents.[4]

Spinal tumors and brain tumors can also cause mobility problems. Lymphoma is a cancer that stems from overproduction of immune system cells called lymphocytes, and it creates severe mobility issues if it spreads to the spinal cord. Advanced imaging tests (CT, MRI) can help confirm a diagnosis.

If an older cat suddenly develops swelling and lameness that affects only one leg or one shoulder, my mind jumps to trauma first, then to a type of bone cancer, called *osteosarcoma*. Radiographs and biopsy help with the diagnosis. Osteosarcoma can't be cured, but amputation removes the source of pain and gives cats a better quality of life. Cats with three legs do well and can be active and happy! In one study, cats who had osteosarcoma lived for a range of about 9.5 months to 30 months after amputation, even though the cancer had spread to other parts of the body in 40% of the cats.[5]

Despite all these problematic possibilities, the mobility issues that most commonly bother geriatric cats include overgrown claws, arthritis, obesity, and sarcopenia (muscle loss associated with aging).

Toenail troubles

Broken or overgrown toenails are irritating and can be painful and cause lameness. Geriatric cats who are less active and infrequently "sharpen their claws" (scratch to remove their nail sheaths)—possibly because they have other joint pain—may have nails that grow under and into their footpads. In addition, geriatric cats may not fully retract their claws because of joint or tendon weakness, and partially retracted, overgrown claws hamper a cat's traction on slippery floors, which could lead to further injury. Regularly trim (or ask your veterinary team to trim) your cat's claws to reduce snagging on carpet, furniture, blankets, and your clothes and help prevent joint strain or a stumble.

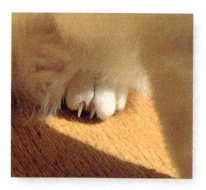

This geriatric kitty couldn't fully retract two claws on her left hind foot. This problem can make the nails appear longer than they are, so take care to not cut them too short (avoid the pink part—called the quick—that contains the blood and nerve supply) during trims.

Arthritis

Arthritis (also called *osteoarthritis* and *degenerative joint disease*) means joint inflammation. It not only causes mobility problems, it is painful and can make cats grumpy. Perhaps more than 60% of cats will have arthritis in their lifetime,[2,6] and it's an even more widespread problem in geriatric cats.[7] Cats most often have arthritis in their elbows and hips, but their knees, ankles, shoulders, and wrists can also be affected.

> **Where bones meet**
>
> Usually two (and sometimes three) bones meet at a joint. Joints typically allow movement and flexibility, with a few exceptions. Cats have hundreds of joints, and there are three types:
>
> - Fibrous joints are made of fibrous tissue, and they don't allow movement. The joints between the bones that protect the brain are fibrous joints.
>
> - Cartilaginous joints contain cartilage and allow some movement. For example, the joints between the bones in the spine are cartilaginous and allow flexibility.
>
> - Synovial joints are surrounded by a capsule that contains a lubricant called *synovial fluid*. These joints, such as the knee, hip, elbow, and shoulder, allow the most movement; the ends of the bones that meet in synovial joints are covered in thin cartilage.

Changes that lead to arthritis

Cats and people tend to develop what's known as *primary arthritis*—arthritis that develops because of degenerative, wear-and-tear changes in the joints that occur with advanced age.

Other factors may be associated with arthritis in cats. In one study of 238 cats whose owners said their cats exhibited mobility changes, cats who were overweight or obese, were neutered at 6 months of age or later, had previous trauma (e.g. had fallen or jumped from a tall structure, had been hit by a car, had been bitten by a dog or cat), or were allowed outdoors were twice as likely to have signs of degenerative joint disease by the time they were 6 years old (as reported by their pet parents) than cats who did not experience these things.[8]

Joint instability from inherited growth deformities (such as hip or elbow dysplasia) and from knee problems (such as cranial cruciate ligament injury, called an *anterior cruciate ligament* [or *ACL*] *tear* in people) or patella luxation (kneecap dislocation) can also cause arthritis, although these problems aren't common in cats.

Regardless of the cause—whether it's injury, infection, overload, hereditary conditions, degenerative changes, or (rarely in cats) cancer or an overactive immune system that attacks the joints—inflammation and other changes in the joints trigger thinning of the cartilage. Then the joint capsule, ligaments, and tissues around the joint may thicken to help stabilize the joint, and swelling from fluid buildup in the joint occurs. At this point, stiffness and pain enter the scene. Cartilage contains no nerves, so as more cartilage wears away, pain results from bone-on-bone friction.

Identifying arthritis

To diagnose arthritis, veterinarians start by asking questions such as:
Does your cat...

- chase toys?
- run normally?
- walk up and down stairs normally?
- jump up to and down from furniture, perches, tables, counters, etc. normally?[9]

Has your cat shown changes in:

- using the litter box?
- self-grooming?
- using a scratching post?
- climbing a cat tree?
- social interactions and mood?

Then veterinarians do a thorough physical examination, which includes assessing your cat's weight and muscle condition, feeling your cat's joints and checking their range of motion, and evaluating nerve function. They'll also take x-rays, and cats may also need blood tests or joint fluid evaluation.

Calvin couldn't squat to eliminate because of his arthritis. It's a common sign of discomfort, but pet parents often don't notice.

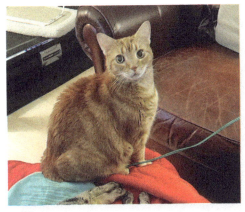
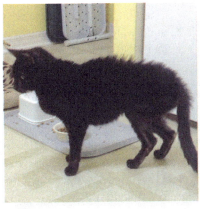

Spencer has arthritis in his spine. The messy fur that's slightly sticking up along his backbone indicated that he couldn't easily groom there, which alerted his mom that something was wrong.

Lance groomed himself less because he had arthritis.

Treating arthritis

Sadly, no cure exists for arthritis once it's established, so earlier diagnosis and earlier intervention is best. For example, surgery corrects deformities and repairs traumatic injuries, antibiotics treat joint infections, and other types of therapies slow progressive degenerative joint changes. Veterinarians often recommend multiple management options that work best together, starting with weight control—which means staying on the skinny side of normal body condition. Veterinary therapeutic diets formulated for weight loss and weight management help, along with low-impact exercise such as taking a stroll—cats can be trained to walk with a harness and leash—on land and even in shallow water on an underwater treadmill!

Additional helpful therapies may include veterinary prescribed:

- anti-inflammatory and pain relief medications (never give medications intended for people to your cat);
- polysulfated glycosaminoglycan, a disease-modifying osteoarthritis drug;
- frunevetmab, a monoclonal antibody that binds to nerve growth factor and blocks its harmful signals (quick deets: nerve growth factor contributes to painful conditions in adult animals, and monoclonal antibodies are molecules that mimic some of the body's natural disease-fighting abilities);[10-12]
- omega-3 fatty acids from fish oil;
- therapeutic diets formulated for cats with joint disease;

- rehabilitation therapy exercises;
- underwater treadmill activities;
- therapeutic massage;
- laser therapy;
- therapeutic ultrasound; and
- acupuncture.

Whew!

Bottom line: Even once arthritis is established, it's a manageable condition. For overweight or obese cats who have arthritis, veterinarian-guided gradual weight loss (to avoid triggering feline fatty liver disease) with a lifelong nutritional plan to maintain a lean body condition and support muscle mass is the single most important therapy. For more information on how to tell whether your cat is chubby, see Chapter 9 "Body condition and nutrition: Helping senior cats eat better and feel better."

Activity is still key for cats with arthritis. So if cats don't have another medical condition that precludes moderate activity, take advantage of the times of day your cat is motivated to scout about (like before mealtimes!). Try daily leash walks to explore the outdoors, short play periods with different types of toys, and teaching new tricks. Work up to longer walks and playtimes gradually, to avoid stiffness and soreness. Also talk with your veterinarian about whether additional pain relief medications will help.

Does my arthritic cat need glucosamine?

Supplements that contain glucosamine and are intended for joint support in pets abound, but studies that confirm glucosamine's benefits in pet cats with arthritis do not. In one study in 59 cats with degenerative joint disease, glucosamine didn't help more than a placebo (a "sugar pill" without glucosamine) did.[13] In another study of 30 cats over 8 years of age who had chronic osteoarthritis, the cats who received glucosamine did not improve compared with cats who received a veterinary nonsteroidal anti-inflammatory drug.[14]

More studies may settle whether glucosamine helps cats with arthritis, but for now the benefits remain unconfirmed. If you're considering giving a joint support supplement to your cat, talk with your veterinarian about their recommendations, and look for supplements that follow National Animal Supplement Council (NASC) and Current Good Manufacturing Practice (CGMP) guidelines.

Obesity: Less food for thought

I'm pounding on this topic a bit because being overweight can contribute to not only arthritis, but to mobility issues of all types and to other health problems in pets.

Cats with mobility issues who are also overweight are more reluctant to exercise. So you'll need to gradually introduce a new or enhanced exercise regimen. One potentially fun option: veterinary rehabilitation therapy centers offer training and programs for obese cats to do underwater treadmill workouts to help them slim down! Whichever "workout" activities you choose, ask your veterinarian about medications to reduce your cat's discomfort so she can be more active and reach her target weight at an appropriate rate.[15] Pain-free exercise, along with environmental enrichment activities that promote appropriate food intake—such as food puzzles or scatter feeding—are also good for your cat's overall attitude and general health.

 YES–cats can do underwater treadmills!

 Clifford is 8 years old in this picture and looks cozy, but his obesity will likely cause issues later in life!

 My cat Mingo is missing a back foot and has arthritis in her spine, so she is on a weight loss program to help ease her discomfort.

201

 Jake was as an obese boy and was unable to groom himself, so he had severe matting and skin irritation (with physical discomfort and poor emotional well-being). Fortunately, Jake was adopted and cared for!

 Marmot is fed with a slow-feeder bowl to make him work a bit for his food.

While exercise boosts weight loss and improves mobility, an obese cat's path to a healthy weight begins with her family dishing out less food and treats, or with serving a veterinary-prescribed food for weight loss in the right amount. About 90% of weight control involves the amount of calories consumed, and about 10% involves calories burned through increased activity. Cat parents and other family members are fully in charge of helping their feline friends get lean, both by limiting calories and by helping them burn calories by encouraging activity.

Sarcopenia and cachexia

I talk more about these two muscle wasting processes in Chapter 9 "Body condition and nutrition: Helping senior cats eat better and feel better," so I'll give a quick review here.

Sarcopenia is muscle loss that occurs with aging, and cachexia is muscle loss triggered by diseases such as congestive heart failure or cancer. Muscle loss hinders strength and contributes to mobility problems. Geriatric cats who have chronic diseases may have both sarcopenia and cachexia. Muscle loss is not as easy to spot in cats who are overweight.

The most effective way to help cats who have cachexia is for veterinarians to treat the underlying illness and help you provide supportive care. Supportive care for cats with sarcopenia or cachexia helps them stay strong and may include:

- **EXERCISE!** Resistance exercises increase strength and muscle mass and can slow or reverse muscle loss, and endurance exercises build power that allows the muscles to better use oxygen for energy.[16] A balanced resistance and endurance exercise program done three days a week is physically and mentally beneficial for pets.[17]
- **MIRTAZAPINE (MIRATAZ) OR CAPROMORELIN (ELURA).** These appetite stimulants help cats get the calories they need.
- **OMEGA-3 FATTY ACID SUPPLEMENTS.** These may help reduce inflammation, decrease muscle loss, and improve appetite.[16] Ask your veterinarian about the right type and dose for your cat.
- **OPTIMAL NUTRITION.** This involves feeding a diet that is appropriate for a cat's life stage, or feeding a therapeutic diet to manage a chronic disease, if indicated—along with using assisted feeding techniques such as a feeding tube, if needed.[16]

Until veterinarians know more about the best ways to combat or reverse sarcopenia and cachexia, it appears that an exercise program tailored to an individual cat's needs and limitations, along with diet changes or supplements, if needed, are excellent options. Your veterinarian can suggest an appropriate exercise program or help you find a veterinary rehabilitation therapy specialist, and can evaluate whether your cat needs additional therapies.

When to see your veterinarian

Limping is an obvious sign of a mobility problem, but a cat's signs can be subtle, such as no longer luxuriously stretching after their nap, or jumping on a chair first to get up to or down from their perch, rather than jumping directly to where they want to be. Cats who get grumpy or become less social or who lash out could have pain associated with mobility troubles, or they may be afraid of not being able to move away from people or other pets quickly.[18]

Keep an eye out for these signs as your cat ages. The earlier you spot mobility issues, the sooner your veterinarian can find the cause and have a better opportunity to provide effective treatments to keep your cat strong and stable. Cats with mobility issues may:

- walk slower to greet you;
- be reluctant to jump up to or down from furniture or favorite perches (for example, first jump onto a chair, then onto the table instead of jumping from the floor to the table with ease);
- climb or descend stairs slower;
- "bunny hop" while descending stairs;
- play less enthusiastically;

- reluctantly run or chase toys;
- show less interest in social interactions with human or pet family members;
- spend more time sleeping;
- spend less time grooming;
- stop using their scratching post;
- have decreased range of motion (seem less flexible and show more stiffness) or limp;
- hesitate to get up;
- no longer get up to greet you;
- have trouble getting into position to urinate or defecate;
- have a hard time getting into or out of the litter box, or stop using the litter box;
- eat or drink less because of pain or because their bowls are inconveniently located (for example, must use the stairs to get to their food or water);
- have difficulty getting on or off the couch or the bed;
- be more irritable, aggressive, or fearful when being petted or in similar; situations—may swat at someone trying to pet them, or dodge being groomed even though they previously enjoyed these interactions
- stumble or otherwise be unsteady;
- have fecal incontinence (this can be a sign of a nerve problem that also affects mobility); and
- be constipated (cats who have spondylosis deformans, especially if it occurs in their lower back, are more likely to have constipation than cats who have normal spines).[19]

It helps to take short videos that demonstrate your cat's mobility troubles at home and share them with your veterinarian. Cats often behave differently in an exam room, so their signs of discomfort may be less obvious during a veterinary visit.[20] If you are a gadget fan, Fitbit-like activity monitors are available for cats that allow you to track changes in your cat's movement habits and objectively gauge their response to various treatments. One fitness monitor recently developed in Japan can even track the number of a cat's jumps and tell the difference between a cat's resting and sleeping times.[21]

Helping senior cats move along

Reduced mobility, especially if it's accompanied by discomfort can adversely affect a cat's quality of life. In the remaining sections of this chapter, I'll share strategies to help you help your cat be more comfortable, get around easier, look better, and safeguard his mental well-being, as well as possibly help your cat socialize more, be in a better mood, and have more energy and enthusiasm.

Keep in mind that your cat's personality affects how well you can administer medications and how often you can make veterinary healthcare visits. If car trips or giving pills to your cat make your cat especially fearful, anxious, or frustrated, the benefits of treatment and your bond with your cat may be negatively impacted. Work closely with your veterinarian to balance the pros and cons of each type of treatment with your cat's comfort and your bond to find alternatives as needed and ensure your cat and you experience the fewest stressors associated with treatment.[22]

Pain relief medications

Relieving pain that often accompanies short- or long-term mobility problems is a big component of managing these cats, along with addressing whatever underlying issue may be contributing to the problem. Pain relief not only helps cats want to stay active, it improves their quality of life. Chronic, unrelieved pain causes emotional distress, along with physical changes in the spinal cord that heighten pain sensation, making pain more difficult to treat. Pain is the number one reason that pet parents elect to euthanize their pets.

It's important to learn how to recognize whether your cat has discomfort so you can tell your veterinarian, who can make treatment adjustments. For a closer look at signs of pain, see Chapter 20 "Pain: If only our cats could talk about discomfort, malaise, anxiety, and suffering." Keep in mind that arthritis and other types of mobility-associated pain may flare up periodically, so adjustments in pain medications will likely often be needed.

A sneak peek at a critical take-home from the chapter on pain: **Never give your own anti-inflammatory or pain relief medication to your cat**, closely follow the dosing schedule for the medications your veterinarian prescribes, and tell your veterinarian about any other medications or supplements your cat is receiving.

Rehabilitation therapy

The goals of veterinary rehabilitation therapy are to stabilize, renew, and support a cat's optimal function and quality of life in relation to mobility, while minimizing the signs and limitations caused by their condition, disease, or injury.[17] A variety of exercises, treatments, and massage are available to improve cats' flexibility, range of motion, muscle strength, balance, and endurance. Rehabilitation therapy helps cats who have a wide range of mobility issues, including those related to nerve damage.

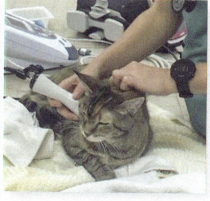

 Dr. Tammy Johnson helps JJ use a balance disc to improve balance, coordination, and leg strength during rehabilitation therapy.

 Sweet 13-year-old Tullah had arthritis in her right forelimb and benefited from laser therapy.

We know that after nerve injury in people, evidence backs using a combination of rehabilitation therapies to promote quicker and better recoveries.[23] Similarly, a general recommendation for managing pets who are recovering from certain neurologic disorders suggests that combination therapy may provide the most benefits—for example, combining a rehabilitation therapy program with neuromuscular electrical stimulation (using a low-frequency current to trigger a nerve to induce muscle contraction) and acupuncture.[23]

I cannot say enough about veterinary rehabilitation therapy exercises, underwater treadmill therapy, laser therapy, massage, and acupuncture to help pets who have mobility issues. Starting treatments sooner rather than later is advisable. While trying these therapies is worthwhile at nearly any stage, waiting until mobility is badly compromised makes managing it more difficult. Veterinarians who have this extra expertise can also teach you how to do specific exercises and therapeutic massage that's appropriate for helping your cat at home. I list resources at the end of this chapter to help you find people who can develop the right rehabilitation therapy program for your cat.

Part of this kitty's rehabilitation therapy for arthritis included a home cavaletti setup— elevated poles that cats are trained and enticed to step over to promote strength and balance.

CAREGIVER TIPS AND HOME HACKS

Adjusting the home environment and using mobility aids as needed so that cats with mobility issues can more easily navigate their space go a long way in improving their quality of life. It also keeps cats safer by helping to prevent injuries and extra veterinary visits.

LOW-ENTRY AND EASY ACCESS LITTER BOXES

Replace standard size litter boxes with roomier (at least 1.5 times the length of your cat) and shorter ones. For examples, see Chapter 14 "Incontinence and other potty problems: Thinking outside the box." Or add a slip-resistant bath step in front of a standard size litter box as a transition step to ease your cat's climb into and out of the box. Bath steps have rubber feet and a rubber top to provide stability and traction.

Place litter boxes in the locations that are easiest for your cat to access. For example, if your cat has trouble navigating stairs, they may stop using their basement or upper level litter box. Consider adding a litter box or two so your cat has more potty options. And you may need to reduce the litter depth to one or two inches, because some cats with mobility problems have trouble maneuvering in deeper cat litter.

A ROOMY TAXI

Not all cats will cheerfully enter (or willingly exit) their cat carriers. So if your cat isn't trained to go in and out on command (or is, but still balks), take care not to cram him into his carrier, and don't drag or shake him out of the carrier. Use a carrier that has ample room to easily place your cat inside, and one that allows a gentle way to lift your cat out (a sufficiently wide and tall side door or a top-opening door) in case he refuses to exit on his own. Place a comfy pad inside, one that also provides traction during transport.

NO SLIP SLIDING AWAY

Slippery surfaces can be a hindrance for cats with mobility issues. The more slippery the floor is, the more effort a cat will need to stay steady on it. And this means less exercise overall because they hesitate to run and play, plus they have a higher risk of stumbling or sliding awkwardly and tweaking a muscle or ligament in the process.

MAKE 'EM STICK

Create a path on slippery floors that helps cats get a grip, walk and run confidently, and remain safe.

FLOORING

When it comes to creating a slip-resistant pathway, the key is to buy heavier products with high-quality rubber backing. If a bath mat or area rug is flimsy, you may trip over or slide on it yourself. Your home may not look exquisitely decorated while you're making accommodations for your geriatric cat, but your cat won't mind!

- **Yoga mats.** Lining slippery floors with these provides wonderful support for cats. Bonus: They're easy to clean! You can purchase large rolls and cut the mats to fit your needs. Also place a mat at your cat's food and water bowls so she can stay steady while she eats and drinks.
- **Bath mats/rugs.** Because most bathroom floors have nonporous surfaces like tile, bath mats usually have a non-skid rubber underside. Like yoga mats, you can place them on slippery pathways throughout your home, but the topside is fluffy and comfy for cats to lie on.
- **Ruggable.com.** This website has beautiful, water-resistant, stain-resistant rugs in all different sizes and colors that feature a non-slip rubber bottom and a machine-washable rug top. They keep cats steady and protect hardwood floors!
- **Gym flooring.** These interlocking, square rubber floor tiles fit together like a puzzle and are popular in gyms and children's play areas. They're squishy and comfortable to lie on. greatmats.com
- **Carpet stairs.** For wood or tile stairs and landings, place a carpet runner or carpet stair treads on a staircase, and add non-slip mats at the top and bottom.
- **Gritty stickers.** Similar to those '70s era, non-slip, flower-power stickers for the shower, non-slip stickers or sticker strips work great for slippery surfaces and outdoor steps.

FOOT CARE

- **Grooming.** Trim your cat's nails and keep them short. This can be the

 Spike likes to drink in the sink, but arthritis made him slip. His mom stuck gritty stickies in the sink so he sips with a grip!

least expensive (but not always the easiest) measure to help keep your cat steady.

- **Anti-slip socks.** Depending on your cat's mobility issue and tolerance-for-wearing-things level, your cat may benefit from sporting one or more socks with grip pads on the soles during certain times of the day—say, for scheduled exercise or play times, or for visits to the veterinary rehabilitation therapy center. Choose socks that securely stay put, are not too heavy, and can breathe a little. Remember to take these along when you visit a friend's home or the veterinary clinic so your cat can strut with added confidence.

HARNESSES

In general, wearing a harness while walking on a leash is more comfortable and safer for a geriatric (or any age!) cat than wearing a collar.

For cats who have severe mobility issues I recommend only one type of harness, the Help 'Em Up Harness: **helpemup.com/**. I have tried many different harnesses for pets, and this one is worth every penny. (Remember, I don't receive monetary or other compensation from companies whose products I recommend in this book!) It's built with high-quality materials, is thoughtfully designed, and comes in a configuration that allows pets to urinate without soiling the harness. The Help 'Em Up Harness is wonderful for pets with front- and hind-end mobility issues.

 Cats who need lift support during outdoor excursions can wear the X-Small Help 'Em Up Harness (it's designed for dogs that weigh 10 to 25 lb, but it works for many cats).

WHEELCHAIRS AND DRAG BAGS

Cats may need a scooter or wheelchair when their mobility is so badly affected that they can barely walk or are completely paralyzed. Cats may also benefit from using one so they can continue to explore the outdoors with you. It can help keep up their strength and improve their quality of life—and help you maintain yours! Manufacturers that I suggest include:

- Walkin' Pets Walkin' Scooter (indoor use)
  handicappedpets.com/walkin-scooter/
- Walkin' Pets Walkin' Wheels (outdoor/indoor use)
  handicappedpets.com/walkin-wheels-cat-wheelchair/

- K9 Carts (outdoor/indoor use) **k9carts.com/cat-wheelchair/**
- Eddie's Wheels for Pets (outdoor/indoor use) **eddieswheels.com/gallery/4/0/Cats**)

It's extremely important that you work with the manufacturer or veterinary rehabilitation therapist to get the best fit possible. They will also walk you through how to get your cat accustomed to the assist device so your cat learns to appreciate it and uses it to their full potential.

Cats who can't walk may prefer a drag bag instead of a wheelchair. This covering prevents skin lesions that result from cats dragging themselves around and helps them stay cleaner. One example: **barkertime.com/product-category/drag-bag/** My cat Goldie preferred to zoom across our tile floor 'au natural' without a drag bag, but this accessory is an excellent option for some cats.

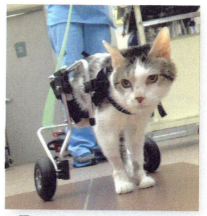
Juno is learning to walk in her new cart.

PET "RVS"

It's not uncommon to see cats in pet strollers, perhaps because they never took to harness and leash walking or because they insist on walking at their own pace off the beaten path. Cats with limited mobility also benefit from strollers and other vehicles of adventure so that they can continue to enjoy the scents in the air and the wind in their fur, even if their owner does all the work!

Walking strollers, jogging strollers, and bike trailers that have sturdy wheels and a big cabin window, and specially designed pet carrier backpacks and bicycle baskets are all options so you can stay active while entertaining your workout buddy.

Lestat enjoys strolling in a Texsens Backpack Pet Carrier (texsens.com/desktops) and looks dapper in a Rabbitgoo harness (rabbitgoo.com/collections/best-cat-harness).

STEPS AND RAMPS

Cats with mobility issues still need to be allowed access to their favorite vertical (higher up) spaces and perches, in order to preserve their sense of safety and ability to retreat. A wide variety of pet steps and pet ramps are available to help your cat reach the windowsill, bed, couch, or cat tree—or you can build your own! Ramps can also be a good alternative to the stairs around your home. Alpha Paw offers sturdy, adjustable pet ramps: **alphapaw.com**.

 Bumble, who has arthritis, uses stairs that help him get up to and down from his favorite sunny window seat.

 Spike shows off his climbing skills. His mom set up several mobility boost options throughout their house to help Spike live comfortably with arthritis.

 This kitty couldn't jump from the floor onto his cat tree bed anymore, so the family arranged the furniture so that he could get on the couch, on the end table, and up to the napping spot.

 This kitty appreciated the addition of a stepstool next to the sunny cat seat.

 A simple, single step stool can create a helpful intermediate step for your kitty.

If your steps are too steep for your cat, consider a ramp instead, placed next to or over the steps. Keep in mind the physics of going uphill and downhill for our furry friends. As they walk uphill, most of their weight shifts to their hind end. And when they walk downhill, their weight shifts to the front end. Weakness or pain in either area can still make it difficult for a cat to use a ramp or steps, so a gradual incline is best wherever possible.

 This family placed a ramp to help their senior kitty get to the couch.

Ramp and step training

If your cat isn't inclined to use a ramp, begin training by placing the ramp flat on the ground and using treats or toys to entice them to walk on it—like a wide balance beam. Do this for one week. Then create a slight incline by placing a brick under one end of the ramp. Teach them to walk on the raised ramp until they are comfortable. Then prop one end of the ramp on a stairstep to increase the incline and teach them to use that. Continue to increase the incline until your cat is using the ramp to get where they need to be.

Similarly, use treats or another of your cat's favorite enticements to train them to use pet stairs. Place a treat at the base of the stairs, and when your cat takes that, place a treat on the first step. Repeat this until your cat comfortably takes a treat off the first step. Then place a treat on the first and the second step. Practice until your cat comfortably stands on or walks up each step and takes the treats from each one. Remember to reward at the top—your cat should get a treat for standing on the bed or couch. Repeat this process to train your cat to comfortably walk back down each step. You can gradually decrease the treats and reward only at the top or bottom of the stairs. Once your cat is fully confident, reward them at random intervals for using the steps to help hold their interest.

MISCELLANEOUS MOBILITY CONSIDERATIONS

- **Bedding.** A cat with mobility issues may struggle to get in and out of an overly cushy or fluffy cat bed. Instead, consider an orthopedic pet bed that is comfy yet provides adequate support. Water-resistant baby "nests" are appropriate for some cats.

    o If your cat is bedridden, be vigilant about warding off pressure sores—these can develop on your cat's elbows, shoulders, hocks, knees, hips, and head. Pressure sores are uncomfortable and can become irritated and infected. Help your cat turn over—from one side, then to the middle, then to the other side—so they can rest in a different position every two or three hours. Use appropriately

 Duncan loved his orthopedic bed!

sized memory foam pads under bony contact points and help your cat maintain normal, neutral, non-stress body positions. Memory foam is available in many sizes and shapes, and some can be cut and customized.

One pet mom created a ramp to a wide perch so her kitty could still enjoy the windowsill.

- **Access.** Most senior kitties still love to gaze outdoors, so create a safe and sturdy perch for them to scout their territory!
- **Warmth.** The temperature range in which our feline friends don't have to burn extra calories to stay warm or cool off is called the *thermoneutral zone*, and it's 86 F to 100 F (30 C to 38 C).[24] This is not surprising, because cats routinely seek sunbeams, warm laps, and other toasty spots. So ensuring access to extra warmth is probably even more important for cats with mobility issues who are less active, underweight, or have muscle loss from sarcopenia or cachexia.[25] I know many geriatric cats

Senior cats love sunny window beds!

Bumble in his other favorite spot: on the (cool-touch) electric fireplace next to the window.

who nap in sunny windowsills and slumber in their heated cat beds! (A comfy cat bed placed halfway over a floor heating vent is an option, too.) Just be sure your cat can freely move off of a heated bed and has another comfy sleep option when they prefer one.
- **Safety.** Sometimes cats with severe mobility issues can get into difficult situations. Create a safe spot where you can leave your cat unattended when necessary and where she's unlikely to get hurt if she stumbles or gets stuck.

Similarly, cats with arthritis may have anxiety related to physical discomfort, and in turn, anxiety may aggravate pain. Anxiety can also arise from fear of not being able to quickly escape from a stressful situation, so be sure your cat can easily retreat to his safe space (including his vertical spaces) when he wants solitude. Consider installing an interior pet door so your cat can access his safe room on his own terms. If your cat is irritable or aggressive related to discomfort or fear, supervise your pet's interactions with visitors. You may need to move your cat to another room while you have houseguests, especially when young children visit.

 Spike's elevated, angled food and water bowls make dining more comfortable for him.

 Spike also had the option of sipping from a Magic Feline Fountain.
mylovelyfeline.com/products/the-magic-feline-fountain

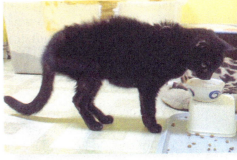

 Luther began eating more of his meals after his food bowl was raised.

- **Food and water bowls.** Elevating a cat's bowls to the height of their elbows can reduce neck, elbow, and back pressure and strain.
- **Pheromones.** These calming chemical messengers (such as Feliway and similar products) delivered via room diffusers, sprays, and collars can help alleviate anxiety and promote grooming behavior in cats.[25]
- **Scratching posts.** Continue to encourage your cat to use these. Cats with osteoarthritis benefit from scratching behavior and stretching.[25] So in addition to providing a traditional tall, sturdy, vertical scratcher, explore horizontal or angled scratching posts with different scratching surface options: cardboard, sisal fabric, or wood, or a firewood or driftwood log that stays put. Place scratching posts next to your cat's favorite sleeping spots, because they love to stretch and scratch when they first wake up.
- **Emergency pit stops.** Place disposable pet potty pads or cat litter pads near or en route to the litter box in case your cat can no longer hold it long enough to make it to their box. Place one in your cat's carrier in case of an accident during a trip.
- **Ice packs.** Icing arthritic joints is great after activity such as playing a gentle game of laser toy chase. Use the blue flexible type and keep them in place (NEVER place them directly on the skin; wrap them in a dish towel or pillowcase) for at least five minutes and ideally for 15 to 20 minutes. You can also wrap an ACE bandage around an elbow to provide additional compression. You can make your own flexible ice pack by mixing two parts water and one part rubbing alcohol in a freezer bag and placing it inside another freezer bag and then in the freezer. Don't use bags of frozen corn or peas because they contain too much air so they aren't cold enough for the cold to sufficiently penetrate the tissues.
- **Grooming and hygiene.** Cats with arthritis or other mobility troubles often can't reach all areas to self-groom effectively, so help your cat stay spiffy with gentle-touch grooming by using a soft comb or brush once a day. And if your cat has trouble washing her face and behind her ears after meals, she may learn to appreciate your help with this—use a warm, damp washcloth, then pat dry with a soft cloth, followed by a quick, light comb. If your cat persistently gets mats in spots she can't reach, consider trimming or clipping the fur in those areas.

Some cats with serious mobility issues have hygiene issues, especially if they have fecal or urinary incontinence or if they cannot posture properly to eliminate. To help reduce the mess, give a sanitary haircut by trimming the fur around the areas where urine or feces can linger, especially for medium- or long-haired cats. Keep pet wipes or unscented hypoallergenic baby wipes handy. Use pet pee pads or cat litter pads, perhaps along with baby changing pads, to help keep incontinent cats clean and comfortable and their beds and resting spots dry. Remember that cats who have fecal incontinence are more susceptible to urinary tract infections. Keep their rear ends clean and keep an eye out for signs of a urinary tract infection, such as urinating small amounts frequently or in odd locations.

Ending on a good note

Cats who have arthritis and some other types of mobility issues can't be cured, but comfort and a good quality of life are key. End-of-life decisions for cats struggling with mobility issues can be especially hard, but there may come a point when pain can no longer be managed. Routinely assessing your cat's life quality with respect to mobility, mood, discomfort level, physical appearance, social interactions, vitality and energy, and overall physical and mental well-being helps you monitor how well your support and treatments are working.[26] In turn, this allows you to work more closely with your veterinarian to adjust therapies as needed and, when the time comes, make a thoughtful, informed end-of-life decision.[25]

 ## Questions to ask your veterinarian

- What examinations or tests will my cat need?
- What can I expect to happen with my cat's condition? Will my cat regain normal mobility or activity levels again?
- Will my cat benefit from surgery?
- Is my cat overweight or obese? (Take no offense if the answer is "yes.")
- Has my cat lost muscle mass?
- Will diet adjustments or a veterinary therapeutic diet for weight control or joint support help my cat?
- What types of environmental alterations will my cat need?
- What types of exercise or environmental enrichment activities will help my cat?
- Will my cat benefit from pain relief medications?
- How will I know whether my cat's pain medications are working?
- Will nutritional or other types of supplements help my cat?
- Will my cat benefit from veterinary rehabilitation therapy or acupuncture?
- Do you offer rehabilitation therapy services? If not, will you refer me to a veterinary rehabilitation therapy practice or telemedicine service?

- Do you provide special padded bedding for my cat who has arthritis or mobility issues while my cat stays here?
- If my cat will be anesthetized for a procedure (for example, a professional dental cleaning), how can you ensure his position will be comfortable so he's not stiff and sore when he recovers?
- Can my cat be scheduled on a day when she can have a morning appointment or procedure and be discharged soon after? (So she doesn't have to wait in the clinic all day.)
- If my cat is especially stressed when I give him medications or travel frequently with him for his treatments or recheck appointments, what alternatives are available (such as different medication formulations or flavors, pre-appointment anti-anxiety measures or medications, in-home veterinary visits, telemedicine recheck appointments)?

READING RECOMMENDATIONS

- Arthritis & Degenerative Joint Disease in Cats. International Cat Care. icatcare.org/advice/arthritis-and-degenerative-joint-disease-in-cats/
- What's Your Pet's Score? Assessing Muscle Condition. Clinical Nutrition Service. Cummings School of Veterinary Medicine. Tufts University. vetnutrition.tufts.edu/2017/11/mcs/
- Global Nutrition Toolkit. (Contains links to information on assessing body condition, muscle condition, and nutrition in cats, and more.) World Small Animal Veterinary Association Global Nutrition Committee. wsava.org/wp-content/uploads/2021/04/WSAVA-Global-Nutrition-Toolkit-English.pdf

RESOURCES

- Information about amputation in pets. Tripawds. tripawds.com/
- American Association of Rehabilitation Veterinarians rehabvets.org/
- American College of Veterinary Sports Medicine and Rehabilitation — Search for a Specialist. vsmr.site-ym.com/search/custom.asp?id=5595

CHAPTER 17:

Cognition: Cross my mind... or not

"How do you run from what is inside your head?"

— Unknown

 Me and Bodhi

Bodhi, a skinny grey tiger cat, stared at me from behind the window of the pet food store. He was up for adoption with 20 other cats from a local rescue organization. I could tell he was a "teenager" (13 or more years old!) just by looking at him, and that alone drew me to him. Puffball kittens cuter than buttons clambered all around in the cages next to Bodhi's. But to me, Bodhi was the most attractive cat of the bunch.

I wasn't in the market for another pet, but I couldn't get Bodhi out of my mind. His cage card described how he had been found in a mall parking lot with a broken leg (that had since been repaired and healed) and that he was receiving subcutaneous (under the skin) fluids every day to manage his kidney failure. I thought, "Who will want this old cat with kidney disease when they have all these kittens to choose from?" The answer was obvious—it was going to be me!

Bodhi easily integrated into my household. He didn't pick fights with my other dogs and cats, and he was a loving lap cat—which was just what I needed. He must have been a big cat in his prime. But when I adopted him, he weighed

8 pounds, and he had the build of a typical geriatric cat with kidney failure: skinny, muscle wasting, and thin skin. I could easily feel the points of his skull, backbone, shoulders, hips, and knees when I petted him. Still, Bodhi was active, alert, and full of life.

Bodhi was awesome! He always wanted to be near me and didn't ask for much more than my lap to snooze in. His age was a mystery, but I guessed he was around 14 years old when I adopted him. Although I missed out on all his prime years, I was blessed to have him in my life. I frequently help families manage kidney failure in their cats, and Bodhi was easy for me to care for.

But about two years after I adopted Bodhi, he started to howl LOUDLY at night. It's a sound that I learned to dread. He'd usually begin at around 2 a.m., and he called like an old tomcat searching for his next mate. A long, deep howl (meeee-yowwwl!), then a 10-second pause, then another one. And another. And another... At first he howled only a few times, but eventually he went on for a good hour every night.

Bodhi's kidney disease was under control, and I was unable to find another illness that would cause his new and progressively worsening nighttime behavior. This was my first personal experience with cognitive dysfunction.

FUN FACT:

The Middle English words "cater" for tomcat and "waul" for mournful cry or "wauwen" for howl are the origins of the word "caterwaul."[1]

Signs of brain aging and cognitive decline

Many of my patients' families expect that their cats will experience age-related changes such as impaired vision and hearing, sleeping more, and playing less. But many pet parents are not aware that their cats can exhibit out-of-character conduct that shouldn't be chalked up to "normal aging," because it may be caused by changes in their cats' brains.

At any age, changes in a cat's typical behavior, activities, or temperament are good indicators of illness or a new behavior problem. But some senior cats exhibit odd behaviors and signs of mental deterioration that cannot otherwise be attributed to underlying medical or behavioral problems, nor to typical age-related sensory decline.

The behavior changes may be subtle at first, and pet parents tend to attribute them to their cats "just getting old" or "having senior moments." Affected cats sleep more than usual during the day and may be awake and restless or anxious at night. They may be more clingy at times and start sleeping in unusual places. They may weirdly meow randomly, especially at night. They sometimes seem confused and wander between rooms or try to wander away outdoors. They may have more accidents outside the litter box. Their thrill of playing or hunting for treats disappears, and they act grumpy or disinterested when other animal friends want to play. Of course cats who have fatigue, discomfort, or vision or hearing problems related to a variety of ailments can show these changes, too; but in senior cats, these signs may indicate diminished mental processes.

Some senior cats with these signs may have physical changes in their brains, such as tissue shrinkage and nerve loss,[2,3] buildup of protein fragments called beta-amyloid plaques, and twisted fibers of another protein called tau.[3-6] Such behavior changes, structural brain abnormalities, and toxic protein buildup correlate with some of the symptoms and brain changes that people with Alzheimer's disease have.[3,7]

In cats, these signs of age-related mental decline and possible brain abnormalities are called *cognitive dysfunction syndrome*, and it tends to progress with age, seriously affecting the cat's and family's daily quality of life. Affected cats may:[2,7-11]

- meow loudly or yowl randomly, especially at night;
- seek more attention, be more affectionate and seem more clingy;
- seek less attention and seem more aloof;
- become more irritable or aggressive toward other cat or dog housemates;
- sleep more during the day and in unusual spots;
- be more agitated or restless, especially at night;
- eliminate outside the litter box;
- wander aimlessly from room to room or wander away outdoors;
- seem confused or disconnected;
- not recognize their owners;
- be anxious about being left alone;
- have an increased fear of new environments; or
- be more reactive to sights and sounds.

Recognizing the signs of cognitive dysfunction earlier in the course of the disease gives cats and pet parents a better chance to effectively manage their cats' signs and relish more happy, good-quality-of-life days together. Apparently healthy cats can show signs of cognitive impairment as early as 8 years of age,[10] and abnormal changes in cats' brains have been seen as early as 6 years of age.[7] Cognitive deficits tend to progress, but the rate of these changes varies—they may progress slowly or quickly.[10] One way to track whether your cat may have changes related to cognition is to use the "Cognitive Assessment Checklist for Cats" at the end of this chapter. Monitor your middle-age and older cat, especially during her senior years, and go over it with your veterinarian if you notice changes.

How common is cognitive dysfunction?

Of cats who are 11 to 15 years of age, 28% have signs of cognitive dysfunction, and of cats who are older than 15, the percentage affected jumps to 50%.[8] According to the American Veterinary Medical Association (AVMA), in 2020 there were between 60 and 61.9 million pet cats in the United States.[12] And according to data from the AVMA in 2016, about 46% of pet cats are 6 years old or older, and 19% of these cats are 11 years old and up.[13] So these numbers suggest that more than three million senior cats in the U.S. have signs of cognitive dysfunction.

Is it cognitive dysfunction or another condition?

Because a diagnostic test isn't yet available to pinpoint cognitive dysfunction, veterinarians must make a *diagnosis of exclusion*. This means we look first for another medical or behavioral problem that could be causing the pet's signs. Your veterinarian may ask you to complete a questionnaire or checklist designed to screen senior cats for signs of cognitive dysfunction (similar to the checklist at the end of this chapter).

If your cat has signs of cognitive dysfunction, the problems your veterinarian may concentrate on ruling out first include:

- impaired hearing, vision, or smell that could be related to aging or other diseases;
- kidney disease;
- bladder or other lower urinary tract problems (inflammation, infection, stones, cancer);
- pain stemming from arthritis or dental, intestinal, or pancreatic disease;
- overactive thyroid gland (called *hyperthyroidism*);
- high blood pressure;
- diabetes;
- liver disease;
- viral or parasitic diseases such as feline immunodeficiency virus, feline leukemia virus, or toxoplasmosis (*Toxoplasma gondii* is a parasite cats can get from eating infected prey or raw meat);
- brain tumor;
- other types of behavior problems such as separation anxiety; or
- a side effect of a medication your cat is receiving.

Your veterinarian rules out these other conditions by taking a good medical and behavioral history, performing a thorough physical examination, and running routine blood and urine tests. Sometimes imaging exams (x-rays, ultrasound, computed tomography, or magnetic resonance imaging) are also helpful, as well as additional tests to assess heart, liver, kidney, or other organ function. Your veterinarian will also ask about all medications (including supplements or nutraceuticals, herbs, or over-the-counter drugs) your cat is receiving and any previously diagnosed behavior problems.

> **What's a nutraceutical?**
>
> A product formulated from bioactive compounds such as vitamins, minerals, probiotics, dietary fiber, herbal extracts, or other food substances—alone or in combination—and consumed to support health or well-being.

If your veterinarian identifies another condition, it can be treated or managed first to see whether your cat improves or the symptoms resolve.

Occasionally, diagnostic testing for other conditions can't be done because of a pet parent's budget limitations or because the cat needs immediate help to mitigate his symptoms. In that case, veterinarians may suggest starting therapy to alleviate signs of cognitive dysfunction, and then assessing the cat's response to therapy. If the cat doesn't respond as expected, additional diagnostic tests may still be needed to further explore the cause of the cat's symptoms.

What are the risk factors?

Our relationships with and caregiving for cats have progressed, along with vast improvements in pet nutrition and continual advances in veterinary diagnostics and treatments. It's wonderful that cats have longer lifespans as a result! And, not surprisingly, because cats are living longer, their risk of developing cognitive dysfunction increases as they age. In fact, age is the biggest risk factor for developing cognitive dysfunction.

People and dogs with various types of cognitive impairment have been studied more extensively compared with cats. So we don't know as much about the risk factors associated with this ailment in our feline friends. People who have conditions that hamper blood flow in the brain have a higher risk of cognitive impairment. And chronic illness and chronic stress are risk factors in people because they can lead to oxidative injury that damages many different cell types in the body, including in the brain. The same may hold true in pets. For example, people who have long-term painful conditions show faster cognitive decline than people without pain do, so it seems prudent to assess and monitor for cognitive impairment in cats who have chronic painful problems such as osteoarthritis.[14] One study in cats aged 8 years and up found an association between cats who lived in a rural community and having a reduced chance of cognitive dysfunction.[7] The authors stated that this finding suggests that more studies are needed to explore air pollution as a risk factor for cognitive decline in senior cats, as well as to uncover other risk factors.

FUN FACT:
USE THE DEEP SLEEP CYCLE TO CLEANSE YOUR BRAIN

Studies show that when people are sound asleep and experiencing heavy non-rapid eye movement slumber, our brains enjoy a gentle-waves bath of cerebrospinal fluid (fluid that protects and nourishes the brain and spinal cord) that washes away beta-amyloid and tau, two toxins that build up in the brain and are linked to Alzheimer's disease.[15,16] It's reassuring to me that pet cats are champs in the realm of catnaps!

Preventive measures and management

Identifying cognitive abnormalities earlier and starting supportive measures sooner may slow cognitive decline, which helps you maintain a happy relationship with your cat while fortifying your cat's overall well-being and quality of life.[10] And regardless of your cat's age or cognitive ability, cognitive support can be provided!

Hard fact: Cognitive dysfunction can't be cured. The goals of therapy are to lighten the physical and emotional toll on cats' daily activities and slow disease progression if possible. Caregiving requires patience and flexibility to find what works best for an individual pet and all affected family members.

To prevent or delay cognitive decline in cats, a multifaceted approach should provide the most benefit, and it includes:

- fine-tuning the home environment;
- giving supplements and perhaps transitioning to a different diet;
- administering medications when indicated;
- bolstering social interactions; and
- encouraging mental engagement.

That's a lot! So it's important to assess the level of emotional and financial investment you are willing to commit.

Below I outline measures to help you mitigate the effects of cognitive dysfunction in your cat. Keep in mind that as with many things, moderation is key! Making extreme changes to try to slow cognitive decline in a cat who is already moderately or severely affected may have the opposite effect. For example, if you bring a new kitten into your lifelong single-cat household in hopes of encouraging your older cat to be more active, or if you take your senior cat for a walk and your cat is not accustomed to being outside, you may introduce stress that intensifies your cat's signs of cognitive dysfunction. On the other hand, I have heard stories of geriatric cats who "act like kittens again" in response to families making such big changes!

In any case, consider your cat as an individual and introduce novel situations gradually and patiently. If you must make substantial changes to your cat's environment or routine, such as moving, traveling, boarding, or welcoming a baby or other new family member, do so as mindfully and slowly as possible so that your cat has time to acclimate well. For example, take your cat's most familiar, most favorite things along when changing locations, and expose your cat to a new family member's scents and accessories in small doses before their first face-to-face encounter.

Nutritional support

Certain nutrients are crucial in maintaining brain structure and function, so some dietary changes or supplements that attempt to prevent or correct detrimental changes in aging brains may ward off or slow cognitive decline.[10] We know that specific vitamins and other antioxidants, triglycerides and fatty acids, proteins (including amino acids and enzymes), plant extracts, minerals, and other nutritional support factors may act alone or together to influence brain processes. Such nutrients have many effects on cells and tissues, including reducing oxidative stress, assisting normal nerve function, influencing neurotransmitters (the chemical signals between nerve cells), changing blood vessel diameter, guiding gene expression, generating ketones (an alternative to glucose as an energy source), and enhancing mitochondria (the energy-producing mechanism in cells) function.

Diet

The brain uses glucose (sugar or carbohydrates) as its primary energy source, but senior brains don't process glucose as well.[10] In fact, dogs as young as 6 years of age (remember, dogs with cognitive dysfunction have been studied more than cats have been) may already be processing glucose less effectively in their brains—before they even show outward signs of cognitive decline!

Fortunately, the liver makes ketones (from fat in the diet or from body fat) that the body can use as an alternative energy source when glucose is in short supply, and the brain's ability to use ketones for energy stays steady during aging. *Ketogenic, or keto diets* shift the body's metabolism away from using glucose as energy and toward using ketones. Traditional ketogenic diets for people are extremely high in fat (70%) and low in protein (20%) and carbohydrates (10%).[10] People use keto diets for weight loss or to manage certain neurologic problems, but we have a hard time sticking with keto diets, and they can cause nutritional deficiencies.[10]

We know that traditional ketogenic diets don't work for dogs because dogs don't produce the same high levels of ketones that people do in response to these diets.[10]

However, supplementing the diet with specific types of fat molecules (called *medium-chain triglycerides;* MCTs) can promote ketone production in dogs without protein or carbohydrate restriction and perhaps supply energy that fuels cognitive function. MCTs have been shown to enhance cognitive function in healthy dogs and in dogs with cognitive dysfunction,[17,18] as well as reduce seizure frequency in dogs who have epilepsy.[19] Concentrated formulations of MCTs are included in some dog diets and supplements.[10] MCT-based ketogenic diets are also becoming popular with people because they don't require such a high-fat diet and are easier diets to stick to. Perhaps in the future, MCTs will be further studied to evaluate whether they support brain health and cognitive processes in cats.

Another pickle that crops up when the brain processes glucose less efficiently is oxidative stress. And oxidative stress—an imbalance between harmful and protective oxygen-containing molecules involved in cell metabolism—is associated with degenerative nervous system diseases and cognitive decline.[10] Thus, antioxidants—substances such as certain vitamins and other compounds that inhibit or slow oxidative stress—are a component of nutritional support for cognitive function. A one-year study in healthy middle-aged and older cats showed that cats who ate a diet supplemented with a nutrient blend of fish oil, arginine, B vitamins, and antioxidants (vitamins E and C and selenium) performed better on three of four tests of cognitive function than did cats who ate the same diet that didn't contain the nutrient blend supplement.[20]

So if your cat has cognitive dysfunction, talk with your veterinarian about which diet is best. Veterinary insight is important, especially if your cat has other medical conditions that influence which diet or supplements your cat can safely receive. A specific diet for cats who have cognitive dysfunction is not yet available, but I list examples of a few diets that may be beneficial at the end of this chapter.

If you need to switch to a new diet, do it gradually (see Chapter 9 "Body condition and nutrition: Helping senior cats eat better and feel better") to prevent your cat's gastrointestinal tract from going "cold turkey," which can cause distressing diarrhea and vomiting. And whenever possible, switch to a new diet when your cat is feeling relatively good. If your cat feels crummy when you try out a different diet, your cat may refuse to eat the new food and never venture to taste it again.

It's more than a gut feeling, it's a microbiome!

Did you know that the gut "talks" to the brain and that the brain responds? Research has revealed that the gut and the brain "discuss" many more things than whether you're hungry, say, for ice cream, or whether you're full and regret eating the entire carton.

In some ways, we've known this for a long time. Think about common expressions we use such as having "butterflies in my stomach" before performing, needing to "trust my gut instincts" when making some decisions, and getting a "sinking feeling in the pit of my stomach" in hazardous situations.

Cats' digestive tracts—and ours—contain billions (probably trillions) of tiny organisms: bacteria, viruses, fungi, and others. These itty bitty critters make up an ecosystem that functions as a metabolically active organ known as the *gut microbiome*.[21] The two-way communication between the gut microbiome and the brain is known as the *gut-brain-axis*. Their complex "conversation" occurs directly and speedily through the nervous system and via various hormones and other molecules that the microbiome organisms influence or produce.

The microbiome is shaped and affected by food and other dietary components, drugs such as antibiotics, and beneficial, live organisms known as *probiotics*. The balance between the good and not-so-good organisms that make up the gut microbiome is important for digestive health, but this balance also has a broader influence. The microbiome and brain also communicate about immunity, metabolism, and mood.

For example, people who have irritable bowel syndrome (IBS) have a higher rate of depression and anxiety compared with people who do not have IBS. Physicians used to think that depression and anxiety contributed to IBS. But evidence suggests that the gastric system nerves in people who experience the bloating, pain, and stool abnormalities of IBS send signals to the brain that can spark mood disorders.[22]

Researchers now know that mental processes aren't regulated only by the brain and spinal cord, and that the gut microbiome influences cognition and several brain disorders in people, including depression,

> anxiety, and Alzheimer's disease.[23] The microbiome may play a role in triggering dysfunction of the immune cells (called *microglia*) in the brain, which contributes to amyloid buildup. Amyloid buildup can be found in the brains of people with Alzheimer's disease and in the brains of cats with cognitive dysfunction.
>
> And in cats, the good, or probiotic, gut bacteria called *Bifidobacterium longum* are associated with anxiety relief.[10] Probiotics are available as nutritional supplements for cats, such as Calming Care (Purina Pro Plan Veterinary Supplements).
>
> The "discussions" between the brain and the gut will continue to be explored in people and in pets. We have much more to learn about the many ways nutrition may be used to influence brain health and well-being.

Supplements and nutraceuticals

In people, limited evidence shows that some supplements may preserve or enhance cognitive function, but, as with drug treatments, an individual's response can be influenced by genes, their health and nutritional status, and other factors.

Overall, studies of nutritional interventions in cats with cognitive dysfunction are also limited, and it can be difficult to conclude which supplements or dietary modifications will benefit affected cats. Nutrients likely work better in combination than does a single nutrient.[10] In any case, supplements alone likely will not relieve a cat's signs of cognitive dysfunction and may work best when given along with other cognitive support measures.

Your veterinarian can suggest appropriate supplements or nutraceuticals and proper doses for cats with cognitive dysfunction. Nutraceuticals may include several ingredients such as vitamins, minerals, and antioxidants. It's important to ask your veterinarian for advice because supplements or nutraceuticals that are designed for dogs may not be appropriate for cats—or may even be toxic in cats, such as alpha-lipoic acid. And some supplements formulated for people may be dangerous for pets (e.g. some melatonin supplements contain xylitol, which is best avoided in cats). It's likely important to keep up with supplementation for the long term and as directed by your veterinarian in order for a product's benefits to be seen and sustained.[10]

Supplements that may support cats with cognitive dysfunction include:

- L-theanine, an amino acid found in green tea leaves. Products formulated for cats include Anxitane (Virbac), Solliquin (Nutramax Laboratories Veterinary Sciences), Composure (VetriScience), and Calmex (VetPlus).

- Gamma-aminobutyric acid (GABA), a naturally occurring amino acid and neurotransmitter that slows nerve impulses in the brain, which may reduce anxiety and stress and promote sleep. (Note: GABA is not the same as gabapentin, a drug that veterinarians may prescribe for pets to treat pain, anxiety, and seizures, or to provide mild sedation.)
- Gingko, an extract from maidenhair trees, contains antioxidants that may improve cognitive function and enhance blood flow to the brain.
- Melatonin, a naturally occurring hormone produced by the pineal gland in the brain of many animals. Melatonin may help with sleep disturbances in cats who have cognitive dysfunction. In people who have dementia, sunset can bring increased confusion, frustration, and agitation, and it is often referred to as *sundowner's syndrome* or *sundowning*. Some cats with cognitive dysfunction can show similar signs at or shortly after sunset. One theory is that cats produce less melatonin as they age. Melatonin is a hormone produced in response to darkness and helps with circadian rhythms (the body's 24-hour internal clock) and the normal sleep-wake cycle. So melatonin supplementation is sometimes recommended for cats with cognitive dysfunction whose sleep-wake cycle is reversed.[2] Most supplements contain a synthetic version of the hormone. Avoid giving melatonin supplements that contain xylitol to pets.
- Omega-3 fatty acids, which may support cognitive function through their anti-inflammatory and antioxidant effects.
- Resveratrol, a chemical produced by some plants that has antioxidant, anti-inflammatory, and blood vessel-widening effects that may help cognitive function.
- S-adenosyl-L-methionine (SAMe), made in the body from methionine, is an amino acid found in food. It helps regulate hormones and many cell activities. As a supplement, SAMe is a synthetic molecule (Denosyl–Nutramax Laboratories Veterinary Sciences) and is used to support liver and brain health in cats.
- Senilife (Ceva Animal Health), a multi-antioxidant blend (phosphatidylserine, pyridoxine, ginkgo biloba extract, resveratrol, and d-alpha-tocopherol), is formulated for use in senior dogs to help reduce behaviors associated with brain aging, but veterinarians may suggest its use in cats.[24]
- Alpha-casozepine (Zylkene–Vetoquinol) contains bovine-sourced hydrolyzed milk protein, an ingredient that has calming properties and may be used in cats to provide support related to anxiety disorders and enhance overnight sleep.[25]
- Probiotics such as Purina Pro Plan Veterinary Supplements Calming Care offer support for cats with anxiety.

> ### Does CBD help cats with cognitive dysfunction?
>
> Cannabidiol (CBD), is usually made from hemp. Hemp is a cannabis (marijuana) plant that contains only a small amount (less than 0.3%) of tetrahydrocannabinol (THC), the compound that produces a "high" in people and can cause intoxication in pets at certain doses.
>
> CBD has been promoted by the manufacturers of CBD products for pets to help calm pets and reduce anxiety. But clinical studies that evaluate CBD to reduce anxiety in cats or to evaluate its effects in cats with cognitive dysfunction are lacking.[26,27] At the time of this writing, only two studies have explored the safety of various doses of CBD in a small number of healthy adult cats who lived in research facilities.[28,29] See Chapter 23 "Course of action: Therapeutic options and gaining acceptance from your senior cat" for more information about CBD.

Drugs

Selegiline is an FDA-approved drug for dogs with cognitive dysfunction syndrome, but veterinarians may prescribe it off-label for cats. It increases the availability of a neurotransmitter called dopamine. It may take six weeks or more to see an improvement in signs of cognitive dysfunction. Because other medications may pose an interaction hazard with selegiline, your veterinarian needs to know about all other drugs and supplements your cat is receiving. This helps ensure drug interactions won't be a risk if your cat receives selegiline treatment.

Some cats with cognitive dysfunction may benefit from an antidepressant or anti-anxiety drug such as fluoxetine, alprazolam, trazodone, gabapentin, or buspirone.[2] If your cat does not respond to a drug, your veterinarian may recommend increasing the dose or switching to a different drug—with an appropriate amount of time between stopping the previous medication and starting the new one. It may take a few weeks to see improvement, so patience and flexibility are key. Some antidepressant and anti-anxiety drugs (and many other types of medications) should not be given to cats who are receiving selegiline because adverse drug interactions may occur.

Researchers are studying the effects of telmisartan (Semintra, made by Boehringer Ingelheim) in cats who have cognitive dysfunction.[2] This drug is FDA-approved to treat high blood pressure in cats. It is being explored to treat cats with cognitive dysfunction because other studies show it protects neurons and cognitive function in mice and rats.

Researchers are also exploring whether vaccinations and stem cell therapies may be useful to treat Alzheimer's disease in people, and these studies are ongoing. Some of this research may show promise for pets in the future.

Acupuncture

Acupuncture may be a helpful adjunct to drug therapy in people who have Alzheimer's disease.[30] Acupuncture's effects have shown promise in a small study in mice that naturally exhibit accelerated aging.[31] However, not much is known about the effects of acupuncture in cats with cognitive dysfunction.

Activity and sleep

Cats with cognitive dysfunction may experience sleep-wake cycle disturbances. Help your cat be active during the day or in the early evening hours. This exposes them to sunlight, which helps reset their body clock and also tires them out, both of which reduce nighttime restlessness. If your cat tends to yowl in the wee hours to be fed, do not inadvertently reward them by feeding them to keep them quiet or they'll insist you continue to supply their midnight meals. I learned this the hard way with Bodhi! Feed them a small meal before bedtime instead, or program an automatic feeder to deliver a wee-hours snack.

Just like for children and for us, your cat benefits from a pre-sleep routine and consistent bedtime. Dim the lights a couple hours before bed to signal the body to produce melatonin, the sleep-promoting hormone. Provide a comfy sleep environment. Talk to your veterinarian to learn whether a melatonin supplement might help your cat.

If your cat wakes up during the night, try to avoid turning on bright lights. Light signals the body to stop producing melatonin. Use nightlights and flashlights on low instead, which will help you get back to sleep faster, too. Don't punish your cat for waking you up. Punishment increases her anxiety. Keep in mind she may be confused and need reassurance. And keep in mind that she may have thought she had a good reason to alert you to something she heard or smelled. It's perfectly acceptable to pet, cuddle, and calm your cat to provide reassurance to help her get back to sleep.

If you and others in your household still aren't able to get your much needed sleep, your cat may need a comfortable room of his own with a warm bed, food and water bowls, and a litter box. Consider using a baby video monitor so you can check on your cat without waking him. And in some cases, you may also need to talk with your veterinarian about prescribing a mild sedative such as gabapentin to help your cat sleep through the night.

Environmental and emotional comfort and physical and mental exercise

Cats with cognitive dysfunction benefit from a familiar, safe environment with furniture in its usual places, their necessities (bowls, beds, litter boxes) in their ordinary spots, and hazards blocked off if needed, such as closets they may get stuck in or stairs if they can't traverse them)—and especially pools they can fall into. Cats take comfort in a stable daily routine with predictable times for meals, play, sunbathing and naps, window gazing, outdoor exploring (if applicable), and treats. But you and your cat don't need to relive monotonous "groundhog days" either!

Cats who have cognitive dysfunction can still do—and enjoy!—most of the things they love to do. Going for walks or riding in a stroller, chasing toys, sunbathing, exploring, being petted and brushed, and hunting for treats are all feasible. Simply engage in activities at a more leisurely pace and with extra care, monitoring, and patience. And add variety to spice up your cat's life. Promoting physical exercise and mental stimulation that your cat enjoys can be therapeutic for both of you!

If your cat is a little unsteady or unable to reliably jump up on or down from usual sleeping spots, consider adding small ramps or steps to help him along. For cats who are a bit pained by arthritis or other muscle conditions, a certified pet rehabilitation therapist or a certified animal acupressure and massage practitioner may be available in your area.

Cats who were social bunnies before they started to slow down should still be allowed opportunities to visit or play with people and animal friends they're comfortable with. Gauge their endurance and tolerance levels to avoid overstimulation and stress.

It's probably beneficial to periodically review the commands your cat knows. And consider teaching her new ones! You may also want to teach your cat hand signals that communicate your commands.

Always use training techniques that positively reinforce desired behavior with treat or toy rewards and love, not methods that use confrontation or punishment. Clicker training works well for cats. It's a positive reinforcement training technique wherein a distinct clicking sound is used to signal that the cat exhibited a desired behavior. The click must be timed exactly at the moment of the desired behavior and immediately followed by a treat (or a favorite toy or praise).

Keep in mind that you may also need to review litter box training with your senior cat if she seems confused about where to potty:

- Take her to the appropriate location frequently to potty.
- Reward her immediately (profuse praise or a tiny treat) after she eliminates in the box.

Spike loves to play with his maze! Some cats like solitary play with new toys such as these, or even with old toys they haven't seen in awhile.

- Confine her while you can't watch her—use a comfy kennel or small area of a room where she's less likely to want to eliminate.
- Don't punish her for having accidents.

Food puzzle toys, games of chase and hide and seek, and scent enrichment opportunities allow cats to express their exploratory nature. These activities provide fun distractions and additional time to bond with your cat.

Calming music, cat rehabilitation therapy or massage, aromatherapy, and videos made to engage your cat can be terrific ways to help your cat relax and stimulate their senses.

Other measures to consider

- Gentle pressure garments that help reduce anxiety in cats such as ThunderShirt (Thunderworks)
- Pheromone diffusers, sprays, or collars (e.g. Feliway–Ceva, Comfort Zone–Central Garden & Pet Company)

 ## Questions to ask your veterinarian

Some veterinarians may not routinely screen specifically for signs of cognitive dysfunction in senior cats, so if you notice these signs in your senior cat, it's important to alert your veterinarian and ask whether your cat's signs may be attributed to another medical condition, to cognitive dysfunction, or to both. Like elderly people, it is common for senior cats to have multiple conditions.

Use the "Cognitive Assessment Checklist for Cats" at the end of this chapter to monitor your cat, and go over it with your veterinarian. Based on your discussion, you may want to know:

- What diagnostic tests will my cat need?
- What supplements, therapeutic diets, or medications might my cat benefit from?
- What physical and mental enrichment activities will help my cat?

CAREGIVER TIPS AND HOME HACKS

- Stick with your cat's usual routines (e.g. meal times, medication timing, play, bedtime).
- Keep your cat's food and water bowls, beds, and litter boxes in easily accessible, familiar spots.
- Avoid rearranging the furniture.
- Keep closet doors closed (unless a closet is a familiar hangout spot or litter box location for your cat).
- Block off access to hazards such as a swimming pool, and to stairs if needed (use a baby gate if your cat won't try to jump over it).
- Maintain a bedtime routine—feed a snack or meal, turn down the lights.
- Provide comfy, not too warm, not too cool sleeping and napping spots, and consider providing a heated cat bed (that your cat can move off of if he wants to), especially during the winter months.
- Reassure elderly cats who seem confused and vocalize; help calm them. Consider reducing the area they have access to if they seem to get lost.[32]
- Take 10 to 20 minutes each day to love on your cat—groom her or simply sit and pet her or give gentle massage. This also helps you stay attuned to any new lumps or bumps. Remember to regularly trim your cat's nails.
- Adhere to your cat's routine veterinary visits for examinations, diagnostic tests, and wellness care such as vaccinations and parasite preventives. Work with your veterinarian to successfully manage any other underlying health conditions your cat has.
- Minimize stress associated with veterinary visits. Speak to your veterinary team for pointers. Your veterinarian may prescribe gabapentin or trazodone for you to give to your cat before you travel to the clinic.
- Provide socialization times with other familiar calm cats and human friends.
- Intermittently explore new areas on leash walks if applicable.

- Review known training commands if applicable and teach hand signals for them.
- If your cat has seemingly forgotten his litter box training, retrain him, or retrain him to potty on an absorbent pad. Reward him for eliminating in the new location. Don't punish him for having accidents.
- Allow opportunities for your cat's favorite activities—chasing toys, hunting for treats, climbing, going for leash walks outdoors, watching the sights and sniffing the air through a screened window, and sunbathing.
- Intermittently offer new toys and puzzle toys or rotate old toys to keep them "new."
- Launder your cat's bedding or covers frequently, such as on the same schedule that you launder your bedding. Cats love "clean sheets" as much as we do!
- Use security cameras to check on your cat throughout the day.
- Monitor your cat during outdoor time to prevent escape, and keep an ID tag with your contact information on his harness. If your cat does not have one already, consider having a microchip implanted. And remember, you or your veterinarian must register the chip. A microchip is not a GPS tracker and is useless if it isn't registered to you.
- If your cat typically receives only dry kibble at mealtimes, consider introducing a "Sunday/Wednesday dinner special" wherein you mix in a small portion of canned food one or two days a week. If possible, use the canned food version of your cat's dry food to help prevent stomach upset. Some cats will enjoy this novelty. Or canned critical care diets such as Purina Pro Plan Veterinary Diets CN Critical Nutrition Canine & Feline Formula or Hill's Prescription Diet a/d Wet Dog/Cat Food are especially tasty.
- For especially picky eaters, try cutting or otherwise forming your cat's food into small squares or tidbit-sized chunks, and then serve them spread out on a flat, washable surface (such as a cheap plastic cutting board or plate) rather than in their bowl. The new "serving platter" may make them more eager to snarf down what you're offering as well as provide another novelty at mealtimes to promote their sense of hunting for food! It also removes the constant sensory stimulation that occurs when a pet's whiskers touch the sides of the bowl, which may irritate some cats.
- Use feline pheromone sprays or diffusers.
- Use a HATCH Baby Rest Sound Machine Night Light that you can control from your phone.
- Use an automatic feeder for nighttime beggars. Set it to dispense about 15 to 30 minutes before your cat typically wakes you up.
- Set up a room of your cat's own to sleep in at night to ensure you get the rest you need and preserve your bond with your cat.

- Play soothing music, nature sounds, or even talk radio on low. Music created especially for pets is available, such as iCalmPet (BioAcoustic Research), and Pet Tunes Feline (Pet Acoustics).
- Hang a sign on your front door that instructs people not to ring or knock if this makes your cat anxious.
- Use a tracking device to keep tabs on your cat, which is particularly useful if your cat often gets losts in your home. My father loves using a Girafus Pet Tracker to help keep an eye on his cats.

Fun enrichment ideas to help stimulate the brain

- Cut a few small holes that are slightly larger than your cat's treats or kibble along the length of an empty cardboard paper towel roll. Staple one end of the tube together and pour treats or kibble in, then staple the other end together. Your cat will need to roll the tube around for the food to drop out. Supervise your cat whenever he uses it to make sure he doesn't chew up and eat the cardboard or the staples.
- Engage your cat in short play sessions with wand or laser toys to help hold her interest, and allow your cat to play while she lies on her side or back. It may seem lazy to you, but your cat still gets the benefits of play!
- Install a bird feeder or pollinator garden (or potted outdoor plants) near a window to invite flying creatures nearby that your cat can watch from one of his elevated perches, from the floor, or from a chair placed next to a patio door.
- Drape a hanging shoe organizer over the back of a chair and put treats in each reachable shoe compartment for your cat to find.
- Fill a small plastic dish with no-sodium chicken broth or broth made specifically for cats (such as Tiki Cat Savory Broth or Purina Fancy Feast Broth) and freeze it or warm it slightly, whichever your cat prefers. Give it to your cat as a treat; it keeps her engaged and occupied while she licks or laps it.
- Instead of feeding your cat's meals in his bowl, place the kibble in a trail around the edge of a wall or around the kitchen so he has to track his food. The hiding spots don't need to be elaborate!
- Use a Snuffle Mat for cats to feed your cat or to place treats on.
- Place treats in an empty egg carton and cover each compartment with a ping pong ball to see if your cat will hunt for the treats.
- Place a few treats under a newspaper page or a small towel so your cat has to hunt for them.
- Toss treats one at a time so your cat has to listen and look for the spot where each one lands.

- Allow your cat to explore cardboard boxes and paper bags (cut the handles on the bags to prevent your cat from getting her head stuck or twisting a handle around her neck) of various shapes and sizes. Hold onto her favorites and rotate them often to maintain your cat's interest, and intermittently offer each new one you acquire from parcel deliveries, grocery stores, and fast food restaurants.
- Offer scent enrichment activities: open a screened window, bring leaves and sticks indoors, provide catnip and other herbs such as parsley, rosemary, and dill.[33]

Quiet, but not peace

Although I loathed what the sound meant, I would give almost anything to hear Bodhi's nightly howl once again. I had adapted to his loud "mee-yowling" and could sleep through it most nights, but I was not alone in my house. I'd often be nudged awake to "do something about Bodhi" when he wouldn't stop howling. It can be stressful for caregivers and all family members to live with a pet who has cognitive dysfunction. So I'd get up and comfort Bodhi, or sit with him on the patio for a bit while he surveyed his backyard kingdom from the patio furniture. That always calmed him down.

It had been three years since I adopted Bodhi when I lost him unexpectedly, during a night that I didn't awake to his howling. I was devastated to find him forever gone the next day. I had expected to have Bodhi in my life for a while longer. And worst of all, I was not there to tell him I loved him when he earned his wings.

PRODUCT RECOMMENDATIONS

Diets that may be beneficial for cats who have cognitive dysfunction:[2]

- Feline Adult 7+ (Hill's Pet Nutrition)
- Pro Plan Adult 7+ (Nestlé Purina)
- Calm (Royal Canin)
- Prescription Diet Urinary Care c/d Multicare (Hill's Pet Nutrition)

Probiotic for cats:

- Purina Pro Plan Veterinary Supplements Calming Care

Omega-3 fatty acids (from fish oil):

- Nordic Naturals:
  nordicnaturals.com/petVet

Music for cats:

- iCalmPet (BioAcoustic Research)
  icalmpet.com/
- Pet Tunes Feline
  petacoustics.com/

Snuffle/slow feeder/foraging mats for cats:

- **catschool.co/products/snuffle-mat**
- **petparentsbrand.com/pages/forager-comparison**

Girafus Pet Tracker:

- **girafus.com/en/security-devices/girafus-pro-track-tor-pet-safety-tracker-rf-technology-dog-and-cat-tracker-finder-locator/**

 RESOURCES

- Information about animal acupressure and massage. National Board of Certification for Animal Acupressure and Massage.
  nbcaam.org/
- Information about veterinary rehabilitation therapy.
  - American Association of Rehabilitation Veterinarians.
    rehabvets.org/training.lasso
  - American College of Veterinary Sports Medicine and Rehabilitation.
    vsmr.org/

Copy and complete this "Cognitive Assessment Checklist for Cats" and share it with your veterinarian during your cat's semi-annual examinations. Schedule a veterinary visit sooner anytime your cat's signs concern you, or if your cat exhibits any of these signs once a week or more. Scan this QR Code to access additional assessment forms:

Cat Cognitive Assessment

Cognitive Assessment Checklist for Cats

Date	Cat's Name	Male/Female	Age

Current known medical or behavioral conditions

Category	Sign	Does not occur or is not applicable	Occurs once a month	Occurs once a week	Occurs once a day/night	Occurs more than once a day/night
Vocalization	Vocalizes more than usual during the day, evening, or night (meows or yowls)					
Interactions	More clingy/seeks more attention/more interest in being petted					
	Hiding/sleeping in unusual places					
	Less clingy/less interest in being petted					
	Irritable or aggressive with family members or housemate pets					

Category	Sign	Does not occur or is not applicable	Occurs once a month	Occurs once a week	Occurs once a day/night	Occurs more than once a day/night
Sleep/wake cycle	Asleep more than usual during the day					
	Awake more than usual during the night					
House-soiling	Urinates or defecates inappropriately in the house/outside the litter box					
Disorientation	Appears lost/wanders between rooms without purpose					
	Paces back and forth excessively or circles					
	Stares into space or stares absently at the floor or walls					
	Gets stuck under or behind objects					
	Doesn't seem to recognize family members or housemate pets					
	Walks or bumps into doors or walls					
	Less interested in or less reactive to sights and sounds					
	Has trouble finding food or water bowl					
Anxiety	Increased anxiety when pet parents are away/doesn't like being left alone					
	More reactive to sights and sounds					
	Agitated or restless during the day, evening, or night					

Category	Sign	Does not occur or is not applicable	Occurs once a month	Occurs once a week	Occurs once a day/night	Occurs more than once a day/night
Activity	Less or no interest in play, toys, or exploring					
	Less or no interest in self-grooming					
	Exhibits repetitive behaviors (excessive grooming, licking inanimate objects)					
Learning and memory	Seems to have forgotten trained commands, routines (such as feeding times), verbal cues, or name					
	Decreased focus/hard to get and retain pet's attention					
Additional health concerns						

CHAPTER 18:

Endocrine disruption: Glands and hormones out of whack

> "Prowling his own quiet backyard or asleep by the fire, he is still only a whisker away from the wilds."
>
> —Jean Burden, American poet

The term *endocrine* refers to a variety of glands (mini organs), including the pituitary, thyroid, parathyroid, and adrenal glands, and the pancreas, ovaries, and testicles. Endocrine glands monitor, produce, regulate, and secrete hormones (chemical messages) that sail through the bloodstream to coordinate many different body functions in cats, dogs, people, and all other mammals. Hormones help direct growth, mood, blood pressure, metabolism, sleep, reproduction, and more.

If an endocrine gland goes haywire—which can occur for many reasons, including autoimmune disease, cancer, aging, genetics, infection, and injury—or if the cells that should respond to a hormone no longer do, the gland may produce too little or too much hormone. A hormone imbalance affects specific body functions and can further disrupt the gland's activity. Depending on a pet's species and their symptoms or age, veterinarians run diagnostic tests to check whether certain hormones are out of whack.

Glands gone astray

Ask any veterinarian to name the most common endocrine disease of older cats, and their responses will undoubtedly be a tie between diabetes and hyperthyroidism.

In cats with diabetes, the pancreas doesn't make enough insulin (a hormone) or the body doesn't respond to insulin normally. Insulin helps the body process glucose–a vital sugar that the body uses for energy. With too little insulin, too much glucose builds up in the bloodstream, and serious health issues follow. In cats with hyperthyroidism, the thyroid glands shift into overdrive and secrete too much thyroid hormone, which negatively impacts health.

Interestingly, diabetes and thyroid gland problems are common in dogs, too, but dogs usually have underactive thyroid glands (called *hypothyroidism*) rather than overactive ones. Diabetes and overactive or underactive thyroid gland disorders are also among the most common endocrine diseases in people.

Several endocrine disorders can affect cats, but here I'll stick with the top two that affect middle-aged and older cats: diabetes and hyperthyroidism.

A primer on the pancreas, thyroid, and parathyroid glands

The pancreas sits in the upper abdomen, and it not only produces insulin, it secretes a hormone called *glucagon* that boosts blood glucose when it gets too low. It also secretes a hormone called *somatostatin*, which inhibits the release of other hormones. On top of all that, the pancreas boasts a separate set of cells that secrete special proteins called *enzymes* that help with food digestion (and when these enzymes leak inappropriately within the pancreas itself, pain and other havoc associated with pancreatitis ensues).

Two small thyroid glands sit on each side of the trachea (windpipe) below the larynx (voice box) and secrete hormones that help regulate growth and metabolism: thyroxine (also called T4), triiodothyronine (also called T3), and calcitonin (calcitonin lowers blood calcium). In addition, each thyroid gland sports two tiny parathyroid glands that make parathyroid hormone (PTH), which increases calcium and helps regulate phosphorus in the blood.

Lilu's clue

My first pet cat who had diabetes was my little girl Lilu (two of my dogs have also had the disease). I didn't pick up on Lilu's signs right away because she shared a water bowl and litter box with my other cat Bodhi who had chronic kidney disease. Excessive thirst and increased urination are telltale symptoms of many problems, and kidney disease and diabetes are two of them. Bodhi drank water like crazy and peed a boatload, so I attributed the frequent water bowl refills and heavily soiled litter boxes primarily to his doings. But one day I spied Lilu drinking eagerly from a planter saucer outside after a rain, and she had never shown a preference for the taste of rainwater before.

Lilu looked good; she wasn't obese—her body condition score was normal, as was her muscle condition score—and her appetite, weight, and energy level hadn't changed for years. But when I saw that unusual drinking behavior, I knew that Lilu needed blood and urine tests. Sure enough, her results showed she had an abnormally high blood glucose concentration (*hyperglycemia*) and glucose in her urine (*glucosuria*).

 Lilu showing off her great body condition score! She likely had diabetes when this photo was taken, but I hadn't diagnosed it yet.

So why was Lilu drinking more because of diabetes? Let's first consider how the body gets energy and uses glucose, and what happens in pets who have diabetes.

Fuel to function

Energy propels the cells in our pets' (and our) bodies. Most of the energy the body needs comes from carbohydrates, proteins, and fats supplied by dietary grains, vegetables, fruits, meat, eggs, and dairy products. The main form of energy the body uses is glucose, a simple sugar that's naturally packed into many plant-based carbohydrates (grains, vegetables, and fruits)—thanks to sunlight, water, and air. But when needed, the body can make its own energy by breaking down glycogen—a form of glucose the body stores primarily in the liver—and by breaking down fat, and, as a last resort, by breaking down muscle.

Dogs and people are omnivores, so we can get energy and necessary nutrients from eating plants and animals. Cats are strict carnivores—they must get their energy and nutrients from eating animal proteins. Cats use protein to build and maintain muscle mass and fuel various other body processes, but cats also rely heavily on protein to supply the energy they need to maintain their blood glucose levels.

Glucose circulates in the blood after food is digested, but to be used for energy, glucose has to enter the cells. I often tell pet parents that glucose needs a "taxi" to get into a cell. And that taxi is insulin.

Diabetes: Two types, several symptoms

In cats (and in people and dogs) who have diabetes, either the pancreas doesn't manufacture enough taxis (insulin) or the body's cells won't let the taxis (insulin) in. When the pancreas doesn't make insulin, it's called *Type 1 diabetes*. Type 1 diabetes is common in people (especially young adults, teenagers, and children) and in dogs. When the pancreas makes insulin but the cells don't respond to it, the overworked pancreas eventually falters and makes less and less insulin, and this is called *Type 2 diabetes*. Type 2 diabetes is common in people (especially older adults) and in cats. Either way, glucose can't get into the cells, so the cells become starved for energy, and glucose builds up in the bloodstream.

Meanwhile, those little wonders the kidneys work overtime to get rid of the excess blood glucose by sending it out with extra water through the urine. This in turn causes dehydration, which leads to excess thirst. Drinking more than normal is called *polydipsia*. Drinking more water plus sending extra water out in the urine adds up to peeing more than normal, which is called *polyuria*. Polyuria and polydipsia are the two most common symptoms we see in pets who have diabetes.

In early stages of diabetes we may also notice cats eating more, because the cells aren't getting enough energy from glucose. Yet despite eating more, cats often lose weight because the body starts breaking down fats and proteins to fuel the cells instead.

When to see your veterinarian

Key reasons to spot and successfully manage diabetes as soon as possible include avoiding disease complications and increasing the chance of disease remission. A fascinating fact: after starting successful treatment, some cats with Type 2 diabetes will have disease remission within six months, so they may no longer need insulin injections! (Even so, diabetes can recur in cats who experience remission, so pet parents should still stay on the lookout.) The signs of diabetes in cats include:

- drinking more water than normal;
- drinking water from unusual sources;
- urinating more—you may notice larger-than-normal litter clumps, a wetter or heavier litter box, or that the clumps seem sticky and the litter box is harder to clean;
- urinating in places other than the litter box;
- bigger appetite—may beg for food;
- weight loss;

- odd standing and walking postures—stands flat-footed (called *plantigrade stance*), walks on heels/ankles instead of on toes;
- difficulty jumping; and
- decreased activity, increased fatigue.

During the later stages of untreated diabetes, cats' appetites decrease, they lose more weight, and their fur lacks luster. They experience further health issues as the disease advances or if their diabetes is inadequately managed.

Fair warning: Cats who have an extremely high blood glucose concentration can experience *diabetic ketoacidosis*. With this condition, the liver breaks down fat (to make ketones for energy since glucose isn't being used) too quickly, and too many ketones rapidly build up in the blood. Signs of diabetic ketoacidosis in cats include not eating, vomiting, diarrhea, extreme lethargy, icterus (yellowish skin, gums, and eyes), and hypothermia (low body temperature). If this emergency happens, a cat needs to be hospitalized for a few days—or longer—to control their blood glucose, provide intense supportive care and monitoring, and help them get back to eating adequately and feeling well again.

How veterinarians diagnose diabetes

If your cat has signs of diabetes (or is visiting for a routine checkup), your veterinarian will do a physical examination and run routine blood and urine tests to check whether your cat's blood glucose is higher than normal. Additional blood and urine tests may also be needed to help rule out other possible reasons for your cat's symptoms or point to concurrent ailments such as chronic kidney disease, hyperthyroidism, pancreatitis, urinary tract infection, or inflammatory bowel disease. If indicated, your veterinarian may also suggest an abdominal ultrasound exam to evaluate whether your cat's pancreas looks swollen.

Lilu was a great patient (for some things!); she patiently and happily let me examine her (most of the time!).

> ### Sidebar: Is my cat at risk for developing diabetes?
>
> Obesity and inactivity are big risk factors for Type 2 diabetes in cats (and in people). Fat cats are four times more likely to develop diabetes than cats who balance the scales at an optimal weight. Many mechanisms by which excess fat contributes to insulin resistance have been proposed, but they aren't precisely known.[1] In people, we know that aerobic exercise, strength/resistance training, and fat loss decreases insulin resistance. Obese cats have disturbances of the gut microbiome (bacteria, protozoa, viruses, and fungi that live in our and our pets' digestive systems) that may also play a role in diabetes.[2]
>
> Other risk factors for insulin resistance in cats include being male; being older than 5 years; being a Maine Coon, Russian Blue, Siamese, Burmese, domestic longhair, or Norwegian Forest cat; and receiving long-term treatment with corticosteroids such as prednisone, prednisolone, methylprednisolone, or dexamethasone.[3] Other ailments can shore up insulin resistance, too, including acromegaly (another type of endocrine disorder wherein the pituitary gland produces too much growth hormone), hyperadrenocorticism (a rare endocrine disorder in cats wherein the pituitary gland or adrenal glands propel overproduction of cortisol hormone), hyperthyroidism, bacterial infections, pancreatitis (inflammation of the pancreas), and kidney, liver, or heart disease.

Treating diabetes and monitoring your cat

Successfully treating diabetes means controlling blood glucose concentrations and easing your feline friend's symptoms. We want to prevent high blood glucose concentrations caused by the disease and avoid low blood glucose concentrations caused by insulin overdose or inadequate feeding. We also want to alleviate the signs and prevent complications associated with diabetes. Your veterinarian will cover your cat's specific needs, but diabetes treatment and monitoring measures include:

- addressing contributing factors if needed, such as stopping corticosteroid treatment when possible and identifying and managing other ailments;
- encouraging cats to exercise or increase their activity level to help fight insulin resistance and/or to promote carefully controlled weight loss in cats who are overweight or obese;
- stopping weight loss in cats who are not obese or overweight;

- giving insulin injections under the skin each day at regular, specific times (in some cases oral medications may be needed);
- feeding a veterinary therapeutic diet;
- monitoring blood and urine glucose levels at home and/or in the veterinary clinic;
- checking weight frequently; and
- monitoring water intake and appetite.

Topics your veterinary team should cover (or things to ask about)

Your veterinarian or veterinary nurse will show you:

- what type of insulin and syringe to use
- how much insulin to give;
- where on your cat's body you can give insulin, and how to alternate the injection locations;
- how to give insulin injections;
- how to keep track of meal timing and the amount your cat eats as well as when you give the insulin injections (date, time, amount) or other medications you're giving; and
- how to check and track your cat's blood and urine glucose.

Your veterinarian or veterinary nurse will tell you:

- how to store the insulin;
- whether you need to gently shake or roll the vial before drawing it into the syringe;
- when to feed your cat and when to give the insulin;
- what to do if your cat doesn't eat a meal;
- what to do if you miss giving a dose of insulin;
- what to do if you give an extra dose of insulin or the wrong dose;
- what to do if your cat has signs of hypoglycemia (low blood glucose) such as trembling, lethargy, incoordination, seizures, or unconsciousness (coma); and
- what follow-up tests and visits your cat will need and how often.

The insulin injection is given with a tiny needle under the skin, it's simple to learn, the process gets easier with experience, and most cats tolerate it well and seem to barely feel it.

One client I learned of had two tuxedo cats—Frankie and Jesse—who were sister and brother littermates. When the cats were 12 years old, they were both diagnosed as having type 2 diabetes. The client had serious health issues and was bedridden, and visiting nurses helped care for him. But every morning and every evening when their dad called them, Frankie and Jesse would dash in and jump right up into bed with him—where he fed them and gave them their insulin injections, along with extra doses of loving attention.

I will admit, my cat Lilu was less enthusiastic and grew tired of getting her insulin injections. She was the type of cat who liked to be touched only on her terms, for a certain amount of time, and only in certain places. So I know firsthand that it isn't always a piece of cake. But with time, you'll develop a comfortable rhythm and confident speed when giving the injections. Always remember to end with a reward—a tasty tidbit, extra love, playtime, guided outdoor exploring, or all of those! Whatever your cat fancies most.

Your schedule and your cat's temperament will affect how well your cat's diabetes can be managed. But with medications, the right diet, supportive care, attentive monitoring, and timely veterinary rechecks, cats who have diabetes can have a good quality of life for many years.

CAREGIVER TIPS AND HOME HACKS

- Schedule mealtimes and give insulin as directed by your veterinarian, and keep a daily treatment log.
- Use only the syringes that came with the insulin prescribed (don't reuse syringes).
- Store insulin on a shelf inside your refrigerator. Don't store it in the door of the fridge because the temperature is not consistent.
- Alternate injection sites each time, and give your cat a treat and lots of praise each time.
- Check with your trash removal service about how to dispose of needles and syringes. You can purchase FDA-cleared sharps disposal containers online and at pharmacies and medical supply companies. Or you may be able to use an empty laundry detergent or bleach bottle, or any other strong plastic container. Don't use empty water bottles because a needle can penetrate the plastic. With an indelible marker, write 'Household Sharps—Do Not Recycle' on the container. When it's about three-quarters full, seal it well (with a tight-fitting, no-leak, puncture-resistant lid), and you may be able to throw it away in the trash. Do NOT place it in your recycling bin.
- Keep a close eye on your cat's appetite, water consumption, urine output, and weight.
- Monitor your cat's blood and urine glucose at home as directed by your veterinarian.
- Keep your cat moving—engage him in play and exercise for five to 10 minutes a few to several times each day, and on a consistent schedule.

- Keep up with all recommended routine and recheck veterinary visits, and call your veterinarian if your cat shows signs of high or low blood glucose or other out-of-character changes.

Hyperthyroidism: Senior cat calls and zoomies?

I'm not referring to the web conference meetings when your cat steals the show (although cats with hyperthyroidism may interrupt those even more frequently)! But did you know that many senior kitties—about one in 10 cats aged 10 years and older—have hyperthyroidism?[4] With this disease, one or both of the thyroid glands are enlarged–usually because of a benign (mostly harmless) tumor, or rarely because of a malignant (harmful, cancerous) tumor—which makes the cells secrete too many thyroid hormones. Thyroid hormones running amok may be making your senior cat feel stressed and strung out, so you may hear new yowling cat calls at night and see them randomly zoom around the room like they often did as a youngster. An overabundance of thyroid hormones can also harm your cat's heart, cause high blood pressure, generate muscle wasting, and damage their vision and kidneys.

Other than advanced age, we don't precisely know what causes hyperthyroidism in cats.[5] Theories that have been explored include:[4]

- autoimmune disease (the body's immune [disease-defense] cells mistakenly attack healthy cells);
- environmental agents (such as certain compounds [called endocrine-disrupting chemicals] found in house dust, which cats ingest by self-grooming [interestingly, long-haired, non-purebred cats have an increased risk of hyperthyroidism compared with purebred and non-purebred short-haired cats[5,6]];

Noodles has hyperthyroidism and kidney disease, but both diseases were well managed.

251

- dietary influences (from naturally occurring marine plant substances found in fish-flavored canned cat food[7]);
- infectious disease; and
- genetic predisposition (born with genes that increase vulnerability to the disease given the right circumstances, such as exposure to certain environmental factors).

Cat breeds that are less likely to develop hyperthyroidism than other breeds are Persian, Burmese, Siamese, Abyssinian, Tonkinese, and British shorthair.[6]

When to see your veterinarian

As soon as you notice any out-of-character changes, of course! Signs of hyperthyroidism may seem minor at first, but cats experience further health issues as the disease advances. The signs mimic those seen with many other ailments in cats and include:

- weight loss;
- bigger appetite (may beg for food);
- drinking more water than normal;
- drinking water from unusual sources;
- urinating more (you may notice larger-than-normal litter clumps, or a wetter, heavier litter box);
- urinating in places other than the litter box;
- increased activity, pacing, restlessness, crankiness, different sleep patterns;
- excessive vocalization (frequently yowling for no good reason);
- unkempt, greasy, or matted fur;
- vomiting; and
- diarrhea.

Your veterinarian will feel your cat's neck to check for an enlarged thyroid gland, and use blood tests to measure thyroid hormone levels and look for other potential causes of the symptoms, such as chronic kidney disease, diabetes, or inflammatory bowel disease. Your veterinarian will also assess your cat's body and muscle condition, listen to your cat's heart, measure blood pressure, and may do an eye exam to look for retinal damage related to high blood pressure. Additional tests may be recommended to check for heart problems.

Taming overactive thyroid glands

You can choose from four options to treat hyperthyroidism, and your veterinarian should discuss the advantages and potential disadvantages of each one with you.[8] The most appropriate treatment for your cat depends on your cat's age, whether your cat also has other ailments, whether you can give medicine to your cat, whether the treatment is readily available, the treatment cost, and other household considerations. Treatment aims to reduce thyroid hormone concentrations to normal ranges. Here's a quick overview of the treatment options:

MEDICATION. Drugs called *methimazole* (also known as *thiamazole*) and *carbimazole* block the production of thyroxine, a thyroid hormone. Lifelong treatment is needed, and the medication can be given orally as a syrup or tablet, or given topically in a gel rubbed on the cat's skin just inside the outer ear. When giving the medication orally, the risk of a person absorbing the drug is low,[9] but it's still recommended that you wear gloves or finger cots when giving the medication. Pregnant caregivers (or those intending to become pregnant) must wear them to protect against birth defects that could be caused by antithyroid medication. When applying the gel form of the medication, *all* pet parents (not expecting, expecting to expect, and expecting!) must wear gloves or finger cots to protect themselves from absorbing the drug through their skin.

Initially it takes two to four weeks of daily treatment for the medication to reduce thyroid hormone levels, and your cat will need a blood test to check how well the treatment is working. After that, your cat will continue to need daily treatment and regular follow-up blood tests to check her thyroid hormone levels.

SURGERY. Surgically removing the affected thyroid glands or tissues can cure hyperthyroidism, and referral to a board-certified veterinary surgeon is recommended for this delicate surgery. Your cat's surgery team along with your cat's primary care veterinarian will ensure careful patient assessment and stabilization before surgery and monitor for complications after surgery. Cats with advanced hyperthyroidism who also have heart or kidney disease may not be good candidates for this surgery.

DIET. Without dietary iodine, the thyroid glands can't make thyroid hormone. So an iodine-restricted veterinary therapeutic diet, Hill's Prescription Diet y/d Thyroid Care, has been formulated to tamp down overactive thyroid glands. It's available in canned and dry formulations. This lifelong treatment means that a cat with hyperthyroidism can't eat anything else—no other cat food, no table food, no mice or other prey, and no treats. Feeding this diet is an easy and convenient way to manage hyperthyroidism, as long as your cat likes the taste, doesn't reject eating only one food for the rest of his life, doesn't have another ailment that requires a special diet, or has other cat or dog housemates whose food he could easily chow down on.

RADIOIODINE. With this treatment, your cat will be sedated and receive a small injection of radioactive iodine (also called iodine-131 or I-131) under the skin. The radiation destroys the abnormal thyroid gland cells, but the normal thyroid gland cells should continue to function. Your cat won't gain new spidey senses or glow in the dark, but radioiodine treatment has a high cure rate (only 5% to 10% of cats need a second injection or further alternative treatment[10,11]),

 Simon has one eye, hyperthyroidism, and inflammatory bowel disease, but with supportive care, medications, and a therapeutic diet, he's enjoying life at age 16.

and it is not invasive, as surgery is. But up to 50% of hyperthyroid cats who receive radioiodine develop hypothyroidism after treatment, so veterinary clinical researchers are evaluating individualized radioactive iodine dosing protocols based on specialized patient assessments to help reduce the risk of this complication.[11]

Your cat will need a referral to a specialty veterinary hospital that provides radioiodine treatment. (Insider tip: A study showed that gabapentin [a medication used to relieve pain and anxiety] is safe to give to hyperthyroid cats, and when it's given an hour before their trip to the veterinary hospital for radioiodine treatment, it helps cats be more relaxed and easier to work with.[12] So if your cat gets stressed by car trips and veterinary visits, ask your veterinarian about it.) Your cat will stay in the hospital for a few to several days after treatment, until his radiation levels are safe enough for him to go home. After discharge from the hospital, you'll need to limit contact with your cat for a couple weeks and follow specific protocols for several weeks for cleaning your cat's food and water bowls and scooping his litter box and disposing of waste. Follow-up blood tests to monitor your cat's thyroid hormone levels and kidney function are needed, and can be done at your primary care veterinary practice.

> ### A funky fact about hyperthyroidism
>
> Excess thyroid hormones boost blood flow to the kidneys, so the kidneys filter waste products faster. This makes it harder to tell whether chronic kidney disease is lurking in cats who have hyperthyroidism. So after hyperthyroidism is treated, kidney disease may be revealed (and can be appropriately managed). And if a cat's thyroid hormones drop so low that hypothyroidism occurs, kidney function can deteriorate more and shorten a cat's nine lives. So it's important for your veterinarian to assess your cat's kidney function before treating hyperthyroidism, and to closely monitor your cat's thyroid hormone levels and kidney function for at least 12 months after treatment.[5,13]

ADDITIONAL TREATMENTS. If a cat with hyperthyroidism also has high blood pressure, heart disease, or kidney disease, additional therapies will likely be needed. Some great news: some ailments may improve or resolve with successful treatment of hyperthyroidism!

 Questions to ask your veterinarian

- What are the advantages, disadvantages, and costs of each potential treatment for my cat's hyperthyroidism?
- Will my cat need specific follow-up tests and exams related to hyperthyroidism and its treatment, and if so, how often?
- What will happen to my cat if I choose not to treat this disease?

CHAPTER 19:

Cancer: Things that go bump in senior cats

> "Research has beaten polio, research has beaten smallpox, research is beating HIV and one day research will beat cancer. And the more research we do, the sooner that day will come."
>
> —Cancer Research UK Video

Roughly six million new cancer diagnoses are made in dogs and cats each year.[1] About one in five cats will receive a cancer diagnosis in their lifetimes. In a survey conducted by the Morris Animal Foundation in 1998, cancer was said to be the biggest cause of death related to disease in dogs (47%) and cats (32%).[2]

I wonder whether these percentages are a bit low. In early 2022, I partnered with VetSuccess (a veterinary practice metrics analysis company) to evaluate data from 3,587 veterinary practices and learned that over 55% of geriatric cats are not seen by their veterinarian during the last 18 months of their lives. Therefore, many undiagnosed cases of pet cancer probably exist.

Entire books have been written about cancer in pets, so I feel I do this topic an injustice by devoting only one chapter to it. But my goal is not to cover every type of cancer and its treatment options. I want to cover the basics, list abnormalities to watch out for, and suggest questions to ask your veterinarian. And if your cat has a cancer diagnosis, I hope to provide some insight and comfort as you navigate that news and your cat's care.

Rogue cells: the building blocks of destruction

Cells are the basic building blocks of the body and contain thousands of genes. Cells divide all day every day to grow, to repair themselves, or to replace abnormal cells. When a cell divides, it follows a stringent set of "rules," and a copy of its genes is passed along to the new cell. However, sometimes cells go rogue and begin to grow and divide without rules! These rogue cells are referred to as:

- a growth, a mass, or a tumor—tumor means "swelling or protuberance" or "abnormal cell growth";
- a neoplasm, or neoplasia—which means "new growth of abnormal tissue"; or
- cancer—which refers to a tumor or to neoplasia that is malignant.

Tumors and neoplasia may be benign (self-limiting) or they may be malignant (invasive). By definition, the term cancer always means malignant.

These rogue cells can grow so large and numerous that they crowd out normal cells and an affected organ can no longer function properly. The rogue cells can also invade neighboring spaces, and they can even travel to other parts of the body through the circulatory system and cause havoc far from where they started. In some cases, the rogue cells also continue to function but overproduce the substance they are supposed to make, such as a hormone, which causes illness.

A tumor is usually described by the organ it affects and named after the type of cell it originates from. For example, in oral squamous cell carcinoma, the affected tissue is the oral cavity, or mouth. And squamous cell carcinoma means that the tumor originates from squamous epithelial cells—cells that line body surfaces such as the skin, blood vessels, and some body cavities.

Many of the tumors and cancers we see in cats are the same that we see in people. Some tumors grow slowly, and we may not catch them until they have done years of damage. Some tumors grow extremely quickly and seem to appear out of nowhere. Some stay put and some travel. Some can be treated with surgery, while others need chemotherapy or radiation therapy or a combination of all of those things. Cancer is tricky!

Lumps and bumps

Cancer cells often form a cluster that becomes a mass, growth, or tumor. Veterinarians need to take a sample of the tumor to identify the cell origin and evaluate whether the cells are benign and self-limiting or malignant and aggressively invasive. It's important to evaluate every single lump and bump on a cat!

In fact, my good friend and veterinary oncologist Dr. Sue Ettinger started a program for veterinarians and pet owners called "See Something, Do Something: Why Wait? Aspirate!" (Visit her website at **drsuecancervet.com/why-wait-aspirate**.) This memorable phrase signifies that if you, or, for some cats, your groomer (sometimes they find bumps first!), or your veterinarian *sees something* like a lump or bump on your cat that is the size of a pea or larger and it has been there for a month, then your veterinarian needs to *do something*—evaluate it. Veterinarians can evaluate a lump or bump by removing cells from it with a needle (called a fine-needle aspirate) or by performing a biopsy (surgically cutting a small sample from the mass or removing the mass entirely) and looking at the cells under a microscope.

One of my senior feline patients had a walnut-size lump on her belly. Her owner told me, "It's only a fat bump, doc!" And sometimes, pet parents are right about these benign fatty growths (called *lipomas*). Except in this case the bump turned out to be a malignant mammary tumor (breast cancer). These tumors and the mammary tissue need to be surgically removed. Only about 10% of mammary tumors are benign, so the vast majority are malignant and extremely aggressive. The cat's owner was grateful that we aspirated and evaluated her cat's bump to identify what type of tumor it was.

It's important to be proactive and test a lump or bump and not simply "keep an eye on it." And if the test results show that the growth is indeed "nothing" (benign), then that's the best news to receive, and the best news is always well worth the cost—it's priceless peace of mind.

So remember the "see something, do something" rule, and schedule a veterinary visit to evaluate every single lump and bump!

Tumor behavior

Benign tumors stay put and don't invade other tissues, so if the tumor has been confirmed to be benign, they are usually fine to leave alone. But sometimes they can get aggravated or can obstruct or put pressure on surrounding tissues. For example many lipomas stay small and don't cause trouble, but some grow extremely large and hamper movement, or they may become infected if they irritate the pet and the pet licks or scratches them excessively.

Squamous cell carcinoma was discovered on The Muffin Man's ear, eyelids and nose when he was 15yrs old. After having the cancer removed, he is still quite handsome, and happy, at 17!

Malignant tumors can be slow or fast-growing. Their cells can invade neighboring tissue or catch a ride in the bloodstream or in the lymphatic system (a network of vessels, tissues, and organs that help fight infection, maintain fluid balance, and remove toxins) and can spread to anywhere in the body (called *metastasis*). The treatment options include surgery, chemotherapy, radiation therapy, and others—or a combination of treatments. And you may also decide not to treat it at all.

> ### Overview of lumps and bumps that may affect older cats
>
> **BENIGN BUMPS**
>
> - **Adenoma.** Affects the gland cells in many areas of the body including the skin (e.g. sebaceous gland adenoma), thyroid gland, intestine, and mammary gland.
>
> - **Hemangioma.** Involves the cells of the blood vessels and can occur in the spleen.
>
> - **Hematoma.** Informally known as "blood blisters." They occur if blood vessels rupture because of an injury, clotting disorder, or after surgery, and the blood collects in a pocket. I mention them here because hematomas typically occur as a swelling under the skin or on the outer ear.
>
> - **Lipoma.** Consists of fat cells.
>
> - **Meningioma.** Originates from cells that line the membrane that covers the brain and spinal cord.
>
> - **Papilloma.** A small, round cauliflower-like wart sometimes caused by a virus.
>
> - **Peripheral Odontogenic Fibroma or Epulis.** These masses stem from structures in the oral cavity and are found in gum tissue.
>
> - **Sebaceous gland adenoma.** A small, round tumor that stems from the skin's oil-producing glands.
>
> **MALIGNANT MASSES**
>
> - **Adenocarcinoma.** Start in gland cells that produce fluids or secretions that keep tissues moist. They can affect many areas of the body, including the nose, throat, trachea, lung, stomach, intestine, gallbladder, or salivary, anal/perianal, sweat, and mammary glands.

- **Fibrosarcoma.** Stems from cells called fibroblasts that make up the body's fibrous soft tissue. These tumors can occur in the mouth or be felt as lumps under the skin between a cat's shoulders or elsewhere on the trunk or on the legs.

- **Glioma.** Originates from one or two types of brain cells.

- **Hemangiosarcoma.** Affects cells that line the blood vessels.

- **Lymphoma.** Involves rogue lymphocytes (white blood cells involved in immunity). This cancer can affect the gastrointestinal tract, skin, nasal cavity, chest, kidneys, bone marrow (a specialized tissue in some bones that produces blood cells), lymph nodes, spinal cord, liver, and spleen.

- **Mammary gland adenocarcinoma or carcinoma.** Stems from breast tissue gland cells. Primarily affects female cats who are not spayed.

- **Mast cell tumor.** Involves cells that produce histamine, a chemical released in response to allergy and causes itchiness. Mast cell tumors are most commonly found on the skin, but can affect the spleen, intestines, liver, and bone marrow.

- **Melanoma.** Stems from the pigment-producing cells of the skin, and can also involve the eyes and mouth. (Some melanomas may be benign.)

- **Osteosarcoma.** Originates from bone cells and most often affects a hindlimb but can also occur in the mouth, hips, ribs, and spine.

- **Squamous cell carcinoma.** Stems from skin cells and often occurs in the mouth in cats.

- **Transitional cell carcinoma.** Involves urinary tract cells and most often affects the bladder.

Tumor staging and grading

In addition to identifying the type of tumor and whether it is benign or malignant, veterinarians often need to identify the grade and stage of a malignant tumor. The grade tells us how aggressive the cancer cells are. The stage tells us whether the cancer has spread, and if it has spread, where it has gone and to what extent. Grading and staging help veterinarians identify the cancer's severity and treatment options as well as give a prognosis—a forecast about a cat's chance of recovery, the course of their disease, and expected survival time.

Grading involves sending a biopsy or tissue sample to a veterinary pathologist who evaluates the tumor cells under a microscope to see how abnormal the cells look compared with normal cells of that type. Cancer cells in low-grade tumors look and organize themselves more like healthy cells. Low-grade cancers have a better prognosis because they are usually less aggressive. The more abnormal and unorganized the cells look, the higher the grade. High-grade cancers are usually more disruptive and have a worse prognosis.

Staging means finding out how much cancer is present in the body and where it's located. It may involve special testing of the blood or cancer cells, imaging exams (radiography, ultrasonography, endoscopy, computed tomography, or magnetic resonance imaging), and biopsy of other tissues.

Follow-up tests may also be needed during and at the end of treatment to see how well the treatment is working. This may be accomplished by repeating some of the initial tests done for staging and comparing the results.

Tumor treatments

Treatment options depend on the type, location, and severity of the cancer, along with treatment availability. Some treatments may need to be provided at other practices or at veterinary specialty hospitals. Another important factor involves carefully considering your caregiving and financial abilities.

Many cancer treatment options are available and more than one type of treatment may be needed. Some treatments can be curative, others can delay the cancer's growth or spread, and some may not work against the cancer at all. Keep in mind that a certain treatment that worked well for a friend's cat may not work for your cat—every patient is different and not all tumors respond to treatment in the same way.

In addition to treatment for the cancer, cats often need supportive treatments that may include pain relief medications, anti-nausea medications, appetite stimulants, antibiotics, probiotics, nutritional supplements, and subcutaneous or intravenous fluid therapy.

Surgery

If a tumor can be surgically removed, the surgeon attempts to take out the entire tumor along with enough tissue around the tumor to obtain "clean margins." This means that normal cells are present at the edges of the removed tissue and presumes that no tumor cells have been left behind to continue growing.

Veterinarians are fairly good at evaluating where a tumor starts and stops, but we still can't use only our naked eyes or simply feel a tumor to know how far the tumor cells reach. So we also use established surgical guidelines for tumor removal to decide how much tissue around the tumor to remove. Then we send the tumor and tissue to a veterinary pathologist who uses microscopic examination to identify whether the tumor has "fingers" that extend from the tumor and, if so, how far. If the pathology report says "clean margins," that means no tumor fingers extend to the edges and the tumor has been adequately removed! If tumor cells are present at the margins, another surgery or a different type of treatment may be needed.

For patients who have tumors that are too extensive to completely remove or are too close to vital structures, the surgeon removes as much of the tumor as possible. This is called *debulking*. It's also sometimes done to alleviate a patient's discomfort or to reduce the number of cancer cells, which can help us better attack the remaining cancer cells with other treatment methods, such as chemotherapy or radiation therapy.

Chemotherapy

A wide variety of chemotherapeutic drugs are available and are used to attack fast-growing cancer cells. Depending on the drug, your cat may need to take pills or receive injections into the blood (intravenous), under the skin (subcutaneous), or into the muscle (intramuscular). Many of the drugs used to treat cancer in cats are used to treat cancer in people.

Cats usually tolerate chemotherapy well. About 80% to 90% of cats experience no side effects from chemotherapy. Less than 5% of cats need hospitalization related to chemotherapy side effects.[3,4] Side effects can happen because chemotherapy agents often also attack fast-growing normal cells like those in the gastrointestinal tract, bone marrow (which produces blood cells), and hair.

The side effects that occur in 10% to 15% of cats are typically milder than those that occur in people. Reduced appetite, nausea, and diarrhea are most common. Often we can provide medications that alleviate some of those side effects, and I suggest giving them regardless of whether those side effects occur. It's easier to keep discomfort at bay than to try to chase it away!

Many pet parents are surprised to learn that hair loss is not a typical side effect of chemotherapy in cats and dogs as much as it is in people. The hair growth cycle of pets differs from ours. But cats who have shaved areas during chemotherapy (perhaps because of surgery for tumor removal) may regrow the hair in that area quite slowly, and the regrowth may be a different color. Cats who receive chemotherapy may lose their outer haircoat and their whiskers but retain their soft undercoat. Hair loss is not a sign that chemotherapy should be stopped, and the hair that is lost during chemotherapy typically regrows afterward.

Some chemotherapy drugs cause bone marrow suppression, so fewer blood cells are produced. The blood cells most often affected are neutrophils (a type of white blood cell that helps fight infection) and platelets (cells that form blood clots to prevent excessive bleeding). A low number of neutrophils circulating in the blood is called *neutropenia*, and a deficiency of platelets is called *thrombocytopenia*. Veterinarians will monitor these cell counts during chemotherapy and adjust the timing of treatments if needed.

A few of the chemotherapeutic drugs can cause organ-specific side effects like heart or kidney injury, and veterinarians monitor cats closely for indicators of these problems as well.

Radiation therapy

For some types of cancer, delivering high doses of radiation to the tumor is the best option. Radiation is targeted to the tumor, and usually no other organs are damaged, although surrounding skin or mucous membrane irritation can occur. Radiation therapy requires multiple treatments, and the cat must be anesthetized each time because the cat has to stay still while the radiation is delivered.

Immunotherapy and light therapy

Veterinary-specific treatments that recruit a cat's immune system to fight some types of cancer may be available for cats, such as monoclonal antibodies and vaccines.[5-7] Monoclonal antibodies used in cancer treatment are molecules that act like the body's natural antibodies to recognize cancer cells and tackle them in a variety of ways. Vaccines include inactive components similar to those within cancer cells, and these components teach the body to recognize them so the body can launch an immune response against the cancer cells.

Researchers are also studying nanobody-targeted photodynamic therapy as a potential treatment for oral squamous cell carcinoma in cats. This treatment involves administering a chemical that makes specific tumor cells light-sensitive, followed by using a special light that precisely kills those cancer cells.[8]

A veterinary cancer specialist (oncologist) can provide information about the most current treatment options available for your cat, so consider asking your veterinarian about a consultation.

Do (somewhat) nothing

Another option is to not pursue cancer treatment. I hesitate to say "do nothing," because you won't truly be doing nothing—you will still be caring for your cat by treating and managing their symptoms and evaluating their quality of life.

Regardless of the decisions you and your family make about treating your cat's illness, you are making the right decisions for your situation. Every cat, every cancer, every family, every circumstance is different. In order to make the right decision and know that you have done so, it's crucial to first gather all the information, and then make an informed decision.

Seeing a veterinary oncologist

A primary care veterinarian (like myself) can help identify, stage, grade, and even treat many cancers in cats. However, some cancer treatments require specialized knowledge and skills as well as specialized equipment, such as specially ventilated areas where chemotherapy drugs are prepared, advanced imaging technology like computed tomography or magnetic resonance imaging, or a linear accelerator, which is a machine that delivers radiation therapy. So your primary care veterinarian may recommend that you visit a veterinary oncologist.

Veterinary oncologists are invaluable. They have the latest and greatest cancer knowledge and medications plus access to advanced equipment. They also know the treatment outcome statistics better than anyone. Each of my own pets who have had cancer have been evaluated by a veterinary oncologist, even if it was only for me to consult with the oncologist about my pet's options and prognosis. Consulting with an oncologist helps you make an educated decision about your cat's treatments—even if you decide not to treat. A consultation may also help you avoid regrets about not starting treatment sooner.

Your veterinarian can recommend an oncologist closest to you. Depending on where you live, they are not always nearby. Pet parents sometimes drive hours to see a veterinary oncologist. Your veterinarian may also consult with an oncologist using a teleconsulting service. Oncologists can work directly with your veterinarian to provide information and treatment options and help guide them during treatment when appropriate. To find an oncologist near you, you can also search the Veterinary Cancer Society website: **vetcancersociety.org**.

See your veterinarian if your cat:

- has a mass that's the size of a pea or larger that has been there for a month or more;
- has a wound that won't heal;
- has a mass that changes shape, color, or size;
- constantly licks, rubs, or scratches at a spot;
- has nose bleeds;

- frequently paws at his nose or mouth;
- sneezes excessively;
- has bad breath or trouble chewing;
- drools excessively or has pink- or red-tinged drool;
- has pale gums;
- has a swollen belly;
- exhibits abdominal pain—cats with belly pain may curl up, have a hunched posture, or stretch out in a "prayer position" with their front legs extended on the ground in front of them and their hind end in the air; ats with abdominal pain may also cry out or resist being picked up;
- strains to urinate or has discolored urine;
- has seizures; or
- exhibits other signs of illness: vomiting, diarrhea, having accidents in the house, behavior changes, coughing, unexplained weight loss, weakness or exercise intolerance, shortness of breath, lameness, rough or thin hair coat or hair loss.

Questions to ask your veterinarian (or veterinary oncologist)

- What diagnostic tests will be needed? What are the costs?
- Does my cat need to be sedated or anesthetized for the diagnostic procedures?
- Why does the aspirate, biopsy, or tissue sample need to be sent to a pathologist?
- What will happen if I choose not to do tests?
- How long will my cat live without treatment?
- How will the disease progress if I choose not to pursue treatment?
- Does my cat need to visit a veterinary oncologist?
- Will the treatment cure my cat? How long will my cat live with treatment? Will the treatment help my cat feel better?

 Cena wearing his 'F' cancer hat!

- What treatments will be needed, how will they be given, how often, and for how long?
- What are the side effects of treatment? Will the side effects subside? Can the side effects be treated?
- What signs or problems do I need to watch out for?
- What do I do if problems occur after regular business hours?
- How will we know whether the treatment is working? How long before we know whether it's working?
- What follow-up tests and exams will be needed and how often?
- Does my cat need a special diet or nutritional supplements?
- Will other therapies such as acupuncture help my cat in addition to standard treatment?
- Will my cat benefit from rehabilitation therapy?
- If a standard cancer treatment is not an option, is my cat eligible to participate in a cancer treatment clinical study?
- Will my cat benefit from hospice treatment now or in the near future?

CAREGIVER TIPS AND HOME HACKS

- Provide a cozy, supportive bed and comfy sleeping area.
- Keep food and water and litter boxes easily accessible.
- Provide non-slip walking surfaces and ramps or steps where needed.
- Keep a cat health journal to track your cat's attitude, appetite, activity, and medications and responses to treatments.
- Treat your cat's pain, nausea, and diarrhea by staying ahead of their symptoms and giving prescribed medications consistently and on schedule.
- Limit your cat's stress, and stick to routines.
- Provide calming feline pheromones. Ask your veterinarian about calming supplements and mild sedatives if needed.
- Take a few minutes every day to engage your cat in an activity she enjoys.
- Feed highly palatable foods appropriate for your cat, and feed canned food or moistened kibble if needed. Talk with your veterinarian about diet options.
- Comb or brush your cat regularly to help him groom, give him extra attention, and check for lumps and bumps.

RESOURCES

- Morris Animal Foundation. **morrisanimalfoundation.org/**
- Veterinary Cancer Society. **vetcancersociety.org/**
- Pet Owner Resources compiled by veterinary oncologist Dr. Sue Ettinger. **drsuecancervet.com/pet-owner-resources/**

CHAPTER 20:

Pain: If only our cats could talk about discomfort, malaise, anxiety, and suffering

> "And even if an animal could talk, would we listen?"
> — Virginia Morell, American science writer

Saksy was a geriatric cat who lived in Newport Beach, California. I was called to her home for a hospice appointment because she was urinating and defecating right in front of her litter box. Her pet parents had taken her to see their primary care veterinarian, who diagnosed arthritis and prescribed pain relief medication. Saksy's owners told me the medication seemed to help, but they had trouble getting her to take it. They also said they didn't refill Saksy's prescription because they looked up the drug on the internet and were worried about its potential side effects.

Saksy's owner directed me to the master bedroom first, because they had set it up for Saksy's comfort. They had added a set of pet stairs so Saksy could climb into and out of their bed, several cat toys were scattered about because Saksy still liked to play, and their bathroom had been converted into a kitty restroom. It was clear that Saksy could at least make it to the restroom, because piles of evidence on the bathroom floor (her poop looked normal though!), a strong odor, and a clean litter box betrayed that Saksy was not using the facilities properly.

Saksy calmly watched me from her perch on the bed. Although she had long, beautiful fur, she had tons of dandruff on her hindquarters along with bald spots where her mom had cut off Saksy's matted hair. It appeared that Saksy couldn't effectively groom her back end and no longer liked to be brushed, so her fur was tangled and matted. When I attempted to gently palpate her hindlegs and hips, she immediately turned her head toward my hands and then tried to bolt away from me (both are signs of pain).

Saksy's scenario illustrates how some pet parents miss signs of chronic pain. Saksy didn't limp or yowl; she simply stopped grooming her hindquarters, stopped jumping up on their bed, resented being touched on her hindquarters, and pooped (and peed) outside the litter box! Her family finally knew something was amiss when she stopped using the litter box. It was obvious to me that we needed to readdress Saksy's long-standing pain caused by arthritis. I was hopeful that with a little more help, we could enhance her quality of life and extend her lifespan, and that she may not be a hospice candidate.

Understanding the pathway that pain travels

When we badly stub a toe, the nerve endings, called *nociceptors ("pain receptor" from the Latin nocere 'to harm or hurt')*, in our skin, muscle, and bone sense it. Nociceptors detect mechanical, thermal, and chemical tissue damage. (Nociceptors are also present in our organs.) The pain signals travel as electrical impulses from the nociceptors along nerve fibers to the spinal cord. These signals relay the physical pain that we and other animals experience.

In an area of the spinal cord called the dorsal horn, the signal travels between neurons through junctions called *synapses*. In the synapses, chemical messengers called *neurotransmitters* are released. Neurotransmitters send signals back down to your toe as a reflex (and you jerk your foot back!) and, at the same time, send signals up the spinal cord to a part of the brain called the *thalamus*.

From the thalamus, the message is distributed to many different areas of the brain for additional processing so you know where the pain came from and how much it hurts; whether to be sad, angry, or afraid (or all of those!); and whether you need to take further action. The brain also begins to process how that particular pain will be remembered. Physical pain carries a negative emotional element (called an affective component).[1,2] What's more, unpleasant emotions can be a form of pain,[3] and positive emotions can reduce pain (called affective analgesia).[2]

The part of the brain responsible for physical sensation is called the *somatosensory cortex*. The part of the brain responsible for emotions is called the

FUN FACT:

Research shows that not only mammals—but also octopuses, fish, and crabs—avoid pain and dangerous locations, and that some animals exhibit empathy, such as cows who become distressed when they know their calf is in pain.[4]

And did you know? Rats exhibit empathy-related pain responses (called *observational contagious pain*) when they see a cage mate in pain.[5,6] Rats also console their distressed buddy by grooming them and by licking their injury.[5,6] Interestingly, rats who aren't cage mates don't show these responses, unless one stranger (non-cage mate) has just recently experienced pain and sees another stranger in pain.[7] This suggests that similar past pain experience produces pain empathy even in rats who don't know each other.[7]

Rats also stop pulling levers that deliver their favorite treats if pulling that lever also mildly shocks another rat,[8] they free cage mates who are trapped in a small tube,[9] and they grant access to dry land to cage mates who have been forced to swim in a tiny pool.[10] Rats are teaching us a lot about the empathy people have (or not!) for others.

limbic system. And one of many parts of the brain responsible for personality and consciousness is called the *frontal cortex*. All or some of these parts of the brain become involved in the pain pathway and influence how the body responds to pain!

What's the point of all this messaging?

Pain allows us to know that something harmful has happened and that we need to respond to it to make it stop. Processing pain messages helps us avoid, prevent, and remember unpleasant incidents or encounters and protect ourselves from more hurt. In this way, pain messages are beneficial. But if pain lasts a long time and isn't adequately relieved or if it is extremely severe even for a short time, pain messages can become harmful and provide little or no benefit.

A peek at some of the many causes of physical and emotional pain:

- physical trauma such as falling or getting hit, cut, or bitten;
- thermal (heat or cold) trauma such as sunburns, frostbite, or heating pad burns;

- chemical trauma such as burns from corrosive substances;
- internal organ problems such as pancreatitis (inflammation of the pancreas), gastritis (stomach inflammation), urinary tract blockage, or an intestinal tumor;
- skin, ear, and eye infections;
- surgery such as tumor removal, tooth extractions, broken bone repair, or removal of foreign bodies (e.g. toys, hair ties, bones, fishing line or hooks) from the stomach or intestine;
- degenerative and inflammatory conditions such as arthritis;
- brain or spinal cord problems such as tumors; and
- isolation, fear, frustration, separation anxiety, depression, helplessness, boredom, anger, or grief.[3]

Short-term pain vs. long-term pain

When it comes to pain, veterinarians (and physicians) generally distinguish between two types—acute and chronic. Acute pain is sudden and typically lasts until the insult is removed and the injury has healed. Chronic pain is long-term and accompanies an ongoing condition (like arthritis) or continues after an injury has healed.

Another way to describe pain is to use the terms *adaptive pain* and *maladaptive pain*.[11] Adaptive pain is beneficial; it's necessary for survival and results from the "early warning" nociceptors that signal damaging stimuli such as high heat, blunt force, and inflammation associated with tissue damage. Adaptive pain is usually reversible or self-limiting if it's treated correctly. Maladaptive pain isn't beneficial; it results from nerve damage or nociceptive system malfunction, and it contributes to decreased pain thresholds and increased sensitivity to painful or nonpainful stimuli.[11]

Acute pain

People usually describe acute pain as a sharp pain, and it can last a moment or for a day—or several weeks. Acute pain in pets can result from trauma (e.g. hit by a car, cat fight), surgery (e.g. to repair a wound or remove a foreign body or tumor), or disease (e.g. dental infection, bladder inflammation).

Acute pain occurs because of tissue damage, and the nerves in the area send signals to the brain to tell us to avoid the source and help prevent us from using the injured area and doing more damage while we heal. Even so, acute pain must be managed! In fact, pain control is known to help speed healing. Pain control also, of course, improves quality of life.

Chronic pain

Chronic pain persists. The pain signals keep coming long after the injury has healed, and the pain can last months or years. (In people, chronic pain is often described as pain that lasts longer than three to six months.) Chronic pain can also stem from long-term health problems that continuously cause damage.

The most common chronically painful condition I see in cats is arthritis, also called *osteoarthritis* and *degenerative joint disease* (see Chapter 16 "Mobility: The creaky, shaky, and unsteady"). Often, the cat's family doesn't notice the subtle signs.

Like acute pain, chronic pain must be managed. Pain relief improves quality of life for cats and prevents or helps reduce the long-term effects of chronic pain, such as worsening of pain and anxiety, and long-term stress. Pain relief improves mobility in cats with arthritis. Pain management also helps maintain a healthy, happy, interactive bond between pet parents and cats. Recognizing and managing chronic pain can be lifesaving for pets because chronic pain that is inadequately identified and poorly managed can lead to premature euthanasia.[12]

The unhelpful effects of chronic pain

Pain stimulates stress responses that involve hormones and other chemical messengers, which are good in the short term because they help an animal decide whether to fight or flee the source of the pain. These chemical messengers also stimulate other cells that are recruited to help with healing. But long-term pain and stress responses can be damaging. In fact, in people, moderate to severe persistent pain (which may indicate chronic pain) was associated with faster memory decline and increased risk of dementia.[13]

Chronic stress suppresses the immune system so the body can't fight off infection and heal its wounds as well. Stress may even promote cancer spread, as studies in mice have shown.[14] Stress-related changes you may notice in your cat include muscle weakness, hair changes, and weight loss. Hair changes?! People often say, "I'm losing my hair from stress!" Cats can experience this coat-depleting characteristic as well, or self-groom excessively and pull their fur out because of stress-related chemical reactions in the body induced by chronic pain.

Another uncomfortable effect of chronic pain: the central nervous system (brain and spinal cord) can overreact to pain. The nerve fibers that carry pain signals and the nerve fibers that carry touch signals end in different locations in the brain. But with chronic pain, chemical signals stimulate some nerve fibers to grow, and the pain and touch fibers become intertwined like a hair knot. This allows the touch nerve fibers to signal pain to the brain in response to normal, nonpainful touch. This is called *hypersensitivity* or *allodynia*. It explains why some cats hiss or lash out in response to simply being petted, when previously they would have welcomed a good love session! Even something as benign as a fan blowing on a cat may cause pain if the cat has allodynia.

The pain nerve fibers can also grow and expand in different directions, which increases the size of the painful area. And pain receptors can become more easily stimulated, which lowers the pain threshold and increases the amount of time that the pain lasts. When this happens, what would normally feel like a minor pain feels much more hurtful.

Anticipating and fearing pain

Cats with acute or chronic pain or hypersensitivity can have anticipatory pain, which means the cat responds *before* the painful stimulus occurs because they know it will hurt. For example, you reach for your cat and they growl or hiss before you touch their painful area. It's their way of protecting themselves and saying, "Please don't!"

> **Did you know? Pain, older age, floor surface, and obesity can make hallways look longer!**
>
> A study in people who have chronic lower back or leg pain revealed that they perceived a long hallway to be 30% longer, compared with people who do not have pain.[15] By simply looking at the hallway and estimating its distance (and not walking it), people with chronic pain estimated that the hallway was longer than the estimates made by people who did not have painful conditions.
>
> Similarly, a separate study showed that older adults estimate distances to be farther compared with younger adults' estimates. Older adults also estimate distance to be farther on surfaces that are more difficult to walk on (carpet covered with a plastic tarp vs. carpet alone) than younger adults do.[16]
>
> Furthermore, another study found that people who are overweight or obese estimate distances to be farther than normal weight people do.[17] The researchers stated that these results suggested that because heavier people perceive their environment differently, they may choose to do less demanding tasks that affect their lifestyle choices than normal weight people do.
>
> While we can't ask cats to estimate distances, the results of these studies make me wonder whether these factors also similarly affect our cats' willingness to participate in certain activities including walking on slick surfaces.

Detecting and assessing pain in cats

Cats may show outward signs of pain that are obvious to us. They may hiss, flinch, growl, bite, hide, or limp. And did you know? Cats who are stressed because of pain may even purr. So keep in mind that cats who are in pain may also still purr, eat, sit on your lap, be happy to see you, or even try to jump with an injured joint. Many clients who brought their arthritic cats to me for evaluation would tell me, "Well, she's eating and still purrs when she sits on my lap, so I don't think she's in any pain."

FUN FACT:

In 2001, a researcher recorded and analyzed the purr sound frequencies of domestic cats, cheetahs, ocelots, servals, and pumas. She proposed that purring may act as an internal self-healing mechanism that works while cats rest, to bolster their recovery time and keep their muscles and bones strong.[18]

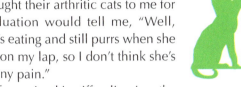

If an animal is stiff or limping, the animal has pain. If an animal has inflammation, the animal has pain. If your cat has an injury or condition that would clearly be painful if you or I had the same problem, your cat is in pain. Unless their pain is extreme, cats who have pain often still have an appetite. And eating and purring are not diagnostic tools that confirm the absence of pain (but oh, how I wish they were!).

To further complicate matters, cats who are in pain often hide. So because cats normally rest and sleep for 80% of the day,[19] you may not notice signs of pain in your cat.

Putting pain on a scale

Veterinary medical caregivers use pain scales to evaluate pain and decide whether to adjust a patient's pain treatment protocol. For example, Colorado State University's Veterinary Medical Center developed a pain scale to assess signs of acute pain in cats.[20] A cat's facial expressions, body postures, specific behaviors, and responses to touch are evaluated and correlated with a scale of 0 (no pain) to 4 (extreme pain).

A feline grimace scale has also been developed to evaluate signs of acute pain in cats based on their facial expressions.[21] Pain scales help veterinary medical caregivers decide whether to adjust a pain treatment protocol for an individual patient.

To help you recognize some of the subtle to more obvious signs of pain that cats may be communicating, I've highlighted components of the Colorado State University Feline Acute Pain Scale along with the Feline Grimace Scale. You can also download a Feline Grimace Scale app on your phone to score your cat at home.

A cat with a pain score of 0
(therapy to relieve pain is not needed):

- appears quiet, content, and relaxed; looks bright- and wide-eyed; holds ears facing forward; has a relaxed and rounded muzzle with loose and curved whiskers; holds head above the shoulder line; is comfortable when resting
- is curious and interested in the surroundings; or
- has minimal body tension and does not mind being touched.

A cat with a pain score of 1
(needs veterinary-prescribed therapy to relieve discomfort):

- appears more quiet than usual, looks less bright-eyed and holds eyes partially open, holds ears pulled slightly back and apart, has a slightly tense muzzle with mildly tense and slightly curved whiskers, holds head level with shoulder line;
- shows less interest in the surroundings, may rest or sleep in out-of-the-way places (e.g. under a bed, in a closet); or
- has mild body tension and may react when a painful area is touched.

A cat with a pain score of 2
(ask your veterinarian about adjusting or adding therapy to better relieve pain):

- appears quiet, seems less alert, keeps eyes partially or mostly closed or squints, flattens and rotates ears outward, has a tense elliptical-shaped muzzle, holds whiskers straight and slightly pointed forward, holds head below the shoulder line, may tuck chin toward the chest;
- seeks out-of-the-way places to rest, sits tucked up or lies curled up with all four feet under his body, keeps tail curled tightly against his body, hunches shoulders, may look unkempt or have a fluffed up coat;
- is less responsive, may still perk up when petted if the painful area is not touched, turns toward the painful area if it is touched and may meow, hiss or growl or try to escape; or
- has mild to moderate body tension, may excessively groom the painful area, has little to no interest in food.

A cat with a pain score of 3

(ask your veterinarian about further adjusting or adding therapy to better relieve pain):

- may growl or hiss even if left alone or when petted in a nonpainful area, may bite or chew at a painful area, pulls away immediately or may growl or bite when a painful area is touched; or
- has moderate body tension, lies crouched or hunched up and is reluctant to move.

A cat with a pain score of 4

(ask your veterinarian about further adjusting or adding therapy to better relieve pain):

- lies flat out on one side, is unresponsive, appears unaware of surroundings and hard to distract from the pain; or
- is moderately to severely tense, may remain still and rigid because it is too painful to move, may even seem more tolerant of contact and not respond to touch.

Check out and compare the images of cats in pain and not in pain:

This cat is in pain after a dental surgery: eyes are partially closed, ears are pulled slightly back and apart, muzzle and whiskers are tense, body posture is moderately tense, overall demeanor is quiet and less alert.

No pain in Eddie's face! He has wide-open, bright, round eyes; tall, forward-facing ears; a relaxed, round muzzle; loose, curved (and magnificent!) whiskers; and he holds his head above the shoulder line and is fully alert and curious.

Before Smokey received pain medication (left photo) after surgery on his hindleg, he showed clear signs of pain: he squinted and kept his eyes mostly closed, his ears were partially flattened and turned down and outward, his muzzle was tense (because he was grimacing) with his whiskers held straight/horizontal and slightly pointed forward, he held his head slightly lower than his shoulders, and he was quiet and less alert. After Smokey received pain medication (right photo), his eyes were much more open, his ears were up and facing forward, his muzzle is more relaxed, his whiskers are slightly more relaxed (more space between them) and curved, he held his head higher, he had a more relaxed body posture, and he looked brighter and was more alert.

Malaise

Sometimes cats may not be feeling well and have malaise: discomfort, tiredness, weakness, and uneasiness. Malaise differs from acute or chronic pain but should be addressed. Nausea, dehydration, high blood pressure, diarrhea, acid reflux, congestion, fever, toxins in the bloodstream, and anemia are only a few of the problems that can cause malaise. For example, nausea may not be considered to be painful, but I think it's as serious as the pain that occurs with arthritis, and, in some ways, nausea is worse.

I broke my foot a few years ago and it was painful! It swelled and turned purple, was ugly to see, and I could not walk on it for weeks. I took pain relief medications and sat on the couch with my leg propped up. I could watch TV, talk on the phone, eat the meals brought to me, and work from my laptop. I could tolerate the foot pain and I knew it would be better in a few weeks.

Two months after my foot healed, I caught a bad case of the flu. I had a fever of 103 F, chills, no appetite, and extreme fatigue. All I could do was lie in bed and moan about getting over the flu! I didn't feel like watching TV or reading, and working was out of the question. I remember being absolutely miserable and thinking that I would rather have *two* broken feet than have the flu! This was malaise, and to me, it was worse than pain. And at times, the malaise was even worse—I was suffering!

Anxiety

Medical conditions can cause or contribute to various types of anxiety in cats. Cognitive dysfunction and diseases that cause respiratory distress are at the top of that list for cats, just as dementia and breathing trouble can cause anxiety in people. Many geriatric cats have increased anxiety in a variety of situations, likely because they become less adept at responding to environmental changes or social cues as their body systems age and lose resilience.[22] In turn, anxiety can exacerbate pain, so take care to alleviate stressful situations that can lead to anxiety, such as aggression between housemate cats or punishment for undesirable behavior.[23] Anxiety can increase pain, and pain can increase anxiety–it's a vicious cycle!

Anxious cats tend to hide, and they may vocalize, tremble, become irritable, compulsively groom themselves, pace, and eat less. To me—and many of my colleagues agree—anxiety is a form of mental pain and suffering that cats may experience and it should be treated to address the underlying cause and manage the cat's responses.

Suffering

Nearly every pet parent tells me, "I just don't want my pet to suffer." And I concur! I do not want any animal to suffer. When veterinarians take the veterinary oath, we swear to prevent and relieve suffering.

But what is suffering? We all have a general idea that suffering is to feel or undergo pain or distress, but the definition of suffering can be varied and highly individual. It can also carry religious and philosophical perspectives.

Suffering may involve a wide variety of extreme unpleasant experiences that stem from physical or psychological stimuli.[24] Physical suffering may include pain, hunger, thirst, illness, and the process of dying. Mental suffering may include grief, anxiety, and loneliness. Unrelieved pain can cause suffering.[24] For me personally, suffering is a state of being where I can't think of or do anything besides concentrate on my pain, whether the suffering is from physical pain (what the pain itself feels like—such as throbbing and aching, stabbing and sharp, burning or constricting), or from emotional pain (how the pain makes me feel—such as uneasy, anxious, depressed, afraid, or isolated). When I broke my foot, I experienced physical pain. When I was ill with the flu, I experienced physical and emotional pain. When I lose a pet, I experience emotional pain, yet in some ways, it also feels like physical pain. I admire how Cicely Saunders (a physician and pioneer in human hospice care) approached the concept of total pain—a mix of physical, emotional, and spiritual discomfort—which we now more commonly call suffering.

An easy way to think about suffering is that it is the opposite of happiness or pleasure. My broken foot was painful, but I still experienced happiness and didn't suffer. It is really hard to be happy while one is truly suffering.

Can animals be happy? I once was discussing happiness in animals with a group of veterinary students in Oregon, and one of the students asked, "Dr. Mary, aren't you anthropomorphizing when you say that animals can be happy?" I replied, "No, I am not. Animals can feel pleasure. They can be happy, and they can suffer."

As you navigate whether and how to treat your cat's illnesses and make their end-of-life decisions, you may think, "I don't want my cat to suffer," which can be hard for you to define. Instead, consider thinking, "I want my cat to be happy." Whether your cat can regain happiness or pleasure in life may be an easier attribute to strive for and an outcome that is clearer to visualize. (Also see Chapter 30 "Life quality: 'Doc, when is it time?'")

When to see your veterinarian

Pain, malaise, anxiety, and suffering can be alleviated. Recognizing these problems in your cat and seeking treatment for the underlying cause as well as treatment for the pain itself helps preserve the bond you and your cat share. Please see your veterinarian if your cat exhibits evidence of pain based on the pain scales included above or any of the following signs:

- no longer jumps up or is reluctant to jump up on the couch, bed, or favorite perch like before;
- is reluctant to go up or down stairs;
- is reluctant to be picked up;
- has an unkempt coat (especially cats who are reluctant to reach their hindquarters to groom) or coat appears "puffed up";
- is reluctant to be groomed;
- moves away while being petted or shies away from being touched in certain areas;
- exhibits personality changes, such as more fatigue, less activity (no longer chases toys), being quieter or depressed, being more irritable;
- begins having urine or fecal accidents in the house;

- excessively scratches or licks certain areas of her body;
- shakes, paws, rubs at, or scoots on a painful area;
- drools;
- has diarrhea or constipation;
- eats or drinks less;
- hides, or rests or sleeps in unusual places;
- has tense muscles or postures;
- has trouble posturing to eliminate;
- has trouble using or no longer uses their scratching post;
- limps;
- stands or walks with a tucked abdomen or arched back;
- stretches out in a "prayer position" with front legs extended on the ground in front of him and his hind end in the air—like a bow;
- is less bright-eyed—may have a sleepy, squinting, or vacant look; pupils may be enlarged;
- is lethargic or reluctant to move;
- prefers to eat or drink lying down;
- exhibits restlessness—repeatedly lies down and gets up again; may occur especially at night;
- has unusual vocalizing—howling, hissing, or growling (and some cats who are stressed or in pain will purr);
- is slower to get up or lie down;
- avoids walking on tile or hardwood floors;
- shows a new preference to lie on tiled floors (may be seeking cooler surfaces to ease joint or muscle pain);
- holds head or tail lower than normal;
- shifts weight to one side while standing;
- shakes or trembles;
- breathes faster than normal or pants (beyond what you would expect in relation to exercise or warm temperatures);
- persistently paces; or
- is hesitant to lift head or turn head to one side or the other.

AN IMPORTANT TIP: Your veterinarian will greatly appreciate seeing short videos of the concerning signs your cat is showing, along with videos that show how your cat moves–walking, playing, using stairs, jumping onto and down from furniture or their cat tree, and getting into the litter box.

Veterinarians may ask pet parents to complete quick checklists to help catch signs of joint pain in their cats. On the next page is a fun example of one that your cat (and you) can do together:

Illustration by Dusan Pavlic. Checklist adapted from: Enomoto M, Lascelles BDX, Gruen ME. Development of a checklist for the detection of degenerative joint disease-associated pain in cats. *J Feline Med Surg*. 2020 Dec;22(12):1137-1147.

Managing pain

Response to pain varies tremendously among individuals and is influenced by many factors, including species, age, health status, sex, genetics, previous experiences, and breed.[24] For example, young animals may have a lower acute pain tolerance than mature animals, but may also be less likely to have anticipatory pain. Animals who are ill have a lower pain tolerance than healthy animals, and severely ill animals may experience severe pain but may be unable to exhibit signs of pain and, therefore, it may go unnoticed and untreated. An individual cat's response to various forms of pain relief also varies.

Offense is better than defense, so the sooner we address pain, the better! Chronic pain is harder to treat, and multiple attempts that involve different therapies (called *multimodal therapy*) may be needed.[24] Whenever possible, taking care to not allow pain to develop in the first place is especially important. For example, veterinarians (and physicians) often provide *preemptive analgesia* by giving pain medications and drugs that relieve anxiety before surgery. This ensures that medications are "on board" *before* the pain and anxiety stimuli occur. And sticking to an optimal pain medication dose and on-time administration schedule after surgery, injury, or illness (and adjusting it as needed) allows pain medication to be reliably and continuously "on board," giving pain less opportunity to break through and send uncomfortable messages to the brain.

It's crucial to avoid repetitive pain signals because the nerves become more excitable and remain overreactive. This is called pain *wind-up*. When wind-up occurs, pain is more difficult to relieve. It often requires higher drug doses to control, and additional medications may be needed, which can result in added expenses, more stress for a pet who doesn't tolerate medication administration well, increased caregiving time, and additional side effects. Pain wind-up can also contribute to unremitting chronic pain.

I always say it's easier to keep pain away than to chase it away. Preventing or alleviating pain can also increase your cat's lifespan, which is invaluable.

Other than resolving the underlying disease or condition, there is not one best way to address pain or malaise. Achieving comfort is the goal, and it's important for pet parents to recognize that completely eliminating pain is unusual, particularly in pets with chronic pain. In fact, it's helpful to think about chronic or maladaptive pain as a disease itself that must be managed.[11]

Always work with or ask your veterinarian which medications and other therapies are right for your cat and your cat's ailment, and do not give your cat your own medications or another pet's medications.

I usually attack pain using a multipronged approach that includes one or more medications with or without non-drug treatments that work together, such as[25]: (Also see Chapter 23 "Course of action: Therapeutic options and gaining acceptance from your senior cat.")

- Drugs used to relieve pain or malaise:
  - gabapentin;
  - amantadine;
  - non-steroidal anti-inflammatory drugs (NSAIDs; e.g. veterinary-specific drugs such as robenacoxib or meloxicam; also, do not give NSAIDs for people to your pet because they can be extremely harmful, and never give acetaminophen or aspirin to cats);
  - frunevetmab (the brand name is Solensia, made by Zoetis) a feline-specific monoclonal antibody (a laboratory-made protein that acts like the body's cells that fight invaders and harmful processes) that recognizes and stops the body's signals that promote inflammation and pain[26,27];
  - opioids (several types are available; tramadol is an opioid but isn't recommended for long-term pain management);
  - corticosteroids;
  - local or topical anesthetics;
  - alpha-2 agonists;
  - sedatives and tranquilizers (some of these drugs provide little to no pain relief, but they decrease anxiety and the emotional component of pain or boost the effectiveness of other pain medications);
  - anti-nausea medications;
  - intravenous or subcutaneous fluid therapy; and
  - anti-anxiety medications or antidepressants.
- Omega-3 fatty acids
- Environmental modifications (see the "Caregiver tips and home hacks" sections in Chapter 16 "Mobility: The creaky, shaky, and unsteady" and in the chapters specific to your cat's conditions)
- Nutrition and therapeutic diets, including weight management
- Rehabilitation therapy:
  - encouraging the cat to be active and exercise as appropriate;
  - massage therapy and passive range of motion exercises;
  - cooling or warming packs;
  - laser therapy;
  - therapeutic ultrasound;
  - pulsed electromagnetic field therapy (a device sends invisible targeted pulses to tissues, which induce electrical changes around and within cells to influence cell behavior); and
  - transcutaneous electrical nerve stimulation (a device sends a small electrical current through the skin to activate nerves and reduce pain).
- Acupuncture

Questions to ask your veterinarian

- What are the signs of pain associated with my cat's condition?
- How will I know whether the treatment to manage my cat's pain is working?
- The pain associated with my cat's chronic condition can flare with stress or overactivity, so can my cat be scheduled on a day when he can have a morning appointment and be discharged soon after? (So he doesn't have to stay in the clinic all day.)
- Can I bring my cat's favorite toy or blanket to ease stress or anxiety associated with visiting the clinic or being hospitalized? (The answer should always be yes!)
- Do you use pheromones in the clinic to help calm anxious animals?
- Do you provide special padded bedding for cats with arthritis?
- If my cat is especially stressed when I give him medications or travel frequently with him for his treatments or recheck appointments, what alternatives are available (such as different medication formulations or flavors, pre-appointment anti-anxiety measures or medications, in-home veterinary visits, telemedicine recheck appointments)?
- If my cat will be anesthetized for a procedure, will you ensure careful positioning and comfort so as not to inadvertently aggravate my cat's painful condition?
- What steps do you take to assess my cat's risk related to sedation or anesthesia (blood tests, radiographs, urinalysis)?
- Do you use topical anesthetic creams before catheter placement?
- Do you use local anesthetics in addition to other analgesics during procedures when possible?
- Do you proactively use pain medications (e.g. before surgery and before my cat shows signs of pain)?
- Do you use sedatives and analgesics to help reduce the amount of general anesthesia needed?
- What steps will you take to reduce my cat's risk related to sedation or anesthesia during my cat's procedure? Do you have specially trained veterinary anesthesia nurses or technicians?
- Will my cat receive pain medications after a procedure? For how long afterward will my cat receive pain medications?
- How will you monitor my cat for pain after a procedure?
- If my cat needs to stay in the hospital, can I visit?
- Will my cat benefit from rehabilitation therapy or other pain management therapies such as acupuncture, nutritional management or supplements, or environmental modifications?

Saksy's relief

I talked with Saksy's pet parents about her condition and eased their worries about the possible side effects of her previously prescribed pain relief medication. I complimented their pet stair accommodation for Saksy, which allowed her to continue sleeping where she was comfy, and their efforts to keep her active with toys. I also suggested that they purchase a larger litter box with a low entry point, because it would allow Saksy to more easily get into the box, turn around in it, and get out of it.

Saksy's pet parents agreed to swap her standard-size litter box for a larger, low-sided litter box, and to give her the pain relief medication again. I prescribed it for Saksy right away. I asked the pharmacy to mix the medication with marshmallow flavor to entice Saksy to more eagerly gobble it up.

Saksy didn't object to receiving the medication this time and even seemed to enjoy it. The owners were relieved that they could reliably give it! She began using her new litter box right away. These two simple changes relieved Saksy's pain and dramatically improved her (and her pet parents') quality of life. Saksy also began grooming herself again, and she even allowed her family to gently brush her again. Saksy lived for another two years after my initial visit with her!

Saksy was very wobbly on her back legs, but she was still determined and did her best to walk around her home!

CAREGIVER TIPS AND HOME HACKS

The household modifications and other environmental comforts you can provide for cats who have painful conditions often overlap, but they also may differ depending on your cat's underlying disorder. For more guidance, please refer to Chapter 16 "Mobility: The creaky, shaky, and unsteady" as well as the chapters that address your cat's specific conditions.

An extra tip to keep in mind: Even after a pet's pain is alleviated, behavior changes that stemmed from a painful condition may be difficult for some pets to unlearn, especially if the behaviors helped the pet change the outcome of a painful situation.[28] For example, if your cat continues to pee or poop outside the litter box or is still irritable, this could indicate either ongoing pain or a learned behavior. Schedule recheck veterinary exams or phone consults to assess your pet's response to pain management treatments, and, if needed, ask your veterinarian whether behavior modification techniques may also be beneficial for your cat.

READING RECOMMENDATIONS

- Animal Pain Awareness. International Veterinary Academy of Pain Management.
  ivapm.org/animal-owners/animal-pain-awareness/
- Feline Acute Pain Scale. Colorado State University Veterinary Teaching Hospital.
  csu-cvmbs.colostate.edu/Documents/anesthesia-pain-management-pain-score-feline.pdf
- Evaluating acute pain based on cats' facial expressions. Feline Grimace Scale.
  felinegrimacescale.com/
- Therapeutic Massage and Your Cat by Dr. Robin Downing. VCA Animal Hospitals.
  vcahospitals.com/know-your-pet/therapeutic-massage-and-your-cat

Part three:
AGING WELL AND CARING FOR TIME-HONORED TABBIES

Being prepared for and getting the right help in caring for elderly cats who have advanced ailments or terminal illnesses can be game changers in improving the lives of cats and their caregivers. In this section we'll explore insights and tools that will help you focus on and enjoy the wonderful moments still to be shared with your fantastic feline friend. You'll learn how to senior-pet-proof and wellness-enhance your home, journal your cat's health, simplify medication administration, and recruit the best support team. I also answer questions that pet parents frequently ask me about veterinary exams, such as:

- "Why should my geriatric cat keep up with veterinary visits?"
- "Is my cat too old for anesthesia?"
- "What do I do when my cat stresses out about going to the vet?"
- And I address the most critical question pet parents ask me when they sense the remaining days with their cats are dwindling: "When will I know it's time?"

In most pet parents' lives, there comes a point in caring for your geriatric or ailing cat when you'll question whether your cat is happy and enjoying life and wonder whether it may be time to say goodbye. And these questions often aren't comfortably discussed with family members and friends. People with good intentions may try to reassure you when they say, "Don't worry, you'll know when it's time." But what I do know, as a veterinarian and as a pet parent, is that you will not always simply "know" when that time has come. And I know that this period is full of heart-wrenching planning and decisions, plus one moment we wish would never come.

When treasured days are limited, time seems to pass in overdrive. So in the later chapters of this section, my goals are to help you lighten the load that caregiving may bring and assess what's most important to you as you face the end of your cat's life. I describe the benefits of pet hospice care and give you options for confidently assessing your cat's unique life quality.

CHAPTER 21:

Safety and environmental enrichment: Creating senior-cat-friendly homes

> A cat needs a place as much as it needs a person to make its own.
>
> —Doris Lessing, British novelist

Ah, a cat's life! Meals prepared and served on time every day. Cozy cat beds and cushions to nap on all day. Sunny windowsills to luxuriate on. Warm laps and human affection available (mostly) on demand. No laundry to fold, work timelines to meet, or rent to pay. How many of us have dreamed we could have a life like theirs? But stop and consider a moment—we've brought them into our homes, and many cats are left to their own devices.

All cats—young, middle-aged, and old—need a safe, comfortable, and stimulating environment with caregivers who monitor and attend to their health and interact with them daily. But as seniors, cats often need extra help to successfully navigate their environment. In addition, being left alone can sometimes be boring, dangerous, unhealthy, and even a bit scary for geriatric cats.

In that spirit, we can alter our own homes, routines, and attentiveness to help our senior cats (and ourselves) live better. This chapter overlaps a bit with some topics included in other chapters, but it gives a high-level view of creating a senior-cat-friendly dwelling. In other chapters, I recommend additional environmental modifications and caregiver tips related to specific conditions common in senior cats—including mobility issues, kidney disease, cognitive dysfunction, and more—so also refer to the chapters specific to your cat's needs.

A cat's-eye view to an aging-friendly abode

Home is familiar, comforting, and safe to your cat. But similar to the home safety and accessibility concerns that arise as people age, the home environment can become more challenging and contain hazard zones for older cats. For people, the American Association of Retired Persons published a free "HomeFit Guide" to help create an "aging-friendly" current or future home, no matter a person's life stage.[1] And companies that specialize in assessing an elderly person's home can be hired to help organize, remodel, or install a wide variety of smart technologies to reduce accidents and make life easier for "aging in place." In the feline arena, don't worry—you don't have to substantially remodel your space for your geriatric kitty! First, visualize the environment from your cat's perspective. Step into his or her paws and take it all in from your home's front door to the back door, including where your cat eats and sleeps, the litter boxes, where you and other household members sleep, where fur siblings eat and sleep, the windowsills, your car and yard (if applicable), and even the neighborhood.

- What does your cat see?
- Does something look scary?
- Can your cat get to where he needs and loves to be?
- Can she manage daily living comfortably and safely?
- Is he inconveniencing family members?

Once you've had a look, consider ways to make things more convenient for your aging cat. Keep in mind that your human housemates may find the environmental adjustments troublesome, even though the changes may be OK for you. Keep your own safety in mind, too. For example, if you need to place pet steps next to your bed, keep them out of your walking path so you don't risk tripping over them in the middle of the night. Let's look over some potential improvements.

Safety

Many environmental hazards exist for a cat living with aging ailments. A staircase presents peril to cats with severe mobility issues, and cats of any age can fall into a swimming pool and drown when no one is watching. Slippery tile or wood floors provide little traction for unsteady geriatric cats. All cats need sure-footing, along with a safe place that is all their

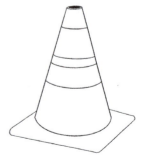

own to retreat to and rest. A senior cat's beloved perch may be too high to easily jump up and down from. It breaks my heart when I visit clients' homes and see elderly cats sitting hunched up in a tiny sun spot on a cold tile floor because there's nothing nearby to give them a step up to the windowsill.

Senior cat home safety and comfort checklist

- ❑ Provide easy access to food and water bowls, cat beds, and litter boxes. Add more of each if needed so your cat has even easier access. Cats may not like to eat side-by-side in close quarters. Some cats prefer their water bowl located a few feet away from their food bowl rather than right next to it. Cats with mobility issues may eat and drink less than they should or eliminate elsewhere in the house if they have to use stairs to access these necessities, so adjust their locations if needed. Make sure another pet in the household doesn't block access to these things, either.
- ❑ Provide elevated (feline elbow height) bowls for senior cats who have arthritis.
- ❑ Consider offering a water fountain (in addition to the regular water bowl) for cats who like to drink from the faucet.
- ❑ Consider offering an orthopedic cat bed to provide another option for comfort while your cat is resting. Geriatric cats may appreciate the warmth and comfort of napping with a housemate cat, or if they have a painful condition, they may prefer a bed to themselves. Monitor your cat's interactions to determine preferences.
- ❑ Furnish a heated cat bed or fluffy blanket as well as access to a cool surface as relaxation options when needed, making sure your cat can get on or off these spaces of her own accord.
- ❑ Offer a variety of sturdy horizontal, vertical, or angled scratching posts with different types of scratching material according to your cat's preferences. Ensure that the scratching posts won't wobble, roll, or tip over. You may need to get creative and place a weight in or on the bottom platform, or otherwise secure one or two sides of the platform to prevent movement.
- ❑ Place scratching posts near cats' resting areas. Cats especially like to claw-mark their territory when they wake up, and geriatric cats may not want to venture far from their resting areas.[2]
- ❑ Provide diverse resting and climbing areas for cats. This is important for all cats, and especially in small living spaces and households with more than one cat, because cats do not necessarily use all space available to them or share space equally.[2]
- ❑ Create a safe haven, which may be a separate room or access to an elevated resting space (cat tree, cat shelf, wide windowsill, back of a couch

or recliner) that your cat can retreat to when she needs quiet time, or segregate pets for short rest periods each day (making sure they still have access to litter boxes and water).
- Block access to stairs with baby gates if needed (if your cat won't try to jump over it and potentially injure themselves) or place a wide ramp if possible.
- Place non-slip rugs or mats on slippery floors and slip-resistant carpet stair treads on wood stairs (and keep your cat's nails trimmed to optimize traction).
- Keep walking paths free of clutter (e.g. toys, shoes, magazines, books, cords).
- Train your cat to use ramps, pet stairs, sturdy boxes, ottomans, or cat cubbies to access favorite spots that may be too high to jump up and down from (bed, couch, window, cat tree) in one leap. It's preferable if cats are accustomed to using a ramp, pet stairs, or other assistance methods before they have mobility issues.
- Place padding on sharp edges that a cat with visual problems might bump into.
- Create a comfy, easy-to-clean area that limits your cat's access to the rest of the house while you are unavailable to supervise her activities.
- Adjust where your cat sleeps if he risks falling off your bed. Consider adding baby bumpers or moving the bed against the wall as a barrier.
- Place nightlights in hallways and stairwells and near litter boxes.
- Offer plenty of interaction and playtime to your elderly cat as well as to younger pets who may be too boisterous to play with their ailing geriatric housemate.
- Keep window blind cords out of reach.
- Add stickers/reflectors to glass doors at eye level so your cat doesn't bump into the glass.
- Restrict and always supervise access to swimming pools, ponds, streams, and lakes.
- Prohibit access to fireplaces, candles, and outdoor firepits.
- Monitor your senior cat's interactions with other human and furry family members and visitors to avoid startling or uncomfortable experiences that may result in conflict or injuries. In multicat households where stress or conflict between cats occurs, placing a cat-safe collar with a bell on the cat who sparks conflict alerts the other cat to the aggressor cat's whereabouts.
- Consider dispensing feline calming pheromones (available as room diffusers, sprays, or collars) during stressful periods such as moving, gaining or losing housemates, traveling, hosting visiting pets, or recovering from surgery—or for day-to-day issues of living with serious chronic health

problems. Pheromones are chemical signals unique to each animal species, and they affect the behavior or emotional state of other members of the same species.

❑ Try to keep a routine feeding, activity, and bedtime schedule. If you rearrange the furniture or move, take extra time to help your cat adapt and learn the new layout.

❑ Properly secure your cat in a carrier for trips in the car and for visits to the veterinary hospital. Be sure to train (or retrain) your cat to trust the carrier as a safe space. Leave the cat carrier out in your home with a comfy pad or bed inside. Feed treats, offer catnip, and play with toys near and in the carrier to allow your cat to come and go at will. Place the carrier in an area your cat regularly hangs out in. Also consider placing it on a sturdy table or bench that they can access, to provide the sense of safety cats derive from watching the world from an elevated post.

Hurricane is 17 years old and has a special entrance to a room with her food and water bowls and litter box—no dog housemates allowed!

Sanitation

Keeping elderly cats and their surroundings spiffy can become a big challenge, especially toward the end of their life. Kitties who can no longer easily use their litter box tend to find a "bathroom" wherever they can—perhaps a bath mat or your bed. Senior cats often have trouble grooming themselves, and longhaired or obese cats especially may have feces caught in their fur if they can no longer position appropriately in the litter box or reach their hindquarters to groom.

Aged cats may have incontinence, and if they have mobility issues, they may end up lying in their urine and feces, which creates a much bigger cleaning issue. (See Chapter 14 "Incontinence and other potty problems: Thinking outside the box" and Chapter 16: "Mobility: The creaky, shaky, and unsteady" for additional precautions and tips.) The more accidents they have, the more cleaning they need. Cats with severe mobility issues who cannot easily move and rotate on their bed can get bed sores that lead to infections.

Sanitation checklist

- ❏ Keep your cat combed or brushed and mat-free, nails trimmed.
- ❏ Provide assistance to help your cat get to the litter box if needed, and provide a large litter box that has at least one low-entry side or access point.
- ❏ Provide easy access to your cat's litter boxes, and add one or more new litter boxes if needed so your cat has less distance to travel. Litter boxes should be at least two feet away from food and water bowls and sleeping areas.
- ❏ Carefully trim or shave the hair around your cat's hind end and hind legs, tail, and groin if urine or feces collects there.
- ❏ Use potty pads and diapers as needed for incontinent cats, and prevent bed sores and skin infections in cats who have severe mobility issues and difficulty getting up and away from their accidents.
- ❏ Keep cleaning supplies handy. Good items to have at the ready include pet wipes or unscented, hypoallergenic baby wipes (keep a pack in your car, too) and floor cleaning tools.

Beating boredom and suppressing stress

Hand in hand with a cat's senior lifestyle is often a lack of new things to contemplate (read: boredom), and an unwavering reliance on familiar routines and spaces, which sometimes morphs into concern: "What was that sound outside?" "What's prowling around in the backyard?" "Did Mom just get home?" The concern can result in unease and stress.

Cats can experience chronic distress if they're repeatedly exposed to stressful events for a prolonged period, or if they're continuously exposed to a tolerable but stressful situation that never stops.[2] Conflicts with other furry family members, chronic health problems, frightening sounds, active and noisy children, or being left alone repeatedly for long periods are examples of stressful situations. Add on a cognitive disorder that some geriatric cats suffer from, and the stress compounds.

Throughout this book I mention that exercise, mental stimulation, and environmental enrichment are important to maintain your cat's health and even extend their lives. Environmental enrichment means providing stimulating activities (plus opportunities to be alone) that encourage animals' natural behaviors and social interactions. Environmental enrichment stimulates thinking, reduces boredom, and helps animals deal with minor stresses. All too often, I've seen families who assume their cat is "just getting old," so they no longer play with their cat or try to include their cat in family activities. But these interactions are just as important for aging cats as they are for young cats. Case in point: many assisted living facilities and nursing homes for people feature game nights, movie nights, arts and crafts, reading rooms, music rooms, resident or visiting cats and dogs (sometimes even farm animals!), gardens, gyms, pools, off-site dining events, community field trips, and group vacation getaways.

The key to enrichment for senior cats is in striking the right balance between the comforts of familiarity and the disturbances of novelty. Senior cats especially appreciate predictable routines and may have difficulty coping with change. Inconsistency can induce stress that negatively affects senior cats' physical and emotional well-being, so introduce new experiences in small doses and make transitions gradually. Provide reassurance, encouragement, and rewards, and stay attuned to and respect your cat's pace of acceptance or reluctance.

Environmental enrichment categories

As we investigate ways to bring enrichment into your home, let's turn to the wild side for examples. Zookeepers enhance their animals' environments in a variety of ways to boost the animals' physical and mental health. Mimicking the animals' natural habitat is just one aspect they've embraced. The five general enrichment categories are social, cognitive, physical, sensory, and food,[3] and the categories may overlap. Enrichment recommendations that the veterinary field applies to cats follow the same general principles. And when it comes to geriatric cats, most of the same enrichment tips for younger cats still apply.

SOCIAL: SOMEONE TO HANG OUT WITH! Zoo animals may live with fellow animals of their own kind or even other animals found in their natural environments. For cats, social stimulation may include interacting with other furry housemates or dates with other familiar cat or dog playmates. Most importantly, social stimulation means interacting with you and other human family members or friends, preferably on a routine schedule. Daily petting, napping next to you, grooming, play, and training all count! Does your cat appear out of nowhere to knead your lap while you talk on the phone? That counts, too!

COGNITIVE: NEW THINGS TO STRETCH THE MIND! Puzzles to solve and toys to play with bring variety and fun for many zoo animals, and the same applies to pets. Add new toys! Cat subscription boxes are a fun option, such as Meowbox, Pet Treater, RescueBox, KitNipBox, and many others. Also rotate your cat's old toys to keep them interesting, and consider making your own toys. Use positive training techniques to teach new commands, tricks, or activities to give cats tasks and boost their cognitive processes.

📷 A towering new scratching post inspired 16-year-old Fleur to reach for new heights!

PHYSICAL HABITAT: MAKING HOME FEEL LIKE HOME! Zoo animals benefit from spaces that mimic the animals' natural environments, such as perches, water features, bushes, boulders, objects to climb, and hiding places. Senior cats, too, appreciate a space of their own to retreat to for rest and quiet. While social interaction is vital, having time to themselves is also important for cats.

SENSORY: NEW ENCOUNTERS FOR THE FIVE SENSES! Zookeepers introduce new smells, interactive toys, novel sounds, and more to help keep the animals they care for curious and engaged. Senior cats may enjoy being combed or given a light massage, chewing on a new safe herb such as fresh catnip or cat grass, munching veggies such as zucchini, watching videos designed to hold cats' attention, listening to music composed for cats' discerning ears,[4] and sniffing out strange scents in the yard or smelling new avenues during leash walks or cruises in a pet stroller.

FOOD: A CHANCE TO FORAGE! Zoo animals benefit from searching for food in a variety of ways and tasting new flavors. Senior cats benefit too, such as deciphering food cubes, wobbler toys, ball treat dispensers, complex activity centers, foraging mats, mouse-shaped kibble holders to hide around your home, and even simply sniffing out tasty treats scattered around the room. DIY food puzzle construction ideas abound on the internet, many using recyclables such as empty cardboard rolls and boxes, egg cartons, and plastic yogurt containers.

Going out for a change of scenery

The great outdoors—natural chances for enriching endeavors are simply a step outside, or even easy breezes bringing faraway scents through a screen door.

THE BACKYARD. If your cat is adventurous, take time to interact, play, explore, and change things up outdoors. Sniffing plants, lounging in the grass, patrolling the perimeter, hunting treats that you disperse around the yard, mini senior-cat-accessible activity courses, and more await. The backyard brings bountiful times for supervised bonding moments with you, whether you use a leash, screened patio, or catio (an outdoor enclosure designed for cats).

Cats can be taught to wear a harness and walk on a leash in the yard, or they may enjoy a screened-in enclosure. Because some pets may not be outdoors as much as they'd like or other pets may not get out at all, provide a place to perch in front of open windows with secure screens during temperate weather to allow enriching sensory stimulation. Consider planting a pet-safe indoor herb garden that your pet can peruse, or bring in a tub of soil or sand they can nose and paw around in from time to time.

WALKS. If your cat is up for it and doesn't have exercise restrictions for medical reasons, you may have already built in regular walks with her, which is a wonderfully enriching activity. Walking about with a trusted human friend brings the chance to spy and smell new things at various times—morning, afternoon, evening, or night. "Where did that moth go? Was that a toad?! What's that rustling in the leaves? Let me sniff out the trail …."

Walks for older cats may need to be shorter duration, but continue to offer regular outings for their exploratory treks with you. Change up your walk routine by allowing a little more freedom in noncongested areas, or you might use an extra-long lead to allow your cat to choose the areas she wants to scout (within reason!) and to saunter, sniff, and lounge at her own pace.

Staying in and changing scenery

Enriching indoor entertainment opportunities abound, too.

TRAINING. Old cats can learn new tricks. Learning new things remains intriguing for elders of the four-legged variety. Sit, high-five, bat at a crinkle ball pitched their way, ring a bell for a treat, fetch a foam ball, jump up to perch, and more.

TREATS. Treats as an enticement are an integral part of training in cats, but enticing them with a device that requires their manipulation to get to a treat can be enriching, too. Many treat toys dispense bits of yum as a cat bats the toy about on the floor. Some pet parents give their cats all of their meals in such food-dispensing devices. Kibble can be tucked into dispensing toys and hidden around the house or placed on a foraging mat. You'll activate their instinct to search for a food reward. It's more active. It takes more futzing around.

Enrichment central!

Some senior cats have reduced senses of smell and taste, so feed especially aromatic, delectable treats. Experiment with what most entices your cat. And remember, cats are smart! They will figure out the quickest wins in the food puzzles, so try several different types of puzzles and switch them out periodically. What's old can be new again!

TOYS. The cat accessories aisle in supermarkets or pet specialty stores often doesn't match the abundance and variety of products found in the spoil-your-dog aisles, but you can still find fuzzy, feathery, colorful, fantastical toys there. Also look for other clever and creative options available through online pet retailers.

Cats appreciate toys in different sizes, shapes, and textures and with a variety of movements. They like boxes, paper bags, toys to chase and toys that promote hunting behavior. Your senior cat may still enjoy playing shorter games of laser pointer pursuit and casually batting at a teaser wand toy. If your cat loses interest after playing with a toy for a few minutes, try switching to another toy. And rotate the toy options to keep cats interested. Let your cat hold onto a toy and tear up the feathers or fur from time to time, even though it means buying a new toy sooner.

MATINEES AND MOVIE NIGHTS. How do many of us pass the time at the end of a long day? The TV! Cats, too, can find entertainment on the tube. Internet streaming services such as YouTube host channels specifically designed to entertain cats for hours, which is a great resource to keep their minds occupied when cats must be left at home on their own. You'll find videos of birds flying in and out to snack on birdseed, dogs running along a forest trail, kittens romping, and so much more. Cats may even key in on a fellow feline or other animal on the screen, perk up their ears and twist their heads when it makes a noise (woof! meow! tweet tweet!)—and try to search around the side or back of the TV if it flies or runs off screen. You'll be as entertained as your cat by watching your cat being entertained by these moments!

Fleur, the calico in the foreground, is 16 years old, and her housemate Jack-Jack is 1 year old. They both enjoy online videos of birdwatching for cats.

A cautionary note: avoid the angry cat videos, because hissing and yowling will likely rile or frighten your cat, and such videos can pit housemate cats against each other. No one needs that kind of excitement!

Enrichment queries

- ❏ Does your cat have a variety of engaging activities and experiences to keep her occupied?
- ❏ What activities or experiences do you need to avoid or prevent so your senior cat does not get overly excited, irritated, scared, or repeatedly stressed?
- ❏ What sounds occur throughout the day that you may need to help your cat avoid because they unsettle your cat?
- ❏ If your cat is left alone for long periods or is confined to a restricted access area when you're not home, do you provide enrichment opportunities that he can engage in on his own?
- ❏ Is someone available to spend at least an hour a day with your cat for physical activity and social interactions?

This baby gate has a small cat door at the bottom to keep the dogs (and kids) out of the cat's safe zone!

A Door Buddy adjustable strap and latch allows cats to retreat to where small children and large dogs can't reach.

READING RECOMMENDATIONS

- An excellent book on cat behavior written by veterinary behavior specialists that includes information on environmental enrichment: *Decoding Your Cat* by the American College of Veterinary Behaviorists; ME Herron, DF Horwitz, C Siracusa, eds. (2020, Houghton Mifflin Harcourt).
- Check out all the ways pet parents play "mind games" with their cats: Feline Enrichment Facebook Group. **facebook.com/groups/610891845701943/**.
- Review lists of plants that can make cats sick and plants that are safe for cats: Toxic and Non-Toxic Plant List - Cats. American Society for the Prevention of Cruelty to Animals (ASPCA). **aspca.org/pet-care/animal-poison-control/cats-plant-list**.

CHAPTER 22:

Journaling: Tracking your cat's health

"Write hard and clear about what hurts."

—Source unverified
(the internet attributes this quote to Ernest Hemingway)

A day in the life of your cat changes as their golden years progress. An occasional accident. An unsuccessful leap to the back of the couch. A turned-up nose to a favorite treat. Sometimes subtle changes can signal a serious issue.

You know your cat's attitude, activities, and behavior best, and I can't emphasize more how helpful it is for you to keep track of these things and mention changes you notice or any concerns you have to your veterinary team. In fact, as your cat ages, your veterinarian will likely ask you more questions during appointments about how well your cat is eating and moving about, whether your cat's interactions with you or other family members have changed, and what your cat's sleep and litter box habits are like.

During veterinary visits or in times of illness, it can be hard to remember the nuances about changes you've noticed in your cat. So it's helpful to keep a senior or geriatric cat health journal—one that also includes methods to track your cat's symptoms, treatments, and schedule changes. Such tracking will help you better evaluate and make decisions about managing the complexities that come along with caring for a geriatric or terminally ill cat.

As a companion to this book, I've created a complete workbook for pet parents to journal their geriatric cat's health and many other aspects of care. Scan this QR code for more information (**amzn.to/3dNvAkg**):

Cat Journal Book

Create a geriatric cat health journal

To keep a cat health journal, write your general observations about the types of behaviors, changes, and symptoms I list below and anything else that concerns you, or create your own checklist. Include stories or notes about activities and other things your cat enjoys so you can track whether their enthusiasm has changed. Add photos of your cat taken at six- to 12-month intervals, and date each one to help you and your veterinarian monitor changes in your cat.

Health observations:

- **EATING/DRINKING:** What are your cat's favorite foods? Favorite treats? Have her food preferences changed? Has her appetite decreased? Are special enticements or is other assistance needed to get her to eat? Does she drop food while eating or have trouble chewing or swallowing? Does your cat have an increased thirst? Any vomiting?
- **WEIGHT:** Has your cat lost weight without being on a diet or without getting extra exercise? Has your cat been gaining weight?
- **SLEEP:** Where does your cat prefer to sleep? How many hours does your cat sleep during an average day? Does he sleep peacefully? What does your cat do if he gets up during the night? Does he sleep more during the day than he used to and less at night?
- **ACTIVITY LEVEL:** What are your cat's favorite activities, toys, and games? Who are your cat's favorite people? Who are your cat's least favorite beings (squirrels, visitors, neighborhood cats)? Does your cat have favorite animal friends or playmates? Has your cat's activity decreased? If so, over what time period—the last few days, weeks, or months, or during the last year?
- **STRENGTH AND VITALITY:** Has your cat's energy decreased in the last year? Does she seem less interested in exercise or exploring? Is she weaker during exercise or less tolerant of exercise?
- **MOBILITY:** Does your cat "bunny hop" down the stairs? Any difficulty jumping on or off the bed or couch or climbing his cat tree? Any changes in his scratching post use or preferences? Has his gait changed (slowness or limping)?
- **URINE, FECES, AND LITTER BOX USE:** Have you noticed an increase or decrease in urination? Any urinary or fecal accidents outside the litter

box? Urine leakage where she rests? A change in fecal appearance? Diarrhea? Fecal incontinence? Constipation? Does she groom her hind end more often?

- **EARS, EYES, NOSE, MOUTH, THROAT, AND BREATHING:** Have you noticed a change in your cat's hearing? More reactive to noises? Less reactive to noises? Vision problems in bright light? In dim light? At night? Up close? A runny nose or sneezing? Bad breath? Does his meow sound different? Does he purr more often than usual? Does he breathe faster or heavier, breathe with an open mouth, or pant? Cough?

- **SKIN, COAT, AND CLAWS:** Does your cat have increased or excessive itching? Lumps or bumps on or under the skin? A bad smell? Is she licking or chewing her skin or fur? Is her skin flaky, dry, or oily? Have you noticed whether she has longer claws? Does your cat enjoy being brushed or combed? Does your cat groom herself normally? Is her coat unkempt, thinning, or dull? Any patches of hair loss or mats?

- **TEMPERATURE AND OVERALL COMFORT:** Does your cat seek out new or unusual areas to rest that are warm, cold, soft, sunny, or hard? Does your cat's fur seem fluffed up? Does your cat frequently sit in a hunched position? Does your cat shiver or tremble?

- **MENTATION:** Is your cat less interested in greeting you when you get home? Has your cat been less interactive with the family? Or more clingy or anxious? Does your cat pace during the day or night? Stare off into space? Seem irritable or act more aggressively? Does he seem disoriented or distant? Become agitated at certain times of the day? Get stuck in odd locations or appear lost? Yowl at night for no apparent reason? Has he had a seizure?

To help track 17-year-old Hurricane's habits, her mom set up a motion-activated Ring camera near Hurricane's food and water bowls. It keeps a close eye on Hurricane, especially when her mom isn't home, to help her assess how well Hurricane is eating and drinking.

Symptom tracker

In Chapter 30, "Life quality: 'Doc, when is it time?'" I discuss how to annotate symptoms to help pet parents evaluate end-of-life decisions for their cats. But tracking your cat's symptoms throughout her senior years, starting well before she reaches her final weeks, helps you remember and realistically assess whether she's improved, stayed stable, or declined. This can help your veterinarian construct a veterinary care plan for your cat and remodel it as needed along the way. Tracking symptoms also helps your veterinarian better predict the course of your cat's condition, because knowing how your cat functions in her daily activities gives supportive context for interpreting diagnostic test results and physical examination findings.

Use the health observations questions above to uncover the symptoms your cat may have. Write your cat's symptoms in your cat's health journal or type them into a spreadsheet, as in the example below. First list the symptom, and then its frequency and time of day. Does it happen every day? In the mornings only? Evenings only? How many times a day?

Next note any circumstance that seems to be associated with the symptom, if applicable. For example, does your cat vomit only after you share your half-and-half with her in the morning? Does your cat yowl at night only after your return from a vacation? Has a new medication helped resolve an ailment?

Symptom severity is the next aspect to document. Is it mild and your cat doesn't seem too bothered by it, or does it affect him for the rest of the day? You can also note whether it is a mild, moderate, or severe issue for you as the caregiver.

Finally, note improvements—what helps alleviate the symptom? Does your cat play more when she finds better traction on the floor? Does your cat sleep through the night when a nightlight is plugged in? Does she eat more when you soften or warm her food?

Date each entry to help you monitor your cat. You'll see trends starting sooner rather than later, so you'll be able to make environmental or therapeutic adjustments faster or schedule a veterinary visit sooner.

When tracking your senior cat's symptoms, keep in mind that with the exception of some conditions that may be treatable and resolve, you are not necessarily looking for perfection or a return to normal. You're looking for ways to help slow the progression of your cat's symptoms and help him live well by alleviating as much discomfort as possible—to provide care and love to the best of your abilities. All of these efforts are to help your cat feel better and have a good life quality—and help yourself do so as well.

SYMPTOM TRACKER

Pet's Name

Date	Symptom	Frequency and Time of Day	Association	Severity	Improvements

TREATMENT TRACKER

Pet's Name

Date	Medication (and other therapy) or Change in schedule	Dose	Frequency and Duration	What it's for	Result

Treatment tracker

Keeping good notes about your cat's medications, other therapies, and schedule changes is as important as tracking her symptoms. This is a handy reference for treatments you've tried and their effects.

Keep a log of each drug name, dose, frequency (how many times a day it's given) and duration (how long it's to be given), what it's used to treat or manage, and the result (whether it helped or if you noted side effects or new symptoms). If you adjust a dose or frequency of administration, note that as well (note: all prescription medicine adjustments should be made according to your veterinarian's advice).

Remember to include medications, supplements, or nutraceuticals that you purchase over-the-counter. Also note any other therapy such as acupuncture, surgery, massage, chemotherapy, and grooming, and note major schedule changes such as boarding, daycare, or a pet sitter. For more information about therapies commonly prescribed or recommended for senior cats and tips for giving them, see Chapter 23 "Course of action: Therapeutic options and gaining acceptance from your senior cat."

This journal I developed had a number of tools, checklists, questionnaires and more to help you manage your aging cat's ailments as well as your caregiving goals.

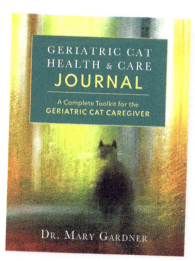

Cat Journal Book

CHAPTER 23:

Course of action: Therapeutic options and gaining acceptance from your senior cat

"We can not only add years to their life but life to their years."
—Dr. Marty Becker

Obviously our cats can't help themselves stay healthy in every way that will help them. So all measures that must be taken to give medications, nutraceuticals, supplements, and other forms of therapy usually become activities of daily living, loving, and caring for senior cats. It can sometimes feel like you're running a senior cat assisted-living home (for too-often uncooperative residents)!

In this chapter, I give a basic overview of the therapies I often use or recommend in my geriatric and hospice patients and my own senior cats—treatments that your veterinarian is also likely to prescribe or suggest. I first briefly describe the legalities of prescribing drugs and then cover therapeutic categories and a few of the individual treatments, including some non-drug, non-supplement therapies that aging cats may need.

I don't cover all potential treatments here—such as antibiotics, drugs used to treat heart failure, anti-cancer agents, and surgeries (that would take at least one more book!)—but I mention many additional therapies in the chapters that address individual conditions. At the end of this chapter I include questions to help you partner with your veterinarian in determining which types of treatment are most likely to help your cat and to help you assess the benefits vs. the potential negative impacts of highly intensive or invasive treatment options.

The first key to successful treatment: Keep your veterinarian in the know

Always tell your veterinarian about all the medications, vitamins, supplements, nutraceuticals, herbs, and other therapies your cat receives. We need to know so we can make well-informed decisions about your cat's care and help prevent serious drug interactions and ensure that your cat's therapies support each other. The vital take-home message here—some drugs or supplements just don't work well together and can do more harm than good when they're combined.

To successfully treat your cat, your veterinarian also relies on you to carefully follow medication instructions and treatment plans. Always let your veterinarian know if you're having trouble following through, because adjustments can usually be made.

An important alert: Stop before giving a medication or supplement to your cat on your own without consulting your veterinarian, even if it is one that you know is used in cats. And hold off on sharing medications among your cats. One cat's prescription is not necessarily your other cat's remedy! Ask your veterinarian first.

The prescriptions for writing prescriptions

Medications are normally a part of an older cat's care toolbox. They can boost comfort, decrease anxiety, improve mobility, enhance sleep, increase appetite, hasten healing, and provide many other benefits. Pet parents may not realize that veterinarians must follow a few rules to prescribe certain therapies for cats. For example, medications approved for use in cats, dogs, or other animals by the U.S. Food and Drug Administration (FDA) Center for Veterinary Medicine are legally available only by prescription from a licensed veterinarian. And in order to legally prescribe a medication in most states, veterinarians must have an existing, valid relationship with the client and the pet (called a VCPR, for short).

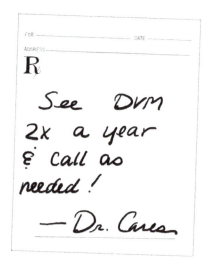

A VCP-what?

A veterinarian-client-patient relationship (VCPR) means that a veterinarian:

- knows a pet well enough to be able to diagnose the pet's problem and oversee the pet's treatment;
- keeps a medical record of the pet's care; and
- discusses treatment benefits and risks with the pet's owner.

A VCPR also means that the pet parent agrees to follow the veterinarian's instructions.

Each state's Veterinary Practice Act (which describes regulations for practicing veterinary medicine) may define the VCPR a bit differently. In most states, knowing a cat well enough to prescribe a medication means that the veterinarian must examine the cat in person to assess the cat's health and the cat's need for medication. The vet must also see the cat regularly for healthcare checkups (for example, at least once a year) and be readily available for follow-up if needed. Those are some important rules!

The VCPR is the reason why if your cat is ill, your veterinarian needs to examine her in person before prescribing medication. It's also the reason why if your cat has no medication refills left and hasn't had a veterinary visit for over a year (or if your cat has missed follow-up tests needed to check her response to the medication), she must be examined before your veterinarian can approve a prescription refill.

Because veterinary telemedicine services have gained more popularity, regulations related to the VCPR may change in the future.

A prescription that doesn't follow the label: Extra-label or off-label drug use

Fortunately, some drugs have undergone rigorous studies and been approved by the FDA for use in cats with specific diseases or conditions. But not all medications have been studied in more than one species, or for more than one disease, or at different doses, or in more than one way to give them. So some drugs that veterinarians prescribe for your pet may not be FDA-approved for that particular use.

When an FDA-approved drug is prescribed for use in a way that's not listed on its label, it's called *extra-label* or *off-label* drug use. This occurs, for example, when your veterinarian prescribes a drug for your cat that has been FDA-approved for use in dogs (or in people), or prescribes a drug at a different dose or for a different disease than the drug label says it's used for. But don't be alarmed, extra-label and off-label uses are acceptable and legal when certain conditions are met and are a common practice in veterinary (and human) medicine.

This doesn't mean veterinarians (or physicians) prescribe these drugs haphazardly among species or diseases. Off-label or extra-label uses are typically evidence-based and supported by scientific research, patient studies, and clinical experience published in the medical literature.

Changing the form of medications: Compounding

Medications come in many forms: pills, capsules, liquids, patches, ointments, tablets, chewables, and injectables. So changing a drug's FDA-approved formulation to tailor it to the needs of a specific patient—such as making a liquid from pills to make it easier for a cat to take—is called compounding. Compounding is also considered an extra-label drug use, and it is legal when certain conditions are met.

Other examples of compounding include mixing a drug with a flavor enhancer, combining two drugs into one, or formulating a drug into a dose that isn't available from the manufacturer. But not all drugs can be altered in these ways, and some compounded formulations may not have the same effectiveness as a drug that's administered in its original form.

To obtain compounded medications, veterinarians typically use local veterinary pharmacies or online veterinary pharmacies. Pharmacies for human drugs may offer some types of compounding for pet medications as well.

A peek at some common meds

Let's meet a few of the medications that might be coming your way as your cat's golden years progress.

Pain management options

Most pet parents will encounter a need to give drugs (or their veterinarian to administer drugs) to manage their senior cat's pain. (We all know, aging can be a pain!) Thankfully, many options are available—from cat-specific nonsteroidal anti-inflammatory drugs and a feline monoclonal antibody to anti-nausea medications and nutritional supplements.

Given as directed by your veterinarian, pain management therapies can work together to help relieve both components of pain—physical (what the pain feels like–sharp, dull, aching, stabbing, burning, throbbing) and emotional (how the pain makes your cat feel–anxious, fearful, uneasy, sickly).

NONSTEROIDAL ANTI-INFLAMMATORY DRUGS. Veterinarians prescribe nonsteroidal anti-inflammatory drugs (NSAIDs) to manage inflammation and pain associated with arthritis, surgery, urinary tract problems, and other conditions. Most NSAIDs work by blocking an enzyme called cyclooxygenase that the body needs to make prostaglandins. Prostaglandins are hormone-like lipid (fat) compounds that contribute to pain and inflammation. Meloxicam (brand names are Metacam and Rheumocam) and robenacoxib (brand name is Onsior) are two NSAIDs approved for use in cats.

NSAIDs can adversely affect kidney, gastrointestinal, or liver function, so be sure to follow your veterinarian's instructions on how much of the medication to give and how often, whether to give it with food, and how long to give it. Also follow through with all your veterinarian's recommended follow-up blood or urine tests. Let your veterinarian know if your cat has a loss of appetite, vomiting, diarrhea, lethargy, increased thirst or urination, black feces (which signal blood coming from the gastrointestinal tract), or yellowish skin, gums, or eyes.

NSAID CAUTIONS AND ACETAMINOPHEN ALERT

Cats are rarely treated with an NSAID and a corticosteroid at the same time because severe side effects can occur. Receiving both medications should be done only when medically required and with extra-close veterinary supervision.

Never give the NSAIDs you may have available in your own medicine cabinet (ibuprofen, aspirin, naproxen, or others) to your cat because NSAID medications for use in people can cause serious or life-threatening side effects in cats.

Acetaminophen (Tylenol), also called paracetamol, is not an NSAID, but I mention it here because it's a pain and fever reducer that most people have at home. **NEVER** give acetaminophen to cats because it causes severe illness and can be deadly.

CORTICOSTEROIDS. Often called "steroids," corticosteroid medications such as prednisone or prednisolone are synthetic (manufactured) versions of a glucocorticoid hormone called cortisol that's produced naturally by the adrenal glands. Corticosteroids are not anabolic steroid drugs—the "roids" that pet parents often think of when veterinarians mention steroids. (Anabolic steroids are synthetic versions of the male sex hormone, testosterone, and they are not often used in veterinary patients.)

Corticosteroids reduce inflammation in cats with arthritis, inflammatory bowel disease, asthma, or allergies. They also suppress the immune system, so they're used to treat conditions such as immune-mediated anemia in which the immune cells mistakenly attack the body's own red blood cells. Corticosteroids also help slow the progression of some types of cancer.

The risk of side effects from corticosteroids increases with high doses and include weight gain, drinking more water (thus, urinating more often), increased risk of infection, diminished healing ability, and gastric ulcers. Corticosteroids are helpful in managing many conditions, and some of their side effects aren't necessarily dealbreakers. It's just good to be aware of the side effects so you can let your veterinarian know if you have concerns about your cat's response. The side effects should diminish as the dose decreases and should resolve after treatment.

Suddenly stopping a corticosteroid disrupts the body's cortisol hormone balance, which can cause other problems, so the dose is gradually reduced over several days or a few weeks. It's vital that you follow your veterinarian's instructions for giving and gradually stopping a corticosteroid.

POLYSULFATED GLYCOSAMINOGLYCAN (PSGAG). Polysulfated glycosaminoglycan (brand name Adequan), an FDA-approved drug to control signs of arthritis in dogs and horses, is an extract made from cow cartilage. Veterinarians may prescribe it extra-label for cats who have arthritis and sometimes for cats who have bladder inflammation. It's an injection given in the muscle (at the veterinary clinic) twice a week for four weeks, and possibly continued at a maintenance dose after that. It can also be given under the skin, so your veterinarian may teach you how so you can give it at home.

GABAPENTIN. How gabapentin works isn't completely understood, but it's thought to inhibit nerve activity. It's approved for use in people, so it's used off-label in veterinary patients to treat pain, anxiety, and seizures. Studies have shown that gabapentin may not effectively treat pets' pain as well as we initially thought, but the jury is still out and more studies are being done.[1,2]

Gabapentin is often prescribed to be given to cats at home about two hours before they make a trip to the veterinary hospital to ease anxiety during the drive and visit. Palliative care and hospice veterinarians also sometimes prescribe it to be given to their cat patients before they visit them in their homes. Placebo-controlled clinical studies in healthy cats and in cats with hyperthyroidism show that gabapentin makes cats more relaxed and easier to work with during veterinary visits.[3,4] Gabapentin also eases fear in cage-trapped community cats in trap-neuter-return programs who undergo spay or neuter surgery.[5] (*Community cat* is another term for an unowned, free-roaming, outdoor cat—otherwise known as a stray or feral cat.)

Gabapentin also helps stimulate appetite in healthy cats as well as mirtazapine (an appetite stimulant) does and better than a placebo does for up to eight hours after spay surgery.[6]

The main side effect of gabapentin is sleepiness, which can vary among cats. Veterinarians may prescribe gabapentin to help cats with cognitive dysfunction sleep better. I prescribe a low dose to start, given only at night. This helps all family members benefit from their cat's good night's sleep! I usually reassess the cat's response after three weeks to determine whether a dose adjustment is needed.

AMANTADINE. Amantadine is an antiviral drug approved for use in people that also influences nerve activity. It is used off-label in cats to relieve pain that can develop after the central nervous system ramps up to respond to pain but then becomes overly sensitive to stimuli. In addition, compared with a placebo in clinical studies, pet parents perceive that amantadine improves quality of life in cats who have osteoarthritis.[7] Side effects are uncommon in cats and may include soft stools or diarrhea.

OPIOIDS. Opioids are natural or manufactured derivatives of the poppy plant. They influence receptors throughout the body and have many effects, including effects within the nervous system that help relieve pain. They're often used in human medicine and are usually used to treat short-term pain in cats, but they can also be given to manage long-term pain.

Because of opioid shortages related to drug abuse in people and because of the potential for opioid abuse in people, veterinarians must often look for alternatives to these drugs to manage pain in cats.

Tramadol is one type of synthetic opioid approved for use in people. It appears to have few pain-modifying effects in dogs and cats, so it is not recommended for long-term pain management in pets. It can make cats sleepy, so some people assume their cats feel better, but they're simply sleeping more.

BISPHOSPHONATES. Bisphosphonates are approved for use in people to prevent or slow the loss of bone density. Veterinarians use bisphosphonates extra-label to provide pain relief in pets who have bone cancer or to treat high levels of calcium in the blood. This medication must be administered intravenously in the veterinary hospital, and cats who receive it long-term should be monitored for bone destruction that can occur in the jaw.[8]

Medications to treat nausea and prevent vomiting

Nausea sometimes causes as much suffering as other painful conditions and negatively affects a cat's quality of life. Medications commonly used to treat nausea and vomiting in cats include:

MAROPITANT. The brand name is Cerenia and it's FDA-approved for use in cats to treat vomiting. It's an injection given under the skin or into a vein. It blocks the action of a neurotransmitter in the central nervous system that stimulates the vomiting reflex.

METOCLOPRAMIDE. One brand name is Reglan and it's approved for use in people, so it's used off-label in cats. It's an oral medication that's most often given to boost gastric motility (move food faster from the stomach to the intestine) in cats.[9] It can also block the sensation of nausea in the central nervous system.

ONDANSETRON. One brand name is Zofran and it's approved for use in people. It blocks a receptor for a neurotransmitter called serotonin that signals nausea. It's used off-label in cats and can be given orally, in a gel that is absorbed through the skin, or as an injection.

Stomach acid blockers and protectants

Famotidine and omeprazole are oral medications sometimes used off-label in cats to reduce stomach acid or treat gastric ulcers associated with a variety of medical conditions.

Sucralfate is also used off-label in pets to help treat ulcers. It coats and protects the stomach lining. Sucralfate is given on an empty stomach and not at the same time as certain other medications because it can block their absorption. Follow your veterinarian's dosing instructions closely.

Nutraceuticals or supplements

Nutraceuticals are nutritional supplements formulated from bioactive compounds (substances that have an effect in living beings) such as vitamins, minerals, probiotics, dietary fiber, herbal extracts, or other food substances—given alone or produced in combinations—that are used to support healthy pets (or people) or those who have an ailment.

> **Did you know?** Nutraceuticals don't undergo FDA review for safety and efficacy as drugs do, so a nutraceutical manufacturer cannot claim that their product prevents or treats disease. In fact, the FDA doesn't recognize the term "nutraceutical" and considers these products to be dietary supplements.[10]

As I mentioned earlier, it's vital to tell your veterinarian about any supplement, nutraceutical, or other over-the-counter medication you give your cat. It may contain an active ingredient that counteracts or enhances the effects of other medications, or it may have other unintended effects in the body. Nutraceuticals or supplements may provide benefits for some cats. Let's take a look at a few examples:

GLUCOSAMINE AND CHONDROITIN. These building blocks of cartilage occur naturally in some joints. Glucosamine and chondroitin are used to repair cartilage and inhibit further cartilage destruction, and they provide mild anti-inflammatory effects.

These substances can be extracted from animal cartilage or shellfish shells and green-lipped mussels (sciency-wiency name for these New Zealand-exclusive mussels: *Perna canaliculus*), or they can be made synthetically. They are formulated as supplements and nutraceuticals or added to some cat foods and marketed to support joint health in cats.

Veterinarians may recommend glucosamine and chondroitin in addition to other treatments (e.g. NSAIDs, weight loss, rehabilitation therapy) for patients with arthritis or after joint surgery. Studies have been done in people, dogs, cats, horses, and other animals, and their effects have been hotly debated. The bottom line is that the potential benefits of glucosamine and chondroitin remain questionable.[11]

Several brands formulated for cats that contain glucosamine or glucosamine and chondroitin are available. Among these products, the active ingredient sources and amounts, other added nutrients, manufacturing processes, and research done to support their effects often differ. Whether veterinarians recommend glucosamine and chondroitin or which brand they suggest depends on their assessment of these factors.

MELATONIN. Melatonin is a hormone produced in the brain, and most melatonin supplements contain a synthetic version. It may help with sleep disturbances in cats. Do not give melatonin supplements that contain xylitol (xylitol is toxic to dogs and it's best to avoid giving xylitol to cats).

OMEGA-3 FATTY ACIDS. Omega-3 fatty acids (called *eicosapentaenoic acid* [EPA] and *docosahexaenoic acid* [DHA]) from fish oil have multiple beneficial effects for cats. They're available as supplements, and some cat foods contain added amounts. They play a vital role in cell membrane health to keep cells functioning normally. Only use omega-3 fatty acid supplements made from fish oil and manufactured by reputable companies, and avoid flaxseed oil and cod liver oil.[12] My favorite brand is Omega-3 Pet by Nordic Naturals. And fair warning: gradually introduce fish oil supplements to your cat over three weeks, because they can cause diarrhea!

RESEARCH REVELATION: A FATTY ACID THAT MAY GAIN POPULARITY

Palmitoylethanolamide (PEA) is a fatty acid amide (a combo fatty acid plus an amine [an amine is a nitrogen compound]) present in soybeans, peanuts, eggs, and other foods. It also occurs naturally within and affects the body's endocannabinoid system (which I describe later in this chapter). PEA is being studied and may play a role in the future in managing cancer, chronic pain, skin disease, and cognitive dysfunction in pets.[13,14]

Probiotics. Some of the beneficial bacteria that live in your cat's intestines can be given as supplements known as probiotics. They help digestion and boost the immune system, and are used to help treat diarrhea, irritable bowels, and intestinal inflammation.

Probiotics are available as powders, chewables, and capsules. Be sure to obtain a probiotic from a reputable company and one that lists the bacteria it contains on the label. Two brands I often recommend for cats are FortiFlora by Purina Pro Plan Veterinary Supplements and Proviable by Nutramax Laboratories Veterinary Sciences.

Vitamin B12 (cobalamin). Vitamin B12 is involved in many of the body's processes. Cats with gastrointestinal disorders may have a B12 deficiency because they can't absorb it sufficiently from their diet. Weekly injections of B12 may be recommended.

Anti-anxiety medications

Many conditions or situations can make cats anxious, but in geriatric cats, anxiety often results from cognitive dysfunction syndrome (see Chapter 17 "Cognition: Cross my mind… or not"). Drugs used off-label to manage anxiety in cats include fluoxetine, alprazolam, trazodone, gabapentin, or buspirone. Many anti-anxiety medications interact adversely with selegiline, a drug that is sometimes used to treat cats with cognitive dysfunction. So, again, be sure your veterinarian knows about all the medications your cat is receiving, in order to avoid side effects from drug interactions.

FUN FACT: PURR THERAPY?

When cats purr, they produce consistent vibrations as they breathe in and out. These vibrations range in sound frequency from 20Hz to 150Hz,[15] and some researchers speculate that purring vibrations may help cats heal themselves after bone or soft tissue injury.[15-17]

Likewise, bone healing in people responds to frequencies of 25Hz to 50Hz, and our skin and soft tissue healing processes respond to about 100Hz.[15] So in addition to the calming effects we derive from cat purrs, maybe their purring can help us heal in other ways. Some people even report migraine relief after resting their head close to a purring cat![17] (Now that's my kind of supportive therapy!)

Cannabidiol (CBD): A drug becoming more common

In the past few years, the CBD industry has skyrocketed for people and pets. But what is it all about?

CBD, terpenes, and tetrahydrocannabinol (THC) occur naturally in cannabis plants (marijuana and hemp). CBD and THC are compounds called *cannabinoids*, and terpenes are aromatic substances that give plants their scents (for example, lavender, orange and lime peels, and, of course, the unmistakable scent of marijuana). Terpenes also influence cannabinoids. In short, CBD, THC, and terpenes have a variety of effects in people and in pets. These compounds affect us because cannabinoids also occur naturally in our bodies.

We (and our cats) make our own cannabinoids (called *endocannabinoids*) that work as neurotransmitters (substances that signal nerves), and we have special receptors and enzymes that interact with cannabinoids. Collectively, this whole kit and caboodle is called the *endocannabinoid system*.[18,19] Our endocannabinoid system helps regulate mood, appetite, pain, immunity, sleep, and more. So when we consume cannabinoids from plants or synthetic sources, they influence our internal endocannabinoid system.

Marijuana vs. hemp and THC vs. CBD: Effects and uses

Of the hundreds of varieties of cannabis plants, the two broad categories are marijuana and hemp. Marijuana encompasses cannabis plants that contain more than 0.3% THC. Hemp encompasses cannabis plants that contain 0.3% or less THC. (Remember, both marijuana and hemp also contain CBD and terpenes.)

This distinction between the amount of THC a cannabis plant contains is important because THC produces a "high" (euphoria, intoxication) in people, but CBD does not have these same intense mental effects. Marijuana is illegal according to federal law (at the time of this writing), but several states permit its sale for medicinal or recreational use in people. THC has been studied and approved for limited therapeutic use in people. Synthetic forms of THC called dronabinol and nabilone are FDA-approved to treat specific types of nausea, vomiting, and inappetence in people.

Marijuana use in pets is not legal, and because of its higher THC content, it can cause toxicity and serious adverse effects in pets.[20] If cats eat their caregivers' weed or edibles, inhale secondhand pot smoke, or consume synthetic THC, they can become woozy and wobbly, lethargic, disoriented, and hypersensitive to sound or motion. They may dribble urine, drool, vomit, vocalize, or have slow heart and breathing rates. They can also have seizures or become comatose. No FDA-approved THC medications are available for cats.

Conversely, hemp is legal according to federal law, but not all states permit it to be grown. Most CBD products are made from hemp, and CBD is federally legal as long as it contains 0.3% or less THC. But CBD is not legal in every state, and in some states its sale or purchase has restrictions.

Hemp contains very little THC, and it is thought to be beneficial because hemp contains over a hundred cannabinoids (including CBD) and terpenes that can interact with our (and our pets') endocannabinoid system. Research suggests that CBD and terpenes may be beneficial in helping manage anxiety, pain, inflammation, seizures, and more in people and in rodents.[21,22] In fact, one CBD oral solution called Epidiolex is a drug that has been approved by the FDA for treating rare forms of epilepsy in people.

Two studies in a small number of cats showed that hemp-based CBD appears to be safe when given to healthy cats.[23,24] But no clinical studies have been done (at the time of this writing) to assess whether CBD has therapeutic effects in cats—for example, to evaluate whether CBD helps manage cats' inflammation, pain, or anxiety.[25]

Despite the multitude of CBD products marketed for cats—available as oils, chews, capsules, and treats—none are FDA-approved.[26] In fact, on a federal level, CBD cannot legally be marketed as a supplement or be added to food because it has already been approved by the FDA as a drug (Epidiolex), and, per FDA rules, drugs cannot be used in supplements or foods, *unless* the drug was a supplement *before* it became a drug.[27] (It is confusing!) So the only way veterinarians can legally prescribe CBD for cats would be to prescribe the human drug Epidiolex off-label.

Should senior cats receive CBD?

The FDA cautions against using CBD in cats and recommends that cat owners talk with veterinarians about other appropriate treatments. Remember, CBD products cannot legally be marketed to prevent, diagnose, treat, or cure disease.

If you decide to use CBD in your cat, do your research and use only CBD products made for cats. CBD products made for people are not formulated in pet-specific CBD doses, and they may contain ingredients that are harmful for cats, such as chocolate. And always remember to check that the CBD product you choose doesn't contain more than 0.3% THC. Consider CBD products made only by companies involved in studies that investigate the effects of CBD in pets, that provide a Certificate of Analysis for their products that detail the amount and types of all ingredients, that follow National Animal Supplement Council (NASC) and Current Good Manufacturing Practice (CGMP) guidelines, and that are recognized by your veterinarian.

Once again, always tell your veterinarian if your cat is receiving CBD, in an effort to avoid adverse interactions with other medications your cat receives and avert other potential problems related to your cat's underlying ailments such as kidney disease, heart disease, or seizures.

Why mum's the word for CBD and veterinarians

CBD use in cats is new, and clinical studies of CBD's effects to manage health problems in cats are nonexistent at the time of this writing. In the vast majority of states, veterinarians are not permitted to prescribe, recommend, or even discuss CBD with their clients. Even in states where cannabis is legal for people, these laws do not apply to animals.[26] So veterinarians may not talk with their clients about CBD use in cats because of legal concerns. In addition, veterinarians may prefer to wait on results from clinical studies that support CBD use in cats before discussing it with their clients. If you ask veterinarians about CBD, they may discuss potential benefits and harms of using it in cats, but they cannot recommend CBD products.[28]

Tough pills to swallow?

In an online survey of over 2,500 cat owners around the world who were asked about their experiences medicating cats, 79% said that their cats spit out tablets, 72% reported that their cats refused medication in food, 53% said that their cats tried to run away from them, and 77% reported that their cats tried to bite or scratch them during medication administration.[29] Most of the cat parents said they preferred giving liquid medications to tablets, and they reported that insulin injections and topical medications were easier to administer.[29]

Let's all be honest here—no one wants to give medications to a cat! A dog will eat almost anything (including cat poop and freshly vomited cat food) so giving medications is light-years easier with a dog. But getting medications down your cat's gullet can be the biggest problem!

Even pilling-wizard veterinary nurses have challenges getting kitties to take their meds, so don't feel bad if it's difficult for you. I have struggled with my own cats! Cats quickly become pros at not taking pills, so medicating them can be nightmarish. However, there are ways to make it better!

First, for oral medications, avoid putting them directly into your cat's regular food, because one displeasing bite can make a cat reject that food from then on. Ask your veterinarian:

FUN FACT

In the early 1960s, songwriter Robert Sherman's 5-year-old son's experience with getting the oral polio vaccine at school inspired a beloved song in the "Mary Poppins" movie, "A Spoonful of Sugar" which is of course widely known to help medicine go down (at least in people!).

- to teach you how to give tablets or capsules directly to your cat on the back of their tongue;
- to teach you to give tablets or capsules using a pill popper (also known as a pill gun or pill shooter);

- to teach you to give liquid medications using a syringe;
- whether flavored formulations are available; and (if you know you'll be unable to give a medication as directed or have tried it and are unsuccessful)
- whether different formulations or delivery options are available, such as putting a tablet in a capsule, giving the medication as a liquid instead of a tablet, administering the medication as a topical, or giving it as an injection.

Many helpful YouTube videos demonstrate different tricks that cat parents have tried for medicating their cats. But when cats are nearer to the end of life, they sometimes become even less accepting of taking their meds, especially pills. It's crucial to let your veterinarian know if you're unable to give oral medications to your cat and to ask for help. In the survey of cat pet parents I mentioned above, 50% reported that their veterinarian 'sometimes' or 'never' told them how to give the medication,[29] so don't hesitate to ask how best to give a medication, whether it should be given with food, whether a capsule can be opened or a tablet can be crushed, whether the medications are bitter-tasting and can be stored in the fridge to diminish their flavor and/or be placed in a gelatin capsule, and any other questions you have about your cat's medication. The **International Cat Care** website has links to helpful YouTube videos for cat owners such as "**How to give your cat a tablet**" and one directed to the veterinary team on "**Administering oral products to cats.**"

For oral medications, my preference is to start by trying a variety of tasty disguises to get cats to voluntarily take their pills, capsules, or liquids. But if your cat needs to lose weight or is prone to pancreatitis or stomach upset, avoid high-fat treats and save dairy-based disguises (such as yogurt and butter) for special occasions, because cats have trouble digesting lactose, the naturally occurring sugar in dairy products. And use only no- or very low-sodium treats for cats with heart disease or kidney disease (many cheeses and deli meats are high in sodium).

In fact, if your cat has heart disease, food allergies, diabetes, or another chronic condition, always check with your veterinarian on the best ways to conceal your cat's medications.

Given those caveats, here are a few suggestions for disguising your cat's medications:

1. pill-hiding pet treats such as Feline GREENIES Pill Pockets (by Mars Petcare);
2. Churu Cat Treats (by Inaba);
3. Kong Stuff'n Easy Treat for Cats;
4. deli meat: Try different meats and get thin slices that are easy to roll the pill in. Thick slices tend to make "taco pills" that don't fool cats as well;
5. plain yogurt (avoid yogurt that contains xylitol);
6. steak cubes or chicken cubes;

7. peanut butter (don't use peanut butter that contains xylitol);
8. processed cheese spread (e.g. Cheez Whiz);
9. small (cooked) ground turkey meatballs;
10. hot dog bites;
11. tuna;
12. baby food (meat puree);
13. marshmallow;
14. canned cat food (or meatballs made from canned cat food) that isn't your cat's regular food;
15. liverwurst; and
16. honey (stay away from honey that contains xylitol).

If your cat gets wise to your tricks, prepare their "treats" when they're not nearby. Seeing and hearing you open the medication container puts them on alert and may send them scurrying. Wash your hands after handling their meds to diminish a suspicious scent.

You can also try giving a treat first (without the pill), then give a treat with the pill, then follow up with another treat (without a pill). Or try fooling them by feeding a treat-disguised pill from your own dinner plate.

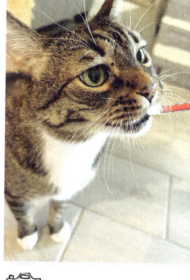

Spike doesn't mind getting his yummy liquid meds via a syringe.

Butter up your kitty!

One of my mentors, Dr. Sheilah Robertson, taught me a "sneaky butter patty" method for giving pills, tablets, or capsules to cats. First check with your veterinarian to make sure your pet's pill or tablet can be crushed or that the drug can be removed from its capsule (some drugs have special coatings that help with proper timing of absorption from the gastrointestinal tract, so they shouldn't be altered).

To make sneaky butter patties, soften (do not melt) the butter, then crush one tablet (pill crushers and pill splitters are available at pet retailers) or open one capsule and mix the medication evenly into the softened butter. Roll this into a small log (like you did as a kid with Play-Doh) and freeze it.

A sneaky butter patty log, ready for the freezer.

 Cut the frozen butter-plus-medication log into sneaky butter patties to feed to your cat.

When you are ready to give the "pill" to your cat, cut the frozen butter log into small patties, and make sure your cat eats the entire log that contains the dose they're supposed to receive. Most cats like the frozen patties and don't notice the sneakiness! If butter doesn't work, try a different base, such as Cheez Whiz, baby food, cream cheese, or tuna. Because butter and cheese are high in calories, try a tuna or baby food meat puree base if your cat needs to lose weight.

More on medi-CAT-ing

Did you know? Cats also need to drink water after taking a pill!

Will cats drink to that?

Have you ever had to take a pill or capsule without water? It's difficult and uncomfortable, right? It can also be treacherous and cause lasting damage if it sticks in your esophagus.[30]

Most pet parents don't realize that making cats "dry swallow" pills can be harmful. In cats, it should only take 10 to 20 seconds for liquid or food to pass through the esophagus and into the stomach (known as *transit time*). But dry medications don't travel through the esophagus and into the stomach fast enough. Veterinarians have studied this. They recorded tablet and capsule transit times in 30 healthy pet cats by using a special radiographic technique.[31]

After a dry tablet swallow (the tablet alone), the tablet stayed put in the esophagus for much too long: up to five minutes in 11 cats, and for *longer* than five minutes in 19 cats! But after a wet swallow (the tablet followed by 6-ml water) the tablet traveled to the stomach within 30 seconds in 27 cats. In the remaining three cats, the tablet made it to the stomach within 90 seconds.

After a dry capsule swallow, the capsule remained in the esophagus for longer than five minutes in 25 cats. After a wet swallow, the

capsule passed into the stomach within 30 seconds in 29 cats and within 60 seconds in the last cat.

A tablet or capsule that sits in the esophagus for a couple minutes or more causes irritation and inflammation, which can permanently damage the esophagus and make it difficult for your cat to eat and drink normally.

So every time you give your cat a tablet or capsule, it's crucial to follow up by giving them a small sip—at least 6 ml (a little more than a teaspoon)—of water. You can slowly squirt 6 ml of water from a syringe into the side of your pet's mouth or tempt them to voluntarily drink a low-sodium meat broth or flavored water supplement such as Hydra Care (Purina Pro Plan Veterinary Supplements). (Or give 6 ml of the tasty beverage by oral syringe if needed.)

If following up with a sip doesn't work, try feeding a high-value treat such as baby food or Churu Puree by Inaba. This makes them swallow more times and moves the pill along with the food. **inabafoods.com/collections/churu-puree**

Another helpful technique is to put a bit of butter on the cat's nose right after you give the medication. This stimulates them to lick their nose and swallow. Swallowing expedites the passage of the pill into the stomach!

 A spoonful of sugar may not work for cats, but a "noseful" of butter helps the capsule go down!

Medication organization

Giving senior cats their medications can become so routine and repetitive that you'll have moments when you can't remember whether you gave your cat their medication. You may be certain you did. But wait... maybe that was yesterday? It has happened to me!

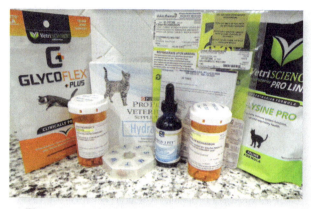

 Cena's medicine shelf.

I love using pill organizers to help track my cat's daily medications. They're available at any drug store. If your cat needs only twice-a-day medications, then a standard "morning/evening" container will do. For additional daily doses, you'll probably need a four-compartment case. Some multi-dose pill boxes organize up to seven-times-a-day medications!

Also consider creating a "Treatment Tracker" as a handy reference to note various therapies and their effects in your pet. See Chapter 22 "Journaling: Tracking your cat's health."

When I was treating Lilu with insulin (an injectable medication that must be kept refrigerated), it became so automatic that there were some days when I would stand in front of the fridge and could not for the life of me remember whether I just gave the insulin. And insulin must not be missed or overdosed!

 Bruce's mom kept his meds in one place—easy to get to! (The canned food is kept refrigerated after it's opened.)

A simple visual reminder tool helps you track feeding or twice-daily medication administration.

Phone apps and fancy medication reminder timers are available, but what worked for me was a simple slider tracker—simply move the slider on the appropriate day and time spot after you give the medication.

Beyond the pillbox: Veterinary rehabilitation therapy

Not all treatments involve medications or supplements. A number of non-pharmacological options categorized under the umbrella of veterinary rehabilitation therapy (which is similar to physical therapy in people) are available that your veterinarian may suggest for your senior cat.

Veterinary rehabilitation includes various therapeutic exercises that strengthen muscles and improve flexibility and balance as well as passive range-of-motion and stretching exercises. It also includes therapies such as an underwater treadmill, hydrotherapy, laser therapy, ultrasound therapy, pulsed electromagnetic field therapy, acupuncture, and massage.

But how do you tell a cat to do specific exercises? It's not easy, but those who are trained to do it are like Jedis—they possess a special "Force"! Cats do best with rehabilitation therapy exercises that promote play or hunting and involve treats, and they also do well with manual, hands-on treatments to manipulate their joints or massage their muscles.[32] Cats also often tolerate electrophysical therapies (such as laser therapy, pulsed electromagnetic

Dr. Tammy Johnson performing physical therapy.

field therapy, and ultrasound therapy) well.[32] Rehabilitation sessions for cats sometimes need to be shorter than sessions for dogs.[32]

Special certification is required to provide veterinary rehabilitation services. Ask your veterinarian or search for an expert near you at the American Association of Rehabilitation Veterinarians website **rehabvets.org/** and the American College of Veterinary Sports Medicine and Rehabilitation website **vsmr.site-ym.com/search/custom.asp?id=5595**.

As my love for working with older pets grew, I recognized how helpful rehabilitation therapy could be for so many pets. Although rehabilitation is most often thought of to help injured or postoperative orthopedic patients return to their original function,[33] it's also used to slow progression of chronic issues. The goal is to help patients, especially those with nervous or musculoskeletal system disorders, attain the best level of function, independence, and quality of life possible.

The vast array of therapeutic exercises and passive range of motion exercises would take another book to cover, so in this section I highlight a few of the other therapies used in veterinary rehabilitation: massage, laser, acupuncture, and pulsed electromagnetic field.

Massage therapy

I love a good spa day or massage! I know not everyone likes massage, but studies in people suggest that regular, frequent massage helps prevent stiffness and pain from arthritis, improves blood circulation, increases blood oxygenation, and boosts energy. Massage also decreases muscle spasms,] and may "trick" the spinal cord and brain into feeling the good sensations over the pain. Massage therapy is used in pets for pain relief, rehabilitation after orthopedic injury or surgery, managing swelling, intensive care support, managing working and athletic activities, and palliative and hospice care.[34-36]

A study of more than 500 dogs (again, no similar studies in cats yet!) treated by practitioners trained in clinical canine massage therapy showed that 95% of the dogs had substantially reduced musculoskeletal pain after three massage therapy sessions over three to four weeks.[37] The dogs' posture, gait, daily activities, and behavior improved. At the beginning of the study, 40% of the dogs were reported to have a positive quality of life, and this increased to 66% after the first massage therapy session, 83% after the second session, and 92% after the third session.

What I love most about animal massage therapy is that pet parents can learn some components of it from veterinary rehabilitation practitioners to use at home. Massage therapy also promotes the human-animal bond. Ask your veterinarian about veterinary massage therapists in your area.

Laser therapy

Laser therapy is also known as photobiomodulation therapy. Light energy in the visible (400–700 nm) and near-infrared (700–1100 nm) electromagnetic spectrum is delivered to a specific area of the body with a laser or light-emitting diode. Research suggests that laser therapy may help decrease inflammation and pain and accelerate healing.

In a nutshell, the light energy reaches cell mitochondria (a cell's "engine") to promote production of adenosine triphosphate—the molecule that facilitates energy transfer within a cell. Free nitric oxide is also produced, which is a powerful vasodilator (widens blood vessels) and an important signal involved in other normal body functions. Vasodilation improves circulation, so this increased blood flow better delivers oxygen, salts, vital sugars, and proteins to and removes wastes from damaged tissue. In addition, reactive oxygen species are produced, and these molecules affect many of the body's important signaling pathways, including the inflammatory response.

Safety goggles are important for animals receiving laser therapy.

Therapeutic lasers may provide benefits in treating a number of conditions in senior cats, such as arthritis, pain from nerve dysfunction, inflammation, and infections. Laser therapy can only be performed by a veterinarian. A treatment can last a few minutes to about an hour, depending on the size of the treatment area and the intensity of the laser. It's not recommended to use laser therapy in patients who have widespread cancer or to use it directly over a cancerous tumor.

Calvin enjoyed chin rubs along with his laser therapy to help manage his arthritis.

Acupuncture

Acupuncture has been used for thousands of years in people as a component of Traditional Chinese Medicine and is now commonly practiced worldwide. In cats and dogs, acupuncture is also commonly practiced around the world as a component of Traditional Chinese Veterinary Medicine. Very thin needles are inserted at specific points in the body to produce a healing response. Cats have dozens of acupuncture points and each point has a specific action when stimulated.

Intensive training is required to be certified in veterinary acupuncture, and only a licensed veterinarian can administer acupuncture. Certified veterinary acupuncture practitioners may use acupuncture to help cats who have arthritis, various types of pain, nerve dysfunction, respiratory problems, gastrointestinal disturbances such as diarrhea, and even anxiety.

Acupuncture usually requires two treatments a week for a few weeks, then once a week, and then every other week. Cats tolerate acupuncture extremely well and often fall asleep during treatment.

 Can't get much more relaxed during acupuncture than this!

Tullah, a 13-year-old kitty with arthritis and intermittent lameness in her right front leg enjoyed her electroacupuncture (tiny electric currents transmitted through acupuncture needles) treatments so much that she never got angry with the veterinary team at the rehabilitation center (a stark contrast to her attitude toward the team at her primary care veterinary practice!), and she ignored the dogs (even though she hated dogs!) who were receiving therapy nearby on the underwater treadmill.

Pulsed electromagnetic field therapy

Pulsed electromagnetic field (PEMF) therapy sends invisible targeted pulses to tissues, which induce electrical changes around and within cells to influence cell behavior. Some evidence suggests it helps decrease pain, inflammation, and anxiety and enhances healing[38]; it may also have benefits in cats after spinal cord and peripheral nerve injuries.[39,40]

At the time of this writing, the Virginia-Maryland College of Veterinary Medicine is conducting a study to assess the effect of PEMF to treat pain in cats with arthritis using an Assisi Animal Health PEMF device.

vetmed.vt.edu/clinical-trials/current-studies/feline-osteoarthritis.html
youtube.com/watch?v=HHic3DqZnQU

So much help for senior cats

Many treatment options are available to help keep your cat comfortable during their golden years! Some treatments may work better than others for your cat and, more often than not, more than one type of therapy will be needed. Patience and communication are key as you partner with your veterinarian to find the best approach. If only we could talk to our cats about how the treatments they're receiving may help them—and if only they could listen, understand, and happily be on board!

Questions to ask your veterinarian

Your veterinary team and/or pharmacy should provide this information orally and/or in writing for each medication prescribed for your pet, But it can be a lot to absorb during a visit and you may forget some components by the time you get home and need to give your pet the next dose. Having answers to these questions will help you remember the basic but important points about your pet's treatments, and help you avoid making follow-up phone calls, or worse, making incorrect assumptions:

- What is the name of the medication?
- What does the medication look like? (It's important to confirm that you've been given the correct medication, and to know what it looks like in case you inadvertently receive the wrong medication when you refill a prescription. Always speak up if a medication differs from what you were prescribed previously and ask why it is different.)
- Why does my pet need to receive this medication?

- How do I give the medication (by mouth, on the skin, as an injection), how much do I give, how often do I need to give it, and for how long does my pet need to receive it?
- Will you teach me how to give the medication to my pet?
- Are there any mild or severe side effects associated with this medication, and if so, what do I watch for in my pet and what should I do if something occurs?
- Are there special precautions or advice for how to use and store this medication?
- What do I do if I miss giving a dose to my pet?
- Does the medication need to be given with food? Can I break, crush, or dissolve the medication if needed?
- Do I need to avoid giving this medication with any other medication or supplement my pet is receiving?
- Are there any special precautions or warnings regarding this medication according to the manufacturer?
- Do you have a handout I can take home for reference about this medication or is there another resource you recommend?
- Will I need to refill this medication?
- Does my pet need follow-up visits or tests while my pet is receiving this medication, before this medication is refilled, or after this medication is completed?

RESOURCE

- Medication information for pet owners. Veterinary Partner, powered by the Veterinary Information Network.
  veterinarypartner.vin.com/default.aspx?pid=19239&catId=102894

CHAPTER 24:

Building your support team: Don't go it alone

"Wouldn't it be easier if we just named all the cats Password?"
— FROM "THE FRIEND," A NOVEL BY SIGRID NUNEZ

A cat's later years are often accompanied by one or more sudden, short illnesses or progressive, long-term ailments, and you may not have control over many aspects of their health outcomes. Having the right team around you is one thing that is controllable. Finding the right team to help you navigate your cat's geriatric challenges, whether your cat is starting to require more daily care or approaching the end of life, takes on vital importance. So let's look at who you'll want to team up with!

Your veterinary clinic pro team

Veterinarians. Veterinarians are the pros in primary care veterinary practice! We spend six to eight years total in undergraduate and graduate school, learning most things about dogs, cats, and farm animals—and many things about other furry, feathery, or scaly family members and wildlife. After graduation, our education continues. We keep up with new developments in animal health, diseases, diagnostic tests, surgical procedures, medical treatments, and other ways to make animals' lives better, and we must fulfill specific continuing education requirements each year in order to renew our state licenses to practice veterinary medicine. Veterinarians may work in clinical practice, research, teaching, media, diagnostic laboratories, public health, and more.

Because I developed a keen interest in and love for geriatric pet veterinary care, I have several years' of focused experience with amazing elderly cat patients. I also stay caught up on new findings in human geriatric medicine and end-of-life care and am always on the lookout for opportunities to translate those concepts to help senior cats live better. This book is one of my labors of learning and desire to share this knowledge with all who share their homes with aging feline family members.

Communicating well with your veterinarian is paramount. Veterinarians want to hear your concerns and questions about your cats. We have ideas and options that can help. If we get too sciency-wiency as we discuss your cat's health, let us know. I give examples of questions you may want to ask your veterinarian throughout this book, so don't be shy about having your question list ready! Your veterinarian should also welcome your wish to seek a second opinion from another primary care veterinarian or to see a veterinary specialist if you'd like. It's our goal to give you options for your cat and access to the level of healthcare support you are comfortable with.

Board-certified veterinary specialists. These veterinarians have completed advanced training in a specific area of veterinary medicine and passed an additional examination to specialize in that area. Veterinarians can become board-certified specialists in anesthesia and analgesia, behavior, cardiology, dentistry, dermatology, emergency medicine and critical care, internal medicine, neurology, nutrition, oncology, ophthalmology, pharmacology, radiology, sports medicine and rehabilitation, surgery, zoo medicine, and more. Phew—that's a true A to Z! These specialists typically practice in private veterinary specialty referral centers and university teaching hospitals. Pharmaceutical companies, zoos, and a myriad of other sectors also seek out the super-charged brains of these veterinary healthcare experts.

Primary care veterinarians can also specialize in caring for a specific species such as dogs, cats, birds, exotic mammals, reptiles, or various farm animals. These veterinarians may practice in a species-specific clinic such as a feline hospital, or they may work in a general practice and see other animals as well. And some veterinarians specialize in shelter animal medicine and work exclusively in animal shelters or consult with them.

Your primary care veterinarian may suggest that you seek the advice and care of a specialist. Access to a specialist can be challenging in some areas, so your veterinarian may offer to consult with a specialist by using a telemedicine referral service.

Veterinary technicians/veterinary nurses. Veterinary technicians have two to four years of education after high school and obtain an associate's or bachelor's degree in veterinary technology. They have similar responsibilities to those of nurses and other professionals who work with physicians and to hygienists who work with dentists. These credentialed veterinary team members hold a special place in the heart of a veterinary hospital by monitoring anesthesia and assisting during surgeries, obtaining patients' medical histories and samples for diagnostic tests, providing nursing care, taking radiographs, cleaning and polishing teeth, helping to educate pet owners, and knowing the importance of a personal touch. They are at animals' sides during an outpatient visit or from hospital admission to discharge, helping veterinarians perform medical procedures, administer treatments, and ensure patient comfort.

Veterinary technicians can also specialize by advancing their education, training, and experience in specific disciplines such as anesthesia and analgesia, cardiology, dentistry, emergency and critical care, oncology, zoo medicine, and many more. Technicians who successfully complete the specialty academy requirements are awarded the designation of Veterinary Technician Specialist (VTS) in their discipline. Veterinary technician specialists most commonly work in specialty referral centers, university teaching hospitals, and primary care practices.

Veterinary assistants. Veterinary assistants help veterinary technicians and veterinarians in a variety of ways that ensure those team members can focus on the tasks and responsibilities required of them. So veterinary assistants clean and prep exam rooms, help fill prescriptions, set up lab tests, update medical records, track inventory, and assist with patient nursing care. Veterinary assistants also help educate clients about pet preventive healthcare, and support the client services personnel at the front desk of the veterinary clinic. In the U.S., graduates of an approved National Association of Veterinary Technicians in America veterinary assistant program who pass an Approved Veterinary Assistant examination become Approved Veterinary Assistants. The designation must be renewed every two years and requires participating in continuing education programs.

Your away team

Boarding facilities. If you travel for work or vacation or simply need a pet parent break (it's OK to need a rest!), finding the right team with the expertise to provide the best care for your cat is pure gold. With older cats, it can be a lot of work to manage the numerous medications and special feedings or diet preparations—AND to maintain constant vigilance for medical issues.

Look for professional boarding and day care facilities that can handle not only medication administration but also cats with special medical needs. Do they have non-slip flooring (for cats who don't walk as confidently as they used to)? Can you bring your cat's orthopedic bed (for cats who have sore muscles or joints and need just the right comfy spot)? Do they have night lights for cats who have cognitive dysfunction (throwing a little light on the situation is always helpful for cats whose minds don't react as quickly as they used to)? Do they use pheromone sprays or diffusers (for those cats with anxiety issues)? Are licensed veterinary technicians on the team to assess and monitor the cats?

Many primary care veterinary hospitals have standard boarding facilities that provide routine pet care for daytime and overnight stays. And some of these hospitals offer medical boarding for pets who need special medical care, but most provide this service only during their regular business hours. So if your cat needs around-the-clock monitoring, a stay at a specialty hospital that offers medical boarding *and* is staffed 24/7 will be needed. Ask your veterinary team for recommendations to find the right boarding facility fit for your cat and the level of care he requires.

In-home pet sitters. This is often the best option when you must leave your senior pet, and the one that I prefer. Older cats appreciate routine and familiarity, and they feel more comfortable and safer in their home environment. Staying home helps them avoid the stress of the unfamiliar noises, smells, and distractions at a boarding facility, and their environment can be better controlled. If you can, have a pet sitter stay with your cat the entire time you are away. This adds cost, but in my experience the savings in personal anxiety are well worth it. My personal in-home pet sitter is Jean **facebook.com/leanonjean/**. (I'm sharing her Facebook page not to sell you on her services, but to show you the special care pet sitters all around the country take to keep our furry family members cozy and comfy year round.) I'm so fortunate that she has been there for my dogs Duncan and Sam, my cat Bodhi, and a few of my other grey muzzle and nine-lives loves. I could not have traveled for work as much as I did without the reassurance of knowing Jean was caring for my fur kids at home. Thank you, Jean!

Respite care. In caregiving for people, respite care provides temporary relief for someone who is caring for a family member or friend with a serious health condition. It allows the caregiver to take a break, go on a required trip, or even go to work each day. Respite care isn't widely available in the pet services industry, but you may be able to hire a home cat sitter or veterinary technician who will come to your home to provide this care.

When I lived in Southern California, Disneyland was 15 minutes from my house. I could see the fireworks at night! When my good friend Christian traveled from the United Kingdom with his stepdaughter Chloe to visit me, they—of course!—wanted to go to Disneyland. This would be an all-day adventure, but I had a number of sick pets who could not be left alone for the day. I wanted to go to Disneyland with my friends! I wanted to have fun! And I needed the break! But, alas, Jean was away on her own vacation. I hired a veterinary technician to stay at my house and care for my pets on her day off so I could have a day off. Those 12 hours with my friends in the Land of Magic were gold to me. I relaxed, I laughed, I had fun, and I did not have anxiety about my pets' care. That short break from caregiving gave me the mental energy boost I needed to care for them in the months that followed.

Your cat's glamor team

Groomers. Maintaining a clean, mat-free, tidy hair coat and keeping toenails trimmed isn't all about aesthetics—at least not for your cat. It's about comfort. Overgrown claws and tangled fur can make mobility and pottying more difficult and uncomfortable. Many pet parents can manage these spiffing-up services for their cats, but if needed, keep in mind that professional groomers can help! They have studied the optimal combing, brushing, and trimming methods for dogs *and* cats.

If it's stressful for your cat to travel to a groomer, consider looking for a mobile groomer who comes to you and understands the special care your fragile one needs. Check out their spa-on-wheels first—does it have a non-slip table? How will your cat be dried? (Hand-drying is safer and less stressful than cage drying.)

Your spirit team

Your friends, family, and coworkers. Here is where the heart is. These people know you. They know your pets. They know that as your cat grows older, you're keeping a more careful eye to make sure she still enjoys her sunning spot. Your cat's care sometimes takes a lot of effort and makes you a little overworked and over worried. Find family and friends who have special roles in supporting your spirit—those who listen to you, talk with you without trying to control the situation, and are empathetic.

So many thoughts are running around in your brain. Working through all those feelings on your own can make you feel lonely and isolated. Talk with people who will truly hear you and not simply tell you what they would do to try to fix your situation. Good listeners are patient and wait for you to be ready to talk or cry. They also notice what you're not saying. They ask open-ended questions, reflect back to you what you've said, and allow you to let out the emotions you may be feeling.

Find people who will talk with you about your difficulties and not simply say things that they think you want to hear. People who will ask for stories, let you share at your own pace, and not rush you to feel better and put a time limit on your pain.

Also seek out family members and friends to support you who have gone through experiences with their cats similar to yours. Alternatively, this is an area where pet care support groups can help.

Your walk-on team

Neighborhood friends. Sheilah is the deli clerk at my grocery store. When I visited her to buy a variety of meats to wrap pills in for my dog Sam, Sheilah handed me a slice to taste. I raised my hand as a 'no thank you' gesture and said, "This is not for me, it's for my dog. She's old and I wrap her pills in tasty treats so she'll take them."

Sheilah's eyes lit up and she answered, "Well, then, you must try the liverwurst! I hid my dog's pills in it and he never knew!" She cut liverwurst slices in a variety of thicknesses and insisted that I come back to tell her how it worked. (I did, and Sheilah was right! Liverwurst was Sam's favorite.)

I always ran my deli errands when I knew Sheilah was working. We chatted about Sam and about Sheliah's dog. You can find support in the oddest places! So many pet lovers are out there, and most of them are excited to share their tips! And wouldn't you know it, my cat prefers liverwurst, too, and she enjoys getting a little bit after she takes her medicine!

Social media. One advantage of social media is that people from all over can connect and share experiences that have helped them. For example, Facebook has groups dedicated to animal enrichment and specific cat medical conditions. Of course it's important to always consult with your veterinarian before trying the medical recommendations you find, but mostly you will find people who love their cats and want to help them through their struggles and share what they have learned. You'll find people who understand what it's like to have a cat with the challenges that you're seeking support for. A few groups that I've joined include:

- Cats with Chronic Kidney Disease Facebook group:
  facebook.com/groups/felinecrf
- Cats with Hyperthyroidism Facebook group:
  facebook.com/groups/42301610484
- Feline Enrichment Facebook group:
  facebook.com/groups/610891845701943

Your special teams

We all know too well that all good things must come to an end. And our cats are nothing but good. You will eventually face their death. It may be sudden and unexpected or a planned euthanasia. It's important to begin to think about the options you prefer for your cat and the outcome that you may be able to control, like choosing the right place and the right time and having the right people around you. This will help you manage the grief you will surely experience. (See Chapter 32 "Grief wellness: Anticipating and experiencing loss" and Chapter 36 "Euthanasia: The ending is what matters most.")

Pet loss support groups. These groups of understanding individuals can help while you navigate anticipatory grief and pet loss. Not every town has a pet loss support group, but online support groups may be a beneficial alternative. Lap of Love has free weekly online meetings as well as one-on-one sessions. **lapoflove.com/our-services/pet-loss-support**

Counselors and therapists. Some people find comfort in speaking directly to a professional, and some therapists and counselors specialize in grief counseling. Veterinary teaching hospitals as well as referral or primary care veterinary practices may offer support to their clients provided by a licensed clinical social worker. Some employers also offer employee assistance programs who may offer these services at no charge.

Free, confidential support for people in emotional distress or suicidal crisis is available in the U.S. through the National Suicide Prevention Lifeline by texting or calling 988 or by calling 1-800-273-TALK (8255), 24 hours a day, seven days a week. Other local support is available by calling your doctor's office or 911. Please don't suffer in silence. It's OK to tell someone. People are willing to listen. Please find them.

A beautiful fellowship

I hope you find the right team of people who support you—from your veterinary team to those you interact with every day. A team who is there to help when you need them but also gives you space when you need it. Your support team isn't there to take over your life. You are fully capable—even when you feel overwrought or are grieving and hurting. It's OK to feel those things and to ask for support when you need it. Your support team should be able to recognize if you are about to go off the deep end and will guide you back to calm, shallow water with the reassurance of a warm, comfy, oversize beach towel wrapped lovingly around your being.

RESOURCES

- American Veterinary Medical Association Resources for Pet Owners
  avma.org/resources-tools/pet-owners
- American Veterinary Medical Association List of Veterinary Specialties
  avma.org/education/veterinary-specialties
- Veterinary Technician Specialties
  navta.net/veterinary-technician-specialties/list-of-approved-academies/
- Approved Veterinary Assistants
  navta.site-ym.com/page/vet_assistants
- Suicide Prevention Lifeline website:
  suicidepreventionlifeline.org
  Text or call 988 or call: 1-800-273-TALK (8255)

CHAPTER 25:

FAQs: Why not let your vet see your senior cat?

"You know my method. It is founded upon the observation of trifles."

— SHERLOCK HOLMES
(FROM "THE BOSCOMBE VALLEY MYSTERY"
BY SIR ARTHUR CONAN DOYLE)

"Does my cat really need to go to the veterinarian?"
"What is the vet going to tell me, other than 'Simba is old'?"
"Does my cat really need tests and medications—what good will they do?"
"My cat is old and will probably only live a couple more years. Why should I continue with vaccinations, parasite prevention, and regular checkups?"
"Isn't my cat too old for anesthesia?"
"How can I take my cat to the vet without all the stress?"

Well-meaning families who share their lives with a geriatric cat often ask me questions like these. And to start, I will be straight to the point: Yes! Please allow your cat to have regular veterinary checkups.

In general, pet parents visit the veterinarian with their dogs more often than they do with their cats. In 2016, the American Veterinary Medical Association found that 79% of dog owners report they take their dog to the veterinarian at least once a year for a routine checkup, yet only 47% of cat owners do the same.[1]

Like us as we age, cats tend to have more health issues and need more medical attention during their last life stage. I know many elderly people who are stable but have long-standing health issues, and they see their family physician for checkups every three or four months. That isn't even counting their checkups with the doctors who specialize in their health problems!

Did you know that when cats reach their senior years, routine veterinary checkups are needed every six months? And that applies to *healthy* senior cats.

Like people, cats with chronic medical conditions usually need to see a veterinarian more often than every six months for rechecks. A cat's final years are the most delicate, and your veterinary team can help shore up the precious time you have left with your cat.

Why so many rechecks? Senior and geriatric cats need more routine checkups and health monitoring to help detect conditions and diseases associated with aging. Looking for and addressing health threats in your furry family members can help them live longer and more comfortably, all while allowing them to stay as active and engaged (and as happy!) as possible.

An engaging life, plus good health, or, if good health eludes us, well-managed health conditions, are what we want for our family members, our friends, and ourselves. Welcoming and watching over your cat's ninth-life stage and partnering with your veterinarian in your cat's healthcare can be splendidly life-changing for your cat and for you.

A prescription for the fountain of cat youth

Senior cats (really, cats of any age) may have subtle signs of issues brewing that you may not readily recognize. So once you notice something's amiss, the ailment may be advanced. Older cats are more likely to have months and years of their lives stolen by kidney disease, cancer, arthritis, heart disease, and other health thieves. I always say that it's easier to keep the demon away than to chase it away once it's in the house!

Enlisting a veterinarian's expertise to help catch problems as early as possible and before they progress may help your cat act, look, and feel younger than his age. One of my goals is to help boost the percentage of senior cats who have regular veterinary healthcare checkups, because it will boost the comfort, care, and contentment of so many feline family members—and their pet parents!

How often should your cat see a vet?

I recommend that senior cats see their veterinarian at least twice a year. Between those visits, monitor your cat's behavior, appetite, thirst, urination and defecation, breathing, energy levels, and attitude. Keeping a cat health journal will help (see Chapter 22 "Journaling: Tracking your cat's health"). Bring this information along to each routine checkup or illness recheck, and visit your veterinarian sooner if you notice out-of-character or concerning changes.

What will your vet see in your cat?

Frequent, routine veterinary visits for your senior cat are similar to our own routine checkups. At my most recent annual checkup, my physical examination findings and blood test results were normal (yay!). And I didn't feel like I'd wasted my time or money because my doctor found nothing wrong. My doctor also asked about my stress levels, workload, and safety in my home environment. My doctor recommended that I take a daily calcium and vitamin D supplement to help prevent osteoporosis, gave me a tetanus booster vaccination, suggested I add two (more!) 30-minute exercise activities each week, reminded me to schedule a mammogram, told me I could look forward to a screening colonoscopy within the next year (eek), and scheduled my checkup appointment for next year.

How does this compare to your cat's visit? A senior cat's routine veterinary examination entails:

- reviewing your cat's medical history and discussing physical or behavioral changes you've noted or other concerns you have (write down your questions ahead of the visit and take your cat's health journal along);
- discussing your cat's diet, appetite, caloric intake, and activity levels;
- a physical examination, including assessments of your cat's pulse, breathing rate, temperature, heart and lung sounds, blood pressure, eyes, teeth, skin, coat, claws, musculoskeletal system, cognition and balance, weight, body condition, and muscle condition;
- blood tests—a complete blood count to evaluate the types and numbers of blood cells, a serum chemistry profile to help evaluate organ function, and thyroid hormone measurement to check for an overactive thyroid gland;
- urine test to check for bacteria, blood cells, crystals, glucose, and protein in the urine; and to help assess hydration status and kidney function;
- other diagnostic tests if indicated, such as a fecal examination, radiography or ultrasonography, an electrocardiogram, and testing for heartworm disease, feline leukemia virus, feline immunodeficiency virus, and more[2];
- discussing whether home environment modifications or new enrichment activities would be beneficial;
- prescribing medications and scheduling follow-up tests, procedures, or referrals, if needed; and
- scheduling the next checkup!

All of my own geriatric cats have bloodwork done three times a year and radiographs and ultrasound exams yearly—or any time there is any whiff or sniff of a problem!

Even if you've noticed no changes and your veterinarian finds no problems at your cat's checkups (the news pet parents hope to hear!), your veterinarian can give tips specifically for your senior cat that fit with your lifestyle and your home to keep your cat active and comfortable in the long run.

Research revelation: Most mature cats have multiple health problems

In a study at three veterinary clinics in the United Kingdom, only 22 of 176 (12%) cats who were between 7 and 10 years old received a clean bill of health based on findings from their physical examinations and lab tests.[3] The other 154 cats (88%) had ailments such as orthopedic problems, dental disease, heart murmurs, possible kidney disease, obesity, hyperthyroidism, and high blood pressure. Of these cats, 61 had one ailment, and 93 had two to five ailments.

Out-of-character changes in their cats that pet parents reported that correlated with their cats having chronic disease were having matted fur, being grumpier, sleeping more, and walking away after sniffing their food. Many cat parents (39%) said that their cats vomited at least once a month—usually a hairball.

Over a quarter (27%) reported that their cats wanted more attention or had become more affectionate in middle age, which cat parents considered to be positive changes.

Vaccine routines—are they needed?

I'm a vaccination advocate. I've seen many horribly sick cat and dog patients and many patients who died because they caught an infectious disease that was preventable, but one that they weren't vaccinated against.

Cats who travel or board need to be up-to-date on their vaccinations, not only for their own protection but to protect other cats. You never know who your cat will be exposed to, and senior cats tend to have weaker immune systems.

If your cat lives entirely indoors, never goes outside, and no other cats visit (meaning your cat basically lives in a bubble!), are some vaccinations really necessary? Possibly not, especially if your cat has immunity confirmed by the results of titer testing. Titers are blood tests that measure whether your cat may be protected against some diseases. The results help determine whether your cat needs certain vaccinations, but the tests are not available for every type of infection that vaccines protect against. Ask your veterinarian whether titer testing is appropriate for your cat.

To determine which vaccinations your senior cat needs and when, your veterinarian will also consider other factors such as whether your cat has a chronic disease (diabetes, cancer, kidney disease, certain viral infections) or is receiving medications that suppress the immune system (glucocorticoids, chemotherapy).[4]

And remember, if *you* go out, we know that viruses and bacteria can travel on cats and people, and some of these are readily transmitted. So you could be the unsuspecting source of an infectious bug, even when your cat stays home curled up in your favorite chair!

How many parasite preventives are necessary?

Fleas, ticks, intestinal parasites, and heartworms don't discriminate by age. They love all cats! If your senior indoor cat truly never steps a "toe bean" outside and other cats don't live with you or come to visit, then your cat may not need flea and tick preventives. But heartworm preventives are still needed because heartworms are transmitted by mosquitoes. (See Chapter 12 "Heart: Keeping the beat strong.") I live in Florida, and those wily fliers sneak in, even though I have a screen enclosure!

Is my cat too old for anesthesia?

While it's true that geriatric (and pediatric!) age is one risk factor associated with a patient's complications after anesthesia, age alone is not a reason to pass up a cat's diagnostic test, medical treatment, surgery, or other procedure that requires anesthesia or sedation.

Additional risk factors to consider before anesthesia include a cat's health status (whether the cat has an underlying disease and how severe the disease is), his breed (brachycephalic or "smoosh-faced" breeds such as Burmese, Persians, and Himalayans may have brachycephalic airway syndrome, which increases a pet's risk of complications during general anesthesia), his level of pain and stress, and the type of procedure he needs—because urgent surgeries or long procedures carry more risk.[5,6]

Geriatric cats tend to have underlying age-related diseases and less ability to respond to stress, so they have a higher risk of anesthesia- or sedation-related complications or death.[7] Senior and geriatric cats simply don't have as much *functional reserve*—the remaining capacity for the body to operate normally—as younger, healthier cats have. This means they have a harder time responding to or recovering from stress such as the pain associated with their condition or from a drop in blood pressure or body temperature during anesthesia. A geriatric cat's kidneys or liver may have a harder time filtering and processing the anesthetics or sedatives, and her aging brain, heart, and lungs may be more sensitive to the effects of these drugs.

The good news is that your veterinary team can reduce anesthetic risks by carefully evaluating your cat beforehand and tailoring the anesthetic plan. The benefits your cat gains by undergoing anesthesia to receive treatments or diagnostic tests often far outweigh the risks of anesthesia. And if your cat has a serious medical condition that increases his risk for anesthetic complications, your veterinarian may recommend that you take him to a referral hospital for the procedure or test, where they have staff who specialize in anesthesia.

How can we reduce anesthetic risks?

The veterinary team and cat parents all have roles in helping reduce the risks of anesthesia in senior cats. The veterinary team tailors the anesthesia and monitoring plan to each patient. We consider the patient's age, species, sex, breed, and size. We evaluate the cat's medical history (current diseases and medications, previous responses to anesthesia), perform a physical examination, and assess the results of blood and urine tests, just as your physician would require of you before you undergo anesthesia. Additional tests may be needed depending on your cat's health status. For example, cats with heart disease may need an echocardiogram.

You can help, too, by asking or allowing your veterinarian to schedule this evaluation a day or two before the procedure whenever possible. This helps the veterinary team identify and address abnormalities before a pet is anesthetized or allows us to more easily reschedule a non-urgent procedure if needed, rather than cancel it on the day of the procedure. You can also ask whether your geriatric pet's procedure can be scheduled as early as possible in the morning, so your cat may be able to go home the same day and have a shorter hospital stay.[8]

> **FUN FACT**
>
> Did you know that veterinary technicians/veterinary nurses can become certified in anesthesia? This means they have extra training in anesthetic techniques and monitoring pets undergoing anesthesia.

Your role before anesthesia

Pet parents have a role in the anesthesia plan, too, because it begins before the cat leaves home. For example, you'll likely need to withhold food as directed by your veterinarian to fast your cat before the procedure. You may need to give pain- and anxiety-relieving medications before the trip to the veterinary hospital to minimize your cat's pain, fear, and stress. If your cat tends to get carsick, let your veterinarian know so anti-nausea medication can be prescribed to prevent this. And take one of your cat's familiar toys or blankets along that can stay with her throughout her hospital visit.[9]

The veterinary team's role

At the veterinary hospital, the goal is to keep pets calm from admission to discharge. Minimizing fear, pain, and anxiety helps reduce the amount of anesthetic drugs your cat will need and promotes smoother recovery and faster healing.

The veterinary team performs a preanesthetic patient evaluation (including blood and urine tests if these were not done a day or two earlier). They select the anesthetic, sedative, and analgesic drugs and doses based on these findings and the pet's medical history. Many of the same sedative and anesthetic drugs that are used in human medicine are used in veterinary medicine, as are many of the same types of anesthesia supplies, equipment, and monitors. Giving a sedative before anesthesia helps relieve patient anxiety and decreases the amount of anesthetic needed. Pets also receive tailored supportive care that includes intravenous fluids (keeps them hydrated), supplemental oxygen (keeps them breathing easy), thermal support (keeps them warm), and comfortable positioning (keeps away physical stress).

Keeping pets warm before, during, and after anesthesia is crucial because hypothermia (too cool body temperature) causes prolonged recovery time and can also delay wound healing and affect mental activity.[10] Mild hypothermia is common because anesthetic drugs suppress the brain's normal temperature control mechanisms. Anesthetic drugs also dilate blood vessels, so body heat more easily travels from the body's core to the skin, where heat loss occurs.[11] Pets also lose body heat through their surgical site or from having their mouth rinsed during dental procedures. On top of all that, a pet's internal thermostat can go a little wonky as they get older (see Chapter 10 "Thermoregulation: Cool cats and feverish felines"), making it harder for them to reset to a normal body temperature. Circulating warm-water blankets, forced warm-air blankets, and warm intravenous fluids are some of the measures veterinary teams use to help pets maintain a normal body temperature during and after anesthesia.[9]

Pets are closely monitored before, during, and after anesthesia or sedation. Their heart and breathing rates, pulses, gum color, hydration status, eye position, jaw tone, overall muscle tone, reflexes, blood pressure, oxygen and carbon dioxide levels, heart rhythm, and temperature are assessed throughout. Like older people, older pets have decreased anesthetic requirements, and this is possibly because the brain shrinks with age.[8] The anesthetic protocol is adjusted as appropriate and additional supportive therapies are given if needed.

Most anesthetic-related deaths in pets occur after a procedure during the first three hours of recovery.[8] Therefore, close patient monitoring continues until your cat is discharged from the hospital. You'll also need to keep a close eye on your cat for several days after he returns home.[12] Speaking of which...

Your role after anesthesia

Although most of the effects of the anesthesia or sedation should have worn off by the time your cat goes home, she may still be groggy and a little unsteady. You continue to play a part in helping her fully recover at home by providing a quiet, warm, and comfortable resting spot, gradually reintroducing meals to your cat as instructed, limiting her activity as directed, giving prescribed postoperative medications, and eventually promoting your cat's return to normal activity per your veterinarian's recommendations.

Your cat may sleep more, have less energy, and be a bit sore for a few days after a procedure. You'll need to continue to monitor your cat for signs of complications according to your veterinary team's instructions, and call your veterinarian right away or seek emergency veterinary care if you have concerns.

Anesthetic risk statistics in cats and dogs

Anesthetic drugs (and their reversal agents), anesthesia administration protocols and checklists, and patient monitoring techniques have greatly improved, and anesthetic-related deaths have decreased in veterinary patients since the early 1980s.[12] In 1990, one study showed that 1 in 679 (0.14%) healthy dogs and cats and 1 in 31 (3.2%) sick dogs and cats were estimated to have died as a result of anesthesia.[13]

A 2008 study showed that the risk of anesthetic- or sedation-related death was 1 in 895 (0.11%) for healthy cats and 1 in 71 (1.4%) for sick cats, and 1 in 1,849 (0.05%) for healthy dogs and 1 in 75 (1.3%) for sick dogs.[14] A 2017 study had similar findings, with the risk of death being 0.11% in cats (1 per 900 anesthesia episodes) and 0.05% in dogs (1 per 2,000 anesthesia episodes).[12]

Cognitive decline: An anesthetic complication?

I have heard some pet parents describe their geriatric pets as "not the same" mentally after anesthesia and say that their pet acted "funny," tired, confused, or anxious. Their geriatric pet's odd behavior usually lasted a week or two before it would improve, which is much longer than the "standard" grogginess that we expect pets may have after anesthesia. Such experiences, along with an experience that one of my geriatric dogs had, made me wonder whether the anesthesia caused this strange temporary behavior. So I looked into this topic further...

Research revelation: Is anesthesia linked to cognitive decline in senior people?

Whether anesthesia alone or anesthesia with surgery can be linked to cognitive decline in cats has not been studied, but it has been studied for many years in older people. Concern about anesthesia-associated cognitive decline may stem from the results of earlier studies in rodents that suggested that exposure to inhaled anesthetics may be associated with brain changes similar to those that occur in people with Alzheimer's disease.

However, one 2020 study shows that surgery with anesthesia does not lead to changes associated with Alzheimer's disease in people,[15] and a 2021 study indicates that surgery may contribute to memory decline in people who already have brain changes consistent with Alzheimer's disease but have not yet shown symptoms.[16] Similarly, the risks of slightly faster cognitive decline in people in the years after surgery may be related to the ailments that led to their surgery or to the uncovering of cognitive impairment that was already present.

For now, evidence suggests that people who already have cognitive impairment may have an increased risk of developing postoperative delirium and cognitive dysfunction after anesthesia and surgery. Thus, it's recommended that elderly adults routinely be screened for cognitive impairment before anesthesia to identify their risk. Elderly patients and their families should be properly informed that cognitive dysfunction may be a risk associated with anesthesia, and screening allows the opportunity to discuss other treatment strategies if the patient has a high risk.[17,18]

My 14-year-old dog Sam had spinal lymphoma, so she received radiation therapy once a day for five days, and she was anesthetized for 10 minutes during each treatment. She did great after each one—she ate normally, went for walks, and acted like her usual self. But about three days after she completed radiation therapy, she started showing signs of cognitive dysfunction. She had hours-long episodes of increased anxiety—odd barking and excessive panting—that occurred during the later part of the day, the evenings, and even during the wee hours. Thankfully, with supportive care, most of her episodes stopped within four weeks.

Based on the studies in people, my experience with Sam, and other pet parents' experiences, I think it may behoove veterinarians to consider routinely screening for cognitive dysfunction in geriatric pets before anesthesia to identify whether a pet may be at risk, to discuss a perhaps slight but potential risk of cognitive impairment after anesthesia, and consider other treatment options if needed. In our case, Sam didn't show signs of cognitive dysfunction beforehand, and, knowing what I know now, I still would've gone ahead with her radiation therapy. But it's important to weigh all the benefits and possible risks associated with a procedure to help everyone involved make their best-informed decisions regarding a pet's care.

But my cat gets stressed by going to the vet!

Oftentimes, taking cats—especially cats who detest their carriers—to the veterinarian is easier said than done. (But maybe don't say it out loud, because your cat may try to head for the hills!) Believe me, I understand. I saw and heard about transportation troubles often in general practice, and I was not immune to these difficulties either. So other than scheduling an in-home veterinary visit or a visit from a veterinarian who brings a practice on wheels to your curb, here are tips that may help you more easily get your cat to see their vet.

Dr. Kim Simons in south Florida has a special place in her heart for cat – especially older ones like this orange beauty Annie.

Need help? Please ask!

If you'd like help getting your cat carrier out of and back into your vehicle at the veterinary clinic, let your veterinary team know when you make the appointment and when you arrive. A team member will be happy to come out to assist you when you arrive and when you depart.

For cats with car sickness, anxiety, or fear: Think ahead!

If your cat gets car sick or is anxious or fearful about car trips or veterinary visits, plan ahead and ask your veterinarian to prescribe a medication that you can give an hour or so before you leave to help your cat relax and feel better during the entire experience. Another good tip: spray cat calming pheromone (e.g. Feliway) on your cat's carrier blanket at least 15 minutes before you leave.[8]

During cold weather, warm up your car before your pet makes a trip, and likewise, during hot weather, cool down the interior before giving your cat a lift. Place a pee pad under your cat as a precaution.[8]

For cats who resist their carriers: Think way ahead!

Instead of taking the carrier out when you need to use it, leave it out at all times with the door open and place a comfy pad or blanket inside. For especially wary cats, you may need to start with leaving out only the bottom half of the carrier, and then add the top and the door in separate stages after your cat willingly enters and is comfortable with the previous stage. You can also spray the blanket with a feline pheromone (let it air-dry for 15 minutes before giving your cat access).

Toss especially tempting (but small!) treats near the carrier, and end each treat session by placing a few treats inside the carrier. Do this at least once a day to entice your cat to explore and freely enter and exit the carrier. After your cat is at ease inside, practice with the door closed and give treats during this time. As your training sessions progress, gradually increase the length of time the door stays closed.

Then practice picking up the carrier and setting it down with your cat inside and the door closed (and give a treat). Work up to walking around the room (give treats) and the house (give treats) with your cat in the carrier. Take care to avoid frightening your cat and prevent nausea—hold the carrier level and steady. Don't swing or jostle the carrier or bump into things. Eventually walk to the car (give treats) and come back in (give treats), and ultimately practice taking short car trips (give treats).[19] Be sure to place the carrier on a level surface during car rides, too.

When you're not training, leave the carrier out and open, and your cat may even choose to nap in it. You may also work up to feeding your cat a meal inside the carrier once every few days so she stays comfortable with it.

Don't fear "bad news": Ignorance isn't bliss

I dream of all pets having annual veterinary checkups until they reach their senior years, getting twice-a-year checkups during their senior and geriatric years, and receiving routine and supportive veterinary care at least once in the six months before the visit at which euthanasia becomes a consideration.

Some people avoid taking their pet to the veterinarian—and, likewise, sometimes even neglect seeing their own physician—because they want to avoid potential bad news! While I understand that, it's better to catch simmering troubles sooner. And you may receive the pleasant news or confirmation that your cat is in good or stable health!

Either way, veterinarians can give you information, support, and treatments that will help you and your cat stay bonded and better engaged in the activities you both love during the last chapter of your cat's life.

Questions to ask your veterinarian

- How often do you recommend that my senior cat be seen for routine examinations?
- What tests will my cat need and how often?
- Do you have suggestions that will make it easier for me to bring my cat to see you?
- What accommodations do you provide for my cat with _____ (e.g. mobility, visual, cognitive) special needs?
- If my cat needs to be anesthetized, what will I need to do before the procedure regarding food, water, and medication administration and any other preparations?
- Will my cat benefit from anti-anxiety or anti-nausea medication to be given before we leave home for the visit or procedure?
- Can my cat be scheduled on a day when she can have a morning appointment or procedure and be discharged soon after? (So she doesn't have to stay in the clinic all day.)
- Will you explain the anesthesia process and how my cat will be monitored during and after the procedure?
- Do you have a veterinary anesthesia-certified nurse available to assist during my cat's procedure?
- How will my cat's comfort be addressed with regard to hypothermia, pain management, and positioning before, during, and after the procedure?
- If my cat's health status indicates a high anesthetic risk, should my cat's procedure be done at a veterinary referral center?
- What will I need to do after the procedure to monitor my cat and help in his recovery?
- What will I need to do after the procedure regarding my cat's food and water intake, medication administration, and other post-procedure needs?
- Will my cat benefit from an anti-nausea medication to promote her willingness to eat sooner after anesthesia?

CHAPTER 26:

Bucket lists: The joys of life

> "The bitterest tears shed over graves are for words left unsaid and deeds left undone."
>
> — Harriet Beecher Stowe

Maybe you have a bucket list—a lineup of all of the things you want to accomplish, see, or try before you die. A few of my bucket list items: to visit Kathmandu, sit with orangutans, write books for pet parents of geriatric cats and dogs (check, check!), learn to play drums, become a centenarian, and—dare I even share—be a contestant on the TV show "Dancing with the Stars." (OK, that last one is a long shot, but I can dream!)

The point of a bucket list is to set fun and relevant goals that you're motivated to accomplish! And if it seems daunting, you can start smaller. The meaning of "bucket list" has expanded to include other wishlists, such as a "summer bucket list"—places you want to go before fall arrives, or a "career bucket list"—the different hats you want to wear before you retire.[1]

FUN FACT

In 1999, as Justin Zackham contemplated the things he'd like to do before he kicked the bucket, he made a checklist and called it "Justin's Bucket List." A few years after that, he wrote a screenplay called "The Bucket List." The movie was released in 2007, starring Morgan Freeman and Jack Nicholson.[1] I wonder whether writing the screenplay was on his bucket list?

Build a nine lives bucket list

I often suggest that pet parents create a similar list of all the things they want to do for their cat or allow their cat to experience before they say their final goodbye. I have made bucket lists for my own geriatric fur kids. When you're thinking about the list, consider: What makes your cat your cat? What brings her pure joy? What brings him ordinary happiness? What 10 things do you want her to experience before you say goodbye?

You can of course add to it or make different plans depending on your cat's health status. I recommend starting to check things off while you can both still relish the activities—whether it's weeks, months, or years before your cat earns angel wings. There may be activities your cat simply cannot do at the end.

An outing such as "watch shorebirds at the beach" may have still been doable three months earlier, but if you wait too long, your cat may no longer be able to comfortably take a long road trip or ride in a pet stroller, and they may have little interest in the salty breezes, flapping wings, and breaking waves.

Bucket list items don't have to be grandiose, either. I think it's safe to say most cats, especially seniors, savor the comforts of a stable routine and simple surprises. Two of my cat Herbie's bucket list items were soaking up sunshine in the backyard for at least 30 minutes a day, and being allowed to nap in the linen closet on our clean towels!

CAT TV

WALK OUTSIDE

BACKPACK HIKE

HAVE HIS OWN CAKE

PROFESSIONAL PHOTO SESSION

YOGA TIME WITH MOM

MAKE "BISCUITS"

BEACH VISIT

ICECREAM DATE WITH MOM

MATCHING OUTFITS

STROLLER RIDE

Pet parents can also have extraordinary fun creating their cat's bucket list! (Illustrations by Dusan Pavlic)

Or if you prefer to go all-out, consider making headway on your cat's bucket list with an extra-special celebration. The internet and social media are packed with heartwarming stories of cat parents' bucket list ideas and adventures, from renting an RV for an extra-comfy kitty road trip or building a catio to buying a new cat toy or constructing a feline-size blanket fort.

Specially picked treasures are at the ready as well if you order a surprise toy and treat special delivery from a cat subscription-box service such as Pet Treater, Meowbox, KitNipBox, RescueBox, and many others. A leg up on an idea for cats with mobility troubles—take a stroll using a kitty sling, pet stroller, or bike pet trailer, and then have a picnic! And be sure to take photos to help hold on to all your memories.

I love bucket lists because when it comes time to say goodbye to your cat, having checked activities and experiences off removes so much regret. It allows you to focus fully on the tender moments with your cat in their final hours, and there's nothing better a loving pet parent can do.

If you're looking for a little inspiration in crafting the perfect bucket list for your cat, check out a few of the lists and photos cat parents have shared with me.

Tigger kitty's bucket list—completed.

Weatherby (aka Percy) purred every day!

CHAPTER 26: BUCKET LISTS: THE JOYS OF LIFE

 Ally got a special treat of cookies and ice cream!

 Ally shared a fast food burger with her mom!

 Ally appreciated tender attention and assistance with grooming.

 Ally's favorite perch/hide box and feather toy.

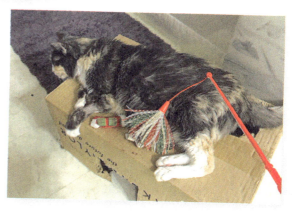

Jot down your cat's joys of living

One of my patients' families created a "joy of living" list for their senior pet, and I appreciate that twist on a bucket list. It's nice to have both lists, for separate reasons.

Bucket lists may contain the familiar favorites plus extra-special things you want your cat to be able to do before they pass. A joy of living list contains all the favorite things that bring your cat joy all the time, such as head rubs, napping on your chest, looking out an open screened window, kneading a clean blanket, and pouncing on the cat treats that you toss to him one-by-one before bedtime every night. A joy of living list helps you better assess your cat's quality of life—do her favorite things still bring her joy? And when most of them do not, maybe that will help you determine when it's time to say goodbye.

I now encourage pet parents to make both a bucket list and a joy of living or favorite things list for their cats. There may be a little overlap between them, but they serve two different purposes.

Many senior kitties love explorer strolls!

Charlie enjoyed beach days!

It's a joy to snuggle in mom's hoodie!

Herbie's Favorite Things:

My cat Herbie's daily joys. (Illustration by Dusan Pavlic)

CHAPTER 27:

Veterinary hospice: Living well until the end

> "You matter because you are, and you matter to the end of your life. We will do all we can not only to help you die peacefully, but also to live until you die."
>
> —Dame Cicely Saunders

For humans, hospice entails physical, mental, and spiritual care for terminally ill patients. Hospice focuses on palliative care—treating a patient's symptoms without treating their underlying illness to attempt to prolong life—and it includes pain control and emotional support. Hospice care can occur at home, in a skilled nursing or long-term care facility, or in a hospital. A patient's care shifts from treating the disease to treating a patient's quality of life. Hospice can also include support related to household duties such as cleaning and shopping, as well as emotional and spiritual counseling for a patient's immediate family.

A surprising benefit of hospice care

Although hospice no longer involves attempts to treat disease, studies show that hospice patients live longer and have a better quality of life than patients who have similar diseases without hospice care. Hospice patients may live longer and better because their individual needs, preferences, and symptoms are managed better, which helps stabilize their condition.[1-3]

Human hospice care: then and now

Although hospice (the word is derived from the Latin word *hospes*, meaning "guest" and "host") was adopted in the Middle Ages by the Roman Catholic tradition as a place of hospitality for the sick and dying, it was not until the mid-twentieth century that the hospice we formally recognize today began. A pioneer in this field was British physician Dr. Cicely Saunders who began work with terminally ill patients in London in 1948.[4]

In 1963 Dr. Saunders introduced the idea of specialized care for dying people that centered around palliation (relieving symptoms) rather than trying to cure the incurable. During a lecture she gave to healthcare professionals, she showed photos of terminally ill cancer patients taken before they entered hospice care and compared them with their photos after they received hospice care, which revealed positive visible differences in the hospice patients' well-being.[4] This began the movement of providing hospice care to patients at the end of life in the United States. Since then, funding for hospice has improved via legislation and Medicare reimbursement, so hospice services have grown and the number of professionally trained hospice caregivers has increased.

In the United States, Medicare and Medicaid provide hospice benefits for people living with an end-stage, incurable illness. Qualifications to receive hospice differ by state, but usually a physician has determined that a patient has less than six months to live. In 2019, 1.61 million Medicare beneficiaries were enrolled in hospice care for one day or more, a 3.9% increase over the number of patients enrolled in 2018.[5] Patients spent an average of 92 days in hospice in 2019. And although patients are eligible for hospice care for at least six months, the median time patients spent in hospice was 18 days—meaning that half of the patients received hospice care for less than 18 days and half received hospice care for more than 18 days.[5]

Unfortunately, experts have predicted that the number of physicians and nurses needed to provide hospice and palliative care in the United States will not meet the future workforce demand and growing aging population.[6-8] Shortages will occur because many hospice professionals will retire, some will leave their profession early because of burnout, and insufficient funding exists for the increased number of advanced educational programs that will be needed to train new hospice and palliative care professionals. This means, for example, that by 2030 there may be only one hospice and palliative care physician per 26,000 patients.[9] These personnel and program funding shortages were identified before the tragic COVID-19 pandemic, yet awareness of the importance of hospice and palliative care and the demand for it has since skyrocketed.[10,11]

> The good news is that a 2018 George Washington University Health Workforce Institute survey of newly trained hospice and palliative medicine specialists revealed that their job market is strong, and that these specialists are enthusiastic and optimistic about their work, with 99% of respondents saying they would recommend the specialty to others.[12] One of my favorite respondent quotes from the survey was from a physician who was reflecting on their fulfilling hospice and palliative care work. They wrote that patients and families often feel overlooked by their doctors during the patients' final life stages of dying and death. They stated that diligently preserving a patient's quality of life to the extent that is feasible and ensuring dignity during their last days or hours allows physicians to bolster the general population's perceptions of doctors, as well as the physician's own humanity. They concluded that well-rounded physicians must recognize that things remain to be done for patients even when death is close.[12]

How does palliative care differ from hospice?

Palliative care can be provided at any time and for any serious illness or condition, one that may or may not be life-threatening. It focuses on patient comfort and quality of life while curative treatments for the underlying disease are given. If a patient is still receiving curative treatments, the patient can receive palliative care. Palliative care and hospice are both patient-care focused, not disease focused. Palliative care is also a component of hospice, but hospice does not begin unless a patient has less than six months to live and curative treatment for an underlying terminal or life-limiting disease has stopped.

Understanding veterinary hospice

Veterinary hospice is similar to human hospice in that we focus on the pet and the family to manage the signs associated with the disease and the end stage of life. We don't focus on curing the disease and no longer administer treatments that are intended as cures. If you've used hospice services for a human loved one, you know that medical aid and other services to make the end of life as comfortable as possible are deeply appreciated, because we all want to experience the true feeling of being "at peace."

The concept of hospice for pets is still relatively new and many people don't realize it's an option. In fact, not all of my veterinarian colleagues understand what veterinary hospice is. Another veterinarian once told me that pet hospice was "just prolonging suffering for our own selfishness." I wondered (to myself) whether he would say that to a human hospice physician or nurse. Did he think that because veterinarians can provide euthanasia, hospice is unnecessary? Did he not understand the benefits hospice provides not only for a terminally ill pet, but also for the pet's family?

Hospice isn't prolonging suffering. It's a medically supervised process that involves carefully watching over a failing patient to help the family provide the necessary comfort and support for their pet. Veterinary hospice is for pets who are facing the end of their life, regardless of their age or the condition that led them there. A young adult cat with acute kidney failure, a senior cat with end-stage congestive heart failure, or a geriatric cat with a number of age-related struggles are all candidates for hospice care.

Pets typically receive hospice care when they have less than three months to live. Unlike human hospice care, government financial support for pet hospice (and other pet healthcare) isn't available. (And similar to human healthcare, private pet health insurance plans differ in the services they cover.)

For cats receiving hospice care, pet parents still of course have the option to choose euthanasia for their cat when quality of life is poor. With that said, when pet parents choose veterinary hospice, they are not required to choose how their cats die (euthanasia or natural passing), but rather they are choosing how their cats live—that is, as comfortably as possible—until they die.

Alleviating a pet's pain and anxiety and helping a family plan for a peaceful exit for their beloved pet are major components of hospice. Veterinarians who provide hospice care work with each family closely to help them understand what their pet ise facing and how they can work together to ensure their pet isn't suffering. Veterinarians know the unknown is scary. Knowing what is coming diminishes dread and fosters calm and courage.

Stopping (or never starting) curative treatment does not mean giving up. Hospice allows you to choose a different care path. Saying no to treating your terminally ill cat's underlying disease while keeping your cat comfortable can allow more time to focus on the time you have left with your cat, and to experience meaningful moments that you may otherwise miss out on.

Five elements of pet hospice

Our terminally ill cats can't readily tell us how they feel, and even if they could, we still may not know exactly what lies ahead. But it isn't known exactly what each dying person's experience will be, either. As pet parents, we can often reasonably infer from a cat's behavior and actions some of the things he or she might be experiencing. Veterinarians have devoted their lives to identifying clinical signs in animals and interpreting their behavior and actions to help pet parents ensure that their animals live their best lives. And part of life is the end of life.

My veterinary hospice care program encompasses palliative care, environmental guidance, caregiver support, quality-of-life assessments, and planning for the end of life. During my initial hospice visit with a family and their cat, I cover all of these topics with pet parents. Veterinary hospice visits, especially the initial one, involve hard conversations. They are delicate, crucial meetings. In his book *Being Mortal*, Atul Gawande, MD, wrote that Susan Block, a palliative care specialist, told him family meetings that involve end-of-life discussions are procedures, and they require as much skill as performing an operation.[13] I wholeheartedly agree.

During subsequent hospice visits or check-ins, I review and reassess these five elements with families and make adjustments throughout their cat's hospice care:

1 Palliative care

Palliative care entails assessing the patient's needs and taking measures to prevent or control signs associated with the cat's illness, as well as the effects related to treating the illness (e.g. surgery, chemotherapy). Components of palliative care include:

- **Managing pain**. Medications and other supportive measures are used to ensure a cat has adequate, continuous pain relief. This includes being able to recognize signs of pain to evaluate whether adjustments are needed.
- **Controlling anxiety**. Anti-anxiety medications and supportive measures are used as needed, for example, to calm a cat who paces and yowls at night or has other sleep-wake cycle disturbances. Controlling anxiety can also help reduce pain.
- **Supporting caloric intake**. Nutritional enticements are used to address a cat's hesitancy to eat, where appropriate.
- **Controlling nausea**. Medications are given to reduce nausea, because nausea may cause suffering similar to that of pain.
- **Maintaining hygiene and preventing infection**. Guidance on grooming and physical assistance are provided as needed. Cats in hospice care may have fecal and urinary incontinence, or they are more likely to have accidents if they can't easily get to where they need to be to eliminate. Sanitary hair trims, brushing or bathing, help to the litter box, frequent repositioning for cats who are bedridden, and using baby wipes, diapers, and waterproof bedding help ensure a cat stays clean so that painful irritation and infections are less likely to develop.

2 Environmental guidance

Assessing a cat's home and making recommendations to ensure the environment is as safe and comfortable as possible for the cat is paramount during hospice care. Throughout other chapters in this book, I've detailed environmental modifications that relate to several specific ailments that cats may face.

3 Caregiver support

Caregiver support involves understanding a family's wishes, hopes, and fears, as well as their physical and emotional abilities and their time and financial resources. This understanding helps veterinarians plan and tailor hospice care for each cat. Pet caregivers have the right to be tired, sad, frustrated, and confused. Pet parents should feel assured that they can choose to stop hospice and elect euthanasia for their cat at any time or to continue with hospice care until natural passing occurs, without judgment.

4 Life quality assessments

These evaluations are vital to hospice care! I discuss and assess life quality in detail with pet parents and other family members, and we create an individualized evaluation method for each cat and family. (See Chapter 30 "Life Quality: 'Doc, when is it time?'")

5 Planning for the end

This challenging conversation entails helping families think through and prepare for their cat's last day, so that the family's wishes are met and that they have the dignified goodbye they hope for.

Would you like sprinkles on top?

One year I returned to my alma mater, the University of Florida College of Veterinary Medicine, to give a lecture on end-of-life pet care to the senior veterinary students. As I walked down the hallways reminiscing, I heard a booming voice behind me. "MARY GARDNER!" I instantly knew who it was. I turned and saw Dr. Gary Ellison, the chief veterinary surgeon at the college, standing there in his white coat and scrubs, a wide smile stretched under his surgery goggles! He was a legend.

As I walked back to greet him, he said, "I am so proud of you!"

(I thought, 'ME?! You're proud of me? You're a rockstar surgeon who saves countless lives!') I gave him a big hug and asked him why.

Dr. Ellison explained, "Well, my father had pancreatic cancer. He was in the hospital for weeks battling it. The cancer also brought on diabetes. So a few times every day the nurses came in to take blood samples to check his glucose level. He hated it! Toward the end, we moved my father to hospice. On the first day of hospice, the nurse came in and he immediately asked, like a curmudgeon, 'What do you want?! More blood from me to check my glucose?' And the nurse answered, 'No, Mr. Ellison. I'm here to find out what your favorite flavor of ice cream is!' And my dad's face lit up! That is what hospice is about, and you are bringing that same comfort to veterinary patients and their families, and that's amazing!"

I was honored that he shared this story with me and happy to know how much hospice had helped his father. Dr. Ellison's admiration of my work in veterinary hospice care meant so much to me.

Finding veterinary hospice care

One of the most difficult parts of practice for veterinarians and their teams is saying goodbye to pets at the end of life and beholding the family's grief. In many cases, veterinarians have been caring for the cat and talking with the pet parents since their beloved feline first joined the family.

Veterinarians understand how cherished cats are in people's lives and want to make sure cats are as comfortable and happy as they can be as they approach and meet the end of life. So in that respect, helping families say goodbye to their cats can also be one of the most rewarding parts of practice.

Veterinarians in primary care practice may provide hospice services that include one or more types of consultations and assessments: in-clinic, telemedicine, or in-home. Not all veterinary hospitals offer hospice care, so if yours does not or cannot otherwise work with you on a hospice care plan for your cat, ask for referral suggestions.

You can also explore the doctor locator at Lap of Love **lapoflove.com/** and the provider directory at the International Association of Animal Hospice and Palliative Care **iaahpc.org/**. Keep in mind these are not complete lists of all veterinary hospice care providers.

Most veterinarians who focus on hospice practice schedule appointments to visit your home at regular intervals during your cat's hospice care. That way all the care, love, and concern can be tended to in the comfort of the cat's own home.

 ## Questions to ask your veterinarian

- Do you provide hospice care and, if so, what does it entail? What are the costs? If not, can you make a recommendation?
- If hospice care is not available in this area, can we work together to create a hospice care plan for my cat?
- Are respite care services or brief periods of hospitalization for respite care available for my cat if needed during hospice care?
- What services or support do you provide in case of an emergency?

Start hospice sooner than later

My Uncle Ed had been receiving prostate cancer treatment for two years, but the cancer had spread to his bones. In the spring of 2021, he was hospitalized because of breathing issues and pain. My sister and my aunt visited him daily, but the hospital had limited visitation because of COVID-19 restrictions, so I had to rely on secondhand information about his condition. When I was finally able to visit him, I was shocked. He was thin, pale, frail, and struggling to get comfortable. Maybe it was because of my work with terminally ill pets, but I sensed right away that he was not going to get through this and get back home.

Uncle Ed talked with me about his radiation treatment and physical therapy, and about going home. I noticed that he had horrible ulcers in his mouth, but he and my family thought they were caused by the oxygen mask. I knew the ulcers were related to his cancer and his treatments.

The saddest part was that for 90% of the time during my visits with him, he just stared at the poster on the wall that had his name at the top, and a 'faces of pain' scoring system from 0 (no pain) to 10 (worst possible pain) at the bottom. He kept telling me his pain was a 7 or 8. I asked him if he wanted to watch TV, and he told me that he couldn't watch TV or read a magazine. It was obvious that he couldn't get comfortable, and all he wanted to do was stare at the poster. I said, "Ed, you are unable to think of or do anything else besides focus on your pain. You are suffering." This broke my heart.

We asked Uncle Ed's doctor if it was time for hospice, and he simply said, "No." I wonder if he felt that hospice meant we had given up or failed, or if he simply didn't want to destroy our and his patient's hope. My family and

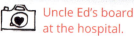 Uncle Ed's board at the hospital.

Uncle Ed's healthcare team kept talking about getting him out of the hospital. I wanted to get him into hospice. It took another week for Uncle Ed's doctors to finally even say the word "hospice."

Uncle Ed was disappointed about hospice, but he hated the hospital. It took a few days to find a hospice care facility that had space for him. He had spent nearly three weeks in a hospital where he was miserable.

Uncle Ed moved into the hospice facility on a Sunday morning, and he was so happy. His chemotherapy drugs were stopped, and his pain management was increased. His room was lovely, with patio doors that opened to a nearby fountain. Everyone focused on his comfort care from the minute he arrived. And he finally got the mouthwash he needed for his oral ulcers. I was happy he was finally being cared for in a place that would focus on helping him live well.

Uncle Ed passed away the next evening. I feel as though he didn't get enough time to benefit more from hospice. If we had gotten him admitted to hospice sooner, he may have lived much better and happier at the end.

I share this story to implore every family not to think of hospice as a failure, but as a way to ensure their pet is well cared for at the end of life. Start hospice sooner rather than later. I wish I had been able to do that for my Uncle Ed.

I'm unsure whether Uncle Ed knew I was holding his hand, but I was grateful to be there with him.

CHAPTER 28:

Goals of care: What matters most in the end

> "Fear helps point to the things that you care about, the things you love, the things you're afraid to lose.... And then that becomes a nice compass for our way forward, how we're going to live until we die."
>
> — Dr. BJ Miller, American physician, author, and speaker

My good friend and human hospice and palliative medicine physician BJ Miller co-wrote the book *A Beginner's Guide to the End: Practical Advice for Living Life and Facing Death*. It's a valuable reference for anyone facing a friend's, family member's, or their own end of life. I've refined a few tools I've been using over the years in my veterinary hospice practice based on some wonderful concepts from BJ's book, including evaluating your "goals of care," which I respectfully share here.

Thinking about goals of care for your cat encourages you to collect and record your thoughts about the things that will influence your cat's and your experiences near the end of his or her life. It helps you examine the situation you are facing with regard to your cat's ailments, which activities are most important for your cat and you, which activities you're willing to give up, and how much treatment you're willing to pursue. It also helps you consider whether your goals for your cat realistically align with your abilities to reach them. I also suggest discussing your goals of care with your veterinarian—this allows them to understand your wishes and direct your cat's care appropriately.

Take a thoughtful self-quiz

I understand that this can be a tough thought process, and you might be thinking, where do I even start? Asking yourself care-oriented questions can help you identify priorities as your pet experiences the limitations and illnesses that aging brings. Based on the care goals exercise that BJ Miller outlines in his book, I advise pet parents to create a "Goals of Care" journal entry like this:

GOALS OF CARE

Pet's Name .... Date: ....

Circumstances

Goals

Compromises

Road Map

- **Circumstances:** Write what you know about your cat's diagnosis or condition, and list the resources available to you. Do you need family members and friends to help? Are they available and willing to help? Can you talk with your veterinarian regularly about your cat's care? As your cat's caregiver, what are your financial, physical, emotional, and time limitations?
- **Goals:** Write what you want to do for your cat and for yourself as his caregiver. Do you want your cat to receive all possible curative treatments? Or would you rather focus solely on relieving symptoms? Would you like to supplement your care with veterinary hospice care? Do you have a bucket list you'd like to fulfill for your cat? Do you want to plan for your cat to die at home rather than at the veterinary hospital? Do you want a veterinarian to end your cat's dying process before active suffering occurs? How would you like to memorialize your cat?

Look at treatment options in light of your goals of care

Chat with your veterinarian as you reflect on whether to OK your cat's proposed treatments, reconsider a proposed treatment, or consider other treatment options. To kick off your discussion, I've adapted the questions below from similar questions proposed by veterinary experts that are intended to help veterinarians weigh how well intensive and costly treatments will benefit their patients.[1]

- Is the recommended treatment in my pet's best interest? Will it improve my pet's health?
- Will the suggested treatment improve my pet's short-term and/or long-term quality of life?
- Is this treatment the least likely to harm my pet or cause suffering, yet still achieve the intended therapeutic goal, or is there another option?
- What is your experience in providing the proposed treatment for pets? Is the treatment a well-recognised option that many other veterinarians would also recommend?
- Do the treatment's expected benefits outweigh the potential for harm and suffering that my pet may experience, or do the potential benefits and negative effects at least balance each other?
- What has been done to minimize the potential for harm to my pet associated with the treatment?
- Will I be able to administer the medications my pet needs?
- Will the recommended treatment positively affect the relationship I have with my pet?
- What does the recommended treatment cost?
- Will the recommended treatment positively affect my quality of life?
- Will my home environment adequately meet my pet's treatment-associated needs?[1]
- **Compromises:** Truthfully draw your line in the sand. What trade-offs are you willing to make and not make? Will you delay travel for months because your cat needs extensive care? Will you allow others to care for your cat if you need to be away? Is it acceptable to you that your cat may urinate on pee pads in her bed every night? Does it work with your schedule and finances to take your cat to rehabilitation therapy or cancer treatments weekly? Are you OK with not trying or not providing certain therapies that may give you more time with your cat? Are you OK with not starting or with stopping certain therapies that are unlikely to help your cat?
- **Road Map:** List your next action items for providing care and meeting your goals within the guardrails of your compromises and limitations. Do you need to provide low-entry litter boxes and pet steps to your cat's favorite perches? Do you plan to investigate veterinary rehabilitation therapy options? Will you start arranging a trip to an exotic, cat-friendly location to fulfill a bucket list item? Do you need to schedule your cat's veterinary examination to provide comfort care or discuss hospice? When will you explore options for aftercare of your cat's body?

Self-quiz retakes

You may need to reexamine your goals of care every month as your cat's condition and your situation change. You may find yourself easily caring for your cat one month, but the next month you may feel like you are drowning in managing his symptoms. As hard as we may try, we can't control all things in the end, but we can take steps to help manage the challenges ahead. Writing down the goals of care for your older cat will help guide you when you're in the thick of things, managing multiple symptoms, emotionally and physically exhausted, and on the verge of being consumed with caregiving. The goals of care can help you to forgive yourself if you reach a breaking point—and allow you to reset and get back to a comfortable state.

Cat Journal

Scan this code if you are interested in a complete workbook to journal your cat's health and other aspects of your cat's care (**amzn.to/3dNvAkg**):

CHAPTER 29:

Caregiver stress, burden, and burnout: When loving hurts

"Love and compassion are necessities, not luxuries. Without them humanity cannot survive."

— The 14th Dalai Lama

Some cats at some point in their lives—perhaps even as kittens—will face an illness that requires intensive care. And, like aging humans, as cats age they're more likely to develop a condition that necessitates a more watchful eye or treatment that requires additional daily care—even if they've been otherwise healthy. Their care may entail multiple medications, a special diet, changes in the home, or more frequent visits to the veterinarian.

In the last decade, I have taken on the role of intense caregiver for many of my pets. I think I have done a good job. Some of my family members and friends may have thought I went a bit overboard for my senior cats and dogs as they see some of the steps I've taken for their care:

- pursuing chemotherapy, acupuncture, surgery, rehabilitation therapy, and massage;
- modifying my house and cars to make them safer and pet-friendlier;
- canceling vacations;
- hiring in-home pet sitters and mobile groomers;
- purchasing nearly every product designed to assist with my pets' special needs;
- rearranging my work schedule;
- sleeping on the hard living room floor for weeks; and
- splurging on nonessentials simply to make my pets' lives more enjoyable.

Have I been an enthusiastic, proud, joyful, and content caregiver? Yes! Have I been a tired, frustrated, mad, and stressed caregiver? Yes! Would I do anything for my cats for as long as they need me to? Yes! And dare I even admit it—have I been relieved when the intense caregiving was over? Yes, but relieved only to have the weight of the work lifted. The weight of losing my pets is far heavier and longer to bear. So I gladly carry the heft of caring for them for any amount of time they need.

I'm fortunate to have a background that has probably allowed me to accept and manage my cats' illnesses a bit easier than many caregivers can. My biggest struggles have been learning to accommodate the viewpoints of others in my home and the need to sometimes place my cats' intense care in their hands. I can manage all the things my ailing cats need quite easily and happily on my own. But if I have to leave my pets with someone who is not as eager to help, it weighs heavy on my heart.

Not until I dealt with the struggles of caring for my own geriatric cats and dogs did I fully appreciate what caregiver burden meant. I empathize so much with other caregivers. It can be so frustrating and tiring. I get it! Caregiving—it's a hard job, even when you love to do it.

Caregiver stress

I'll be the first to admit that I've been stressed by caring for my aging cats. It's important that you and all caregivers don't feel guilty when you're stressed. You aren't alone.

You may feel stress when the demands of your situation outweigh your resources of money, time, physical ability, and emotional capacity—or anything else that you need to care for your cat and to also take care of yourself. I hope that by sharing some of the experiences of my patients' families and my own throughout this book, you can recognize sooner when those resources are diminishing and take away ideas for replenishing your resources when possible or managing them differently. Caregiver tools and support can lighten the stress of caring for your geriatric cat, and you'll better focus on the good moments that remain for you both to enjoy.

Unpacking the burden

Caregiver burden was first described in human medicine and is defined as the cumulative strain of providing care for chronically ill, elderly, or disabled family members. The challenges of caring for a seriously ill loved one can adversely affect the caregiver's emotional, mental, and physical well-being; financial situation; ability to work; and relations with friends and family members.

Caregiver burden has also been described in veterinary medicine and can occur in people caring for sick pets, especially pets who have chronic or terminal illnesses. The first study that examined the toll of caregiving on pet owners used measures of mental health that have been studied in human caregiving relationships.[1] The results showed that compared with caregivers of healthy pets, caregivers of terminally or chronically ill pets had:

- more perceived stress;
- more caregiver burden and stress;
- more symptoms of anxiety and depression;
- reduced psychosocial function (psychosocial function means the ability to maintain work and relationships and pursue one's full potential[2]); and
- poorer quality of life.

Similarly, another study evaluated pet owners whose pets had cancer or suspected cancer. The results showed that pet owners with greater caregiver burden had higher stress levels, more symptoms of depression, and reduced quality of life.[3] Sometimes caring for a pet can make you feel like you're running on empty. Intense caregiving for a loved one—pet or human—can lead to stress, depression, and anxiety.

In people caring for ill human loved ones, the burden of caregiving can lead to *caregiver burnout*, which means that the caregiver's burden has progressed to the point where the situation is no longer doable or healthy for the caregiver or for the person being cared for.[4] Caregiver burnout is also referred to as *caregiver fatigue*.

Based on the signs of caregiver burnout in people who care for ill human loved ones,[5] the signs of caregiver burnout you might notice in yourself or another family member who is caring for an ill pet include:

- feeling cranky and glum;
- no interest in activities formerly enjoyed;
- withdrawal from family, friends, and other loved ones;
- feeling hopeless and powerless;
- changes in sleep patterns;
- changes in appetite, weight, or both;
- more frequent illness;
- physical and emotional exhaustion; and
- feeling a desire to injure yourself or the pet who requires care.

One reason caregivers experience burnout is that they take on unreasonable demands, in part because they view caregiving as their sole responsibility. Another factor that leads to burnout is that caregivers are unable to recognize burnout in themselves and ultimately cannot function effectively. Burned-out caregivers may themselves become sick.[5]

You love your cat, and you will do what you need to do, but it takes a physical and emotional toll. It is no small thing to face your cat's debilitating or terminal disease. In addition to spending a lot of time and money to keep your cat as healthy, happy, and comfortable as possible, the emotional toll in knowing that soon your cat may not be with you is one of the toughest and most sorrowful things to face. Although you dig in and devote all of your resources, you need to remember to care for yourself. Your quality of life matters, too.

Easing the stress and burden

Your well-being is a vital part of the equation that adds up to doing the best you and your family can do for your cat. I suggest five coping strategies that have helped me ease the strains of caregiving.

1. Become an expert. The unknown is often scary. "What's going on with my cat?" "What will happen next?" "Is my cat in pain?" "How will I know if the medications or supportive care are working?" Learn about your cat's disease, its expected effects on your cat and the signs you will see, and how you can treat or manage and monitor those effects. One of my goals in my veterinary career (whether it is this book, my blog, or the videos I make) is to help cat parents with precisely those things. Also talk with your veterinary team. Add to your arsenal against the cloudy unknown you may face and read up on your cat's ailments and the treatments you're considering from other reliable veterinary healthcare sources. Your veterinary team can share insights about the impact care-intensive treatments may have on your life,[6] and can help direct you to additional credible resources specific to your cat's condition.

2. Seek support. Veterinary teams understand their clients' needs for support during their pets' serious illnesses and demanding treatments. Your cat's veterinary team can answer questions about your cat's condition, and they can also offer the support you may need when you're making end-of-life decisions for your cat. Other helpful guides include support groups, counselors, or veterinary social workers.

Another possible outlet—many Facebook groups are centered around specific cat diseases and are full of people who understand your situation. Also seek support from those who will listen and not try to take over your situation and resolve all your concerns. New friends are out there who have a beloved cat facing the same disease your cat has. The internet makes connecting with others who are experiencing the same burden so much easier. For example, one of the wonderful Facebook groups I joined is the Cats with Chronic Kidney Disease Facebook group: **facebook.com/groups/felinecrf**. I have often seen cat owners struggle with decisions about their cats' care, quality of life, and euthanasia, and this group's support enables them to make better decisions or to at least not feel alone in the challenges they face.

3. Accept help from or call on family members and friends who will help. If someone offers to help, graciously accept! You would likely do the same for them if you could. And don't be shy about asking for help when you truly need help. For example, The CareCorrals (**prizedpals.com/canobie**) offers a private online community where pet parents can invite friends and family to join their cat's circle of support.

4. Take a break. Board your cat for a day or half day in the veterinary hospital as needed—the veterinary technicians/veterinary nurses will administer medications and see to your cat's comfort. They may also be available to hire to provide home care for your cat as needed, to sit with your cat overnight for respite care, and more.

5. Set SMART goals. This tool helps you focus on the specific things you would like to achieve and measure your progress. A SMART goal is:

> **S** = **Specific**
> **M** = **Measurable**
> **A** = **Attainable**
> **R** = **Relevant**
> **T** = **Time-bound**

For example, my cat Mingo's appetite fluctuates because of her diabetes, and she eats less on days she doesn't feel well. So instead of saying, "I want Mingo to eat more," my SMART goals for her appetite are:

S = Mingo needs to meet her caloric needs every day despite her intermittently decreased appetite.

M = Mingo's current body condition score is 3 out of 9. She needs to eat a healthy and balanced diet consisting of a minimum of 300 calories each day to reach and maintain a body condition score of 4 out of 9.

A = Mingo can achieve this goal if I measure her food intake and warm her food slightly and administer an appetite stimulant on the days she needs it. I'll also consider placing an esophageal feeding tube if needed.

R = Reaching and maintaining an appropriate body condition score contributes to Mingo's overall health and well-being.

T = I will evaluate Mingo's body condition, muscle condition, and weight in four weeks and again each month thereafter.

By setting realistic, measurable goals and tracking them, you may feel more organized and in better control of the situation. Keeping a pet health journal can help remind you to evaluate your SMART goals every week and determine whether adjustments are needed. These goals will also help you evaluate your cat's quality of life and ease the decision to say goodbye when it comes time.

The number one reason pet parents elect euthanasia for their cat is the cat's decreased quality of life. The number two reason is caregiver burden. My intentions in writing this book are to help you enhance your cat's quality of life and lessen the burden of caregiving—by providing an overview of common feline age-related diseases and ailments and their treatments, giving you a wide variety of tips to better manage the struggles, and giving you ideas for enjoying those last months, weeks, and days with your beloved cat.

Caregiver assessment chart

Caregiver Assessment Chart

I've created a chart to help you identify and reflect on some of the challenges and stressful feelings you may experience as you care for your ailing cat. Remember, you aren't alone in having these feelings. It's helpful to recognize these challenges and feelings and share them with your support team to identify where additional support may be available.

 ## Questions to ask your veterinarian

- What resources do you suggest to help me learn more about my cat's condition?
- What is each medication my cat is receiving used for, and how do I know whether it's working?
- How often and for how long does my cat need to receive each medication?
- Are there medications that my cat has been receiving that can be paused or discontinued?
- Can we work together to better fit my cat's medication and treatment schedules into my daily routine?
- Do you have recommendations for caregiver support groups or a veterinary social worker I can connect with?
- Do you offer medical boarding/daycare or respite care for cats who need extensive care?

 ## RESOURCE

- **PetCaregiverBurden.com** is a website dedicated to the scientific understanding of pet caregiver burden, how this stress affects caring for a geriatric or terminally ill pet, and what can be done to reduce it: **petcaregiverburden.com/**.

CHAPTER 30:

Life quality: "Doc, when is it time?"

> "What you love is nothing of your own: it has been given to you for the present, not that it should not be taken from you, nor has it been given to you for all time, but as a fig is given to you or a bunch of grapes at the appointed season of the year."
>
> — Epictetus

When we think of our cats, we smile and delight in the companionship we've shared with them throughout our lives. We've welcomed them as family members, and they've been through it all with us—putting a purring exclamation point on the happy times, bringing a reassuring headbutt during the sad times … springing straight up in the air in a poof of surprise in those LOL moments!

Then, suddenly, the time we have left with our cats seems like only a moment, and the end of the cheer they bring us nears. If I had the proverbial dollar for every time a pet parent asked me, "How will I know when it's time to say goodbye?" – I could easily afford the geriatric pet rescue facility I dream of owning one day.

The answer is complex, and evaluating a cat's quality of life—also called *life quality*, and the term I prefer—is the most important step. The signs of death's approach can be subtle and overlooked when you're consumed with the daily care of your ailing cat.

Please know that I empathize more than you might imagine when you enter this stage of evaluation and are trying to decide when it may be time to give your cat a peaceful goodbye. The emotions can become incredibly painful, so I hope this chapter helps you through this time and gives you the caring confidence you need in making this agonizing decision. I have helped countless pet parents evaluate their beloved pet's life quality and supported them in their end-of-life decisions. While we can applaud a cat's lifespan, we must attend to a cat's quality of life and consider it even more worthy of celebration.

The life quality conversation: How well is the cat, and how well is the family?

During my conversation with pet parents, we discuss life quality considerations in four major categories: the pet's ailment(s), the pet's personality, the pet parent's personal beliefs, and the pet parent's four essential pet care budgets—financial, time, physical, and emotional.

1. The pet's ailments

We may not always have a specific diagnosis, but learning about the pet's ailments guides me in understanding the expected course of a cat's decline in functioning. Is it kidney failure? Is it widespread cancer? Is it a heart condition? Is another organ failing? Is it a cognitive disorder? Is it a mobility issue? Does the cat have incontinence? Is the cat completely blind? Does the cat not sleep through the night? Does the cat have a number of those things? Based on what we do know about the cat's ailments, I can figure out whether more can be done to manage the ailments, whether the ailments are causing or will cause discomfort or suffering, and whether the ailments are likely to progress quickly or slowly. This information also helps me determine whether the pet's road to the end will be flat and slightly bumpy, winding through hills and valleys, or heading straight to a sheer cliff drop off.

2. The cat's personality

Learning about the cat's temperament and individuality helps me help the family assess how their cat is handling the ailments. How well does the cat take her medications? Are there troubling or annoying side effects from the medications? How well does the cat handle being left at home on her own while the family is at work or school? What are the cat's interactions like with other pets in the home? (Has the younger cat started ambushing her when she uses the litter box?) Is the cat stoic and the pet parent doesn't realize their cat is in pain? How well does the cat handle veterinary visits for treatment?

3. The family's personal beliefs

Not everyone in the family may agree when it's time to say goodbye to their pet. Cultural and religious differences and personal preferences may factor into the decision. Sometimes the pet's function in the family comes into play, for example, an indoor cat with all the latest toys and a catio vs. a barn cat who lives outside to patrol for rodents. When opinions differ, it is important for family members not to judge one another. (See Chapter 31 "A home divided: Conflicts between family members about end-of-life care.")

4. The essential pet care budgets

Each of the four pet care budgets—financial, time, physical, and emotional—are critical in ensuring and assessing a cat's care. They consider not only the cat's life quality, but the family's quality of life.

A. **Financial budget.** To be factored into your care considerations: medications, therapeutic diets, cat sitters, rehabilitation therapy, additional veterinary visits, diagnostic tests, cancer treatments, and more. The additional cost of an ailing cat's care may range from $100 for pet steps and low-entry litter boxes, to thousands of dollars for surgery or radiation treatment for a cat's cancer. A family may struggle to afford a cat's care as age and ailments add up. It's important for a family not to feel unnecessary guilt if they cannot afford treatment. Sort out what is most important to provide and do your best. If you are unable to provide care to keep your elderly cat comfortable, clean, and safe, then euthanasia may be an option to consider.

B. **Time budget.** Time is precious, and we may not have enough of it to take care of ourselves and a geriatric or terminally ill cat. Are there enough hours in the day for you to care for your cat? If you're awake half the night every other night trying to calm a cat who has cognitive dysfunction, your work or personal time and your health will suffer. Are you available if your cat needs medications many times a day or needs help to get around to avoid accidents in the house? Not everyone has a job that allows them to come and go every few hours for these things. And if you have to travel for work or would like to travel with your family, can you find someone who will take care of your loved furry one?

C. **Physical budget.** Consider how well you can physically handle your cat and the effects of her ailments. Cats aren't always easy to manage, and giving them their medications can be a workout. Getting your cat into the car for frequent veterinary visits or prescribed treatments may be burdensome. Or maybe your cat is easy to handle, but keeping her or your house clean is difficult. For example, my mother has severe physical limitations and cannot bend down or kneel, so when her dog became fecal and urine incontinent, it was impossible for her to keep her home clean in a timely manner and without help.

D. **Emotional budget.** Take stock of your emotional bank, in light of everything that's happening. How well are you handling seeing your cat not be his or her normal self, or thinking about when to say goodbye? Are you tired of being a caregiver? Are you fighting with family members about the challenges? Is your cat the last living link to someone you lost? Are you worried or do you have guilt because you think you let another pet go too early, or you hung on too long? The emotional budget is one we tend to discount, but it often weighs more heavily on us than we realize.

For my patients, I support the family's decision to say goodbye to their cat when any one of these budgets is depleted. If they financially can't manage the treatment that may help their cat, that's OK, and I'll help them say goodbye. If they don't have enough time to properly care for their cat, that's OK, and I'll help them say goodbye. If they physically can't manage their cat, that's OK, and I'll help them say goodbye. And if they're emotionally ready, I'll help them say goodbye. I make no judgments, and I don't compare a family's abilities or beliefs to what I would do. It's vital that you don't take on guilt if you've depleted one or more of these budgets. I've seen too many pet owners beat themselves up over not being able to afford their cat's treatment or having to work 12 hours a day so they can't be there for their cat.

A loving rehome

If circumstances prohibit you from continuing to care for your aging cat, but your senior cat is healthy or your geriatric cat has a readily treatable condition, consider rehoming before euthanasia. Many cats can adapt well to a new home—some do quickly, and some require patience and a longer adjustment period. So if your cat could still lead a comfortable, good quality of life, other family members or friends may be willing to welcome your companion. Seeking help from foster, sanctuary, or shelter services are other options. Many people, like me, love adopting senior pets.

The quality of death conversation: How well will the cat pass?

It's a common wish for pet parents that their ailing or geriatric cat will die in their sleep so they don't have to face the difficult decision to euthanize. I was once one of those pet parents. But that is rarely what happens, and if it does, it's usually unexpected or does not happen as peacefully as people imagine. So I prepare pet parents for how their cats may pass if they don't choose euthanasia (see Chapter 35 "Natural passing: What to expect"). I also prepare pet parents who choose euthanasia for how their cats' ailments may affect the time they have with them at the end. The goal for any death is that it be a peaceful passing—one in which the least amount of pain, anxiety, or suffering (for the cat and family members) occurs. I've found it helps for pet parents to understand the different paths their pets' illnesses are likely to take as their pets near the end of life.

Trajectories of decline

Hospice and geriatric care physicians use the phrase *trajectories of decline* to describe the patterns that illnesses take toward the end of a person's life.[1-3] Other than the trajectory of sudden death (advancing from normal function to death with minimal forewarning), the three primary trajectories of decline described in people are terminal illness, organ failure, and frailty. I believe pets experience these trajectories, too, although I refer to them differently.

>**Terminal illness.** During the initial stages of illness (which is typically cancer) patients are physically stable, and then experience a rapid decline in the last few months or weeks of life. Hospice was originally developed for people in the final stage of this decline.[4]
>
>For pets, I call this trajectory "The Dive " or "The Cliff." As in people, cats maintain a relatively well-functioning, steady state until a threshold is reached and the disease accelerates and the body declines quickly. Diseases such as cancer that follow this trajectory typically allow pet parents ample time for pre-planning to ensure a cat's peaceful passing.
>
>**Organ failure.** People with long-term and worsening lung, heart, kidney, liver, and some neurologic diseases experience a slow and gradual decline marked by periods of sudden health crises. The sudden crises are triggered by the underlying disease or by a new problem such as an infection. Each crisis may end in death, or the person may recover with supportive treatment or hospitalization but have reduced function, and so on, with each subsequent crisis.
>
>I call this trajectory "The Winding Road" for ailing pets. Like people, these cats typically experience a gradual decline that involves sudden downturns followed by recoveries. Frequent trips to the veterinarian for "treatment tune-ups" are usually needed. Eventually the

disease takes hold and a time comes when no recovery occurs. Kidney failure, diabetes, or diseases that can cause difficulty breathing such as congestive heart failure and lung cancer may follow this trajectory.

Pre-planning is vital to ensure a pet's peaceful passing, because during any sudden downturn, death may occur. Unfortunately, when a pet progresses to the point of respiratory distress, decline goes south fast and pet parents may not be afforded the luxury of planning a good death. This is why I like to have a preparatory conversation with pet parents so that they can plan as best as possible, which includes me making sure they know which emergency veterinary clinic is closest to their home in case their cat has a crisis at 2 a.m. and is suffering.

Frailty. In people, this decline is extremely slow and the disease may have progressed substantially before a diagnosis, such as dementia, is declared. Or the diagnosis may simply be "advanced age."

In pets, I refer to this trajectory as "The Fade." Chronic and slowly progressive diseases such as arthritis or cognitive dysfunction take a long time for the body to decline. Diseases that progress relatively slowly often afford us time to make the decision about when to euthanize and ensure that the pet's quality of death is good. Pet parents can have a goodbye party and make sure their cats are comfortable and surrounded by love when they pass. But these decisions can also be difficult because the pet's decline is gradual, and pet parents may not recognize how sick their cat has become during an extended period. Although the underlying disease may not directly cause the pet's death, it often causes challenges that deplete the caregiver's physical, time, and emotional budgets.

"The Roller Coaster"

Almost all cat lovers can agree when a cat's quality of life is good and their signs of joy are evident. Most cat lovers can also agree when a cat has intractable suffering and it would be kindest to relieve their suffering and elect euthanasia. But a huge "grey area" chasm lies between those two points where this decision is not straightforward. Making it across that chasm usually entails boarding what I call "The Roller Coaster." And it is like riding a rickety wooden roller coaster where it seems the cars will fly off the rails and you will plunge into a heap of splinters! I have ridden on this coaster plenty of times—right up front, screaming!

On this roller coaster you have good days and bad days as the weeks and months pass. Some Sunday nights you may think, "we had a really bad weekend, and it's time to say goodbye." But then Monday comes and your cat seems much better, so you don't schedule the euthanasia appointment. This roller coaster is no joy ride, and you will struggle. At what point do you decide it's time for the roller coaster to return to the platform so you can exit? If you had a really bad weekend, and on Monday your cat is doing better but you don't want another bad weekend, it's OK to get off the roller coaster and say goodbye.

"The Flicker"

Many times I have seen ailing cats spend days or weeks on a steady downward trajectory, then out of the blue they have a day or two of greatness. They eat better, move around more, climb their cat tree again, sleep through the night, and even play again. You may think a miracle has happened. I call this "The Flicker." However, like a thief in the night, that bounty is stolen and afterward the cats seem even worse than before they perked up. It's helpful for pet parents to know that some cats experience a flicker before their flame goes out.

"You'll know" and "The look"

Many people may tell you, "Don't worry. You'll know when it's time." I don't like this advice because you don't always know! Especially when you're evaluating your own cat. It's hard to understand and recognize all the signs of pain, progressing disease, malaise, or anxiety. We simply don't want to say goodbye, and sometimes it's difficult to assess our cat's physical and emotional life quality.

Other people may tell you, "Don't worry, your cat will give you 'The Look' when it's time." My advice is, please do not wait for this "look." I say this because I'm sure your answer to the question, "Do you want your cat to suffer?" is "NO!" In my experience, if we wait for a certain "look" from our pet, we're waiting for our pet's suffering to be so bad that we can see it plainly. My advice is to try to say goodbye before you would see such a look.

My cat Herbie (the Love Bug!) had a lung tumor that affected his breathing. His disease progressed pretty fast and in about a month he had massively declined. He had always been the epitome of a loving, orange tabby tomcat!

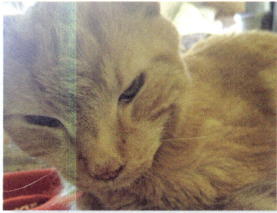

 My boy Herbie a week before he died (left) and on the day he died (right).

He once had a big, round face and seductive eyes. But his lung tumor stole his beautiful look. As his pet mom, I had a really hard time thinking of life without Herbie. But one day, his breathing became so difficult, and he sat on my chest and I realized, "OMG! Herbie has 'The Look.'" I knew he was suffering. I felt such sorrow that I had let my little one suffer. That day I knew I needed to give him his angel wings. We said goodbye outside, on the lawn, in the sunlight, and surrounded by daisies.

Knowing when it's time to say goodbye relies heavily on evaluating a pet's quality of life, which can be a challenge. Differences in how to define quality of life, differences between diseases, differences between caregiver observations (veterinarians, pet parents, other family members, friends), and factoring in the caregivers' potential biases all make evaluating life quality in pets highly complex.

Research revelation: Does science know when it's time?

Many quality of life assessment tools published in the veterinary scientific literature have been designed with dogs[5] or cats in mind, and most are intended to help veterinarians evaluate pets who have a specific issue. For example, such tools are available for cats who have osteoarthritis, chronic kidney disease, skin disease, heart disease, cancer, or diabetes.[6-13]

General quality of life assessments for cats have also been published in the veterinary scientific literature.[14-17] Veterinarians may use them to monitor healthy cats for changes, to assess quality of life in cats who have chronic ailments (and their responses to treatments, if applicable), and perhaps to evaluate quality of life in cats near the end of life.[15] For example, one tool is available online for veterinary practices on a subscription basis, and veterinarians can invite clients to complete these assessments. More information is available at **newmetrica.com/vetmetrica-hrql/**.

So if your veterinary practice does not offer a quality of life assessment tool, where does this leave you in evaluating when it may be time to say goodbye to your cat?

Methods for evaluating your cat's life quality

A wide variety of pet quality of life evaluation tools—surveys with scoring systems, questionnaires with rating scales, and quizzes—are available on the internet. All of them have benefits in considering different aspects of pets' lives, and they attempt to provide pet parents with clearer insight on the subjective quality of life observations that differ for every pet.

Life Quality Tool

I've created a Life Quality Assessment tool for cats, which is available on my website:

Here I'll also cover a few of the other popular assessment methods that you may learn about on the internet, through social media, or from your veterinary team. You may want to use one or a combination of methods to consider your cat's physical, mental, and emotional well-being.

Top Five

One classic quality of life assessment method for pet parents is to list the top five things your pet loves to do and evaluate whether she still loves doing them. Seek out sunbeams, get out in the yard to patrol for bugs, sit on your lap while you watch TV, eat, greet and hang out with friends who visit, watch birds from the window, play laser dot chase, explore a new cardboard box, nap on the back of the couch—whatever activities make your cat your cat. Then—presuming that your cat's pain, underlying disease, or health condition has been treated or managed to the best of your abilities or cannot be further treated or managed—when your cat is not doing three of her five favorite things consistently, it may be time to say goodbye.

A caveat with this method is that with some diseases, your cat may be doing his five favorite things, yet he's struggling throughout the day or night. I sometimes see this in cats with cognitive dysfunction. The cat has a great appetite, enjoys supervised sunbathing outdoors, still interacts with visitors, and loves tasty treats, but he spends half of the day following your every move around the house and becomes overly anxious at night and doesn't sleep well.

One twist to this method is to evaluate four of the cat's favorite activities and one thing that the cat hates. For example, my cat Bodhi hated unfamiliar neighborhood cats and was passionate about them staying away from our windows. The second Bodhi got a whiff or a glimpse of an intruder's tail, he hissed, growled, and spat at the window until the prowler ran out of his sight (or until I knocked on the window to startle the stranger, closed the curtains, and distracted Bodhi!). Sometimes Bodhi would even pee by the door! (And as far as Bodhi knew, it worked, because it kept the strange cat out of his house!) I knew that if the time came when Bodhi stopped being upset about free-roaming outsiders, that would mean he was probably too weak to expend the energy to care, and that he was no longer himself.

The Five Freedoms

As you're evaluating your cat's health status, response to medical treatments, and quality of life, keep these measures of animal welfare top of mind. The "Five Freedoms" were developed in the United Kingdom beginning in 1965 to address farm animal welfare.[18] And they have since been applied to address the physical and mental needs of companion animals living in shelters. These five freedoms also readily apply to the care we provide for the cats we share our lives with:

1. Freedom from hunger and thirst, by ready access to water and a diet to maintain health and vigor.
2. Freedom from discomfort, by providing an appropriate environment.
3. Freedom from pain, injury, and disease, by prevention or rapid diagnosis and treatment.
4. Freedom to express normal behavior, by providing sufficient space, proper facilities, and appropriate company of the animal's own kind.
5. Freedom from fear and distress, by ensuring conditions and treatment that avoid mental suffering.

More good days than bad

One of the most common things I hear from pet parents is, "When my cat has had more bad days than good days, then I will know it's time to say goodbye." In this case, it's important to objectively measure what you're monitoring, because otherwise it's very difficult to determine.

Defining good days and bad days

What constitutes a good day for your cat? This is a subjective determination, and the definition is specific to your cat and to you. Does a good day mean that three things went right? Or one thing? Does it mean that your cat slept through the night? Or does it mean that your cat slept at least four hours straight during the night? Does it mean that your cat ate all of his normal amount of food, or at least half that? Does it mean that he was able to get to the litter box without your assistance? That she had cognitive issues for three hours or less a day vs. more than three hours? That he had only two accidents in the house that day? Or is it a good day only when things are almost perfect?

You also need to consider how well your good day definition matches up with that of other family members. My definition of a good day for my cat differs a lot from that of my partner. To me, a good day for my ailing cat is one that may still require me to provide intense caregiving to ensure my cat is still enjoying life and, of course, does not suffer. To my partner, a good day means our ailing cat has no litter box mishaps, doesn't vomit, and needs no coaxing to eat. Yet my partner can understand my definition, because I provide the majority of our ailing pets' caregiving and I'll never allow them to suffer.

Write down what makes a good day and a bad day for your cat and you. Everyone in the household should agree on the definition of each. Then monitor your cat each day using those criteria to decide whether he's had a good day or a bad day.

Measuring good days and bad days

You also need to decide what percentage of bad days vs. good days means that it may be time to say goodbye. Is 51% good days to 49% bad days OK? Or do you need your cat to have good days 80% of the time? Or maybe having good days 25% of the time is acceptable to you.

Also consider for what period of time you'll monitor your cat, and whether you'll allow leeway for setbacks that your cat may recover from with additional treatment or supportive care. (Remember the ups and downs of "The Winding Road" trajectory I described earlier in this chapter.) For example, let's say you've decided that you won't consider saying goodbye as long as your cat has at least 60% good days and no more than 40% bad days. But then your cat has one bad week where three of seven days (42%) are bad because he has a disease setback or a new problem such as constipation. Yet with additional treatment the problem is managed.

Visualizing good days and bad days

Write your assessments in a diary or on a wall calendar, or post them on the fridge or wherever it's convenient and all family members can see them. Use a big red X to indicate the bad days. This documentation helps you and your family agree on when it may be an appropriate time to say goodbye.

This calendar example shows that the pet is having 42% bad days in a month and 58% good days.

So maybe it would be OK to say goodbye if that ratio is your decision point. But you can also see other trends, not simply declines. In this example, the garbage truck came every Friday morning and the family had not realized how much emotional stress this caused their ailing pet. The rest of the day was horrible for the pet and the family. The calendar allowed the family to see this pattern clearly, and they made sure that someone was home to distract him when the truck came. After that, Fridays got better for everyone! Scan here to download a blank version of a calendar.

Calendar

Discuss good days and bad days with your children, too. One suggestion is to place one jar labeled "Good" and one jar labeled "Bad" on the counter.

Put a penny in the appropriate jar for that day. At the end of your predetermined time period, the jar that contains the most pennies will help you consider your decision. It's a simple visual for children to measure how their cat is doing over time and may help you talk with them when the time to say goodbye is appropriate.

The "Good Day vs. Bad Day" quality of life assessment works well for me and has worked well for hundreds of pet parents who I've helped throughout my career in veterinary end-of-life care. Afterward, you'll look back on your daily diary and see the upward, steady, and downward trends, and be reassured that you made the best decision.

Other quality of life surveys, scales, and quizzes

Dr Faith Bank's QOL Scale

A variety of other quality of life evaluation tools are available on the internet and from other resources, and all of them have benefits.

My friend Dr. Faith Banks is a hospice veterinarian in Canada. In her quality of life evaluations she includes an assessment of the pet's interactions with their family in terms of whether the pet gave love or took love. Is the pet seeking love and attention, and is the pet also providing love? **mmvhs.ca/quality-of-life-scale/**

Photographic timeline

It's helpful to reminisce with photographs and videos of your cat taken a few months or years earlier. This exercise helps you remember what "good" looks like for your cat. We all change as we grow older, so you need to allow for typical aging changes. If I looked at photos of me when I was 18 years old right now, I would wonder where 30 extra pounds and a road map of wrinkles came from! But often, the pictures and videos can illustrate dramatic changes related to our cats' ailments and help us remove the denial googles we sometimes wear.

"Denial Island"

Darby was one of my grey muzzle canine patients years ago, and her mom taught me about a mindset called "Denial Island." Darby's health was declining because of liver cancer. And although Darby's mom used quality of life scales, she scored Darby as nothing but "Excellent" or answered "Everything is fine!" Yet she knew Darby was not doing that well. She told me she was on "Denial Island" and could not evaluate the situation properly. So she asked me to complete a quality of life scale for Darby.

My assessment of Darby's quality of life gave "poor" and "everything is NOT okay" results. We discussed my assessment and I suggested that it would be an OK time to say goodbye to Darby if she was ready. Darby's mom was not ready that day. So I adjusted Darby's medications and she had a wonderful next day. Darby's mom realized that she did not want Darby to experience bad days again. So two days later, Darby's mom asked me to help Darby earn her angel wings.

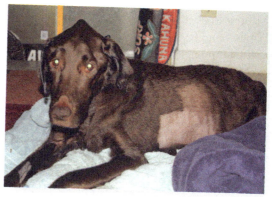

 Darby after her last swim, which she loved so much.

I've been to Denial Island with my own pets. Saying goodbye is heartbreaking and may bring on feelings of guilt about letting go, and denial feels better. I'm pretty sure I've been the Mayor of Denial Island, so if you are there, too, it isn't unexpected. It's the place I go when my head and heart engage in a war, and my heart takes over because I can't bear the thought of not having my cat in my life. So my brain twists circumstances around to protect me from a truth I'm not ready to face. Denial is a helpful coping mechanism, but it can get in the way when you're facing a difficult decision. It's hard to see the reality when you're by yourself. If you find yourself on Denial Island, lean on friends and family, or, as Darby's mom did, ask your pet's veterinarian to help.

If you find a friend or family member stuck on Denial Island, Dr. BJ Miller, a human hospice physician and friend of mine, says that swooping in to try to extract them could seriously backfire. Instead, he suggests asking questions that may soften their denial and see the circumstances more objectively.[19] So I suggest asking questions similar to those he uses to help his patients reflect. For example, when a family member or friend tells me that their ailing cat is OK, I ask, "What is happening with your cat that tells you that?" And, "Do you think there may be something we are missing?" Or, "Is that way of seeing things serving you and your cat well during this time?" Context and tone are vital, because I don't want to sound like I'm coming from "Judgment Island."

Getting to goodbye

Some ailing cats have only a series of good moments sprinkled throughout bad days. Or some ailing cats have only a series of a few good days surrounded by bad days. For pet parents struggling with the decision of when to say goodbye, I suggest thoughtfully considering the activities and experiences that bring joy to your cat. What makes your cat... your cat?

I adore Bucket Lists (a list of experiences you'd like your cat to have before they pass) and Joy of Living Lists (a list of activities or things that bring your cat joy all the time). See Chapter 26: "Buckets lists: The joys of life" for more about these lists. These lists can also help you assess your cat's life quality and whether your cat is enjoying life. Write these things down. Evaluate them often. Be honest. Look at pictures and videos. Be kind to yourself and prepare yourself. My hope is that when it comes time to get off your roller coaster, you won't have regrets. You'll know that not only did you give your cat a great quality of life, but that you also gave them a good quality of death.

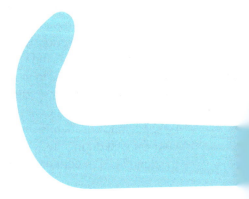

Part four:

ENDURING THE UNENDURABLE— PREPARING FOR AND SAYING GOODBYE

These may be the ... help you consider ho... and, be prepared ... the comple... you and your f... and honor... patients as a... parent, this ... rmingly insi...

CHAPTER 31:

A home divided: Conflicts between family members about end-of-life care

> "Remember, we all stumble, every one of us. That's why it's a comfort to go hand in hand."
>
> — EMILY KIMBROUGH, AUTHOR AND BROADCASTER

During some of my in-home hospice visits, family members haven't been on the same page about the next steps in their pet's care, and sometimes even when I was called there to euthanize their pet. A disconnect or malalignment of beliefs can occur between family members about their cat's treatment and caregiving, and the end-of-life decision. The division may be between partners, or between parents and children—or it may even be a battle you have with yourself every other day. And sometimes this disconnect can get heated.

Love for their pet is the first thing family members can agree on. And this is where healing begins. Finding that thread of common ground. And, usually, everyone loves their cat. So it's a pretty easy place to start.

Walking on common ground

The first step in helping pet parents or other family members come together in agreement about hospice care or euthanasia for their pet is allowing them to acknowledge—to themselves and each other—that they love their pet. I usually start by saying something along the lines of, "It seems to me everyone here loves this sweet kitty beyond measure. Do you all agree?" And this often sparks the family's tears and nods.

Then I ask, "Do you agree that you don't want your cat to suffer?" That's always my next question, because no one ever says, 'No, I'd like my cat to suffer." So when everyone agrees, the family has taken two steps in common: love and avoiding suffering.

Then I ask them each to write down what suffering means to them, whether their cat has signs of suffering, and, if so, what the signs are. I want the family to take time to reflect on their answers and not be swayed by others. Then they each read out loud what they wrote. Typically, their responses are very similar.

I write down the signs of suffering that they each agreed on. And then we talk about the signs that differed. If they then come to agreement on any of those signs, I add those to the list.

Then I ask them to do a similar reflection: "Write down the things that make your cat happy. List the things your cat hates feverishly. Write down the things that make your cat himself or herself. Write down your cat's signs of joy." This usually gets cat parents in a better frame of mind and infuses happiness back into the conversation. And then I ask them to again openly share what they wrote. I ask to see pictures of their cat throughout their life and ask them to share their favorite stories.

My no-judgment rule

My biggest ground rule for the family during these conversations and one that I ask them to uphold during their own follow-up discussions is "no judgment." We discuss that tossing unkind comments back and forth and judging the other person's decisions are roadblocks that divert the family from the path of common ground. I encourage them to always circle back to the fact that everyone loves the cat, so what specific things can they do to better support each other?

Drawing a line in the sand

After we have our definitions of joy and suffering, we discuss setting parameters and drawing a line in the sand. I ask questions such as: How many days can pass without your cat eating before you think it's time to say goodbye? Are each of you willing to help your cat get to the litter box? How many hours of undisturbed sleep must your cat have every night? I write their responses on a big piece of paper and ask everyone to evaluate these things every day—separately and as a team.

Children—include everyone in the discussion

I've found that older children, particularly teenagers, struggle with decisions about an ailing pet's care, especially when the adult believes it's time to euthanize the pet. Children may feel as though the family could do more for their cat, spend more money, and be more patient with the cat's condition. And they may not fully grasp the entire picture about their cat's ailments, prognosis, and caregiving needs. I go through the same steps with children and ask them the same questions so they can take part in these quality-of-life conversations and share their stories. It's best to include children at any age, as appropriate, in the caretaking and decision-making so they can share in the common ground.

Consider hospice care

If you're establishing common ground among all family members on your own and you haven't yet considered whether hospice services are an option for your cat, consider talking with your veterinarian about pet hospice. Once a cat has started receiving hospice care, it can be helpful to create their bucket list and make time to complete and check off the activities, and it's essential to do daily life quality assessments. These endeavors empower family members to participate in the cat's care and encourage everyone to stay on the same road and make decisions as a team. For more on those topics, see Chapter 26 "Bucket lists: The joys of life," Chapter 27: "Veterinary hospice: Living well until the end," and Chapter 30 "Life quality: 'Doc, when is it time?'"

Narrowing the gap

As the "obvious" end of life draws nearer for a pet, disparities that remain between family members about their pet's care narrow. The worst conflict usually occurs during the initial stages of making decisions about end-of-life care. Once a pet's quality of life becomes seriously diminished, decisions about next steps become more apparent to all.

A house that stands together

When pet parents or a family create their cat's "joy list," it's usually long! And the family's "signs of suffering" lists typically agree nearly 100%. I write the signs of suffering on a new piece of paper, then we add measurable parameters that the family agrees on for each one, such as "How many days will your cat show

no interest in sitting in his sunny windowsill before it's time?" And "How many items on this list need to be happening at the same time for us to say goodbye?"

Then comes the hardest part, when I say, "Now let's check our list and evaluate how your kitty is doing today."

Their responses on those lists may show how far their cat has crossed the line in the sand that they indicated would be time to say goodbye. And when that realization takes hold, more tears usually follow. But everyone usually comes together on the same page shortly afterward, and they become calm, relieved, and grateful. Making end-of-life decisions may make us suffer, but when we follow an appropriate course of care, our pets do not have to suffer.

Caregiver tips

Ask these questions of yourself, or use these questions to start a discussion with family or other household members to help get everyone on the same page about your cat's end-of-life care.

The Big Questions list:

- Do you love your cat?
- Do you want to prevent your cat from suffering?
- What do you think suffering means for your cat?
- What makes your cat himself or herself?
- What brings your cat joy?
- What does your cat detest? (The intent of this question is to identify whether things that typically bother your cat—such as unfamiliar visitors, the neighbor's cats, getting claws trimmed, or taking pills—no longer do.)

After you each define your cat's joys and signs of suffering by answering the Big Questions, set parameters that everyone agrees on so you can stay on common ground about your cat's end-of-life care. Then consider how your cat is doing now, and look at the line in the sand you've drawn, and determine:

- Does your cat have any form of suffering? If so, to what degree?
- Is your cat getting enough moments to be who he or she is?
- Is your cat still getting moments of joy?
- Is your cat tolerating things he or she detests because it's easier not to fight?
- Could pet hospice care help?

CHAPTER 32:

Grief wellness: Anticipating and experiencing loss

> "To retain the memory of love's sweetness without letting the pain of parting and loss embitter it is perhaps the greatest challenge for the bereaved heart, and its greatest achievement."
>
> — Maria Popova

Considering the possibility of electing euthanasia for a pet and the emotions surrounding this decision can be overwhelming for many pet parents. Before the impending loss of a pet, many people experience *anticipatory grief*, a variety of emotions that may include sorrow, anxiety, loneliness, fear, frustration, guilt, despair, or anger. I have experienced it with each of my pets, when I knew our remaining time together would be short. Anticipatory grief may be similar to grief that occurs after our pets die, or it may differ.

After learning of our pet's terminal illness or watching the long-term decline of our geriatric pet, grief can begin to manifest. We may not only grieve the forthcoming loss of our pet, but also the imminent loss of the relationship and the security it brings—and the role we have as our pet's caregiver. Anticipatory grief can sometimes drown out the pleasures in the moments we have left with our pet.

Each affected family member or friend may express or handle anticipatory grief differently, and not everyone experiences it. For those who do, anticipatory grief may affect not only one's mental and emotional states, it can result in physical illness. Additional help from a grief counselor or mental health professional can be invaluable, so don't hesitate to seek extra support if needed.

When anger rules

Anger can be a component of anticipatory grief, and pet parents or other family members sometimes express resentment or outrage in response to the news of a pet's terminal illness. I focus on this emotion here because it can be a destructive force in client-veterinarian relationships and in family relationships. This anger may be displaced and inappropriately directed in one or more ways:

Toward the veterinarian. Because veterinarians deliver the news about a pet's condition or diagnosis, a pet's family sometimes irrationally blames the veterinarian for their pet's terminal illness, or for not identifying the problem sooner. Sometimes the cause of a pet's decline and symptoms remain unknown, which can be frustrating for everyone. At times like these, it can be difficult for pet parents to remember that their entire veterinary team loves animals and loves caring for pets. We veterinarians understand that such anger stems from a pet owner's sudden grief and that it's usually temporary. The veterinarians and team members also often experience distress after identifying or learning the news that one of their patients has a terminal condition.

Toward the pet. A pet parent or other family member may blame their pet for imminent desertion. They may reject their cat and refuse to pet or play with their cat again. A cat won't understand why such changes in behavior or routine occurred. A cat needs their family's love and care even more at this time, especially when they're probably not feeling well. Ailing cats benefit from additional reassurance and comfort. Providing extra kindness and support for the pet can help family members begin to heal and avoid regret.

Toward other family members. Children or family members who feel others aren't doing enough for their pet may blame those family members. Children may not realize that their parents sometimes cannot afford treatment or that treatment won't change their pet's outcome. When parents decline treatment or elect euthanasia for a pet, I sometimes hear children blame their parents for "killing my cat."

For this reason, it may be best that parents alone hear their pet's care options and that veterinarians not present treatment choices when small children are present. Pet parents need the option to consider euthanasia when it's an acceptable alternative to their pet's treatment, and to have time to talk with their children about their decisions, without the added stress and guilt that young family members' responses may invoke in the moment.

Toward God or the universe. Whether or not a pet parent has religious beliefs, some will blame a higher power for an animal's illness or death. A pet parent may say, "Why did this have to happen to me? Such awful things don't happen to other people who don't even care for their pets!" In such cases, it's helpful to seek advice and insights from an appropriate religious or spiritual leader.

Toward oneself. This anger often manifests as guilt or blame. "If only I had brought my cat to see the veterinarian sooner." Or "We never should have had this surgery done in the first place." Such thoughts may go through a pet parent's mind when a pet's terminal condition has been diagnosed or when a pet dies suddenly. Pet parents sometimes look for ways in which they or their family members contributed to the pet's condition. This guilt and blame are unjustified because it's highly unlikely that anyone intended willful harm. A pet parent may also feel guilty if they don't have the financial resources to care for their pet without forgoing other family necessities. It's important to not take on guilt that isn't yours. Life brings challenges, disease, and loss that we have no control over. We only have control over how we respond to those things.

Coping before loss

Because grief related to pet loss tends to be less socially accepted than grief associated with a person's death, those who experience anticipatory grief before losing their pet may feel intensely isolated. Pet parents sometimes tell me that they feel like no one understands them or they feel "silly" that they are "being so emotional over losing 'just' an animal." But most pet parents do understand, and it's important that this period of grief is recognized. It's beneficial to share feelings with others who understand what it's like to lose a pet and who can provide support. Veterinary professionals are often able to assist clients in finding support groups or resources during this difficult time.

Anticipatory grief doesn't usually replace or prevent the grief that occurs after a pet has passed. However, an anticipatory grief period can also allow the pet's family time to share activities with their pets that they may have put off in the past. For some, this helps prompt a conscious closure—reflecting on the gratitude one feels for sharing their pet's life and preparing for what is to come—before the loss. Focus on the pleasures you still have, and consider documenting them to help hold your memories and honor your cat.

Dr. Elisabeth Kübler-Ross, a psychiatrist famous for her work in human hospice care and her 1969 book *On Death and Dying*, said that a person who loses someone will experience more grief if they never said "I love you" to that person before they passed. So keep in mind that an anticipatory grief period allows you to say "I love you" to your cat every day. Such an opportunity has certainly helped me cope with the loss of my own cats. It can also help with the sudden, unexpected loss of a pet, which I learned the hard way.

My kitty Goldie was such a special joy in my life. I learned so much from caring for a cat with partial paralysis, and her unending devotion to me was a priceless reward. But because of our household circumstances, I had to give her access to go potty outdoors. Goldie preferred her independence in that way, and she managed getting outdoors and back indoors with ease.

Until one day, when horror struck. A coyote took her. Losing Goldie has devastated me in countless ways. The guilt I carry because I let her go out while I wasn't watching, the sadness of missing my girl, my anger toward the coyote, and my neverending wish to turn back and change the events of that day.

 Me and Goldie enjoying the sun together.

Losing Goldie gave me a more profound understanding of Dr. Kübler-Ross's wise observations. I utterly, regrettably missed that precious opportunity to tell Goldie out loud how much I loved her. So I tell all my families whose pets are in hospice to say "I love you" every day to their pets.

Anticipatory grief can also give you time to prepare for your cat's death and make arrangements that you may not have otherwise considered, such as choosing the day, where you'd like your cat to be, and who will be present.

Neither you nor those around you must forget that the death of a beloved cat changes your life forever. And those changes may start before your cat leaves you.

Dreading a pet's death

If you've planned a day and time to euthanize your cat, you may experience a different sort of stress or anxiety on the scheduled day, during the hours and minutes that lead up to the moment your cat will pass. I believe this differs from anticipatory grief, which relates to anticipating the loss you'll experience after your cat passes. This anxiety that centers on the moment the loss happens seems different.

Even as a veterinarian who has helped countless families say goodbye to their cats, when the time comes to euthanize my own cat, the scheduled day is a day that fills me with much anxiety. My emotions are in high gear and every treasured second lingers on that day. I can't help but think about each of my cat's actions as "the last." The last good-morning kiss I give them, the last breakfast they'll eat, the last after-dinner treat, the last time they'll sit on my lap. I watch the clock all day and count down until the "last appointment": six more hours, four hours, two hours, one hour, 30 minutes, 15 minutes ….

A planned euthanasia can happen at a veterinary hospital, at home, or in another location meaningful to you and your pet. I believe that whenever possible, saying goodbye at home or at another special location rather than at the veterinary hospital may be best for everyone. I prefer to avoid that "last drive" to the veterinary hospital, and the heartbreaking drive home. If everyone can stay home and focus on comfort and love, the process may be slightly easier.

I personally suffer from anticipatory grief and post-loss grief. But the day of my cat's euthanasia is a different type of heartfelt torment. It's hard for me to concentrate on anything else other than the death that's coming. I share this with you to let those of you who feel the same know you're not alone. I do my best to put this anguish aside and focus on making the best of the remaining hours I have with my cat. I encourage you to do the same. Time is a treasure you cannot restore.

Grief after losing a pet

Regardless of whether your cat is old or young when they pass, or whether your cat's death is sudden or expected, grief is a normal and natural reaction. At times you may be so submerged in grief it seems impossible to surface for air, and the grief is so powerful it drowns out the pleasant memories of the lifetime of love you shared.

Dr. Kübler-Ross proposed that people experience five stages of grief when faced with *their own* imminent death, which she wrote about in her book *On Death and Dying*. These stages were later applied to the emotions that survivors may experience after losing a loved one. The five stages of grief have also since been applied to people experiencing a major life change, such as a divorce or unemployment, and applied to society in general in describing people's responses to the drastic changes brought on by the COVID-19 pandemic.[1] You've probably heard of the five stages of grief: denial, anger, bargaining, depression, and acceptance.

The five stages of grief are popularized in media and culture, but evidence that people experience grief in stages is lacking. Studies show that most people don't grieve in stages and don't experience a clear end point that indicates recovery from grief.[2-4] Healthcare professionals and counselors are now discouraged from using these stages as clinical guidelines for their bereaved clients because if they're expected to go through these stages but don't, they may be harmed by feeling that they're grieving incorrectly.[3,5]

Instead, research indicates that grieving is not an orderly and predictable stage-like process, and that grief can involve many different complex, fluctuating "roller coaster" emotions. Toward the end of her career, Kübler-Ross regretted that her stages of grief had been misunderstood and wrote that grief doesn't work in a predictable, linear way.[6]

Different patterns and ways of "normal" grieving exist, along with individual and cultural differences in reactions to loss.[3,7] Most people experience loss in their own way over time. The bottom line is that people who are grieving should not expect or be expected to go through a specific set of stages.

The space of duality

After one of my pets passes, I find myself spending time in a "space of duality" where I'm both wrenchingly heartsick and peacefully content. I miss my pet terribly, and I take comfort in knowing my pet is whole again. Yet it rubs me wrong when people say to me, "She's in a better place, she's not suffering anymore," as if I would allow my pet to suffer and had been holding her prisoner on Earth with me. I understand the good intentions behind sentiments like these, but they don't help me. Instead, it helps me to focus on the pictures and videos of my pets throughout their lifetimes. Their images and my memories of our shared moments make me smile, and they help me imagine and hope for my pet's new state of perfect being, in whatever form that may be.

 ## Questions to ask your veterinarian

- What can I do to help my cat stay comfortable until it's time to say goodbye?
- If veterinary hospice care isn't available in this area, can we work together to create a hospice care plan for my cat?
- What plans or preparations should I make before it's time to say goodbye?
- What options are available during and after regular business hours for in-home or in-hospital euthanasia for my cat?
- Do you have suggestions for aftercare of my cat's body? Do you have a pet cemetery or cremation service you recommend?
- Do you have pet loss information available or resources to recommend?
- Can you suggest a local pet loss support group or grief counselor?

 READING RECOMMENDATIONS

- *Coping with Sorrow on the Loss of Your Pet* (Third Edition) by Moira Anderson Allen (2015 CreateSpace Independent Publishing Platform).
- *There is Eternal Life for Animals* by Niki Behrikis Shanahan (2002, Pete Publishing).
- *Grieving the Death of a Pet* by Betty J. Carmack (2003, Augsburg Books).
- *The Pet Loss Companion: Healing Advice from Family Therapists Who Lead Pet Loss*
- *Groups* by Ken Dolan-Del Vecchio and Nancy Saxton-Lopez (2013, CreateSpace Independent Publishing Platform).

- *Pet Parents: A Journey Through Unconditional Love and Grief* by Coleen Ellis (2011, iUniverse).
- *The Grief Recovery Handbook for Pet Loss* by Russell Friedman, Cole James, and John W. James (2014, Taylor Trade Publishing).
- *Pawprints in the Stars: A Farewell and Journal for a Beloved Pet* by Warren Hanson (2008, Tristan Pub).
- *Going Home: Finding Peace When Pets Die* by Jon Katz (2012, Random House Trade Paperbacks).
- *Goodbye, Friend: Healing Wisdom for Anyone Who Has Ever Lost a Pet* by Gary Kowalski (2012, New World Library).
- *Cold Noses at the Pearly Gates: A Book of Hope for Those Who Have Lost a Pet* by Gary Kurz (2008, Citadel).
- *It's Okay to Cry: Warm, Compassionate Stories That Will Help You Find Hope and Healing After the Death of a Beloved Pet* by Maria Luz Quintana, Shari L. Veleba, and Harley King (2000, Mariposa Press).
- *A Final Act of Caring: Ending the Life of an Animal Friend* by Mary Montgomery and Herb Montgomery (1993, American Animal Hospital Association).
- *The Loss of a Pet: A Guide to Coping with the Grieving Process When a Pet Dies* (Fourth Edition) by Wallace Sife (2014, Howell Book House).
- *When Your Pet Dies: A Guide to Mourning, Remembering and Healing* by Alan D. Wolfelt (2004, Companion Press).

SUPPORT RECOMMENDATIONS

- *Lap of Love Pet Loss Support.* Offers free virtual group support and paid one-on-one support.
  lapoflove.com/our-services/pet-loss-support
- *Two Hearts Pet Loss Center.* A wonderful resource including courses to help with grief.
  twoheartspetlosscenter.com/
- *Center for Loss & Life Transition.* Founded and led by death educator and grief counselor Dr. Alan Wolfelt.
  centerforloss.com/
- *The Association for Pet Loss and Bereavement.* Includes a scheduled online support chat room and an online video support program.
  aplb.org/
- *Everlife Memorials.* Includes a nationwide pet loss support group list.
  everlifememorials.com/Pet-Loss-Support-Groups-s/443.htm

CHAPTER 33:

Young grief: When children bid farewell

> "The tree I had in the garden as a child, my beech tree, I used to climb up there and spend hours. I took my homework up there, my books, I went up there if I was sad, and it just felt very good to be up there among the green leaves and the birds and the sky."
>
> — Jane Goodall

My fur kids—cats and dogs—have always been my only children. And I may have a couple of goat kids in my future! Early in my veterinary career, I struggled with finding the right things to say to children during their pet's euthanasia visit. But I quickly learned that children share tender insights about their pets, and their presence often helps the adults during the experience.

Explaining euthanasia

Every child differs in how they respond to a pet's passing, and every parent differs in how they want to explain death to their child. In general, I like having children present during the euthanasia appointment. I discourage families from scheduling the appointment at a time when their children are at school, or from telling their children that their pet "went to a farm" or "ran away." I also suggest that parents consider whether their children may wish to have time alone with the pet—both immediately before and after the euthanasia, if their children wish.

I, of course, defer to the parents on how best to teach and help their children about their pet's passing, but parents often ask me for suggestions. Foremost, I think it's important that parents themselves understand the euthanasia process beforehand and the changes they and their children may see as their pet passes. I cover these topics in this book; see Chapter 35 "Natural passing: What to expect" and Chapter 36: "Euthanasia: The ending is what matters most." And at the time of the euthanasia appointment—whether the appointment is at your home, at another special location, or at the veterinary clinic—veterinarians typically describe the process and the changes that will occur in the pet. Veterinarians are also available to talk with you before the appointment if you'd like, so don't hesitate to schedule this time.

I speak to everyone in the room and explain the euthanasia process so that each family member feels included in these important moments. For young children who don't understand the concept of death, I usually say that the pet's body is no longer working, and that when a pet dies, the pet doesn't breathe or move, get cold or hungry, or hurt anymore. I remind them that plants die, too, and that it is a natural process. I find it beneficial to talk with them about why their pet's euthanasia is needed and what euthanasia is. I explain that their pet is already dying, and that euthanasia simply helps their dying process progress more peacefully, rather than say we're ending their pet's life. If the pet's euthanasia is needed because of an accident, I explain that their pet was badly hurt and their body cannot heal. If the euthanasia is related to terminal illness or to old age, I explain that their pet's body stopped working because of a disease that cannot be cured, or because the body wore out naturally after a long, happy life.

Parents can help children understand that for pets who will not get better and who are suffering, the pet's family can ask a veterinarian to assist by making their pet's dying process more comfortable and peaceful. Explain to children that euthanasia means "good death." Tell them that for pets who can't be healed, veterinarians help pets experience a good death by giving a medicine that will help the pet relax quietly for several minutes, and then they give a special drug that painlessly slows the body down so the pet passes peacefully.

Let children know that by gently helping pets during their dying process, a veterinarian will help prevent their pet's suffering and allow the family time to tell their pet how much they mean to them. Explain that euthanasia can give the child an opportunity to say goodbye with extra kindness and love. I think it's helpful for children and adults to understand that their pet is already experiencing the dying process, and that I'm, in essence, ending that process rather than ending the pet's life.

If you have a child who has autism spectrum disorder (ASD), you know better than I do, but children who have ASD may have difficulty expressing emotions, or they may have an intensely dramatic emotional response. They may also react in an unexpected way, such as laughing when others are crying. Children who have ASD may ask more questions, or they may seem more disengaged. They may also ask questions that seem harsh, or make declarations that upset or shock other family members. I have learned that it is, of course, important to validate every child's feelings.

I'm by no means an expert with children. As I mentioned, I don't have children myself. I offer guidance based on my experiences in helping families with children say their final goodbyes to their best furry friends. Based on these goodbyes, I typically see that a child's involvement in and reactions to their pet's euthanasia differ among three broad age groups:

2 to 5 years old. Children in this age group usually don't fully grasp the concept of death and its permanence. I suggest that parents involve these youngest children before the pet's euthanasia, such as asking them to draw a picture of the pet or gather flowers for the pet's gravesite. During the euthanasia appointment, children of these ages can be a distraction to other family members. It's often easier for the entire family if a friend or other family member stays with the child in another room while the family concentrates on saying goodbye to the pet. However, it's always up to the parents to decide whether they wish to include their children during their pet's final goodbye, and I support their decision either way.

6 to 12 years old. Children of these ages typically do well in handling an ailing pet's final goodbye. They understand that death is permanent and that their pet won't return to them. They often tenderly want to participate in making the preparations, such as writing letters to their pet, choosing their pet's last treats, making a cake, and selecting music.

Brooks, Jane, Clara, and their mom Connor say goodbye to Thriller together.

They also ask the best questions during my visit. I have been asked: "Where does she go after?" (*I'm not totally sure, but one thing I know without a doubt is that she will live forever in your heart.*) "Will he visit me tonight in my dreams?" (*He may visit your dreams. Sometimes we remember our dreams when we wake up, but sometimes we forget them. So even if you don't remember your dream, it still may mean he visited your dream.*) "How will you know for sure she is dead—can she come back to life?" (*I will listen for the silence of her heart and the silence of her breathing. This means her dying is done, and she cannot come back to life.*) "Can I keep his tail?" (*If you keep his tail, it will change and not be as nice as it was before, so it's better to let him keep it. Plus, he needs it—how will he wag in heaven* [or I'll say—*how will he wag in your dreams?*]) "Are you allowed to do this?" (*Veterinarians are allowed to help end the dying process in animals who are very sick or suffering and who cannot be healed.*) "Can she keep her eyes open during it so we can look at each other?" (*The first medicine I give makes her relaxed and sleepy, so her eyes may not stay open. But she will be able to hear you, so she would like to hear your voice, even if her eyes are closed.*)

Children don't sugarcoat things, so I usually answer them just as directly, and they seem to appreciate it. If they are eager to help me, I may also encourage them to hold my stethoscope, help collect fur keepsakes, and make a clay paw print.

Teenagers. I personally struggle with this age group the most during euthanasia visits. They usually have strong reservations about the reasons for euthanasia and often believe we're giving up when more could be done to help their pet. I highly encourage parents to allow their teens to take part in their pet's caregiving and hospice care long before the euthanasia appointment. This helps them better understand and witness their pet's struggles and decline. Ask teenagers to do their pet's quality of life assessments with you. Talk about the disease and its progression and how it affects the pet. Giving teens more information about their pet's illness and getting them involved in their pet's care sooner helps them better accept why and when it's time to say goodbye.

Explaining what happens to the cat's body

If you plan cremation for your cat, you may wish to explain to children that the cat's body will go to a pet farewell center where the body will be cared for and become a powdery sand called ashes. You may describe that the cat's body turns to ashes after being placed in an intensely heated room (cremation) or by using special heated water (aquamation). Let children know that the cat's body cannot feel this. Tell them you will receive the cat's ashes (if the family chooses to) and you can decide together whether to keep the ashes at home in a memorial container called an urn, bury them in a pet cemetery or in the backyard, or scatter them (if allowed) in an outdoor area that the cat loved to visit.

If you plan to bury your cat's body in a pet cemetery or other location, explain that the cat's body will carefully and lovingly rest in the ground. Let children know that you will place a memory marker there to honor their cat. And tell them how lovely it will be that grass and other plants will grow there naturally to protect their cat's gravesite. Consider having your children help you choose a native grass or native wildflowers to plant at the gravesite.

Tips that may help children cope with pet loss

I cry a lot when my pets die, and I'm not shy about it. I'm a hot mess! My eyes are puffy and red for days from rivers of tears. My other fur kids seem to know I'm not my usual self and they stick closer to me than they usually do. I make an effort to give them extra affection and attention in return.

A parent's reaction to losing a cat often heavily influences a child's reaction. Keep in mind that some young children may be more upset by their parent's reaction than by the cat's death. It's perfectly acceptable for parents to show grief in their children's presence. Let your children know that you're sad because of the cat's death, in case they may think you're sad because of something they did.

In the years that I've been helping families provide pet hospice care, I've seen many ways parents have involved their children in the process of a pet's passing. Here are a few ideas from those experiences, along with other wonderful suggestions I've read about:

- Invite children to help create their cat's bucket list beforehand, participate in the experiences, and mark them as completed.
- Involve children in their cat's end-of-life care.
- Note time with a visual gratitude marker. Children can place a penny or marble in a vase for every day they share with their cat after a terminal illness is identified.[1]
- Ask the child to write a story about their cat.
- Select a pretty bowl or jar to hold colorful scraps of paper on which family members jot down happy memories or funny moments with their cat. Read these together or separately at any time, especially when a family member feels particularly sad.[1]
- Ask the child to write a letter to God about their cat.
- Suggest that the child create a card for their cat, which can go with the cat for cremation or burial if they wish.
- Keep a battery-powered LED candle flickering next to a favorite photo or drawing of the cat.[1]
- Purchase a customized plush animal made to look like their cat. (**mypetsies.com**)
- Involve children in creating memorial scrapbook pages that include their cat's name, a drawing or photo of their cat, and their reflections on why their cat was special. Children can write what they will miss most about their cat, what silly things their cat used to do, why the cat was their friend, the names of others who loved their cat, and what makes them smile most when they think of their cat.[2]
- Frame original artwork created by the child or a large photograph of the cat to be displayed in the home.[1]

- Customize a blanket or pillowcase with the cat's photograph.
- Craft a keepsake of the cat's collar or bowl.
- Involve children in creating a tribute video or digital slideshow of special moments throughout the cat's life—and also in choosing the background music.[1]
- Paint memorial stones (with acrylic paints) to place on the ground at the cat's gravesite.[3]
- Hold a memorial service.
- Take your children along when you pick up your cat's ashes.
- Involve your children in selecting and planting a native tree or shrub, or native wildflowers or grasses in honor of their cat. Plant them at the cat's gravesite or in a specially selected portion of your yard.

My dear friend and pet loss expert, Collin Ellis, created an activity book for children to help guide them through the journey of loss of a cat. It has many activities they can do before and after the passing of their pet and it can help start conversations with children which many parents struggle with.

Forever Friend Activity Book

READING RECOMMENDATIONS

- Helping Children Cope by Moira Anderson Allen. The Pet Loss Support Page. 2007.
  pet-loss.net/children.shtml
- Explaining Pet Loss to Children by Martha M. Tousley. Grief Healing.
  griefhealing.com/article-explaining-pet-loss-to-children.htm
- Pet Loss Support for Kids. Chance's Spot: Pet Loss and Grief Support.
  chancesspot.org/kids-pet-loss/index.php
- Helping a Child Cope with Pet Loss. Grief Support Center at Rainbows Bridge.
  rainbowsbridge.com/Grief_Support_Center/Grief_Support/Chrildren_and_petloss.htm
- Helping Children Cope with the Serious Illness or Death of a Companion Animal. The Ohio State University Veterinary Medical Teaching Hospital.
  vet.osu.edu/vmc/sites/default/files/import/assets/pdf/hospital/companionAnimals/HonoringtheBond/HelpingChildrenCopeFactSheet.pdf

Books about pet loss for children to read, or to read with children

- *Don't Say Goodbye, Just Say See You!* By Patricia Ann Brill (2015, Functional Fitness LLC).
- *The Fall of Freddie the Leaf (A Story of Life for All Ages)* by Leo Buscaglia (1982, Slack Incorporated).
- *Remembering Baymore* by Peter Gollub (2015, Peter E. Gollub).
- *Staying Strong for Smokey* by Corey Gut. (2017).
- *The Next Place* by Warren Hanson (2002, Waldman House Press).
- *Always Remember* by Cece Meng (2016, Philomel Books).
- *Cry, Heart, But Never Break* by Glenn Ringtved (2016, Enchanted Lion Books).
- *When a Pet Dies* by Fred Rogers (1998, Puffin Books).
- *The Heaven of Animals* by Nancy Tillman (2014, Feiwel & Friends).
- *Children and Pet Loss: A Guide for Helping* by Marty Tousley (2014, Our Pals Pub).
- *Healing a Child's Pet Loss Grief: A Guide for Parents* by Wendy Van de Poll (2016, Center for Pet Loss Grief LLC).
- *The Tenth Good Thing about Barney* by Judith Viorst (1987, Atheneum Books for Young Readers).
- *My Pet Died: A Coloring Book for Grieving Children* by Alan D. Wolfelt (Center for Loss & Life Transition).

CHAPTER 34:

Housemates: Furry family members who lose their furry friends

> Help your brother's boat across, and your own will reach the shore.
>
> — Hindu proverb

Families who schedule euthanasia for a cat often ask me, "Should my other pet be present during the euthanasia?" And I usually tell them, "Let's let that pet decide." If the other pet is unlikely to disturb or disrupt the family or the process for the pet who is earning their wings, then I think it's acceptable to have them present, for as much as they wish to be.

I have been amazed by the variety of reactions from other pets in the home during a euthanasia of their "sibling." Reactions range from curious sniffing and hissing to being oblivious. I have come to realize that some of our furry family members may be similar to us in the variety of ways we react to death and manage grief.

A sibling sniffed Petey after he passed.

Weighing grief in pets: What the studies say

In 1996, the American Society for the Prevention of Cruelty to Animals (ASPCA) conducted a Companion Animal Mourning Project and surveyed pet owners about behavior changes they'd seen in their pets after a companion pet died. Of the dogs who were left behind, many were more vocal (63%) or were quieter than normal, and many became more attached to their caregivers and changed where they slept. Over one-third (36%) of the dogs showed less interest in food, and 11% stopped eating.[2] The cats who were left behind showed similar changes. After a companion cat passed, 46% of the remaining cats ate less, 70% vocalized more, and more than half became more clingy with their humans.[2]

> **SAD, SWEET FACT:**
>
> Elephants, birds, whales, great apes, and dolphins are known to investigate and touch a deceased member of their group. Whales, dolphins, and great apes have been seen physically supporting or carrying the body (often a young animal) for hours to weeks.[1]

Another large survey of pet owners in New Zealand and Australia published in 2016 collected information about 159 dogs and 152 cats who had lost a companion pet. The pets' behaviors that were assessed related to affection, territory, vocalization, eating, and sleeping, among others.[3]

In categorizing the pets' responses to loss, the researchers considered grief as a biological response to separation, which has active and passive phases of behavior responses. Active responses occurred during the first phase after loss and involved pets searching and vocalizing. During the second phase after loss, passive responses involved pets reducing activity and withdrawing from the environment, which help animals conserve energy. Animals search and vocalize, then save energy because they expect to see the missing companion again soon and want to help make sure that happens. For example, when farm animal mothers and their offspring are separated during artificial weaning (separation earlier than weaning would naturally occur), they first attempt to reunite by vocalizing more, then they show altered feeding patterns and stop playing.[3]

Similar to the ASPCA survey, this survey showed that many dogs (61%) and cats (62%) sought more attention from their owners or became more clingy. A few pets (13% of dogs and 16% of cats) sought less attention or avoided contact with their owners. Some dogs (26%) and cats (22%) had no changes in affection. The researchers indicated that changes in pets' affection may be a reflection of:

- the pet's grief, anxiety, or distress;
- less competition for access to the pet owner; or
- having fewer opportunities to interact with the owners (if social interactions were previously sparked by the other pet's presence).[3]

When it came to territory-related behaviors, 30% of dogs and 36% of cats kept checking their deceased companion's favorite spots. A few pets (10% of dogs and 5% of cats) avoided those spots. But 41% of dogs and 37% of cats showed no territory-related behavior changes. In addition, 27% of dogs and 43% of cats vocalized more after the loss of their companion.[3]

The researchers suggested that pets who seek out a deceased companion's favorite spots and those who vocalize more may be experiencing the active phase of grief. Alternatively, they stated that pets who check these spots could also be claiming the newly vacated spot as their own because they don't have to compete for it.[3]

Eating less occurred in 35% of dogs and 21% of cats, and eating slower occurred in 31% of dogs and 12% of cats. The amount of food eaten did not change in 58% of dogs and 67% of cats. Changes in the amount the pets ate or how fast they ate were attributed to either a negative effect of a pet losing their friend, or to less competition for food.[3]

Owners reported that 34% of dogs and 20% of cats slept more. Researchers attributed pets' sleep changes to either the passive phase of grief, or to the pet no longer receiving stimulation from their companion.[3] (No more, "Hi friend, whatcha doin'?" inquiries, or "Hey everyone, someone's at our door!" alerts.)

Some pets had the opportunity to see their deceased companion's body. Of these pets, 78% of dogs and 74% of cats sniffed and investigated their friend's body. But 13% of dogs and 18% of cats showed no interest, and 7% of cats hissed or growled (none of the dogs growled).[3]

Interestingly, the behavioral changes reported for pets who saw their deceased companion didn't differ from the behavioral changes reported for pets who didn't see their deceased friend.[3] To me, this finding suggests that regardless of whether a pet views their deceased friend, if the pet left behind is going to be sad, they will be sad, and if they're going to be neutral, they'll be neutral. It also suggests to me that while it may not necessarily help for a pet to be present during their friend's euthanasia, it probably doesn't hurt either. Although we can't be sure how our pets process the "meaning"

My dog Sam stayed close by when I said goodbye to Herbie.

of such an event, being present during euthanasia or seeing their deceased friend when possible and if appropriate may at least give them an opportunity to learn.

The researchers also mentioned that pets who lose a companion from other types of separation (such as sale, rehoming, relinquishment to a shelter) may exhibit many of the same behavior changes. However, they suggested that this type of separation and the behavioral responses to it should be studied separately.[3]

In another survey of more than 400 dog pet parents in Italy, they reported that after the death of one of their dogs, the surviving dog showed changes in sleeping, eating, playing, and fearfulness.[1] The amount of time the dogs had spent together didn't affect the surviving dogs' behaviors. The researchers indicated that changes in the surviving dogs may be related to grief and their owners' emotions. They concluded that the surviving dogs exhibited separation stress after losing their companion dog rather than responding to the death itself, and that more research is needed to confirm whether dogs exhibit grief.[1] No information about cats was included in this survey, but I mention it here because few studies have been published on grief in pets, and because it's reasonable to consider that surviving dogs may show similar responses after they lose a companion cat. For example, in the 2016 survey I described above, whether the surviving pet was the same species as the deceased companion affected only one behavior change: dogs who had lost a companion dog were more likely to eat slower than dogs who had lost a companion cat. In addition, whether the surviving pet was the same or a different species as the deceased pet did not affect the amount of time that the survivor's behavior changes occurred.[3]

Handling pets who experience loss of a companion pet

Even with the limited data from published surveys and my wealth of experiences with my patients families' and my own pets, I'm still unsure whether it helps for other pets to be present when their companion passes. Pets have jumped into my car before I drive away with their friend, pets have lain

Enzo was curious and sniffed at Dwayne's body after he passed.

on top of their friend during the euthanasia, and pets have stepped over their friend as if they didn't notice a difference after their friend passed. But after helping thousands of multi-pet families, I don't think it hurts for other pets to be present. This is why I let the furry friends decide.

In my experience with my patients' families, the pet who is left behind exhibits behavior changes within the first day or two after the loss of their friend, and the changes usually last about two weeks. And I often wonder whether some of the pet's behavior changes occur in response to the owner's grief. In my household I have not noticed a big difference in any of my pets after the loss of a companion pet. However, almost all of them gave me more attention, as if they sensed my grief and knew I needed extra love. I especially remember that when I lost my dog Serissa, I was very sad and depressed and cried a lot for a few days. During that time, all three of my cats laid on me, head-butted me, and just stayed close to me at least twice as much as they normally did.

Yoda (the calico on the left) comforting her friend Teazie.

For pets who exhibit behavior changes and seem to be grieving, conflicting advice on how to help abounds. Recommendations range from sticking to regular routines and refraining from giving the pet extra attention to switching up their routines and providing extra attention. In my experience, giving the pet extra love and attention is never a bad thing. You can try new games, food treats, catnip (for crestfallen cats), and adding walks (for doleful dogs or for cats who are accustomed to walks), or perhaps car rides (if your pet is happily engaged by these). Changing their daily routine a bit may also help, such as taking them for a walk in the late morning instead of in the early morning and feeding them in a different location. The number and types of changes you can comfortably make in familiar routines depends on your pet's health status and age, because as I've mentioned in many other chapters, sticking to routines is beneficial for many senior pets and may be especially important for pets who have cognitive dysfunction.

Calming measures such as pheromone sprays or collars (like Adaptil for dogs or Feliway for cats) may help. Keep the deceased pet's items—such as bedding, bowls, toys, and leashes—in their usual locations for a while. Some pet parents have told me they have placed the deceased pet's collar on the remaining pet and it seemed to help the pet relax.

The bottom line is that the mechanisms that may help a pet adjust to losing their companion and the length of time it takes to adjust will likely be highly individual for each pet. I have no doubt that animals are sentient beings and possess emotions that we may never be able to explain. Anticipating their reactions when another pet passes is definitely worth consideration.

Welcoming a new furry friend

What about bringing a new friend into the family? I believe it's good to first give the whole family time to grieve and adjust to the loss of their friend. When the remaining pet's anxiety has subsided, appetite has improved, and sleeping pattern is normal—and when all human family members agree that everyone is ready—then I think filling the void may be helpful to everyone. Alternatively, consider making play dates with other pets in the neighborhood or with your friends, or perhaps fostering a pet first. Even just a little activity with another animal or different people may bring sparks of joy back into your pet's life.

 READING RECOMMENDATIONS

- How Animals Grieve by Karissa Bennett. Colorado State University College of Veterinary Medicine.
  vetmedbiosci.colostate.edu/vth/animal-health/how-animals-grieve/
- Do Pets Grieve? Grief Support Center at Rainbows Bridge.
  rainbowsbridge.com/Grief_Support_Center/Grief_Support/Do_Pets_Grieve.htm

CHAPTER 35:

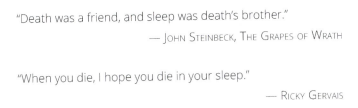

Natural passing: What to expect

"Death was a friend, and sleep was death's brother."
— John Steinbeck, The Grapes of Wrath

"When you die, I hope you die in your sleep."
— Ricky Gervais

I know exactly how I want the passing of each of my pets to go when they pass with my help, and each experience will be unique to them. I always want to be there, making sure they have all the comforts I can provide. Most importantly, I want them to know I am there with them—loving them and thanking them for their love and companionship.

Another part of me wishes that my pets would pass on their own so I don't have to make that decision. And I know many pet parents wish the same thing. They often tell me, "I just want my pet to die peacefully in his sleep."

That is also how I'd like to die—sleeping and dreaming of something great after having had a wonderful dinner with a stack of Oreos to top off the night; to not know I'm dying and to not feel anything. Perhaps you have a similar wish for yourself.

Pondering that final wish

Most of us will die as a result of a disease or an accident or other trauma. We may be able to choose to die at home or in a hospital or a hospice facility. Some people choose assisted death, which is allowed in a few states and countries that have right-to-die laws. Depending on the circumstances, death may be painless and peaceful, or it may be painful and distressing. Euthanasia, which is deliberately and painlessly ending someone's life to relieve suffering, isn't available and is illegal for people in the United States. But for our pets, euthanasia is acceptable, available, and legal. Yet many pet parents wish for their pet's natural passing instead—as long as it occurs without suffering. Many people don't realize that natural passing doesn't always occur quickly or without pain or suffering.

Pet parents occasionally call me for hospice services and tell me they're against euthanasia for a variety of reasons; they believe only in natural passing for their cat. I understand and respect these families' requests for their cats, and I want to make sure each cat's needs are met. Pain and suffering must be mitigated to the best of our ability. I think, and I hope, that most pet parents wouldn't want their cat to suffer, whether they agree with euthanasia or not.

For cats to not endure suffering, pet parents must be able to accurately recognize and acknowledge the signs of pain, anxiety, or suffering in their cats. Sometimes these signs are subtle. Pet parents may also not understand that their cat has a disease that will take years before death to occur naturally and, in that time, their cat suffers if the effects of the disease are not adequately managed. An example is cats who have arthritis and severe dental disease. Walking and chewing may be terribly painful, but that doesn't mean their organs will fail and death will occur.

Properly understanding the disease or condition your cat has, what can be done to treat the disease or relieve the signs, as well as what occurs during the death process will help you determine the best options for your cat and you.

Preparing for a cat's death

Regardless of whether euthanasia or natural passing is chosen, I encourage all owners of geriatric cats or cats who have a terminal illness to make these preparations:

- Learn the signs of the disease or condition your cat has, and understand the effects it has or will have in your cat.
- Know the signs of pain and anxiety in your cat so you can promptly determine how to alleviate them. Your veterinarian or hospice veterinarian can prescribe pain and anti-anxiety medications appropriate for you to give your cat or have on hand, and give guidance on how to administer them. Talk with your veterinarian about the medical concerns you have.
- Know that pet hospice and palliative care in your home is an option during the final weeks or days of your cat's life.
- Consider all methods to mitigate suffering. Although further studies are needed, acupuncture has been reported to help ease pain, tiredness,

insomnia, nausea, dyspnea (difficulty breathing), and anxiety in human hospice patients,[1-4] and it could bring comfort to your cat in their final days. In addition, for people with advanced cancer who experience prolonged shortness of breath, a fan blowing on the face, music therapy, acupuncture, and acupressure are suggested as helpful non-drug additions to the medical treatments these patients receive.[4] Breathing exercises, spiritual interventions, and cognitive behavioral therapy are also suggested in these patients,[4] but these therapies are less applicable to pets.

- Decide whether you'd like to be present when your cat passes. It's an important decision that some pet parents don't stop to consider. Learn about what occurs during natural death, and keep in mind that it may be difficult to witness. If you don't wish to be present but want someone to be present for your cat, consider asking a family member or friend to be available, or reconsider whether euthanasia may be an appropriate choice.
- Consider the wishes of family members or friends involved in the cat's care. Decide whether and how children will be involved and whether they'll be present when your cat passes.
- Consider how you may want to memorialize your cat, and have the proper supplies on hand (such as clay or ink and paper to make a paw print).
- Research options for handling your cat's body. Will your cat be buried or cremated? Where will your cat's remains rest—at home, in a pet cemetery, or at another location? By taking the time to reflect on this information beforehand, it's easier to act on the desired plan rather than having to choose in the moment.
- Make arrangements for handling your cat's body. Identify a cool (below 70 F [21 C]) holding area, decide on transportation, and determine what payment will be needed.
- Consider which arrangements may need to change and how to handle those if your cat passes during the night.
- Try to avoid leaving your cat alone during the final days.
- Learn about the natural stages of dying. It's important to know what changes your cat may exhibit.
- Learn about the changes in a cat's body that occur after death so you're prepared.
- Continue to give love and attention to other furry family members.
- Take care of yourself. Try to get adequate sleep and good nourishment. Ask for help and take time out as needed.
- And remember, if you decide you no longer want a natural death for your cat, you can change your mind. Natural does not mean it will be painless

or nontraumatic to witness. Veterinary in-home or in-clinic euthanasia should remain options. (Keep information on hand for in-home veterinary hospice and euthanasia services, veterinary emergency clinics, and your primary care veterinary practice in case you decide that you no longer want your cat to experience a natural death.)

Keep the unexpected in mind

With natural passing, you won't know exactly when it will happen. So you need to be prepared for the fact that you may not be there when your cat passes, or that it may happen at an inopportune time. Your cat may pass in his sleep or while you're at work. He may pass when you are sitting down to have dinner, or when you're getting your kids ready for school.

Also consider whether being present when your cat passes is your priority, which in-home euthanasia can provide. If you want to be present when your cat dies and are not, this may leave an emotional scar. I have learned that most pet owners want to be with their cats during euthanasia, but many do not want to be present when their cat passes naturally.

An example of the truly unexpected: During the COVID-19 pandemic, many veterinary clinics didn't allow pet owners to come into the clinic to be with their pets during euthanasia. These were agonizing situations for the pet parents and the veterinary teams. So given unprecedented circumstances like this, even if you want to be present and schedule an in-clinic euthanasia or take your cat to an emergency service for euthanasia, it's possible you may not be able to be present. I mention this in the hopes of helping you be prepared for and accept that such circumstances could arise.

The natural death process

Understanding the dying process for your cat and being aware of what you and your family may experience is essential. What happens to the cat naturally in those final days and hours are especially important to consider. The natural dying process has many stages that manifest in different ways as the end of a cat's life approaches.

If your cat still has an appetite or is thirsty, then, of course, continue to provide this support. Don't be alarmed if your cat seems to waste away despite eating a fair amount. His body may no longer fully absorb or process the nutrients normally. Similarly, though he may drink, he may not drink enough to stay hydrated or may become dehydrated because his kidneys are malfunctioning. Keep in mind that it's important to differentiate weight loss and dehydration associated with dying from those signs associated with a treatable illness.

Disinterest in food and water are normal at the end of life. If your cat doesn't want to eat or drink, don't continually place food or water in front of her and don't try to force her to eat or drink. This can cause nausea and other distress. Her body is going through the natural steps of shutting down, and we may cause harm or pain by interfering in this way.

Other changes you may see in your cat as death approaches, and what you can do to help keep your cat as comfortable as possible:

- **Spending time in out-of-the-way locations in your home or seeking to be alone.** Allow your cat to rest where she feels most comfortable. Provide comfy bedding, although keep in mind she may choose not to use it. Keep the environment quiet and calm, and avoid loud noises and lots of activity. Supervise other pets in the household and monitor their interactions with the ailing cat, limiting any interactions if needed. Your pets may prefer to remain close to one another, or they may prefer to stay apart.

Severus's unusual hiding spot

Severus, a 15-year-old orange and white tabby, had been receiving treatment for chronic kidney disease for three years, which included a therapeutic diet and at-home subcutaneous fluid therapy. He also received an appetite stimulant and anti-nausea, analgesic, and other medications as needed, and he would nearly always bounce back to "normal" after receiving this extra supportive care. Over the course of his kidney disease, he also had to stay in the veterinary hospital for a few days on three separate occasions to receive intravenous fluid therapy and supportive medications, after which he would return home and be his usual self again.

These four photos show Severus's change in demeanor despite supportive therapies and intensive care during his final two weeks.

September 20. Severus happily scratches on his usual spot on the deck, getting ready to soak up his daily sun.

September 23. Severus went to his usual spot at his usual dinner time, but his posture clearly shows that he's uncomfortable and feels ill: his head is down, his limbs and tail are tucked in tightly, and his fur is

puffed up. Shortly thereafter he received additional subcutaneous fluid therapy, anti-nausea medication, and an appetite stimulant, and he ate his dinner (a little late) and slept comfortably in his usual sleeping spot in his heated cat bed.

September 27. Severus began resting on the couch, which was unusual for him. So his mom moved his heated cat bed to the couch and placed a space heater nearby. Despite receiving extra at-home supportive care and medications, he wasn't recovering to his "normal" baseline as he usually did, so Severus was hospitalized the next morning for intravenous fluid therapy and diagnostic tests.

October 2. Severus was discharged from the veterinary hospital after receiving four days of intensive care. His blood and urine test results had worsened slightly despite this, so the plan was to continue hospice care at home. He didn't perk up within a few hours after coming home as his pet parents had hoped. He began breathing faster, and his attitude and posture indicated continued discomfort. He chose to hide in a spot he had never rested in or showed interest in before—under a corner bookshelf with a pile of dog toys. His mom placed a small fan and space heater nearby to help keep him comfortable. Severus was euthanized at home that evening, while lying in his mom's lap, getting lots of soothing strokes and reassuring words.

- **Diminished or—on the opposite end—intensified signs of pain associated with the cat's underlying disease.** It's important during this time and until the end to administer pain medications as prescribed by your veterinarian and to consider whether anti-anxiety medications may be needed as well. Talk with your veterinarian about how best and when to administer medications, because in the later stages of dying, swallowing may not be possible. Injectable options are available, or patches can be placed on your cat's skin that deliver medication to give her more comfort.
- **Reduced grooming, then complete lack of grooming in cats.** Light combing or brushing or gentle massage may be acceptable to your pet.
- **Abnormal postures that may look uncomfortable.** Turn your cat every two to four hours or adjust his position as needed if he is too weak to move.
- **Twitching, trembling, and shaking.** Be a reassuring presence.
- **Low body temperature or pale gums.** Keep a warmer room temperature and put a light blanket over your cat—one that doesn't feel too heavy or constrictive of your cat's breathing. Leave your cat's face uncovered.
- **Severe weakness that progresses to little to no movement when awake, then an almost comatose state.** Provide a reassuring presence and quiet environment.
- **Lack of fecal and urine control and no attempt to move away from the soiled area or groom themselves.** Place puppy pads under your cat and help keep her clean and dry by removing soiled pads and gently washing soiled fur and skin.

As time passes, cats will begin to display more drastic changes that lead to the moments right before they pass. These changes are often more difficult to witness than you might anticipate, and they can last for several hours. But it can be helpful to expect that they may occur. They include:

- complete unresponsiveness;
- lack of blinking; their eyes may seem blank and dull;
- restlessness or agitation;
- seizures;
- stretching of their limbs;
- backward arching of their neck or head;
- evacuation of their bowels or bladder;
- vocalization;
- twitching, tremors, or paddling;
- complete lack of movement; and
- long gaps between breaths, progressing to gasping breaths, and then no breathing.

Considerations for the family during the dying process

When the time comes and a cat is passing, it can be difficult to remember what you should be doing. It can be helpful to take a little time to remind yourself and those around you of what you wanted to do during the dying process:

- Continue to talk to your cat and comfort him. Hearing is one of the last senses to fade.
- Don't move your cat if possible. He may react, or it may be distressing or painful.
- Be as present and calm as possible. Focus on the love of your furry family member.
- Remember to say or read or do what you and your family members prepared for these moments.
- Leave your cat's collar on if she is used to wearing one. She may feel more comfortable wearing it.
- Excuse yourself and take a breath if you feel overwhelmed in the moment and it's safe for you to do so.
- Breathe, and remember that the dying process is natural. As difficult as it may be to watch your cat in the final stages of dying, don't try to administer CPR to stop your cat from passing, and don't try to hasten your cat's death as he is passing naturally. If your cat seems to be struggling for a prolonged period, consider using a veterinary service for emergency in-home or in-clinic euthanasia.

What happens after a cat passes

After your cat has breathed his or her final breath and is completely at rest, look for the continued absence of breathing. You may also have been able to feel, hear, or see your cat's heart stop beating.

It's helpful to familiarize yourself with other bodily changes that may occur after a cat has passed. This way you can manage your and others' expectations and be respectful of your cat's remains. You may notice one or more of these changes:

- voiding of feces (or diarrhea), flatulence, voiding of urine;
- muscles twitching in the face and lips;
- open eyelids;
- open mouth;

- cooling of the body— cat's normal temperature is about 100 F (38 C), so it may take a few hours to cool to room temperature;
- change in the pet's odor;
- fluid discharge from the mouth or nose—whether this occurs often depends on what the cat's ailments were, and the fluid sometimes appears frothy and bloody; and
- progressive stiffening of the limbs and body (rigor mortis)—this typically occurs two to four hours after death in cats, which may vary with the ambient temperature.

What should I do after my cat's death?

After your cat passes, you and others present need to take time—within reason, and with respect to your cat's body—to take care of yourselves. You may want to sit with your cat for a few minutes and continue to talk to her. Then take a moment for yourself, reflect, talk to your friends or family, and do what brings you comfort.

Although you feel grief, you may also feel relief that your cat is no longer feeling the effects of his ailments. A part of your own suffering has been relieved. Allow yourself to experience relief. It's a good and normal emotion.

When you're ready, consider the next steps:

- You may want to allow other family pets or pet friends to see and sniff their deceased friend. Because grief in pets hasn't yet been extensively studied, we don't know precisely how pets process being exposed to a deceased companion. According to one study, seeing a deceased companion does not change the behavior of the pet left behind.[5] However, we also don't know whether being present gives pets an opportunity to learn, so we may not want to deny them that opportunity.
- If you planned to make a clay or ink paw print, it is easier to obtain before your cat's body has stiffened. You may want to trim your cat's toenails and fur between the paw pads if needed to provide a better imprint.
- Remove your cat's collar if you would like to keep it.
- Get help moving your cat if you need assistance.
- To contain body fluids and help preserve your cat's body, place her inside a thick plastic bag or wrap her in a blanket, and then place her in a plastic container.
- Move your cat's remains to the appropriate place in preparation for cremation or burial, such as a box, bag, or basket, before rigor mortis has occurred. If stiffness sets in, you may have difficulty placing her in the carrier you've chosen.

- Place your cat in a cool location and chill his body if possible to delay natural decay, which can happen quickly, especially in warmer climates.
- Inform the chosen crematorium or other service who will pick up your cat's body.
- As soon as you feel comfortable, call or write and inform your primary care veterinary practice (and referral hospital, if applicable) that your cat has passed away. The veterinary team will appreciate your sharing the news of your cat's passing with them. It also allows the team to update your cat's medical records and will prevent you from receiving health-care reminders for your cat who has passed.

As difficult as this process may be for you and your loved ones, remember to be kind to yourself and those around you. Prepare as much as possible, but give yourself a break during the extremely difficult moments. It's normal to feel and display a wide range of emotions.

Neo's passing

The day after Thanksgiving in 2010, I went to help a family in Fort Lauderdale, Florida, who requested in-home euthanasia for their cat. They were so grateful that I was working during the holiday weekend. I always say to myself on holidays, and in the middle of the night, and during hurricanes, that death doesn't avoid holidays, wait for a more convenient time, or care about the weather. The appointment went smoothly for the family, and their cat passed peacefully with my help. On the drive back afterward, I reflected on the comfort I had provided for the cat and the family. And as I got closer to home, my thoughts turned to my ailing dog Neo and what to make for his dinner. He had advanced cancer, and at that stage in his illness, he was receiving

 Neo was a pro in his confined area when I had to leave the house.

palliative care and I was feeding him home-cooked meals to entice him to eat better.

Whenever I needed to leave Neo for a few hours, I had to put him in a hallway blocked off with a baby gate and cover the floor with towels in case he urinated—a frequent problem associated with his illness. I hated confining him. But he didn't seem to mind as long as I gave him his squeaky toys, which he happily played with, including that afternoon when I left. And he always eagerly pranced at the gate, happily welcoming me when I got home.

When I returned home and opened the front door that afternoon, silence greeted me. No clicking of Neo's toenails. He wasn't prancing. I thought, "Maybe he's sleeping and didn't hear the door." I felt a slight pang of anxiety as I rounded the corner to look down the hallway.

There was Neo, lying on the floor. I knew immediately that he was not asleep. His handsome body was lifeless. His long legs were outstretched and stiff. Feces and urine were spread over his hind end and on the floor behind him. His eyes were open, completely dull and blank. My heart clenched and seemed to drop into my gut. The shock of his death washed over me, and I sank to my knees and screamed his name.

I had not been prepared for Neo to leave me this way. It was not what I wanted for my boy. I had thought about and planned for his passing. It was going to be in the early evening, when the temperature was a bit cooler so we could be outside. He would have a bowl of ice cream with whipped cream on top. (He loved to share my sundaes!) I would give him a ton of kisses and snuggles to make sure he knew how much I loved him as he sailed forth into his next adventure. That was my perfect scenario for Neo to pass. But now, here he was. Alone, in the hallway, covered in feces. No treats. No farewell love. No feeling of calm. I was devastated for him.

I will always regret not helping Neo to pass peacefully sooner. Now, whenever I think for a second that I wish Mother Nature would take one of my pets, I remember that moment when I found Neo. And I start to plan for a euthanasia instead.

Questions to ask your veterinarian

- What measures (such as pain and anti-anxiety medications, acupuncture, massage) will be most beneficial, given my cat's underlying condition, in the days leading up to my cat's passing?
- What options are available to administer the medications my cat needs?
- Do you offer telemedicine or video conferencing services so I may check in with you if I have questions or concerns while I'm supporting and monitoring my cat?

- What are my options during or after regular business hours for in-home or in-clinic euthanasia services?
- Do you have suggestions for aftercare of my cat's body? Do you have a pet cemetery or cremation service you recommend?

 READING RECOMMENDATIONS ON HUMAN MORTALITY

- *Being Mortal: Medicine and What Matters in the End* by Atul Gawande (2014, Picador).
- *A Beginner's Guide to the End: Practical Advice for Living Life and Facing Death* by BJ Miller and Shoshana Berger (2019, Simon & Schuster).

CHAPTER 36:

Euthanasia: The ending is what matters most

"It's not that I'm afraid to die, I just don't want to be there when it happens."

— Kleinman in Death, A Comedy In One Act by Woody Allen

I never considered I would be good at euthanizing animals, and students certainly don't win euthanasia awards in veterinary school. But providing euthanasia requires skills that rival successfully performing many complex surgical techniques. And as odd as it may sound, I'm good at it. I've learned that I love helping families during these heartrending moments. I'm honored to bring care, comfort, pain relief, and love to animals at the end of their lives. But euthanasia comes with challenges—emotional and technical.

When possible, I've always been the one to euthanize my pets. Not all veterinarians can do this for their own pets, and I can understand that. Believe me, I never want to have to say that final goodbye to my pets, just like you. But when I must, I want to be the one to relieve their struggles and usher them into their next adventure. I know I'll make the last day for each of my pets a really good day, and their last moments will be those of looking at the face of their friend— me. My goal is for every pet to have a really good last day with their family, and to be surrounded by their family's faces and love at the end.

It's helpful for pet parents to better understand the euthanasia process. This knowledge may bring some peace and reassurance to those struggling with or afraid to make this decision. It may provide answers to lingering questions for those who have gone through a pet's euthanasia. In this chapter I'll share important considerations for you in relation to the euthanasia process—whether you experience it with your pet in the veterinary clinic or at home.

The Day

Of course for pet parents, there is no true good day, ever, to lose a pet. But we can do our best to make our pet's last day a good one. Our pets certainly deserve that whenever possible.

Families usually don't think about planning euthanasia for their pets. Most of us tend to delay it for as long as we can. About a quarter of the families who contact Lap of Love Veterinary Hospice schedule their pet's euthanasia on the same day, and about half schedule it for within 48 hours. While this time frame is often understandable and not unreasonable, I encourage families who do have time to plan ahead, to think about and plan for several things in order to make their pet's last day as good as possible.

Start by asking yourself some important questions, then talk with your veterinarian in advance to learn what options are available to you. Where would you like to say goodbye to your pet? In the veterinary hospital? At home? Which room at home? At a park? In your backyard? What time of day? Can your veterinarian accommodate your wishes?

If you prefer to say goodbye to your pet at the veterinary clinic, what are the clinic's business hours? If a veterinarian comes to your home or meets you at a park, at what times are they available and what is the additional fee? If your veterinarian does not make house calls, do they recommend an in-home euthanasia service such as Lap of Love? What happens if you book an appointment and want to cancel? Will there be a fee?

When

All of us at Lap of Love fully understand how difficult the decision to euthanize a pet is. I've pulled into families' driveways and saw them peeking out through their blinds, and then my mobile phone rings because they've called to tell me "we just can't," and they cancel the visit. I usually ask them if I may still come in to say hi to their pet. I offer to assess their pet and discuss hospice care and help with assessing the pet's life quality. I want to make sure their pet isn't suffering. But Lap of Love never charges a cancellation fee. We understand. We know that doubt can be overwhelming, and we want to support the family as best as we can. Some say our policy is a bad business practice, but the gratitude we receive in such situations is payment enough.

Some pet parents want to schedule their pet's euthanasia on a weekend so they can have more time to spoil their pet and have other family members present. Some have to say goodbye during the week because their pet's decline hastens. Many families tell me they want an appointment first thing in the morning so they can "get it over with." That may sound harsh, but usually their pet is struggling and the family doesn't want to wait another hour to relieve their pet's discomfort, or they may want to avoid prolonging their own dread and anxiety about the appointment.

Conversely, some pet parents want to schedule for the last appointment of the day so they know they shared every possible second with their pet. I remember one woman who wanted an appointment toward the end of the day, but before dark. She told me she did not want to immediately be left alone in the dark, and that she needed to have at least an hour afterward, before sunset.

I always do my best to schedule according to the family's wishes. This is why it's a good idea for families to start thinking about The Day, especially before it becomes last minute. Then you can plan to make your pet's last day a good last day.

If you can plan ahead (even if it is within a day), and if your pet has had a veterinary exam within the past 12 months, your veterinarian should be able to pre-prescribe medications you can give your pet at home before the euthanasia appointment. Medications can help alleviate your pet's pain or anxiety, especially if you're planning to travel to the veterinary hospital for your pet's euthanasia. Depending on their medical conditions, pets often experience pain or nausea toward the end of life. Giving a veterinary-prescribed analgesic or anti-nausea drug can ease the experience of getting cats into their carriers and riding in the car. If your cat tends to be aggressive when around other people or in unfamiliar situations, your veterinarian can prescribe a mild sedative to take the edge off. Contact your veterinarian to ask whether your cat can receive one or more of these medications.

Also think ahead about the memorial items you wish to obtain before your cat's passing, whether it's photos, videos, a lock of fur, or a paw print or nose impression. Pre-planning ensures that you capture all the mementos you want.

After your cat is gone, the last thing you may want to have to decide is what you wish to do with your pet's body. This is a personal decision, and it's helpful to decide ahead of time.

Preplanning for prescriptions

Your pet will need to have been seen by your veterinarian within the last 12 months in order for your veterinarian to legally prescribe medication for your pet. This is a requirement of the Veterinary Practice Act in most states. I mention this because in January 2022, I partnered with VetSuccess (a veterinary practice metrics analysis company) to evaluate data from more than 837,000 pets who were euthanized. The data revealed that over 50% of pets had not been seen by their veterinarian during the final 12 months of their lives. So in addition to not receiving veterinary evaluation to determine whether other potential therapies would've been beneficial during their final months, these pets didn't have the option to have medications prescribed before their euthanasia appointment if needed. It's beneficial—for many reasons—for your pet to receive a veterinary examination at least once a year, including when they're nearing the end of their life.

Who

All who wish to be present for the pet's euthanasia are more than welcome. But some pet parents or family members don't want to be there. Again, I respect the family's wishes. I've been left alone with pets for euthanasia, and I've been a guest at a pet's final block party! There is no "right" number of people. What is best is the pet's comfort. And the pet loves their family most!

Some pet parents who can't imagine not being with their pet during euthanasia harshly judge those who don't want to be present. Even some veterinary professionals harbor negative feelings toward pet parents who don't want to be present. But a clear distinction exists between those who don't care to be present because they don't care much for the pet and those who can't bear to be present for their pet's death. In either case, it doesn't matter to me because I'll be there to give the pet lots of love and kisses. For the pet whose owner seems indifferent—and those cases are rare—I get a chance to give that pet extra love. However, many pet parents cannot bear to witness the death of their pet. I understand and accept their position without judgment. They love their pet.

I remember one pet parent, Elizabeth, who couldn't bear to be present during her dog's euthanasia. She also asked that her dog be laid to rest in a special place in her backyard on that day. And she didn't want to return home until after the burial.

I had known Elizabeth for many years and I knew this dog was her whole world. I knew the dog had had a wonderful life. But when it came time, Elizabeth wanted to kiss her dog goodbye and leave.

And so she did.

I was alone with her beloved dog, gently stroking, hugging, kissing, and talking to her as she took her final breaths. I continued stroking and softly speaking to her for several minutes afterward, ensuring her transition was as beautiful as she was.

After the burial, I called Elizabeth to tell her she could come home.

She barely squeaked out her tiny reply, "OK."

Typically, all the family members in the household are present. I love this because I hear stories, I see tears, and I feel the love they have for their pet. I'm thankful for that emotional boost that helps me do this bittersweet work. I'm gratified to witness how much the pet was loved.

Deciding who will be present for a pet's euthanasia is deeply personal. No one should judge you if you can't be present. No one should judge you if you want to be the only one there. No one should judge you if you want to throw a festive neighborhood party. No final farewell playbook exists. Find a veterinarian who will help you achieve the best experience possible.

If you're unable to be present for your pet's euthanasia because of work, school, vacation, or another conflict, ask to attend via a video conference. Once when I was traveling to speak at a conference, my cat Lilu who had diabetes and

I got to tell Lilu I loved her and be with her by video chat during her goodbye.

had been successfully managed with insulin and diet, suddenly got very sick. We learned that she had a severe urinary tract infection that had spread to her kidneys. And although she had the best care at a specialty veterinary hospital, Lilu took a sudden turn for the worse and she stopped producing urine, which meant her kidneys had shut down.

Lilu's condition was life-threatening and irreversible. I was taking a cross-country flight and would not make it home in time. So my wonderful colleague and friend who also provides in-home veterinary euthanasia services picked Lilu up from the speciality clinic and took Lilu back home for her goodbye. My friend video-called me, and there was Lilu on my bed, surrounded by her furry siblings. I talked to Lilu, and I got to see her get her angel wings.

Where

Determining the location for a pet's euthanasia is also a personal choice, but your options may be limited by your pet's ailment or the weather. I believe that pets love their home, and whenever possible, we should try to honor that and say

Dr. Danya says goodbye to her cat Bumble (lying on the couch). Buca, the white and black kitty, was Bumble's rescue mate and close friend. Buca rested his head on Bumble during Bumble's final moments and kept one paw on mom. Katharine Hepburn, the longhaired kitty, climbed on mom's lap to join them. Allowing housemate pets to be near can help them and other family members say goodbye to their friend.

goodbye where they are most comfortable. I have been called to help pets earn their angel wings in thousands of living rooms, hundreds of master beds, many backyards, and a few parks. I have also delivered pets' sendoffs on beaches, under a grand piano, beneath a pool table, in the back of a car at the conclusion of a pet's final joy ride, and on a sailboat!

Daisy's rock-a-bye walk

I experienced an unusual situation with Daisy, a shih tzu who had severe cognitive dysfunction. Daisy lived with her pet parents in a lovely single-story condominium with a small porch that overlooked a gorgeous lake. Daisy's mom was retired and spent nearly every waking moment caring for Daisy. They had a toddler playpen in the living room with all of Daisy's necessities inside so Daisy would be safe if they were not home—which was quite possibly never more than 30 minutes at a time.

Daisy's mom was terribly distraught at the thought of losing Daisy, and the moment I walked into the home, I sensed that her anxiety hit the ceiling. I did all I could do to reassure and calm her, but I soon realized that this would be how her body and mind would handle this moment.

She was standing, holding Daisy in her arms and rocking back and forth, which appeared to comfort her a bit. It seemed to soothe Daisy, too.

I gently asked where she wanted to say goodbye. Her anxiety spiked again. Frantic, she looked around the house—at the playpen, the couch, the patio, and the couch again. Then she looked at me and implored, "I just don't want to have one spot in this house where I look and think, 'That's where she died.'"

She hesitated for a moment and then asked, "Can you just do it with her in my arms, while I stand and maybe walk around a little? This is what we do every night before she goes to bed, and it calms her down."

That request was a first for me. But Daisy was comfortable and her mom seemed certain. I couldn't think of one good reason against it.

So I agreed. "Yes, I can do that."

Daisy's mom's shoulders instantly relaxed, and calmness settled across her wide eyes and tense jaw as her anxiety diminished. I gently asked Daisy's dad to sign the necessary consent paperwork.

I gave Daisy a dab of peanut butter to distract her while I injected a small amount of sedative under her skin. She looked back at me for a second, and then turned forward to continue licking the peanut butter.

Her mom held her and started walking around the living room and into the kitchen. Daisy slowly began to relax and snooze in her favorite place—mom's arms. When I knew Daisy was completely asleep, I told her mom I needed to perform the next step and give the euthanasia solution. Typically I inject it into a leg vein, but other injection sites are acceptable, and I decided to use a different one for Daisy that would allow her mom more time for their final walk.

I asked her mom to stand still for a few seconds, and I injected the final medication into Daisy's liver. Daisy still snoozed comfortably in her mom's arms.

I said, "OK, I gave her the medication. It will now travel slowly to her brain and let her drift off to her final rest. You can walk around as much as you want."

Daisy's mom started to cry, then turned away from me and started back on her path—around the living room, into the kitchen, and back around the living room. She spoke softly to Daisy the whole time.

Finally, she stopped at the sliding glass door and looked out at the lake, gently rocking back and forth, quietly saying sweet things to her little Daisy as she left her world for the next one with a full heart and mind.

Once you decide on a location, make sure it's comfortable for your pet and for you. Does it allow easy access for you to love on your pet? Will the veterinarian be able to perform the procedure? In some cases it may be difficult to say goodbye exactly where you hoped or planned to, especially if your pet is too sick to move. It's best to leave your pet where he or she is most comfortable, even if it's not perfect for you. Your pet's comfort is paramount—your plans and desires come second.

 Goblin on his last day, in his favorite bed with his toys.

If you'd like to choose a public location, select a time of day when it will be the least occupied to provide the fewest distractions for your pet and the most privacy for you. Consider the weather, too, because extreme heat or cold makes everyone uncomfortable, and you want to ensure everyone's comfort—especially your pet. Choose a spot that is sufficiently far from the usual traffic for that time of day and one that allows easy access to your car to transport your pet back to your vehicle afterward. Bring your cat's bed, a blanket, or a basket that will help you carry your pet.

In the veterinary hospital

It's still most common for pet parents to say their final goodbyes to their pets in the veterinary clinic. Some clinics have a comfort room that's used only for pet euthanasia. It makes the experience a little more comfortable and less clinical.

If you say goodbye to your cat at the veterinary hospital, feel free to bring your cat's bed, favorite toy, treats, and other familiar comfort items—perhaps a shirt recently worn by a family member who can't be present. I often suggest that other pets ("siblings") accompany the family to the clinic, if feasible. They, too, are losing a friend. They may also help calm and reassure their friend in their final moments. They will also most certainly provide comfort for the family. The hospital team will support you and will understand that you want to make your pet as comfortable as possible.

 One example of a comfort room at a veterinary clinic.

What about feeding and medicating my pet?

If your cat still has an appetite, then they can eat anything they'd like, including any table food they want on the day you say goodbye. Fish, steak, chicken, bacon, hamburger, ice

 Bumble enjoys the warmth of the sun and a cushy blanket on his last day, along with a bit of fresh catnip and clover with Temptations cat treats mixed in.

Rockstar enjoys ice cream while the family says goodbye.

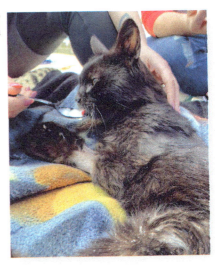

cream, whipped cream, or whatever special treat delights them!

Also give your pet their regularly scheduled medications for that day—whether they're medications to treat pain, anti-anxiety pills, anti-seizure medications, insulin, or others. Your pet's medications won't interfere with the euthanasia process.

The euthanasia process

The process by which veterinarians euthanize pets varies, and there are big differences in some countries compared with the United States. One crucial component is required in all techniques: that veterinarians do not induce suffering.

Sedation

At most veterinary hospitals in the United States, your pet will receive a sedative before the veterinarian gives the euthanasia solution. The level of sedation can vary from mildly drowsy but still alert, to deep anesthesia. If the euthanasia solution is delivered by injecting it into a vein, sedation is not required, but I highly suggest the pet be sedated anyway. It's comforting for all involved to thoroughly relieve a pet's pain and anxiety before we say goodbye. Innumerable times, once their pet is sedated, pet parents have told me, "This is the best sleep he has had in days," or "She seems so comfortable now."

Comfort is the primary benefit of sedation. It also provides a transitional state between being awake and being gone. I believe it's difficult for anyone to see an awake, alert pet one moment and a lifeless pet the next moment. Even as a veterinarian performing euthanasia, I struggle with that. Sedating the pet first provides an intermediate stage that is emotionally gentler for everyone involved.

The sedation injection is usually a combination of an analgesic to relieve pain and a mild sedative to bring relaxation and drowsiness. The injection can be given in a muscle (usually in the rear leg or back), in the subcutaneous tissue (under the skin, like most vaccines), or in a vein. I give the sedation injection in a back muscle or under the skin. The body location, or route of administration, that I choose is based on the patient's body condition and position. By

 I'm reassuring Kaiba, who has been comfortably sedated, before I give the euthanasia injection.

giving the medication under the skin or in a muscle rather than in a vein, the medication more slowly takes effect—usually over a few minutes. This prevents a sudden change from the pet being awake to instantly falling asleep, which can be startling to some pet parents.

Many veterinary teams follow a process in which they take your pet to the hospital's treatment area to place an indwelling intravenous catheter in their leg, and then bring your pet back to the room to be with you. Some teams place this catheter in the room with you so your cat doesn't have to be moved. The catheter allows your veterinarian to easily administer the sedative and the euthanasia solution into the vein. When and how the veterinarian gives the sedative may vary depending on a pet's demeanor and degree of discomfort. Some veterinarians inject the sedative under the skin after they've placed the catheter instead of injecting it into the catheter. That way the sedative's effects are more gradual, and your pet will not be drowsy yet when they return your pet to you in the room.

Instead of giving a sedative, some veterinarians give an anesthetic induction agent called propofol, which is given only in a vein. From a medical standpoint, there is nothing wrong with giving propofol, and we use it in pets before many surgeries. But unless propofol is needed for specific medical or behavioral reasons during the euthanasia process, I'm not a proponent of giving pets this medication in place of a sedative that is given under the skin. Administering propofol immediately induces unconsciousness. This happens quickly and can startle some pet parents. Pet parents often think their pets have already passed, and may get upset if the drug's effects aren't carefully explained beforehand. Again, every veterinary hospital has determined which euthanasia protocol works best for them, and using propofol is not wrong. It's simply not my preference to induce unconsciousness so quickly.

If you prefer that your pet stay with you in the room for the catheter placement, you should feel comfortable asking your veterinarian whether this is possible. Your veterinarian will assess the stability of your pet's condition and your pet's demeanor, as well as the circumstances in the room and discuss the options with you. For example, a toddler who pets and pulls on the pet's legs during catheter placement and a parent unwilling to discourage this makes the veterinarian's job hard to do and is unsafe.

Does the sedation hurt? As most of us know from receiving flu shots or giving blood, a needle penetrating the skin can hurt. Pets who are already in pain may have a heightened sensitivity to pain, so a needle stick may hurt when normally it would not bother the pet. Some cats may not feel a thing, while others may flinch, hiss, or growl when the needle goes through the skin or when they feel the medication being injected. This is not a veterinarian's or nurse's lack of skill; it's a normal reaction in many pets. We do our best to avoid it because we never want to inflict pain. But, fortunately, most

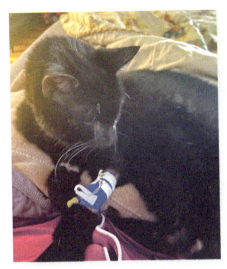

 Bruce has an indwelling intravenous catheter for fluid therapy sessions.

pets don't even notice, especially if they are distracted with a delectable treat. Placing an indwelling catheter also requires piercing the skin with a needle, so it can cause the same reaction, but you won't see that if the pet isn't in the room with you. I do everything in front of the owner, unless they don't wish to be there. I always hope that the pet doesn't react, because I would never want an owner to think I caused their pet a moment of pain. But pets do react to the sedative injection or catheter placement sometimes.

The sedative normally induces a good snooze. Sometimes a pet may still have a blunted awareness. Pets who have respiratory disease or who have a painful condition do not snooze as easily and can be roused. Again, this is normal. And some pets feel really good when the sedation starts to take effect because it's combined with a pain reliever. I've seen pets with incredibly painful hips suddenly be able to get up. And I've seen cats who have had nausea and little interest in food for days mosey to their food bowl. Pet parents sometimes interpret this to mean their pet is telling them, "It's not time." But it's simply a normal bodily reaction to feeling temporarily good. I encourage family members to find comfort in their pets having that moment of comfort.

Although pets are usually calm and comfortable in just a few minutes after one sedation injection, there are times when giving more sedative is needed to achieve a comfortable level of relaxation. So it's not unusual for veterinarians to give two sedation injections.

During my speaking and teaching engagements at veterinary conferences abroad, I learned from veterinarians in European and African countries that they do not routinely give pets sedation before euthanasia. Again, sedation is not a required component of euthanasia if the euthanasia solution is delivered through a vein, so whether sedation is used may simply be a cultural or societal difference.

The euthanasia injection

After the pet is serene and comfortably sedated, it's time to give the euthanasia solution. This injection for euthanasia is an overdose of a barbiturate, an extremely powerful central nervous system depressant. An overdose of this medication travels through the bloodstream to the brain and stops brain function. When the brain activity has stopped, all other bodily functions then stop. I want to assure you that the pet does not have a heart attack, as some people think. The pet simply falls into a deep, irreversible, anesthetic sleep. It's totally painless.

The route by which the euthanasia solution is given varies. It's most commonly injected into a vein. It can be injected through an indwelling intravenous catheter, a butterfly catheter (also known as a butterfly needle), or a syringe attached directly to a needle:

- An indwelling intravenous catheter is a small plastic tube with an injection port and a connector on its external end. The internal end of the catheter is guided into a vein by inserting a needle through the skin and vein. Once the needle and catheter are introduced into the vein, the needle is removed and the catheter remains in place. The catheter is then secured by taping it to the patient's skin. The catheter is not as rigid and sharp as a needle is, so it allows flexibility and patient movement during medication administration, it reduces the likelihood of puncturing the vein during medication administration, and it can remain in the vein for a longer time than a needle can (such as when hospitalized people or pets receive intravenous fluids).
- The butterfly catheter consists of a needle with two attached flexible "wings" and a long, small, flexible tube with a connector on its external end. Although the needle remains in the vein, the wings and long tube allow for more patient movement during medication administration. Because the needle remains in the vein, these catheters are used only temporarily (such as when people donate blood).
- A syringe attached to a needle is simply that, and it can be used to inject a medication directly into a vein, muscle, organ, or body cavity, or injected under the skin. It provides the least flexibility and allows the least amount of patient movement during medication administration.

For my patients, I wait until the pet is sedated and snoozing. Then I locate a good vein for butterfly catheter placement. I place my thumb on the flexible wings to hold the catheter in place and do not need to tape it to the patient's skin.

Regardless of the type of catheter placed or whether it's placed in the pet in the treatment room or in front of you, the pet's veins do not always cooperate. And geriatric pets' veins are very fragile. Often, the vein will "blow." This means that the vein has a tiny rupture whereby blood (and the medication) leak out. Both old age and some medical conditions (such as liver failure or a decrease in the platelet cells that help blood clot) can cause these leaky veins. In some cases, a vein "blows" because it rolls away from the needle as soon as it is pricked, also leaving a tiny, leaky hole and no way to use that vein (until the hole heals, under other circumstances).

If a vein blows, we'll most often try another vein. A butterfly catheter can be placed in a vein in a different leg, in a vein in the pet's paw, or in a vein on the outside of the pet's ear. Veterinarians may need more than one try to access a pet's vein. It can be difficult to do even in healthy animals, but with disease and age, the difficulty triples. If this happens, continue to love up on your pet while your veterinarian proceeds.

If a vein can't be reliably accessed, the veterinarian may choose a different administration route. Or we may prefer a different route based on your pet's condition or demeanor or, as in Daisy's case, based on the situation in the room. Using a route other than a vein is common, and as long as the pet has been adequately sedated beforehand (the pet must be unconscious), using a route other than a vein is approved by the American Veterinary Medical Association. The animal's unconscious state helps ensure that the alternative route injection is painless. I have selected an alternative administration route in all of my own pets. For example, in cats, the most common alternative route is intrarenal administration, which means injecting the euthanasia solution into a kidney. The kidneys are in the abdomen and the veterinarian can feel them along the cat's back behind the ribs. A syringe filled with the euthanasia drug is attached to a small needle that penetrates the skin and is directed into the kidney. It is an easy and quick way to deliver the euthanasia solution. I used this method with my cat Herbie. After injection, the pet usually passes within a minute or two. (Kidneys are harder to feel in dogs than in cats, so I rarely use this method when helping a dog.)

Another alternative administration route is through the liver, which is called intrahepatic injection. Like the kidneys, the liver contains many vessels that shuttle blood to the brain. A syringe with a needle attached is used to penetrate the skin in the pet's midsection below the rib cage, and the euthanasia solution is injected into the liver. With this route, the pet usually takes about 15 minutes to pass. This is the method I used for Daisy.

 I rested next to Serissa as she peacefully passed.

Another route, called intraperitoneal, involves injecting the euthanasia solution into the abdomen—the pet's belly (not the stomach). Because the blood supply differs in the abdomen compared with the blood supply in the organs, intraperitoneal injection takes longer for the pet to pass—usually about 45 minutes. I used this method for my dog Serissa.

An intracardiac route may also be used, which means the euthanasia injection is given directly into the heart. Unfortunately, pet parents are often afraid of this method. But remember, the pet is completely asleep before the injection is given. And keep in mind that veterinarians perform surgery in unconscious pets all the time—surgery that is much more invasive than a small needle penetrating the chest. Also know that the needle itself does not stop the heart. The needle delivers the drug to the heart, where the drug is rapidly carried in the blood to the brain, where it then stops brain function.

I remember using intracardiac injection in Benny, a dog who had end-stage congestive heart failure. His heart disease had caused severe limb and belly swelling, along with liver disease. So his leg veins, abdomen, liver, and kidneys weren't options for delivering the euthanasia drug. And as any veterinarian who has to explain this process to a pet parent knows, this is when our hearts sink because we know intracardiac injection seems odd and can be upsetting to hear. I explained the whole process to the family, starting with the sedation. I told them that after Benny was soundly asleep, I would give the second medication in his chest cavity, where it would go into his heart and travel to his brain, which would stop all body functions. I assured the family that this was the best route for Benny, and I promised he would not feel anything.

True to my word, Benny passed peacefully, with his boxer bestie next to him and his 12-year-old human bestie snuggled in front of him kissing his little black nose as he passed. If Benny were my dog, I wouldn't have done anything differently.

A pet's body's responses during euthanasia

Whichever route we use, the euthanasia medication travels to the pet's brain and stops brain function. Then the pet's breathing stops, and then heart function stops. This usually happens within seconds to a few minutes after brain function has fully stopped. Veterinarians then listen with a stethoscope for a heartbeat, check for a pulse, and also check for a blink reflex by lightly touching the eyelids. When all indicators of life are absent, I say, "Your pet is an angel now."

Euthanasia means "good death"—and it usually is. But some of the body's automatic reflexes or responses may make a pet's passing appear 'not so good' to a pet parent. It's important to know that pets are not suffering when these things occur—they are normal biologic processes. Seeing the body shut down can be difficult, and that's why some people elect not to be present. I think if everyone better understood these natural processes, they wouldn't be as afraid. These same responses occur when a pet passes naturally.

After brain function stops, the body gradually shuts down. I prepare pet owners for two of the body's responses that happen in all pets at the time of passing. First, the bladder relaxes. The bladder wall is muscular and the sphincter that holds urine inside is also a muscle. After one passes, all the muscles relax, including the bladder and sphincter. So if your pet has urine in their bladder, it will leak. This is why we place an absorbable pad under pets before euthanasia. Feces may also pass from the bowel, but this occurs more commonly in pets with diarrhea in the preceding days or who have not defecated in a while.

The second response is that the eyelids remain in a relaxed state. The eyelids require the activity of small muscles to open them wide or to keep them closed. When a pet dies, the eyelids relax, so the eyelids remain half open. You won't be able to keep them closed. This occurs in people, too. It frustrates me to watch scenes in movies when someone runs their hands over a deceased person's open eyes and they stay shut. This is a fallacy. In fact, morticians use glue or other methods to keep a deceased person's eyelids closed for a viewing at a funeral home.

As the body shuts down, other reactions can occur, but they occur so infrequently that I don't wish to frighten pet parents by describing them beforehand. So I don't typically explain them unless their pets exhibit these reactions. Muscles contract, and twitching or tremors may occur as the nerves stop firing and the last electrical impulses leave the muscles. The diaphragm is a large muscle that sits between the abdomen and chest, and when it contracts it forces air from the lungs. And as the brainstem shuts down from lack of oxygen, this may trigger a reflex known as agonal respiration, and it looks like gasping for air. This can startle everyone watching—even myself. Please know that this is not the pet breathing. The jaw muscles also relax at death, and when the air is forced from the lungs, the jaw drops and it looks like a gasp. If this happens, it usually occurs within the first two minutes after the heart has stopped. And it invariably happens after I have declared that the pet is an angel! This raises pet parents' doubts and they sometimes don't believe me.

Very rarely, during the sedation process or right before the pet passes, the pet has a seizure. This has happened to animals I have euthanized only three times in 10 years, but when it does, it's upsetting to everyone. No definitive reason is known, but in people these seizures may be related to lack of oxygen or glucose as the brain shuts down, and it may occur in response to certain medications or in patients with a history of seizures, brain trauma, or brain cancer.[1] Take comfort in knowing that the pet is unconscious and has no knowledge of the experience. Yet if a seizure occurs, the family remembers it. Every veterinarian dreads the rare occurrence when a pet has a seizure during the farewell.

During sedation or euthanasia, some pets may also vocalize. Vocalization is common during any anesthesia process, and even people will chat, moan, or yell as we go under anesthesia. And sometimes the muscle twitching that occurs in pets as the nerves stop firing can result in vigorous leg paddling. Again, this is normal as anesthesia sets in. All of these things can upset a family if they interpret them as the pet suffering. I can assure you that the pets are not suffering. In fact, these responses let me know the medication is starting to work and they are not feeling discomfort. I prefer to wonder what pleasant moments the pets are dreaming about while they're kicking their legs or flicking their tails.

After the medication travels to the brain, it usually takes only a few minutes for the body to shut down. However, there are times when it can take longer. I have had a few patients whose heartbeat gradually slows and stops after up to 20 minutes, even when I give the euthanasia solution intravenously, which is the quickest route.

Talk to your pet

I encourage pet owners to talk to their cats as they are being sedated and as they are passing. I think it's not only nice for cats to hear their humans' voices, it also helps comfort the pet parents to say loving things to them. A study found that hearing still occurs in people who are unresponsive and dying,[2] so one might cautiously presume this is also the case for our pets. Hearing may be the last sense to stop functioning as we (and our pets) die, so use your voice to comfort your pet throughout the end.

CHAPTER 37:

Burial and cremation: A final place to rest and remember

In the 1970s in rural New York where I grew up, it was customary to bury your deceased pet. I don't recall having gravestones—we buried Lump, our family dog, near a tree and planted flowers at her gravesite. But over the years, it grew over and her final resting place was unrecognizable. The stray cats our family had adopted typically just didn't come home at some point, so I don't remember being faced with making arrangements for their remains. I didn't think about pet burial or cremation again until the late 1990s, when I had to decide what to do for my own first dog, Snow White, who you first met in this book's introduction.

Snow White died unexpectedly, so I had not thought about or prepared for what would happen with her body afterward. When that evening came and I sat crying, holding my lifeless friend, I only knew I would need to bury her. At that time, I hadn't heard of pet cremation. I took Snow White home from the veterinary hospital and called friends to help me dig the gravesite and help settle her snugly in her final resting place.

I didn't realize how hard it would be to create her gravesite. When developers built homes near the Everglades in South Florida, they filled the marshland with coral rock. My friends and I took turns using a pickaxe to break through the rock in my yard. It took us three hours to dig a 5-ft-deep hole. We tried to gently lay Snow White at the bottom, which was no easy task. I placed flowers on her body and said a prayer. We filled in the hole, and I placed a special rock on top. A few days later I planted white flowers at the gravesite to honor her resting place. I always thought fondly of Snow White when I passed that spot.

When I sold my house to move to Gainesville, Florida, to attend veterinary school, I lost that space to visit and honor Snow White. The new homeowners never knew the importance of that spot. But I have pictures of Snow White, and her life inspired me to become a veterinarian. Each letter of my DVM degree carries some part of her spirit.

Since then, I also buried my cat Herbie, but all my other pets have been cremated. I don't have a personal preference; my own choice is influenced by each pet and situation. The choice of aftercare is a personal decision, and I support every family's choice. So let's take a closer look at the options available so you can feel more confident, prepared, and at peace with your decision.

Burial

When a body is buried, microbes break down the tissues, and the soil pH can help accelerate the process. Depending on what a pet is buried in, the body may break down within a few months, leaving bones behind. Humans have been burying their deceased pets for centuries. Archaeologists have identified what appears to be a pet dog burial site from 14,000 years ago.[1] Ancient Egyptians mummified and buried their cats, but the sad truth is that while these animals may have been revered, many were deliberately killed—perhaps because they were linked to ancient Egyptian gods or were buried to accompany their deceased owners.[2,3]

Pet burial may be done on the family's property if local regulations permit it, or in a pet cemetery. The oldest and largest pet cemetery in the United States is in Hartsdale, New York. It was founded by a veterinarian in 1896 and now is the final resting place of more than 80,000 animals.[4] A sign of the closeness between

 In 1881, a dog named Cherry was the first of many pets to be laid to rest in what became Hyde Park Pet Cemetery in London, England. Most of the 1000 animals buried there are dogs, but it includes a small number of cats, monkeys, and birds. The cemetery ran short on space and closed to burials in 1903.[6]

 An honored cat mummy at the British Museum in London, England.

pets and their human family members, Hartsdale worked hard on New York law to allow people to place their cremated ashes with their pets in pet cemeteries.[5] Together forever, truly.

Pet cemeteries are not necessarily widely available, so if you prefer this option for your cat, preplanning is wise. A burial and gravesite can cost thousands of dollars and require an annual maintenance fee. Burying your cat in your yard may be acceptable, so here are things to consider first:

- Check your city or county ordinances for restrictions, because not all areas allow pet burial.
- Call your local public utilities office to mark your yard before you dig so you can avoid damaging gas and water lines or other utilities.
- If your household accesses well water, choose a site away from the well.
- Will you need room for future additions (other pets) in the location you choose?
- Are you OK with leaving your cat's gravesite behind if you move?
- Are you physically able to dig the hole, or do you have someone to assist—a family member, friend, or hired help?
- Is the weather cooperative? Burying your pet on your property in Buffalo, New York, in January, or in your yard in South Florida during the rainy season probably isn't feasible. (Tip: Your veterinary clinic or local crematory may hold your cat's body in a chilled facility until the land thaws or dries out.)

If you choose burial, here are some tips:

- If you need to delay the burial by a few days, you may want to place your cat's body in an air-tight plastic container and place it in a refrigerator or freezer.
- When you're ready to bury your cat, wrap your loved one in a small blanket, t-shirt, or pillow case. Avoid plastic bags or boxes because they slow the natural process of absorption into the soil.
- An urn or box isn't necessary, but if you prefer one, a pet crematory can provide options. Paw Pods **pawpods.com/** are an option for biodegradable containers.
- An adequate depth for the hole allows four to five feet of soil to be placed above the cat to prevent other animals from investigating the area.
- Sprinkle 1 cup of lime powder (calcium hydroxide) on the bottom of the grave and 1 cup on top of the coffin, blanket, or pet. Lime can be purchased at most hardware or livestock feed stores.
- Place at least four feet of soil on top of the body or casket. If the pet was euthanized, the euthanasia medications remain in the tissues, and the pet's body can be deadly to or cause severe illness in curious pets or

other scavenging animals. Again, avoid burying your pet in a location near your water supply if your source is well water.
- Use a headstone or decorative piece to discourage future digging in that spot.
- If you elect to have your cat cremated and then bury their ashes yourself, use an organic soil mixture along with the cremains (cremated remains) to create a nutrient-rich mixture that will benefit the earth and help plants around the burial site flourish. Burying cremains alone can adversely affect the soil and inhibit plant growth.

Traditional (furnace-based) cremation

Cremation involves using intense heat to reduce the body to its basic elements of bone fragments. Cremation of deceased people on an open funeral pyre is an ancient tradition and began thousands of years ago. Cremation using high heat in an enclosed space began in Europe and North America in the late nineteenth century.

In the late twentieth century, dedicated companion animal pet cremation centers began opening. Hundreds of pet-only crematories exist around the U.S. today, and some human crematories also offer pet cremation services. Based on nationwide data from Lap of Love's veterinarians and a crematory in South Florida that I co-own, families elect cremation for their pet 80% of the time. Modern-day cremation uses a special furnace that generates extreme heat (at least 1700 F [927 C]) from burners fueled most often by natural gas and sometimes by propane, fuel oil, or electricity. The body is not directly exposed to flames.

Because bodies are about 70% water, the water evaporates in the extreme heat and the remaining tissue breaks down. For a cat, the process takes up to two hours. Any items (toy, blanket, collar) placed in the crematory with the cat will be cremated as well. Metal implants, such as a bone plate that was placed during an orthopedic surgery, do not break down in the heat and are left behind. Small metal pieces such as microchips or thin surgical wires dissolve in the heat.

After a human or cat body is cremated, bone fragments are left behind (many still retain their original shape, but they're very fragile when touched). These bone fragments are then placed in a pulverizer machine and ground into smaller pieces which resemble sand. This pulverized material is what is typically referred to as *ashes, cremated remains,* or *cremains*.

Depending on the wishes of a pet's family, the ashes are then either spread by the crematory or returned to the family. If you plan to spread your cat's ashes after cremation, check your local laws and federal regulations. For example, spreading ashes in national parks or on public beaches is often prohibited.

For people, each deceased person is cremated individually and the ashes are returned to the family in an urn that the family chooses (or multiple urns, if the family wishes to divide a loved one's ashes among family members). For cats, a family can choose a communal, private, or individual cremation. Based on the Lap of Love and my crematory data, of the families who choose pet cremation, 50% elect communal cremation and 50% elect private cremation.

Communal cremation

This style of cremation involves cremating a deceased pet with other deceased pets without separation between them. The pet's ashes are not returned to the pet parents. Without sugarcoating this process, this means that pets are placed on top of each other (sometimes a dozen or more) and cremated. Each crematory may have different protocols regarding the number of pets that they allow to constitute a communal cremation, so it's a good idea to learn about the process for the crematory you select. Communal cremation costs less than private cremation.

The crematory disposes of the ashes of pets who are communally cremated, and this is done in accord with local and federal regulations, which may be stricter in densely populated cities. Such disposal (I hate using that word, but that is exactly what they do) may mean that the ashes are put in the trash. That may sound shocking, but in some places, no alternative way exists to spread ashes. Some crematories spread the ashes (or a portion of the ashes) in a memorial garden, some obtain special permits and may spread them in rivers or oceans, and some bury the ashes on their property.

I want to emphasize that communal cremation does not suggest that the cat was unloved or less loved. Some people are simply not attached to their pet's body and do not want the ashes returned to them. I have known many families who went to the ends of the earth to save their pets, shared their beds with them, cooked for them, and much more, but in the end they did not wish to receive their pet's ashes—a perfectly acceptable preference.

Private cremation vs. true private cremation or individual cremation

This method of cremation means a deceased pet is separated from other deceased pets during cremation, and the family receives their pet's ashes. However, the manner in which pets are separated differs among crematories.

Historically, crematory machines had only one large chamber, called the retort. Multiple pets would be placed in the chamber at one time, and they were separated by distance or by bricks, or pets were placed on individual metal trays. This method could be prone to mistakes if the pets were not properly organized and identified. The crematory's protocol to retain organization and keep pets identified is vital. Mixing of ashes could also theoretically occur. I'm not aware of any scientific studies on whether bone fragments become airborne during cremation, and, in my opinion, not much of this type of mixing occurs. I have seen questionable "private cremation" methods where too many pets were placed in one chamber, too close together. Not everyone agrees with me, but I believe three feet between pets, with bricks separating them is acceptable and can be considered a private cremation. It may seem odd to you, but when my dog Serissa was cremated, I felt some comfort knowing that other pets were close by.

The machines used for pet cremation have dramatically changed over the years. Some have multiple small chambers so that one pet can be placed in an individual chamber, which leaves no doubt that all the ashes belong to that pet alone. Some crematories refer to this as *true private* or *individual* cremation.

Because no regulation exists regarding body spacing and the terminology used to describe it, some crematories use these three terms interchangeably. So you may need to ask for more details about the crematory's process if you prefer a true private or individual cremation.

After a private cremation, the bone fragments are scooped up, pulverized, and placed in a container or urn to be returned to the pet's family.

Aquamation (water-based cremation)

Aquamation is a relatively new type of cremation gaining traction in the United States for both people and pets. Aquamation is a gentle, quiet, and eco-friendly process that uses a combination of heated flowing water and alkaline compounds (sodium and potassium hydroxide) to accelerate the same natural course of tissue breakdown that occurs during burial in the earth. Aquamation is also known as bio-cremation, alkaline hydrolysis, or green cremation.

The crematory I co-own with my brother Allan, Monarch Pet Memorial Services in Boynton Beach, Florida (**monarchpetservices.com**), provides only aquamation. It's a safe, natural, and environmentally friendly alternative to burial or furnace-based cremation. It produces no toxic air emissions and uses a fraction of the energy of traditional cremation.

Aquamation machines provide communal or private cremation. Most have a long metal basket that holds one very large dog, but it also allows placement of metal sheets to separate small pets. The pets and their bone fragments remain in their private chambers and the water passes through all the containers through small holes. Because of the water circulation, whether this can be called true private or individual cremation is debated. With a private aquamation option, each pet is carefully tracked through the process and pet parents receive their pet's ashes back.

The aquamation process can take up to 24 hours, and then the bone fragments need to be dried, which can take another 24 hours. The "bone ash" from aquamation is mostly made up of calcium (bones, teeth) and other minerals. It is softer, whiter, and lighter bone ash and the process produces more ash than that produced by extreme heat cremation. Any non-organic material placed with the pet remains intact afterward. So if a toy is placed with the pet, it will be there after the process. Sometimes we find items that pet parents may not have known their cats had eaten—hair ties, small toys, and more!

Composting

A new, limited option in the United States for pet aftercare is body composting. Like burial, furnace-based cremation, and aquamation, composting breaks down body tissues and bone fragments remain. Pet composting may be done indoors or in a greenhouse, and composting of farm animals has been done outdoors for many years. The pet's body is placed in a special aerated, temperature- and moisture-regulated container with wood chips and soil to promote growth of helpful bacteria and fungi that catalyze the process. Done correctly, the process also neutralizes disease-causing microorganisms and chemicals. This process takes about eight weeks, and the compost that remains can be used in gardens or to plant trees and houseplants.

The body's elemental nature—a recap of aftercare options

Whether a family chooses pet burial, furnace-based cremation, aquamation, or composting, the end result is the same—each body is eventually reduced to its basic elements of bone ash. Apart from cost and availability, the primary differences among these methods are the amount of time the process takes, the catalyst that supports the decomposition, and the environmental impact of the process:

- Burial results in slow decomposition that can take several months to years, is catalyzed by microbes and certain soil conditions, requires land use, and may release toxins into the soil or water.
- Furnace-based cremation for cats takes about two hours, is catalyzed by extreme heat that requires a large amount of energy to produce, creates smoke, and has a high carbon footprint.
- Aquamation (with drying) takes up to 48 hours, is catalyzed by alkaline hydrolysis, and has a small carbon footprint. The byproduct is sterile

water that contains nutrients, salts, amino acids, and sugars. The water is processed the same as other wastewater is.
- Composting takes about two months, is catalyzed by microbes, and has a small carbon footprint. The byproduct is heat.

Viewings

I have attended a few pet memorial services, but memorial services are not as common for pets as they are for people. Because I am a veterinarian focused on end-of-life care, I consider the euthanasia visit to be one element of a pet's funeral. I try to make it as peaceful as possible while providing the family the opportunity to celebrate their cat's life.

Sometimes pet parents want to view their cat again before cremation. They may wish to say one last goodbye, or oftentimes a family member who wasn't present to see the cat before they passed can obtain closure during a viewing. Most crematories can provide a viewing opportunity, and the cat is placed lovingly on a table to allow a family to pay their last respects.

Care of the body and ashes

Veterinary clinics and in-home veterinary euthanasia services typically partner with one nearby crematory (there may be only one option). Pets' bodies are delivered to the crematory directly or kept in cold storage at the veterinary clinic until the crematory picks them up—usually once or twice a week. The crematory returns the ashes to the clinic within a few days to two weeks. The family may pick them up, or the end-of-life-care veterinarian may deliver them to the family. A few veterinary hospitals have their own crematory on site.

 Bruce received a floral tribute before cremation.

Questions you may wish to ask your veterinarian

- If I wish to, may I choose a different crematory than the one you typically use? (This may require that the crematory makes a special trip to the clinic to pick up your cat or you may have to take your cat to the crematory.)
- Has a team member from the veterinary hospital toured the crematory and watched their process?
- If I choose a communal cremation, where will my cat's ashes be spread?
- What memorial items will be returned?
- What options for urns are available?

 ## Questions you may wish to ask a crematory representative

- What are the hours for drop off? (This may affect the time you elect for your cat's euthanasia appointment if you take your cat's body to the crematory.)
- What are my options if my cat passes after regular business hours?
- Do you provide a viewing opportunity before cremation?
- What type of cremation do you offer (water-based aquamation, furnace-based cremation, or both)?
- Are memorial items available?
- What options for urns are available? (If you would like your cat's ashes divided into multiple urns for family members, a crematory may provide this option for a small additional fee.)
- What is your protocol to ensure cats are separated and properly identified throughout the cremation process?

CHAPTER 38:

Keepsakes: Memorializing your cat to honor their life story

> "It's surprising how much memory is built around things unnoticed at the time."
> — Source unverified (the internet attributes this quote to Barbara Kingsolver, novelist)

I've been asked to help families memorialize their pets in many ways. Some are common and traditional, and others are quite uncommon. When someone requests a memorial I haven't done before, I enjoy the challenge of trying to make it happen. The first time a family asked me to take a sample for their dog's cloning, I had no idea what to do, which I confessed to the pet parent. But with help from the company that provides pet cloning, I obtained the sample they needed.

For some families, their thoughts are all they need to remember their pet, while others want physical remembrances. Many companies and artists that produce awesome pet memorials have asked me to recommend them, but discussing such products during euthanasia appointments would be awkward and sound uncomfortably promotional. Instead, this chapter is dedicated to sharing memorial ideas and products I have learned about during my career, and it isn't intended to be promotional nor is it intended to serve as my endorsement of any product, company, organization, activity, or service listed.

I hope you find these suggestions helpful or that they may inspire you to create something different. It's also helpful to think about memorial items you may want before your cat passes so that you can prepare and

Scan to visit my pet memorials webpage

fulfill your wishes when the time comes. Related to the list I've included here, I've created a webpage **drmarygardner.com/resources/memorials** that provides additional examples and direct links to the sources of many of these ideas.

1. Create a paw print impression in clay. I love a good paw print. Air-dry and oven-bake clays are available in craft stores. You may want to trim your cat's toenails and fur between the paw pads to provide a better imprint. Many veterinary clinics and almost all crematories have the supplies to create a paw impression, so just ask.
2. Create a paw print impression with ink or paint. Using ink or paint is a bit messier than clay alone, and it may take a few tries to get a good print. Again, you may want to trim your cat's toenails and fur between the paw pads. You can also have your colorful print scanned and use it to help create jewelry or a tattoo.

ColorBox is one example of many inkpad options you can use to create a long-lasting paw print impression.

Dwayne's nose print and paw prints.

3. Keep your cat's ashes. More than half of families who elect cremation want their cat's ashes returned to them. This gives many people a sense of closure or that their cat is "back." You'll see many keepsakes in this list that can be created to hold or incorporate a cat's ashes.
4. Create a custom memorial blanket. Many internet retailers will create a blanket from one or more photos of your cat.
5. Create custom memorial clothing: t-shirts, socks, scarves.

Socks honoring kitty brothers Albus and Severus.

 I sent this photo of Goldie to have a custom plush toy created by Petsies.

6. Have a plush animal made that looks like your cat. Cuddle Clones and Petsies are two examples of companies that create these.
7. Keep fur clippings. These can be a treasure to sniff and touch to help you remember. Many keepsakes can also be created to hold your cat's fur or can be made from their fur.
8. Hold a memorial ceremony—alone or with a few family members or friends, or invite everyone who knew your cat.
9. Create a scrapbook to memorialize the wonderful moments in your cat's life. We often keep pictures on our phones and computers but don't take time to print them. You can make or order a custom cover for your cat's photo album or scrapbook (e.g. Northwest Gifts Personalized Wood Photo Album in Maple & Rosewood). Prefer not to print? Consider a digital photo frame.
10. Create a nose print. Similar to a clay paw impression, you can make a nose impression in clay. These impressions are easier to make after the cat passes. The nose is even more unique to your cat than their paw—like a person's fingerprint.
11. Make or purchase custom lockets, charms, or other jewelry created based on your cat's paw or nose print impressions.
12. Consider a trip to your cat's favorite spot or spots to sprinkle their ashes or a smidge of their ashes. Check your local regulations before doing this, and think about others who visit the area and how you would want the area treated as well.

 My cat Lilu's nose print... and a print of a bit of her upper lip!

13. Obtain a sample that will give you the option to have your cat cloned. Talk with your veterinarian and the company you choose (ViaGen Pets is one example) before the euthanasia appointment, because specific procedures that require fast action may be needed to preserve the sample.
14. Preserve your cat with taxidermy. Research this option before the euthanasia appointment so that the best preservation can be achieved.
15. Preserve your cat with freeze-drying (e.g. Perpetual Pet). This process differs from traditional taxidermy. It is applied to the whole animal and stops the decaying process by using ultra-low temperature and a vacuum procedure to remove all moisture.
16. Preserve and remember your cat with cryonics (e.g. Cryonics Institute). This process is available for deceased people as well. Research this option thoroughly beforehand because special preparations and fees are required. A cat's body is specially prepared and suspended in a liquid nitrogen tank and must stay at the cryonics facility. With this method, the hope is that one day reanimation of frozen bodies will be possible.
17. Get a tattoo of your cat, their paw print, or their nose print. You may also investigate options to incorporate some of your cat's ashes into the ink.
18. Light up the night sky with your cat's ashes! Ashes can be incorporated into fireworks (e.g. Heavenly Stars Fireworks).
19. Plant new life and boost local biodiversity by planting one or more native trees, grasses, wildflowers, or an entire memorial garden dedicated to your cat on your property. (One book about planting native plants specific to your region: *Nature's Best Hope* by Douglas W. Tallamy [Timber Press, 2020]).

 A bit of Hank's ashes were incorporated into the ink for this tattoo that honored him.

20. Plant new life by donating in memory of your cat to an organization that plants trees in national forests, such as the Arbor Day Foundation.
21. Plant a memorial tree urn. A tree will grow from a special urn that contains some of your cat's ashes. (Keep in mind that if ashes are placed alone in a planting location or gravesite, the ashes can inhibit plant growth, so use special soil mixes or biodegradable urns.)

22. Place a memorial bench in honor of your cat in your yard or garden.
23. Write lyrics and music for a song in your cat's honor, or commission an artist to do this. Websites such as UpWork may be helpful in finding independent artists.
24. Write your cat's eulogy or obituary and post it online. Many websites invite cat lovers to share stories about a cat who has passed.
25. Donate in memory of your cat to a local or national cat rescue or shelter facility.
26. Donate in memory of your cat to a local veterinary primary care or specialty practice that has a charitable fund to help clients who qualify and cannot afford their cat's emergency or chronic illness care. Not all hospitals offer this, but national organizations such as Frankie's Friends also provide this service.
27. Donate in memory of your cat to an organization that researches cat diseases or provides funding for research, such as a veterinary school, Morris Animal Foundation, or EveryCat Health Foundation (previously Winn Feline Foundation).
28. Purchase a personalized cat memorial stone to keep at home or in your garden, or to place on your cat's gravesite.
29. Create a silhouette portrait of your cat made of buttons and fabric.
30. Repurpose your cat's identification tags and have them made into jewelry.
31. Create your own or order a customized cat memorial holiday ornament.
32. Create a special spot in your home dedicated to your cat with photos, battery-operated LED tea lights or flickering LED candles, flowers, their collar, a favorite toy, locks of fur, ashes, or other items.
33. Make a planter out of your cat's food and water bowls.
34. Create felted beads from your cat's hair instead of using wool.
35. Have a bracelet made from your cat's harness, collar, or leash.
36. Make a cat photo collage—a great project to do with children.
37. Write a letter to your cat and send it with them to be cremated.
38. Have a portrait painted or other illustration created from a photograph of your cat. Wonderful watercolor, acrylic, and even cartoon options are available.

 An adored kitty's collar adorns a planter.

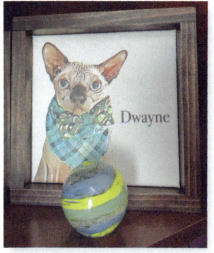

Dwayne's exquisite portrait pays tribute to his stunning self and to his ashes kept inside a lovely glass orb.

My gorgeous girl Lilu, during her bucket list photo shoot.

39. Paint your cat's portrait using a decoupage medium such as Mod Podge, or attend a paint-your-pet class.
40. Commission a portrait painted with your cat's ashes.
41. Incorporate your cat's ashes into a memorial sculpture or stone (e.g. Spirit Pieces).
42. Create your own or purchase a customized cat sculpture.
43. Incorporate your cat's ashes into glass art or jewelry.
44. Incorporate your cat's ashes into a memorial glass paperweight in a form meaningful to you.
45. Place your cat's ashes in a specially made urn hourglass (e.g. **JustHourglasses.com**).

I'll be honest, it's not always easy to get a group shot with a cat. Cats rarely look happy, and even my dog Duncan was losing patience with Bodhi!

46. Have a professional photo shoot done before your cat passes. The directory at **PetMemorialPhotographers.com** will help you find a pet photographer.
47. Create your own or order a personalized flower or floating candle vase.
48. Make a hanging jar candle or other memorial candle with a personal message.
49. Make a framed memorial photograph that includes your cat's collar (e.g. **Pearhead.com**).
50. Get a personalized window decal (e.g **UPrinting.com**)
51. Create a custom coffee cup.
52. Engrave your cat's name on a personalized wind chime (e.g. Pawprints Left By You Memorial Gifts).
53. Send a portion of your cat's ashes to orbit the Earth, or to the moon, or into deep space (e.g. Celestis Pets).
54. Name a star after your cat (e.g. Sparkling Star Register).
55. Create a cat hair keepsake, such as a glass jar, wooden box, or locket.
56. Write a short story, poem, novel, biography, or children's book about your cat.
57. Place your cat's ashes or hair in various resin memorials.
58. Turn your cat's ashes into diamonds (e.g **Eterneva.com**).
59. Turn your cat's ashes into pottery.
60. Include your cat's ashes in an eternal reef (e.g. **EternalReefs.com**). The ashes are incorporated in an environmentally safe cement and dropped in the ocean to erode safely over time.
61. Create a memorial keychain with a photo of your cat or an engraved remembrance.

 Lilu's shadow box, with her nose prints (I couldn't bear to throw out the imperfect prints), fur clipping, and paw prints.

 Jax's custom paw-impression keychain and other items.

62. Create a ring, pendant, or charm with a lock of cat hair with or without flowers and captured in resin.
63. Incorporate cat hair with beads the color of your cat's birthstone to be crafted into a necklace or pendant.
64. Create a pet memorial wall or shelf that features photographs of all your beloved pets who've passed on.
65. Purchase an urn that matches your cat's breed (e.g. **ForeverPets.com**).
66. Have your cat's photograph engraved on drinking glasses.
67. Incorporate your cat's ashes into snow globe art.
68. Complete a special home or personal project, participate in a community charitable event, or volunteer at a shelter or elsewhere in your community to fulfill a personal goal while honoring your cat's memory. Decide how you will commemorate or dedicate your special project to your cat.
69. Organize your own community fundraising or charitable event in honor of your cat, such as a walk or fun run and donate all proceeds to a local pet shelter.
70. Create your own video memorial montage, short film, or movie about your cat.
71. Make or order a personalized memorial bird feeder (e.g. Urns Northwest).

A pendant with an etching of Dwayne.

Charlie's memorial corner includes a custom paw print shadow box, drawing, and plush toy, as well as his collar and other keepsakes.

72. Celebrate your pet's life with a toast, cheers, and customized bottle opener (e.g. Urns Northwest).

73. Paint a birdhouse that resembles your house from a kit and incorporate a small portrait of your pet. (You can also order a custom birdhouse designed to look exactly like your house! e.g. **TheBirdhouseBarn.com**)

74. Honor your beloved pet by adopting a new pet to share your love anew if this is right for you.

 Goblin's shadow box.

CHAPTER 39:

After they are gone: The silence is deafening

"What greater gift than the love of a cat?"

—Source unverified

(the internet attributes this quote to Charles Dickens)

They may inhabit all aspects of our daily lives for only a short precious time, or for a treasured decade, or many years beyond. They become our "furry children." And when the end nears, our lives become even more entwined. To make their remaining time better, we alter our own routines. We cancel vacations, we run home from work at lunch, we come home early after weekend dinners out with family, we sleep in the living room to stay nearby, we don't have friends over because our homes are messy and the carpet is stained…

…. we have constant worry, we scour the internet for answers, we try every product available hoping it'll help our pet a little bit more …

… we offer dozens of delectable new foods so they'll show us they still have an appetite for life, we lose countless hours of sleep, we deal with unholy smells, we have frustrations that no one else seems to understand, we argue with our family members ….

Yet most of us would do it for as long as our pets need us to.

Caring for an ailing pet brings stress, but it can also bring pride, solace, and cheer. Every one of my pets has taught me more about life, disease, caregiving, and loss. Each experience I've had with them has made me a better veterinarian (and human), and I've used that knowledge to help more pets and more families. I thank my pets for the love they provided and for their gifts that I can share.

I've had the amazing privilege of providing end-of-life veterinary care for thousands of pets, and I've met thousands of phenomenal families along the way. People often ask me whether I'm numb to euthanasia because I've done the procedure so many times. My answer has been and will always be, "No!"

I've never visited a home and felt that a pet represented a routine appointment. Every family and every pet brings a new experience, a new love story, and a new set of angel wings I can deliver. Have my technical skills improved in performing the procedure? Yes. I have muscle memory for the process. And this advantage allows me to be more present for the family and their pet. I also send a silent wish with every pet to please say "hi" to one of my fur kid angels above. I feel like I'm sending a friend to all my loves that I miss so much. In many ways, I'm now more affected by a pet's passing and their family's experience than I was when I began practicing so many years ago. And that's OK. The day that I become numb will be the day I need to stop providing this care.

I'm grateful for the treasured lessons I've learned from my patients and their families. My wish for this book is to give families answers, tips, and hope in caring for their aging pets, especially in times when they may feel helpless.

Praise your time together

I often hear pet parents say one of two things as their pet is being sedated or as their pet is passing. Some say, "I'm sorry!" I worry when I hear this, because it sounds like they have regrets. And I wonder—do they feel they should've done more? Or perhaps they're quietly expressing sorrow for their pet's illness. Grief and sadness are expected, but regret seems unjustified. I hope you don't feel regret at the end of your pet's life. Instead, I hope you can say what I hear many pet parents say to their pets, "Thank you!" I hope you can allow yourself to express that you're grateful that your pet was a part of your life. You're all good pet parents. Do what you can for your pets, and be gentle on yourself. Because if your pets could talk, I'm sure they would say, "thank you," right back.

Their spirit survives

I have many pictures and videos of my cats Herbie, Lilu, Goldie and Bodhi. They transport me back to the hectic, heartwarming years and hilarious moments we shared. Sometimes I turn around, still expecting Bodhi to have jumped into my freshly warmed office chair when I get up to refill my hot chocolate. I still have my dog Neo's collar. I saved a lovely wad of fur from my dog Serissa—how I miss her tufts of "snow" that would tumble through my house! I treasure Snow White's pictures. I gave my dog Duncan his angel wings four years ago, and I still cannot bear to throw out his huge multi-dose pill box that contains his heart medications. And shortly before I began this book, I lost my beautiful, smiley, Anatolian shepherd girl, Sam, to spinal cancer. My heart stings when I look down at her vacant spot next to my writing desk.

Our pets share our space and occupy our hearts. When they're gone, the expanse of their absence engulfs us. We miss their greetings, expectant looks, smell, fur on our clothes, drool, nose prints on the windows, and warmth on our lap. We simply glance at their spot on the couch or favorite perch, and the pang of its emptiness breaks like a wave crashing through our being. The bare cat bed, the lone toy in the corner, the treats still in the cabinet—all pierce, yet soothe us, and we can't bear to put these reminders away just yet. The familiar background symphony of our cats' meows for dinner, nearby purrs, soft snores, and claws digging into the scratching post is forever muted. I often pray to hear my pets' special sounds one more time, even if it's only in my dreams. The silence in my house after I've lost a pet is deafening.

How blessed we are to love a pet and to receive a pet's love. Loving a pet expands our capacity to love, and losing a pet doesn't limit it. Still, we know that no matter how much time we have our cats in our life, nine lives are not enough.

Acknowledgments

My everlasting gratitude goes to countless people, pets, and patients who have inspired and motivated me—before and during my voyage to become a veterinarian, and throughout my journey in focusing on aging pet wellness and veterinary hospice care. Every one of you has helped me shape and bring this book and its canine counterpart to life.

Countless thanks to the absolute treasure that is Dr. Theresa Entriken! Years ago, I asked if she was available to help research, thought-tweak and edit my books and she gracefully accepted. Little did I know I found the perfect person to turn my thoughts and words into magic. Years of working together to bring the two books to life has formed a deep respect and friendship for Theresa. I absolutely would not have produced such amazing works without her help, hard work, writing genius and inspiration!

Big thanks for my editing goddess, Mindy Valcarcel; and to my awesome doodlers, Portia Stewart and Moira Stewart.

Deepest thanks to my friends—Holly Russo, Dr. Dave Nicol, Eric Garcia, Dr. Caitlin DeWilde, Nikita Pavlov, and Dr. Faith Banks—for your never-ending encouragement.

Thank you, Dr. Sheilah Robertson, my fellow global guardian of geriatric pets. Your guidance makes me a better veterinarian.

My love and gratitude to my sister, Sharon Sherman, who unceasingly cheers me on in my life's endeavors, and to my brother, Allan Gardner, who is ever-present with helping hands.

Stacy Bennett, my banana split maker! For years you've helped me research all the questions that pop into my head about grey muzzle pets, geriatric people, and age-related conditions. I asked for a scoop of vanilla ice cream, and you brought me a banana split.

Thank you, Suze Orman, for your invaluable, uplifting, no-nonsense, no excuses, get-it-done character, my friend.

To all the families who allowed me to share their stories and pictures, THANK YOU! Each and every one of you and your pets has touched me personally and made me a better human and veterinarian. Your marvelous cats live on and will continue to enhance many more lives.

To my feline fur kid angels above—Bodhi, Herbie, Goldie, and Lilu—you've shared innumerable moments of love, and taught me more each day about all the joy that seals the human-animal bond. I continue to care for you in my heart as I'm caregiving for others, and I think of you all every day!

My heartfelt thank-yous to Dennis. You were my champion throughout my hectic, exhilarating years of veterinary school and a buoy for all my wild ideas. Thank you for loving our cats as much as I did, always trusting me to care for them in the best ways I knew how, and for enduring all the hairballs and litter box mishaps!

References

I have cited many references (indicated by superscript numbers) throughout this book. The references are organized by chapter in numeric order. Please use the QR code below or visit **drmarygardner.com/resources/catreferences** for the reference list.

Index

A

Acetaminophen 284, 315
Acid blockers 318
Acromegaly 90
Activity level 33–34, 92, 94, 139, 147, 189, 248
Acupuncture 27, 170, 173, 194, 200, 206, 217, 231, 267, 285, 309, 329, 330, 332, 377, 428–429, 437
Acute pain 272
Adaptil 426
Adaptive pain 272
Additives 85, 175, 178
Adenoma 260
Adrenal 90, 243, 248, 315
Aftercare 375, 410, 438, 456, 461
Aging 5–7, 19–21, 23, 32–36, 38–45, 49, 57–58, 64–65, 89, 101–103, 108, 122, 130, 140, 182–184, 195–196, 202, 220, 222, 225–226, 229, 231, 243, 292, 297, 309, 311, 314, 336, 344, 347, 364, 374, 377–378, 386, 396, 476, 479
Allergies 54, 93, 106–107, 131, 133, 315, 324
Allodynia 273–274
Alzheimer's 56, 221, 228, 231, 351
Amantadine 284, 317
Anesthesia 18, 57, 82–83, 87, 123, 145, 285, 287, 289, 336–337, 343, 347–351, 348, 354, 447, 454
Anorexia 112
Anosmia 57
Anti-nausea 113, 118, 145, 159–160, 262, 284, 314, 348, 354, 431–432, 441
Anxiety 8, 20, 46, 53, 63, 75–77, 84, 146, 169, 174–175, 205, 215–216, 218, 222, 227–231, 233, 240, 254, 269, 272–273, 279–280, 283–285, 312, 316, 320, 322, 332–333, 338–339, 348, 348–349, 351–352, 354, 366–367, 379, 387, 389, 405, 408, 422, 426, 428–429, 429, 433, 437, 440–441, 444, 447
Anxitane 228
Appetite 33–34, 45, 57–58, 98–99, 102–105, 111–118, 123–124, 141, 143, 145, 147, 152, 155, 157–160, 163, 165, 189, 191, 203, 245–246, 249–250, 252, 262–263, 267, 275, 278, 304, 312, 315–316, 321, 344–345, 379, 381, 391, 426, 430–432, 446, 475
Appetite stimulant 104, 118, 145, 159, 160, 316, 381, 431, 432
Aquamation 6, 416, 460–461, 463
Arthritis 49, 92, 103, 115, 128, 131, 167–168, 170, 172–173, 176, 193, 196–201, 205–206, 208, 211, 215–218, 222, 232, 269–270, 272–273, 278, 285, 293, 314–316, 319, 330–333, 344, 388, 428
ASD 414
Ashes 416, 418, 457–460, 462–463, 466–472
Assessing pain 275
Atopic dermatitis 131
Auditory 69, 76
Autoimmune 55, 83, 131, 243, 251

B

B12 320
Balance 32, 73–74, 110–111, 114, 150, 152, 155–157, 205–206, 213, 227, 248, 260, 297, 316, 329, 345, 375
Bath mats 208
Bedding 213
Beta-amyloid plaques 221
Bisphosphonates 317
Blind 61, 65–70, 294, 384
Boarding 28, 100, 165, 225, 309, 337–338, 382, 388

483

Body condition 33, 92, 93, 95, 101, 103, 117, 146, 187, 199–200, 218, 245, 345, 381, 447
Boots 96
Boredom 67, 94, 147, 189, 272, 296–297
Bowel movement 171
Bowls 63, 67–69, 86, 91, 115–117, 127, 147, 162, 176, 189, 204, 208, 215, 231–232, 234, 254, 293, 295–296, 305, 426, 469
Breath 53, 80, 85, 87, 139, 142, 147, 152, 184, 187, 189, 266, 305, 429, 434
Breathing 138, 182, 429
Bucket list 355, 357
BUN 153–154
Burial 417, 435, 442, 455–458, 460–461

C

Cachexia 33, 101, 102–103, 105, 108, 123, 145–146, 202–203, 214
Calculus 80
Calmex 228
Cancer 27, 32, 43, 45, 54, 56, 64–65, 75, 83, 87, 91, 93, 98–99, 102, 123, 128, 131, 139, 145, 168, 170, 185, 188, 196, 198, 202, 222, 243, 257–259, 261–267, 273, 311, 316–317, 319, 331, 344, 346, 364, 368, 370, 375, 379, 384–385, 387–388, 390, 396, 429, 436, 454, 476
Cannabidiol 230, 321
Cardiac 144–146
Cardiologist 139–140, 144, 146
Caregiver stress 9, 377–378
Cataracts 61, 63–64
Catheter 145, 285, 448–451
Cavaletti 206
CBD 230, 321–323
Cells 39, 44, 45, 51, 54, 55, 56, 58, 74, 81, 84, 99, 113, 121, 122, 124, 130, 132, 133, 137, 139, 150, 154, 156, 182, 183, 196, 225, 228, 243, 244, 245, 246, 251, 253, 257–264, 273, 284, 316, 319, 333, 345, 451
Cellular senescence 45
Cerenia 317
Chemotherapy 27, 84, 258, 260, 263–265, 309, 346, 367, 371, 377
Children 9, 10, 21, 76, 147, 189, 208, 215, 231, 246, 296, 301, 395, 401, 403, 406, 413–419, 429, 469, 471, 475
Chondroitin 318–319
Chronic pain 270, 273–274, 278, 283, 319
Churu 116, 165, 324, 327
CKD 151, 153, 155–157, 161
Cognition 8, 219, 320

Cognitive Assessment 221, 233, 239
Cognitive dysfunction 49, 56, 168, 170, 172, 220–226, 228–233, 237, 291, 316, 319–320, 338, 351, 385, 388, 391, 426, 444
Communal cremation 459, 463
Composting 461–462
Composure 228
Compounding 314
Cornea 61
Corticosteroids 112, 194, 248, 284, 316
Cortisol 90, 248, 315, 316
Coughing 141–142, 181–182, 184, 186, 191, 266
Cremation 9, 410, 416–417, 435, 438, 455, 458–463, 466

D

DCM 109–110
Death 5, 19, 32, 56, 101, 117, 141, 146, 155, 164, 257, 341, 347, 350, 365, 383, 386–388, 398, 406–409, 411, 413–415, 417, 421, 424, 427–431, 434–437, 442, 453
Dehydration 115, 122, 151–152, 154, 157, 246, 278, 430
Dementia 27, 229, 273, 279, 388
Denial Island 396–397
Dental 27, 42, 46, 56, 57, 79–84, 87, 91, 106, 123, 141, 144, 146, 155, 161, 218, 222, 272, 277, 346, 349, 428
Dermatologist 57, 132–133
Dermatology 336
Diabetes 27, 49, 64, 79, 81, 83, 91, 93, 98–99, 106, 122, 128, 131, 151, 168, 195, 222, 243–250, 252, 324, 346, 368, 381, 388, 390, 442
Diabetic neuropathy 195
Diapers 134, 176–177, 179, 296, 367
Diets 42, 89, 95, 105–110, 106, 114, 144, 156–157, 159, 170, 199–200, 226, 233, 235, 284, 385
Dilated cardiomyopathy 109, 140
DNA 38, 44
Dog Aging Project 43
Dragging 210
Drools 85, 152, 266, 281
Duality 410
Dying process 374, 414, 416, 430, 434
Dyspnea 187, 190, 429

E

Echocardiogram 144, 348
Elbow dysplasia 197

Electrolytes 150–151
End of life 100, 114, 117, 324, 335, 364–367, 369, 371, 373, 387, 390, 403, 431, 441
Enrichment 8, 42, 67, 170, 201, 217, 233, 236, 291, 296–297, 301–302, 340, 345
Enucleation 65
Epigenetic 38–39
Epigenetic clock 38–39
Epilepsy 226, 322
Euthanasia 19–20, 140, 273, 341, 353, 366, 368, 380–381, 385–389, 401, 405–406, 408–410, 413–416, 421, 423–425, 428–430, 434, 436–448, 450–454, 457, 462, 465, 468, 475
Exercise 26, 34, 41–42, 97, 103–104, 122, 141, 143, 146, 188, 199, 201–203, 207, 209, 217, 232, 248, 250, 266, 281, 284, 296, 299, 304, 345, 374, 396
Explaining euthanasia 413
Extra-label 313
Eye medications 69–70
Eyes 16, 19, 23, 30, 54, 61–63, 65–66, 69–70, 74, 86, 96, 100, 129–130, 193, 247, 261, 263, 276, 276–278, 305, 315, 340, 345, 390, 416–417, 433, 437, 444, 453

F

Fat 23, 33, 44, 89, 91–94, 97, 99, 101–103, 108, 119, 123, 126, 150, 153–154, 156, 225–226, 245, 247–248, 259–260, 315, 324
Fat mass 93, 103
Fatty liver 99, 200
Fibrocartilaginous embolism 195
Fibroma 260
Fibrosarcoma 261
Fish oil 103, 105, 115, 145, 200, 226, 237, 319
Flicker 389
Fluid therapy 100, 128, 155, 158–159, 161, 163, 165, 175, 262, 284, 431–432, 449
Fragile 30, 32–33, 124, 339, 451, 458
Fragility 7, 29, 31–33, 39, 101
Frailty 31–36, 45, 91, 102, 387
Free radicals 156
Frunevetmab 199, 284

G

GABA 229
Gabapentin 229–231, 234, 254, 284, 316, 320
Glioma 261

Glucosamine 318
Goals of care 9, 373
Grain-free 109–110
Grief 9, 89, 272, 279, 341, 369, 399, 405–411, 413, 417, 421–425, 435
Grief in pets 422, 424, 435
Grimace 275
Groomer 134, 258, 339
Grooming 34, 85, 86, 92, 132, 134, 173, 177, 193, 198, 204, 216, 241, 251, 270, 271, 286, 295, 297, 309, 359, 367, 433
Gums 54, 55, 57, 80–83, 86, 87, 100, 123–124, 130, 143, 152, 188, 247, 266, 315, 433

H

Halo 68
Harness 47, 66, 68, 77, 97, 148, 199, 209–210, 210, 235, 299, 469
Hazards 61, 66, 232, 234, 292
Health journal 46, 98, 147, 189, 267, 303–304, 306, 344–345, 381
Hearing 7, 67, 73–77, 220–222, 305, 325, 454
Heart 16, 27, 32, 43–44, 61, 80–83, 91, 98, 102, 104–106, 109–112, 122–123, 128, 137–152, 142, 155, 162, 182, 187, 189, 195, 202, 223, 248, 251–253, 255, 264, 289, 293, 311, 321–322, 324, 337, 339, 344, 345–349, 366, 370, 378, 384, 387–388, 390, 397, 399, 405, 415, 434, 437, 445, 450, 452–453, 476, 480
Heartrate 139, 142, 144, 146, 150
Heartworms 141, 184, 187, 347
Hemangioma 260
Hemangiosarcoma 261
Hematoma 260
Hip dysplasia 197
Home-cooked 108–109, 437
Hospice 5–6, 9, 19–20, 117, 187, 190, 267, 269, 270, 280, 289, 311, 316, 330, 363–371, 373–377, 401, 403–404, 407–408, 410, 416–417, 427–430, 432, 440, 479
Housemates 51, 221, 253, 292, 294–295, 297
Hydration 122, 150, 155, 162, 345, 349
Hygiene 216, 367
Hyperadrenocorticism 90
Hyperglycemia 245
Hyperkeratosis 130
Hyperthermia 122–124
Hyperthyroid 254
Hypertrophic cardiomyopathy 43, 140
Hyporexia 112

485

Hyposmia 57
Hypothalamus 120–121, 124
Hypothermia 123, 247, 349, 354

I

I-131 253
Ice packs 216
Immunotherapy 264
Incontinence 168–173, 176–178, 204, 216–217, 295, 305, 367, 384
Incontinent 134, 168, 173, 176–177, 179, 216, 296, 386
Infections 54, 56, 58, 65, 74, 83, 99, 102, 112, 124, 129, 131, 134, 136, 139, 151–152, 168, 172, 176–177, 199, 217, 248, 272, 295, 296, 331, 346, 367
Inflammation 45, 49, 51, 54–56, 62, 65, 74–75, 80–81, 93, 99, 101–102, 105, 110, 112, 139, 151, 168–169, 176, 184, 197–198, 203, 222, 248, 272, 275, 284, 314–316, 320, 322, 327, 331, 333
Intervertebral disk disease 195
Iris atrophy 64–65
Irritable bowel 227

J

Joy 356, 360, 388–389, 398, 402–404, 407, 426, 444, 480
Joys of living 10, 360

K

Keepsakes 416, 466, 467, 472
Ketogenic 226
Ketones 154, 225–226, 247
Kidney 27, 32, 45, 61, 83, 98, 102, 105, 112, 116, 119, 122, 128, 131, 138, 144–145, 149–164, 167–168, 170, 175, 219–223, 244, 247, 251–255, 264, 291, 315, 322, 324, 344–346, 366, 384, 387, 390, 431, 451
Kidney transplant 155, 161
Kitty Litter 28, 35, 49, 67–68, 100, 115, 147, 152, 158, 163–165, 167–179, 189, 193, 195, 198, 204, 207, 216, 221, 231, 232, 234, 240, 244, 246, 252, 254, 267, 269, 270, 281, 286, 287, 292, 293, 294, 295, 296, 303, 304, 367, 375, 384, 385, 393, 402, 480

L

Laser therapy 200, 206, 284, 329, 331
Lens 61–64
Lenticular sclerosis 61, 63
Lethargic 153, 281, 321
Life quality 10, 217, 289, 306, 368, 383–385, 389–391, 398, 403, 440
Lifespan 37, 43–44, 46, 91, 93, 100, 270, 283, 384
Limp 204, 270, 275
Lipomas 130, 259–260
Liver disease 98–100, 131, 200, 222, 452
Lungs 8, 104, 137–147, 181–186, 191, 347, 453
Lymphoma 196, 261

M

Maladaptive pain 272, 283
Malaise 278
Mammary gland 260
Maropitant 317
Mast cell 261
MCT 226
Medium-chain triglycerides 226
Medulla 150
Megacolon 100, 172
Melanoma 54, 261
Melatonin 229, 319
Memorializing 9, 465
Meningioma 260
Mentation 305
Message therapy 270, 312, 471
Metabolism 45, 81, 91, 102, 104, 111, 121, 123, 138, 155, 226–227, 243–244
Methimazole 253
Metoclopramide 317
Microbiome 110–111, 129, 227–228, 248
Mixed-breed 43, 45
Mobility 33, 34, 49, 92, 94, 130, 160, 165, 172–176, 178–179, 193–197, 201–217, 273, 291–296, 312, 339, 354, 358, 384
Monoclonal 199, 264, 284, 314
Monoclonal antibody 199, 284, 314
Morris Animal Foundation 43, 257, 268, 469
Muscle loss 33, 36, 83, 98, 101–105, 117, 122–123, 145, 157, 196, 202–203, 214
Muscle mass 33, 41, 101–104, 115, 117, 122, 145, 153, 161, 165, 200, 203, 217, 245
Muscle wasting 33–34, 103, 202, 220, 251

N

Nails 129, 134, 196, 208, 234, 294, 296
Natural passing 366, 368, 428, 430
Nausea 84, 98–99, 112–113, 118, 145, 152, 157, 159–160, 262–263, 267, 278, 284, 314, 317–318, 321, 348, 353–354, 367, 429, 431–432, 441, 449
Neoplasia 258
Nephron 150–151, 155
Neuropathy 195
Nociceptors 270, 272
Nose 39, 51–52, 54–59, 68–69, 86, 105, 113, 124, 130, 132, 134, 136, 182, 185–186, 190, 259–260, 265–266, 299, 303, 305, 327, 435, 441, 452, 466–468, 471, 477
Nosebleed 143
NSAID 315
Nuclear sclerosis 63–64
Nutraceutical 223, 318
Nutrition 7, 10, 45, 58, 89, 100, 105–109, 114, 118, 126, 128, 131, 163, 200, 202–203, 218, 223, 226, 228, 336

O

Obese 90–91, 93–95, 103, 112, 117, 127–128, 197, 200–202, 217, 245, 248, 274, 295
Obesity 89–90, 187, 201, 248
Ocuglo 67, 71
Off-label 230, 313, 316–318, 320, 322
Olfactory 51–52, 56, 58
Omega-3 105, 203, 229, 237, 284, 319
Oncologist 139, 258, 264–266, 268
Ophthalmologists 67
Opioids 284
Oral care 7, 79
Organ failure 121, 387
Osteoarthritis 91, 112, 197, 199–200, 216, 223, 273, 317, 333, 390
Osteosarcoma 196, 261
OTC 106–107
Oxidative stress 55, 156, 225–226
Oxygen 123–124, 137–139, 148, 151, 156, 182–183, 188, 203, 226, 331, 349, 370, 453–454

P

Pain 8, 187, 201, 205, 269, 271–275, 280, 283, 287, 314, 428
Pain management 273, 314
Pale gums 123, 266, 433

Palliative 5, 330, 363–365, 367, 373, 428, 437
Panting 122, 124–125, 186–187, 351
Papilloma 260
Parasite prevention 131, 146, 343
Parosmia 57
Pathology 263
Paw prints 466, 471
PEMF 333
Pet loss 341
Pheromones 53, 148, 165, 175, 178, 190, 267, 285, 294
Pigment 54, 100, 130, 261
Plantigrade 195, 247
Polyps 54
Polysulfated glycosaminoglycan 199
Presbycusis 74
Presbyosmia 57
Private cremation 459–460
Probiotics 95, 99, 111, 223, 227, 262, 318, 320
Propofol 448
Protein 36, 45, 91, 101–102, 105–106, 108, 111, 114, 129, 140, 152, 154–157, 221, 226, 229, 245, 284, 345
Proteostasis 45
PSGAG 316
Purebred 43, 45–46, 251

R

Radiation 27, 84, 253–254, 258, 260, 263–265, 351, 370, 385
Radioiodine 253
Ramps 147, 165, 189, 211, 232, 267, 294, 317
Rapamycin 43
Rehabilitation 104, 170, 173, 194, 200–201, 203, 205–206, 209–210, 217, 232–233, 238, 267, 285, 319, 329–330, 332, 336, 375, 377, 385
Respiration 453
Respite 338
Restrictive cardiomyopathy 140
Resveratrol 229
Roller Coaster 388
Ruggable 208
Rugs 165, 208, 294

S

Saddle thrombus 141, 195
S-adenosyl 229
Safety 62, 69, 71, 76, 211, 230, 238, 292–293, 295, 318, 345

Safe zone 66, 68–69, 301
SAMe 229
Sanitation 295–296
Sarcopenia 101–102
Sedation 447
Sedatives 267, 284, 347
Seizures 106, 150, 229, 249, 266, 316, 321–322, 433, 454
Selegiline 230
Semintra 230
Senilife 229
Snuffle Mat 71, 236
Solliquin 228
Spleen 260–261
Squamous cell carcinoma 83, 259, 261
Stem cell 45
Steps 40, 65, 68, 84, 95, 194, 207–208, 211–213, 232, 267, 285, 292, 347, 375–377, 385, 401–403, 431, 435
Steroids 315
Stones 151, 154, 168, 170–171, 222, 418
Strollers 210
Suffering 8, 146, 187, 205, 269, 279–280, 317, 365–367, 370, 374–375, 384, 387–390, 392, 402–404, 410, 414, 416, 428, 435, 440, 447, 453–454
Sundowner's syndrome 229
Supplements 10, 76–77, 99–100, 105–106, 108, 116–117, 145–146, 161–162, 170, 172, 200, 203, 205, 217, 223–226, 228–230, 233, 262, 267, 285, 309, 311–312, 314, 318–320, 322, 329
Swollen 75, 86–87, 100, 132, 143, 247, 266
Symptom tracker 306–307

T

Tactile 69
Tartar 80, 82, 85
Taste buds 58
Telmisartan 230
Telomere 44
Temperature 45, 84, 86, 115, 120–125, 127–128, 130, 147, 162, 164–165, 186, 189, 214, 247, 250, 345, 347, 349, 433, 435, 437, 461, 468
Terminal illness 117, 387, 405–406, 414, 417, 428
The Look 389
Thermoregulation 8, 119, 349
Third eyelid 63
ThunderShirt 233
Thyroid 90, 112, 128, 131, 140, 144, 151, 155, 162, 222, 243–244, 251–254, 260, 345

Toenail 196, 339, 435, 437, 466
Toxoplasma gondii 222
Transient myocardial thickening 140
Transitional cell carcinoma 261
Treatment tracker 308–309
Tremor 433, 453
Tumors 99, 130, 139, 151, 154, 168, 170, 196, 258–263, 272
Tumor staging 261

U

Ultrasound 99–100, 140, 144, 153–154, 170, 200, 222, 247, 284, 329–330, 345
Unsteady 8, 32, 193, 204, 232, 273, 284, 287, 292, 295, 350
Urinary tract 32, 49, 106, 151, 153, 161, 168–170, 172, 176, 217, 222, 247, 261, 272, 314, 443
Urinate 152, 163, 168–170, 172, 194–195, 204, 209, 266, 375
Urine 83, 132, 134, 136, 149–154, 156–157, 159–160, 168–171, 173, 175–177, 191, 216, 222, 245–247, 249–250, 266, 280, 295–296, 315, 321, 345, 348, 386, 432–434, 437, 443, 453

V

Vaccine 186, 264
VCPR 312–313
Vestibular 74
Vision 58, 62–63, 65–70, 75, 153, 174, 220–222, 251
Vitality 217, 304
Vitamins 99, 108, 111, 156, 223, 225–226, 228, 312, 318
Vocalize 75, 234, 279, 321, 422–423, 454
Vomit 99–100, 306, 321, 393

W

Weakness 32–34, 102, 123–124, 145, 147, 152, 157, 160, 173, 189, 195–196, 266, 273, 278, 433
Wheelchairs 209
Wobbly 8, 21, 102, 194, 286, 321

Y

Yeast 43, 131
Yoga mats 208

Made in the USA
Columbia, SC
07 January 2023